Out to Eat

London 2002

Lonely Planet Publications
Melbourne • London • Paris • Oakland

Lonely Planet *Out to Eat* – London 2002

2nd edition – September 2001
First published – September 2000

Published by Lonely Planet Publications

Lonely Planet Offices
Australia Locked Bag 1, Footscray, Vic 3011
USA 150 Linden St, Oakland, CA 94607
UK 10a Spring Place, London NW5 3BH
France 1 rue du Dahomey, 75011 Paris

Series publishing manager: Peter D'Onghia
Series editor: Donna Wheeler
Series design: Wendy Wright
Coordinators: Amanda Canning & Imogen Franks
Designer: Andrew Weatherill
Cartographers: Sara Yorke & Paul Edmunds
Cover design: Simon Bracken & Jamieson Gross
Photographs: Simon Bracken & Carl Drury

ISBN 1 74059 205 0

text & maps © Lonely Planet 2001
photos © Lonely Planet Images 2001

The images in this guide are available for licensing from Lonely Planet Images.
email: lpi@lonelyplanet.com.au

Printed by The Bookmaker International Ltd
Printed in China

London Underground map reproduced with the permission of the London Transport Museum.

All rights reserved. No part of this publication may be reproduced, stored in a retrieval system or transmitted in any form by any means, electronic, mechanical, photocopying, recording or otherwise, except brief extracts for the purpose of review, without the written permission of the publisher.

LONELY PLANET and the Lonely Planet logo are trade marks of Lonely Planet Publications Pty. Ltd.

Lonely Planet books provide independent advice. Lonely Planet does not accept advertising in its books, nor do we accept payment in exchange for listing or endorsing any restaurant. Lonely Planet reviewers do not accept discounts or free meals in exchange for positive coverage of any sort.

Dis-moi **où** tu manges, je te dirai ce que tu es.
Tell me **where** you eat and I will tell you what you are.

with apologies to Brillat-Savarin

OUT TO EAT – PEOPLE

This book is the result of more than a year's planning, hundreds of meetings and the creative efforts of a hungry team that includes experienced food writers, food-mad editors, designers, cartographers, guidebook authors and a sprinkling of publishers.

Fuelled by a passion for good food and a love of dining out, the core **team of writers** comprised:

David Atkinson, Joe Bindloss, Paul Bloomfield, Amanda Canning, Heather Dickson, Imogen Franks, Abigail Hole, Mark Honan, Claire Hornshaw, Kate Galbraith, Susan Grimshaw, Clay Lucas, Thornton McCamish, Etain O'Carrol, Tim Ryder, David Wenk and Sara Yorke.

For **additional assessments**, thanks to Jolyon Attwooll, Neal Bedford, Sarah Bennet, Katrina Browning, Ciara Clissmann, Liz Corcoran, Robert Devcic, David Ellis, Teresa Fisher, Lorna Gallagher, Janet Gower, Michelle Hawkins, Chris Horton, Andrew Humphries, Kath Kenny, Sarah Long, Claudia Martin, Rebecca Packham, Simon Richmond, Nicky Robinson, Maureen Stapleton, Anna Sutton, Dorinda Talbot and Ryan Ver Berkmoes.

The **features** and **introductions** were written by Amanda Canning, Steve Fallon, Imogen Franks, Susan Grimshaw, Mark Honan, Ryan Ver Berkmoes and Sara Yorke.

From the Publisher
The production of this book was coordinated by Amanda Canning and Imogen Franks. It was edited and proofed by Imogen with assistance

from Abigail Hole, Tim Ryder, Emma Sangster and Amanda. Sara Yorke coordinated the mapping and the maps were designed by Paul Edmunds with assistance from Jimi Ellis, Ian Stokes, Ed Pickard and David Wenk. Andrew Weatherill was the designer, with assistance from Jimi Ellis, and Simon Bracken and Carl Drury supplied the photographs. Simon Bracken and Jamieson Gross designed the front cover, and Adrienne Costanzo, Peter D'Onghia, Donna Wheeler and Wendy Wright provided expert advice from afar. Thanks to Finola Collins and Rachel Suddart for last-minute research and to Bibiana Jaramillo and Andrew Tudor for their quick turnaround of countless hundreds of files. Thanks also to Paul Bloomfield for all his support, to Tom Hall for his geographical expertise and to Tim Fitzgerald for his mapping inspiration.

INTRODUCTION 9
A GUIDE TO THE GUIDE 10
SYMBOLS 12

Central 13

Aldwych, Belgravia, Bloomsbury, Chinatown, City, Covent Garden, Edgware Road, Euston, Fitzrovia, Holborn, Leicester Square, Marble Arch, Marylebone, Mayfair, Oxford Circus, Piccadilly, Pimlico, St James's, Soho, Trafalgar Square, Victoria, Westminster

North 95

Archway, Barnsbury, Belsize Park, Camden, Crouch End, East Finchley, Finchley, Finsbury Park, Golders Green, Hampstead, Highbury, Highgate, Islington, Maida Vale, Muswell Hill, Primrose Hill, St Johns' Wood, Stoke Newington, Tufnell Park, Turnpike Lane, West Hampstead

East 125

Aldgate, Bethnal Green, Brick Lane, Clerkenwell, Docklands, Farringdon, Hackney, Haggerston, Hoxton, Shoreditch, Spitalfields, Wapping, Whitechapel

South 147

Balham, Battersea, Bermondsey, Blackheath, Brixton, Camberwell, Clapham, Dulwich, Greenwich, Kennington, New Cross, South Bank, Southwark, Stockwell, Tooting, Wandsworth, Wimbledon

West 183

Acton, Bayswater, Chelsea, Chiswick, Ealing, Fulham, Hammersmith, Holland Park, Kensal Rise, Kensington, Kensington Olympia, Kew, Kilburn, Knightsbridge, Ladbroke Grove, Lancaster Gate, Mortlake, Notting Hill, Putney, Queens Park, Shepherd's Bush, South Kensington, Teddington, Westbourne Park

FEATURES

Designer Diners	18
Tea Time	50
Dot.com Dining	65
A Taste of History	72
Food with a View	94
Part of the Food Chain	106
Eat, Drink and Dance the Night Away...	136
Farmers Markets	146
Sunday Best	182
A Tipple by the Thames	197
Organic Street Preachers	229

INDEXES	**238**
MAP SECTION	**265**

Map Contents

Outer London	**266**
Inner London	**268**
Map 1 - Central: Soho	**270**
Map 2 - Central: Holborn & Covent Garden	**272**
Map 3 - Central: Fitzrovia & Bloomsbury	**273**
Map 4 - Central: Marylebone	**274**
Map 5 - Central: Mayfair & Around	**275**
Map 6 - Central: City	**276**
Map 7 - Central: Victoria & Around	**277**
Map 8 - North: Hampstead	**277**
Map 9 - North: Islington	**278**
Map 10 - North: Camden & Primrose Hill	**279**
Map 11 - East: Shoreditch & Spitalfields	**280**
Map 12 - East: Bethnal Green & Haggerston	**282**
Map 13 - East: Clerkenwell & Farringdon	**283**
Map 14 - East: Wapping	**283**
Map 15 - South: South Bank to Bermondsey	**284**
Map 16 - South: Clapham & Around	**286**
Map 17 - South: Brixton & Stockwell	**288**
Map 18 - West: Knightsbridge	**289**
Map 19 - West: South Kensington & Chelsea	**290**
Map 20 - West: Notting Hill & Kensington	**292**
Map 21 - West: Hammersmith	**294**
Legend	**295**
London Underground	**296**

Introduction

Long associated with snooty service, unremarkable cuisine and extortionate prices, London has recently metamorphosed into a gastronome's dream. With over 8000 restaurants and over 70 cuisines to choose from at the last count, 21st-century London can cater for every taste, suit every wallet and pander to every whim.

In the centre are the big names – the long-established restaurants offering internationally renowned haute cuisine and the ill-tempered chefs-turned-restaurateurs who continually make the headlines with their antics both in and out of the kitchen. These sit side by side with a huge number of less well-known and generally cheaper eateries that offer a taste (some better than others) of every continent on every street corner. Farther afield, neighbourhood restaurants and ubiquitous chains rule. Previously hit-and-miss affairs, the standard of these restaurants is now rising, prompted by the demand for excellent food at affordable prices in each borough and aided by the escape to the suburbs of West-End über-chefs. Every Londoner can boast a fantastic little local – and they will, given half the chance. Often that favourite is a family-run Italian joint that's been dishing up pasta and pizza staples for years, or it might be a newly renovated gastropub with attitude and carefully crafted ambience in platefuls.

And, of course, in the centre and in the suburbs, the culinary scene just keeps evolving. The passion for buying up disused buildings and turning them into restuarants has gone into hyperdrive this year. We're happily converting banks into multiplex Chinese restaurants, libraries into new-fangled curry houses and hydraulic power stations into modern British canteens. London also finally seems to have woken up to the fact that it has rather a large river running through it and the number of restaurants springing up by the Thames is growing by the minute. Naturally, trends also change in the food we like to eat and hence the dishes served up by restaurants. The interest in organic produce continues to grow apace, spurred on by foot and mouth disease, BSE and concerns over GM (genetically modified) foods. Then there's the gourmet vegetarian, the new breed of vegetarian restaurant that offers veggie fodder that's a cut above (with prices to match). Still, 'modern' cuisine remains the darling of the foodie world, with fresh takes on old classics continuing to pull in the punters.

Out to Eat – London 2002 is for everyone trying to get the most out of this ever-changing restaurant scene – not the easiest of tasks in a city with so many choices. In the best Lonely Planet tradition we scoured London from Bloomsbury to Brixton and from Hammersmith to Hampstead for our favourite restaurants. Top-notch ethnic eateries and fine little neighbourhood joints are listed alongside the 'it' names of London dining. Now in its second edition, this book draws on the vast resources of local knowledge at Lonely Planet's London office and the culinary expertise of our guidebook authors – after journeying to the far corners of the earth, our authors know the difference between a truly authentic dish and a poor imitation. The sum of all this experience is a team of reviewers who are passionate about food and who won't settle for mediocrity. After devouring hundreds of meals and tossing back untold glasses of wine, all the while noting myriad details such as service, décor and ambience, the *Out to Eat* team recommends every restaurant in this book, but we also tell you if a place falls short of perfection in any area. We're free from advertising, we dined under the cloak of anonymity and we paid for our meals, so you're guaranteed uncompromising opinion and a clean read. Bon appetit!

A Guide to the Guide

Organisation
Out to Eat – London 2002 is organised according to locality. The names of the chapters (Central, North, East, South and West) represent convenient groupings of areas and do not refer to actual named districts. Within the chapters, areas are organised alphabetically and reviews are listed alphabetically within that area. Features are sprinkled throughout the book.

Favourites
Because *Out to Eat* includes such a diversity of listings, there are no 'stars' or points scored out of 20. But there are places that we would especially steer you towards in the 'Favourite' list at the beginning of each chapter.

The Listings
Each review offers a snapshot of one reviewer's experience of one or more visits to the restaurant, bar, pub or cafe. The opinion outlined in each listing should be taken as a guide only, and not as hard evidence of what you may expect. Dishes are seasonal, prices change, staff and owners move on. The reviews attempt to encapsulate the spirit of a place and provide an opinion on whether the place delivers what it promises. Every listing is a personal recommendation.

Wheelchair Access Restaurants equipped with a toilet that has been purpose-built or adapted for wheelchair access are the only listings carrying the words 'wheelchair access'. Access suggests wheelchairs will easily get into the restaurant and have ease of movement once inside. We can't guarantee this, so please telephone ahead to confirm facilities.

Certified Organic If a restaurant has been certified by the Soil Association as using organic produce, we've listed the words 'certified organic' in the margin of the review.

Price The starter, main, dessert and wine fields show the complete range of prices on each restaurant's menu. For example 'starter £5-£11' indicates that £5 is the price of the least expensive starter on the menu and £11 is the most expensive. We've also indicated the price of any set menus or special deals (such as pre-theatre meals) that the restaurant offers on a permanent basis. Where prices are only given for set menus and not for starters, mains and desserts, the restaurant only offers set menus. Prices were correct at the time of research.

Credit Cards Abbreviations show credit and debit facilities offered by the restaurant. We've included the following cards: American Express (AE), Diners Club (DC), Japanese Credit Bureau (JCB), MasterCard (MC), Visa (V) and Switch (SW).

Licensing A restaurant with a BYO (bring your own) licence allows you to bring alcohol that you have purchased elsewhere to be served with your meal. Almost all restaurants with a BYO licence allow only bottled wine to be brought in and served. 'Unlicensed' means that it is illegal to consume alcohol on the premises.

Transport In the margin of each review we've listed the tube/rail station or bus line closest to the restaurant. There's a map of the London Underground on page 296.

Maps Each listing has its own map which shows the main route from the nearest transport link to the restaurant. The distance between the two is given in brackets after the transport information for the listing. Please note that these maps have been simplified so the main route is clear – they do not include every road. Most, but not all, of the restaurants also appear on the area maps at the end of the book. The map number and grid reference is indicated in the margin of each review.

Indexes
We've indexed the listings in three different ways – alphabetically (which includes a grid index indicating whether the restaurant has wheelchair access, is child-friendly, is good for a romantic date or a business lunch, has a private room or outdoor seating); by cuisine (which includes a section indicating all the vegan, vegetarian and certified organic restaurants in the book) and by neighbourhood. So whether you're looking for all of the Japanese restaurants in the book, all of the restaurants in Brixton or all of the restaurants that are child-friendly, you'll be able to find them.

Tipping & VAT
Many restaurants now add a 'discretionary' service charge to your bill, and technically this should be clearly advertised so that you do not mistakenly add an additional tip. In places that don't automatically add the service charge you're expected to leave a 10% to 15% tip, unless the service was unsatisfactory. Restaurant menus will already include 17.5% value-added tax (VAT) in their prices.

Example:

Map 6 C4

Tube/rail: Cannon Street (80m), tube: Bank or Monument

 Smoking throughout

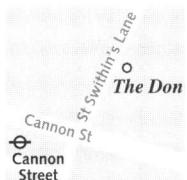

starter £4.50-£6.95
main £8.75-£12.95
dessert £5-£7.75
wine £14.95-£850

AE MC V; SW

Symbols

Totally smoke free

Smoking Text accompanying this symbol explains whether there are smoking restrictions, separate smoke-free dining areas or smoking throughout.

Outdoor seating Outdoor dining options for fine days or nights. Text accompanying this symbol explains where the tables are situated, for example on the pavement or in a garden.

A separate vegetarian menu or excellent vegetarian options.

Various and/or interesting vegetarian options.

Quiet Noticeably quiet, even when busy.

Mid-range Medium noise, not noticeably quiet, and you can generally hear conversation at your own table without straining.

Noisy Can be very noisy when busy (either due to music or the acoustics of the space). You may have to raise your voice considerably to be heard in conversation.

Romantic Make a date. Something about this place makes romance seem very likely.

Business Exercise the expense account. This place is suitable for business occasions. Expect professional table service, compatible clientele, adequate table spacing and comfortable noise levels.

Open fireplace Open fireplace for chilly days or nights.

Air Conditioning

Write to us

Things change – prices go up, opening hours change, good places go bad and bad places go bankrupt – nothing stays the same. So, if you find things better or worse, recently opened or recently closed, please tell us and help make the next edition even more accurate and useful.

Every morsel of information you send will be read and acknowledged by the appropriate author, editor or publisher. The best contributions will be rewarded with a free Lonely Planet book and excerpts may appear in future editions of *Out to Eat – London*, so please let us know if you don't want your name acknowledged.

Lonely Planet Out to Eat
10a Spring Place, London NW5 3BH
email: out2eat@lonelyplanet.com.au

Visit us on the Web

For new reviews and tasty titbits on comings and goings, follow the links from **www.lonelyplanet.com** to Upgrades.

Aldwych
Belgravia
Bloomsbury
Chinatown
City

CENTRAL

Covent Garden
Edgware Road
Euston

Fitzrovia
Holborn
Leicester Square
Marble Arch
Marylebone
Mayfair
Oxford Circus
Piccadilly
Pimlico
St James's
Soho
Trafalgar Square
Victoria
Westminster

FAVOURITE

■ **British**
French House
Dining Room (p78)

■ **Chinese**
Hunan (p68)

■ **French**
Le Gavroche (p58)

■ **Indian**
Rasa Samudra (p46)

■ **Italian**
Sardo (p47)

■ **Modern European**
The Ivy (p35)

■ **South-East Asian**
Mandalay (p40)

■ **Vegetarian**
Country Life (p78)

Central

With boroughs and districts as large and diverse as Soho, Mayfair, Pimlico and the City, central London is a difficult area to encapsulate. From fashionable fusion and heart-stoppingly rich Hungarian to naff caffs and dubious-looking sausages – 'with onions, mate?' – sizzled on street corners, central London's offerings run the gamut from the sublime to the simply substantial. Soho itself, the epicentre of London dining, is a good example of this gastronomic schizophrenia. It does have its detractors, however: it's crowded and dirty and all but impossible to get a table on a weekend night without a reservation. Many of the cognoscenti now eschew the area and head north to Fitzrovia, where there's a wide range of less frenetic options and Italian *trattorie* run by Maltese are a penny a peck, or west to Covent Garden, which is densely packed with places to eat that cater to theatre-goers, pubbers and clubbers. Sandwiched between Holborn's Inns of Court and the B&Bs of Bloomsbury is a small but quality choice of European and Asian restaurants. Mayfair, Piccadilly and St James's Park are big-ticket areas, home to some of the capital's most luxurious hotels and regal residents, so it's no surprise that French cuisine in all its guises is very much in evidence. But we wonder where all those MPs lunch, judging from the dearth of restaurants in Westminster. Maybe they venture to nearby Pimlico with its assortment of upmarket Chinese and some of the finest French restaurants this side of the Channel. To the north is Marylebone and Edgware Rd. The latter is lined with Middle Eastern cafe houses, almost exclusively the domain of men who while away the hours sipping tiny cups of mud-like coffee. And the City, previously an irritating place to find a decent and affordable restaurant that was patronised (or, indeed, stayed open) after the stock market closed, now offers several cutting-edge restaurants that all keep the welcome mat out at dinnertime.

ALDWYCH

The Admiralty
French Regional

☎ 7845 4646
Somerset House, The Strand WC2R

With a delicious irony, The Admiralty, located in the rooms where Lord Nelson planned his campaigns against the French, serves up the cuisine of rural France in one of the most quintessential of English buildings. But tradition is left behind with the slightly off-beat décor, the unusual raised ledges to the tables and the remarkably fast, courteous and knowledgeable service. Take in the views of the Thames, have a drink at the separate bar and then dine in either the green or the orange dining room. There's no denying the food's good – the pâté's smooth and flavoursome (£10.00), the rack of lamb (£16.50) rich and juicy, the butter biscuits melt in your mouth (£5.50) – and the wine list is certainly deserving of comment. But what really makes The Admiralty worth a visit is its originality, in both location and design. This restaurant is definitely one of a kind.

Open: Mon-Sat noon-2.45pm, 6pm-10.45pm, Sun noon-3.45pm; reservations advisable; licensed, no BYO

Map 2 E3

Tube: Temple (150m), tube/rail: Charing Cross

Wheelchair access

 Separate smoke-free dining available

 Terrace tables

starter £7.50-£13.50
main £17-£18.50
dessert £6.50-£7.50
set menu (weekends) £27
wine £12.90-£650

AE DC JCB MC V; SW

Bank Aldwych
Modern British, Liberated French

☎ 7379 9797
1 Kingsway WC2B
www.bankrestaurants.com

Pacy, professional Bank Aldwych produces high-quality twists on classics across the entire spectrum of Franco-British cuisine, fish and chips swimming proudly next to crustacea and sevruga caviar on the menu. A 20-ton chandelier hovers like an alien ship above the cavernous, boisterous canteen. Baltic herrings (£6.95), light in taste and quantity but served with a pleasingly gritty Swedish mustard, were out-shelled by a goodly tureen of mussels (£5.90). Breast of duck (£18.50), with traditional orange sauce, was almost equalled by the ever-so-slightly mushy calves liver and bacon (£16.50), saved by precise cooking and complemented with herb-infused mashed potatoes. The sticky toffee (£5.90), a belter of a pudding, was moist with plenty of substance; ostentatious chocolate crème caramel and citrus salad (£5.90) worked. Helpful service suits the scene.

Open: Mon-Fri 7am-11am, noon-3pm, 5.30pm-11.30pm, Sat 5.30pm-11.30pm, Sun 11.30am-3.30pm, 5.30pm-10pm; reservations accepted; licensed, no BYO

Map 2 D2

Tube: Holborn (450m) or Temple

Wheelchair access

 Smoking throughout

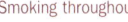

starter £5.50-£12.50
main £8.50-£29
dessert £4.50-£7.50
set menu (noon-3pm, 5.30pm-7pm, 10pm-11.30pm) £15.50-£17.90
wine £12.50-£245

AE MC V; SW

ALDWYCH

Map 2 E2
Tube/rail: Charing Cross (400m)

Dress code: Jacket & tie

Smoking throughout

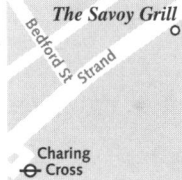

starter £9-£16
main £18-£25
dessert £8
pre-theatre menu Mon-Sat £22 or £29.75
wine £20.50-£800

AE DC JCB MC V; SW

The Savoy Grill
British/French

☎ **7836 4343**
The Savoy, The Strand WC2R
www.savoy-group.co.uk

The Savoy Grill thrives on tradition and a menu that's as conservative as its upper crust clientele. After a perfectly pleasant Jerusalem artichoke soup, laced with truffle, and an adequate caesar salad with a hunk of hickory smoked salmon, we did the right thing and ordered the roast beef. This proved to be a performance of military precision: an advance guard of tail-coated waiters parked a huge silver trolley next to our banquette, while reserves were brought in to carve the roast (nicely pink), dish out vegetables (cracking roast potatoes) and spoon on the red wine shallot sauce. The dining room is lofty and wood panelled, with starched linen tablecloths and place settings just so. This is the sort of place to take great-uncle Cedric for a treat, but remember to put on your best bib and tucker – and reserve your stiff upper lip for the bill.

Open: Mon-Fri 12.30pm-2.30pm, Mon-Sat 6pm-11.15pm; reservations essential; licensed, no BYO

The Conservatory at the Lanesborough (Carl Drury)

BELGRAVIA

The Conservatory at the Lanesborough
International

☎ 7259 5599
1 Lanesborough Place SW1X
www.lanesborough.com

Among the potted palms and bamboo, there's a sedate corner of the Lanesborough hotel that will forever be Victorian England, all high teas and tiffin. Although this setting may attract power-dining Arabs and ladies who lunch on a professional basis, its universal appeal is limited. We found the standard of food to be sorely lacking, especially when compared to the pristine service and lavish surroundings. The spinach cannelloni (£16.50) looked and tasted like a supermarket ready-meal and although the flavoursome Scotch beef (£26.50) would have any self-respecting mad cow mooing its approval, the accompanying large fries were soggy in the middle. The menu is broad, with nods to world-fusion cuisine and vegetarians – though the latter will find it fails to live up to its promise – but quality falls short of impressive. And frankly, at these prices (£8.40 for two glasses of still water!), you would expect better.

Open: Mon-Sat 7am-11.30am, noon-2.30pm, 3.30pm-6pm, 6.30pm-11.30pm, Sun 7.30am-11.30am, noon-2.30pm, 4pm-6pm; reservations essential; licensed, no BYO

Map 7 A1
Tube: Hyde Park Corner (50m)
Wheelchair access
Entertainment: Dinner dance Fri & Sat evenings, pianist Sun-Thurs afternoon and evenings, jazz Sun lunch
Smoke-free dining available on request

starter £7.50-£17.50
main £15.50-£32
dessert £8.50
set lunch £15, £22.50 or £27.50, set dinner £32, Sun brunch £32.50
wine £22-£2,900

AE DC JCB MC V; SW

Mulberry
International

☎ 7201 1905
20 Chesham Place SW1X

Through the lobby of the Sheraton Belgravia Hotel, you'll find green-glass plates and the will-o'-the-wisp woodland known as Mulberry. There wasn't a soul here on our visit – perhaps news hasn't got round yet – leaving the deft, genteel waitress to warm our cockles thoroughly without distraction. One clever concept was the set menu (£18.50 for three courses) with 'coastal cooking' from the shores around Britain, Norway, Denmark and France. Freshly hooked fish came in a variety of disguises, including chock-a-block Claddagh soup and baked cod with parsley-sauce lava and chunky mash. Mermaid-enchanting dishes were nudged by less-aquatic fare such as Danish meatballs with red cabbage or a burly hunk of grilled chicken. To finish was a sugar-frisky sticky-toffee pudding. It's a strangely beguiling place, although the lights needed dimming for an even better thicket effect.

Open: Mon-Fri 7am-10am, 6.30pm-10pm, Sat 7am-11am, 6.30pm-10pm, Sun noon-2.30pm; reservations advisable; licensed, no BYO

Map 7 A1
Tube: Knightsbridge (400m)
Nonsmoking tables available

starter £4.95-£8.95
main £13.95-£23.45
dessert £5.95-£7.95
set dinner £14.50 or £18
wine £18-£40

AE DC JCB MC V; SW

Designer Diners

In the best restaurants everything has to be just right - from the smallest detail to the whole concept, from the placement of the cutlery to the construction of the building itself. The following places stand out with their elaborate, inventive or unusual architecture:

Bibendum (page 230) The former Michelin tyre factory, built in 1911, now helps add spare tyres to the girths of affluent diners, thanks to Bibendum, which has been ensconced here since 1987. Reminders of the tubby Michelin Man are everywhere, from the impressive stained glass windows to the ashtrays - even the chair legs ape his rolls of fat.

Oxo Tower (page 174) This pink-hued Art Deco landmark was once a meat warehouse whose architect side-stepped regulations against advertising by creating a geometric design of neon lights that just happened to spell out the name 'oxo'. The tower was reinvented in 1996 and now houses shops, flats and restaurants.

Parco's (page 127) This double-storey restaurant was built in the 1980s. Its most remarkable feature is an atrium area, dominated by three giant fig trees and topped off by a glass and metal roof.

Wapping Food (page 145) This restaurant resides in a former hydraulic power station, which was built in 1890. The engine and turbine houses were reopened as a restaurant and exhibition space in 2000 with the cavernous halls much as they once were – even the massive metal turbines are still in place.

Even places with an unremarkable exterior can become exceptional with the aid of a few interior design flourishes. Good examples include:

Bank Aldwych (page 15) The restrictive dimensions of this former bank are ingeniously masked. Connecting the front bar and back restaurant is a corridor 'widened' with mirrors. The eye is drawn to vivid murals on the walls and strong colours on the pillars; overhead, vertical sheets of glass alter the hue of the ceiling lights depending on your angle of view.

Beach Blanket Babylon (page 220) Inside what was once an average pub is a fantasy Gothic castle complete with a mini drawbridge, festooned with chains, that leads to an upstairs turret-like room. Flickering candles, roaring fires, heavy drapes - even some Gaudi-esque mosaics - combine to make you forget you're in west London.

The Criterion (page 66) This high-class restaurant is not afraid to offer an unusual Byzantine interior, incorporating arches, pillars and heavy curtains. A splendid mosaic depicting an 'Arabian nights' scene dominates the curve-sided ceiling.

Sarastro (page 38) Entering this unobtrusive restaurant you're immediately immersed in a space crammed with clutter and colour. Opera is the theme here, and some tables are located in cleverly-constructed opera boxes accessed by diminutive wooden stairways. Unusual design accessories range from a mummified demon to dangling ballet shoes.

Mark Honan

BLOOMSBURY

Abeno
Japanese

☎ 7405 3211
47 Museum St WC1A

'Europe's only okonomi-yaki restaurant' presents this Japanese fast-food staple in a surprisingly civilised setting. The centrepiece of each table is the teppan – the hotplate on which the okonomi-yaki (savoury pancakes) are prepared. But first try some of the inventive starters, such as the tofu and avocado gyoza (deep-fried stuffed dumplings; £3.50), an unusual but tasty combination. Once you're ready for the okonomi-yaki (two sizes available), the ingredients of your choice are skilfully mixed and fried before your eyes. The Sapporo mix (squid, prawn, salmon and sweet corn; £8.80/10.80) is deliciously satisfying, with fresh seaweed salad (£4.50) the perfect side dish. There is also a range of mouthwatering desserts – the arashiyama-an (£3.80) is a refreshing platter of green-tea ice cream, adzuki beans, kiwi fruit and sweet rice dumplings. The impeccable food, service and attention to detail result in a near-perfect dining experience – we can't wait to go back.

Open: Mon-Sat noon-10pm, Sun noon-8pm; reservations advisable; licensed & BYO (corkage varies)

Map 2 C1

Tube: Tottenham Court Road (300m) or Holborn

 Nonsmoking tables available

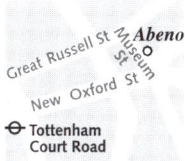

starter £1.80-£7.80
main £5.20-£28.50
dessert £2.95-£5
set lunch £6.50-£16
wine £12.75-£30.25

JCB MC V; SW

Court Restaurant
Modern British

☎ 7323 8990
The British Museum, Great Russell St WC1B
www.digbytrout.co.uk

Drenched in soft light and surrounded by incredible architecture, the Court Restaurant is wonderfully situated at the centre of the British Museum. The most popular tables provide a superb view of the reading room. Choose from the à la carte menu for a hearty and impressive potato and leek soup (£3.30) or a country-style rabbit and pheasant terrine (£4.55) in juniper and blackberry sauce. Main courses were disappointing and tasted as if they had been sitting as long as we had been queuing. The salmon fishcakes (£9.25) were lukewarm and lacked flavour, though the accompanying pea and mint purée was beautifully light and creamy. Overcooked fusilli (£7.95), dowsed in a watery tomato sauce, did nothing to improve our mood. Desserts, however, were excellent and included a wonderfully sharp and tangy lemon tart (£4.75). The long queues move quickly, but get there early for the best of the food.

Open: Sun-Wed 11am-5pm, Thurs-Sat 11am-9pm; reservations accepted for dinner only; licensed, no BYO

Map 2 C1

Tube: Tottenham Court Road (300m)

Wheelchair access

starter £3.30-£5.25
main £7.25-£9.25
dessert £4.75
set lunch £10.50
wine £10.50-£25

MC V; SW

BLOOMSBURY

Map 2C1
Tube: Holborn (300m)
Nonsmoking tables available

Giotto
Italian

☎/fax 7323 0891
52-54 New Oxford St WC1A

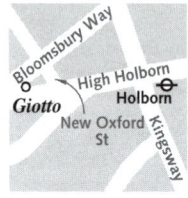

starter £4.20-£6.30
main £5.90-£16.70
dessert £2.90
wine £11.90-£58

AE DC JCB MC V; SW

Salmon-pink walls, crooner music and the relaxed atmosphere of a family-run *cucina* (kitchen) transplanted to the high street – it's easy to see why Giotto is popular with expat Italians and lunching suits. The wine list makes for exciting reading, with a good range of great-value Italian regionals; less so the menu, which favours choice over innovation. Giotto's eponymous rigatoni (£4.20) was a good-size starter of perfectly al dente pasta in a rich tomato and ham sauce, but dry crostini al formaggio (crostini with cheese; £2.50) was unappetising. We regretted a dull mozzarella salad (£5) but loved calamari fritti (£9.80), perfect, juicy hoops of heavily crumbed squid, and saltimbocca (£9.80), three tranches of tender veal in a strongly seasoned sauce. Mains come with a generous platter of homely roasted vegetables. Tiramisù (£2.90) was a little stodgy, but service is good and, as you'd expect, the coffee (£1.50) is excellent.

Open: Mon-Sat noon-3pm, 5pm-11pm; reservations advisable (essential lunch); licensed, no BYO

Map 3 A2
Tube: Warren Street (100m)
Nonsmoking tables available

Lal Qila
Indian

☎ 7387 4570
117 Tottenham Court Rd W1P
www.lal-qila.com

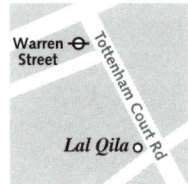

starter £2.99-£5.99
main £4.25-£14.99
dessert £3-£3.50
set lunch £7.99 or £8.99
set dinner £13.99 or £15.99
wine £8.99-£22

AE DC MC V; SW

With curry now London's staple dish, curry houses are ten-a-penny with most catering to the mass-market chicken korma crowd. Lal Qila does try to set itself apart with a good range of speciality fish dishes and an above-average selection of vegetarian options, but it feels caught between innovation and pandering to the post-pub trade. Dishes such as Goan crab (£4.99) attempt to inject some flair to the menu, yet this failed to pack the spicy punch we anticipated. Similarly, muri ghonto (£6.99), a Bangladeshi lentil-based fish curry, sounded exotic but actually tasted rather bland. Still, they were better than the korahi chicken (£6.99) which was even greasier than the kiss curl of our grumpy waiter. Lal Qila's strength lies in offering above-average Indian fare with a flourish of flavour at very reasonable prices, but it falls down with rather surly service and unexceptional quality.

Open: Mon-Sun noon-2.30pm, 6pm-11.30pm; reservations accepted; licensed, no BYO

BLOOMSBURY

Le Bistro Savoir Faire
French

☎ 7436 0707
42 New Oxford St WC1A

Map 2 C1
Tube: Tottenham Court Road (250m)

 Nonsmoking tables available

 Pavement tables

Supreme value for money can be had at Le Bistro Savoir Faire. Proprietors Irene and Max Khorramshahi have set up shop in a strategic crossover zone equally convenient for students and show-goers. And despite sitting at the crux of several major roads, the shallow dining room – with its wittily graffitied ceiling – has a surprisingly sheltered feel. Food is as faultless as you could expect for £12.90 a head (three courses); service is beguilingly ditzy. Well-executed beef julienne preceded baked salmon that was a mite dry but still quite tasty. Vegetarian options are varied and wholesome, our marrow came elegantly presented with side vegetables and drizzled balsamic vinegar. Puddings weren't so hot: lemon meringue pie was too soggy. Savoir Faire's inexpensive and mostly competent classics make it an inviting place to grab a bite when the wallet's light.

starter £2.50-£4.50
main £8-£10.50
dessert £2.90
set lunch £6.90, pre-theatre menu £7.90 or £12.90
wine £8.30-£19.50

AE DC MC V; SW

Open: Mon-Sat noon-4pm, 5pm-11pm, Sun 10.30am-4pm, 5pm-11pm; reservations accepted (advisable Fri & Sat evenings); licensed, no BYO

Malabar Junction
South Indian

☎ 7580 5230
107 Great Russell St WC1B

Map 3 B3
Tube: Tottenham Court Road (350m)

Don't come to Malabar Junction expecting the 30p thali you remember from Khozhikode railway station – you won't get it. What you will get is an excellent wine list and high-end Keralan cuisine served in an elegant dining room. Ghee roast masala (£8), a crisp rolled dosa served with tamarind chutney, and dahi vada (£4), a subtle 'donut' of ground lentils in yoghurt, are typical of carefully prepared vegetarian options. The menu does have some curry-house faves, such as lamb korma, but we stuck to the Keralan offerings: turmeric and green-chilli flavoured cubes of kingfish in the fish moilee (a kind of stew; £8) and Cochin prawn curry (£9.50) with huge king prawns in a tomato and coconut broth. Keralan ingredients continue for dessert too: Malabar coconut (£5) is a slab of unctuous pressed coconut and cashew nuts, and banana fritters (£3.50) have a light, cardamom-flavoured batter.

starter £3.50-£9.50
main £6-£11
dessert £3-£5
set lunch at bar £3.50
wine £10-£27.50

AE JCB MC V; SW

Open: Mon-Sat 11am-3pm, 6pm-11.15pm, Sun 11am-3pm, 6pm-10.30pm; reservations essential at weekends; licensed, no BYO

CHINATOWN

Map 1 C5
Tube: Leicester Square (300m)
Smoking throughout

Aroma II
Chinese

☎/fax 7437 0377
118 Shaftesbury Ave W1V
www.aromarestaurant.co.uk

Aroma II, the second in a group of three, feels rather forbidding. Maybe it's the huge sprawling menu or the searing hospital lights, or maybe it's just the surly welcome. Either way, we weren't put at ease. Moreover, the food came coated in a slimy film of MSG, which killed any chance of savouring the flavour of our cuttlefish with asparagus (£9) or bok choi vegetables (£5.50). Top tip: ask for non-MSG preparation. To its credit, however, the menu does cover a huge range of Chinese regional dishes from juicy Shanghai dumplings (£3.50) to spicy Szechuan king prawns (£9), plus a wide range of unusual dishes (deep-fried pork chitterlings anyone?). The crowd comprises tourists and Chinese families. Best ask the latter's advice when ordering. It could help avoid confusion over the menu (whole suckling pig for £128!) but won't make up for the fact that quality, like the service, is rather lacklustre.

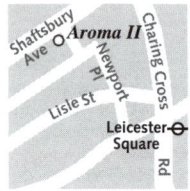

starter £2.20-£28
main £6-£128
dessert £1.50-£4.50
set dinner £12.50, £16.50-£22, pre- & post-theatre menu £9
wine £8.50-£36.80
AE DC JCB MC V; SW

Open: daily noon-11.30pm; reservations advisable Fri & Sat; licensed, no BYO

Map 1 C5
Tube: Leicester Square (200m)
Nonsmoking tables available

China City
Chinese

☎ 7734 3388
White Bear Yard, 25a Lisle St WC2H

After the pretty courtyard leading you from the hustle of Lisle St, the white-walled minimalism of this huge three-floorer might seem a little dull. Fear not – this place offers damn fine, damn authentic dim sum ('fried crab with cheese' aside). Having negotiated the maze of menus, we sampled excellent prawn dumplings with chives (£1.80), Vietnamese spring rolls (£1.80) and stuffed tofu with seafood (£2.80). Our token carnivorous order of 'mixed meats' wrapped in lettuce leaves (£8.50) turned out to be more seafood. We followed it with wonderfully dry deep-fried squid with chilli and garlic (£7) and some boring mixed-vegetable egg-fried rice (£4.50). Custard tarts (£1.80) were small, warm and delicious. Give the house wine a miss in favour of something else from the international list. Staff tend to congregate in the middle of the room – so we'd recommend sitting in their line of vision.

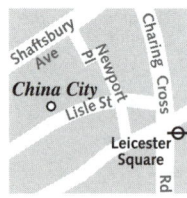

starter £1.80-£11.50
main £6-£20
dessert £2-£3
set menu £11, £15 or £17
wine £8-£38.50
(£10 min) MC V; SW

Open: Mon-Sat noon-11.45pm, Sun 11.30am-11.15pm; reservations accepted; licensed, no BYO

CHINATOWN

Fung Shing
Chinese

☎ **7437 1539**
15 Lisle St WC2
www.fungshing.com

Map 1 D5
Tube: Leicester Square (200m)

 Smoking throughout

The many-stickered door signposts this as one of London's top Chinese restaurants. If the front dining room has a coffee-shop feel, the chandeliered back room is altogether grander. The lengthy menu is full of surprises – not least a fine wine list – and many dishes, such as stir-fried milk with scrambled egg white (£9.50), differ from the Chinatown norm. We started with plump scallops in garlic and soy (£2.40 each), the aptly named aromatic crispy duck (£10.50 per quarter) and prawns in delicious yam batter (£4.50). Venison (£9.50) came with a yellow bean sauce that was a far cry from the sickly ubiquitous version, and both egg-fried rice (£2.50) and Singapore noodles (£6) were exemplary. Crispy baby squid with Chinese sausage (£9.50) was top notch, but the musty oriental flavour didn't appeal to our Western palates. Predictably, puddings were thin on the ground but coconut milk tapioca (£3.50) rounded things off nicely.

Open: daily noon-11.30pm; reservations advisable; licensed, no BYO

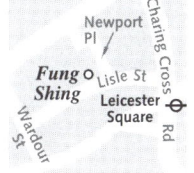

starter £2.30-£16
main £7.50-£26
dessert £2.50-£4
set dinner £16-£30
wine £13.50-£65

AE DC MC V; SW

China City Restaurant (Carl Drury)

CHINATOWN

Map 1 C5

Tube: Leicester Square (300m) or Piccadilly Circus

Smoking throughout

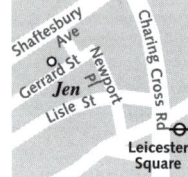

starter £2-£6
main £5-£38
set menu £9-£19 per head
(min 2 people)
wine £11-£39.50

AE MC V; SW

Jen
Hong Kong

☎ 7287 8193
7 Gerrard St W1V

Despite the tatty interior and dingy dining room downstairs, Jen attracts a large number of Chinese diners by virtue of its innovative Hong Kong cuisine. The extensive menu offers not only the standard fare – delicious Peking duck (£24) or chicken and cashew nuts (£5.50) – but also some weird and wonderful alternatives. If you're brave, try the shredded chicken with jellyfish (£8) or sautéed frogs legs with ginger (£7). Soups are a speciality, with over 13 varieties on offer, ranging from fish soup with thousand-year-old eggs, coriander and tangerine peel (£2.50) to superior shark's fin soup (£35). For the best value go for one of the set meals, which offer a selection of dishes at affordable prices. The restaurant is always buzzing and its opening hours ensure that it attracts a mixed crowd: post-pub revellers, after-theatre diners and the night owls of Soho.

Open: daily noon-3am; reservations accepted; licensed, no BYO

Map

Tube: Leicester Square (300m)

Nonsmoking tables available

starter £1.75-£20
main £5.75-£25
dessert £1.70-£2.80
set menu £11-£26
wine £10-£50

AE DC JCB MC V; SW

New World
Chinese

☎ 7734 0396
1 Gerrard Place W1

New World has a 20-page menu packed with everything from fried beef ho-fun with chilli and black bean sauce (£3.60) to pork and yam hotpot (£6.15) and several styles of abalone (from £12.50). But long menus aren't unusual. What's different here are wheeled carts and lots of them. From 11am to 6pm every day, fleets of dim sum trolleys circulate through the vast dining room bearing scores of little dishes, most of which cost £1.75. There's no menu and no need for one as you can point and choose based on what you see. Various steamed dumplings, sautéed greens, deep-fried meats, stir-fried noodles and much more parade past. The whole place seems lifted right out of Hong Kong and the many Chinese families dining are a great endorsement. Since there are more than 700 seats, you'll never have to linger long on the worn red carpet in the entrance.

Open: daily 11am-midnight; reservations advisable; licensed, no BYO

CITY

1 Blossom Street
Modern European

☎ **7247 6532**
1 Blossom St E1
www.1blossomstreet.com

Map 6 A5
Tube/rail: Liverpool Street (400m)
Wheelchair access

 Smoking throughout

Well hidden behind an office, you wonder if 1 Blossom Street chose its name to stop people calling to confirm the address. However, its location doesn't prevent a mass of City folk descending with clients in tow to dine à la carte or more casually at the impressive bar. Vegetarian mains are available as starters, which makes for an impressive selection, offering dishes such as a simple tomato, mozzarella and basil salad (£4.50) invigorated with aioli. Mains include lightly fried sea bass (£16.50), simply served with spinach and potatoes, and succulent medallions of pork (£16.50) with a flavoursome mustard sauce and lurid broccoli florets. An otherwise unadventurous dessert menu (including a miserable crème brûlée; £6.50) is redeemed by a frozen cocktail of Grand Marnier, Baileys and Kaluha (B52; £6.50). Slick service and a pleasant ambience make the bill easier to swallow.

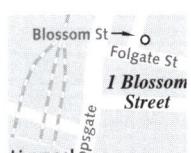

starter £4.50-£9.50
main £15.50-£37.50
dessert £3.80-£6.50
set lunch £19.95 or £24.95
wine £13.50-£85.00

AE MC V; SW

Open: Mon-Fri noon-9.30pm; reservations accepted; licensed, no BYO

The Bridge Brasserie & Bar
International

☎ **7236 0000**
1 Paul's Walk EC4V
www.thebridgerestaurant.co.uk

Map 6 C3
Tube/rail: Blackfriars (250m)
Wheelchair access

 Smoking throughout
Terrace tables

The Millennium Bridge meant to lure people over from the South Bank wobbled and shut, leaving The Bridge's potential customers on the wrong side of the Thames. They're missing out. The interior (cold, canteen-like) is no great shakes but the gaze is directed elsewhere – at the Globe, Tate Modern and, probably to the irritation of the management, at the Wobbly Bridge itself. Sexy-sounding duck and mango spring rolls (£7.00), atop crisp seaweed and red chilli, hint at the chef's ambition but wild mushroom soup (£4.50) is more accomplished. Light pork medallions in Armagnac (£11.50) and supple lamb shanks in red wine (£12.50) are kept level-headed by smooth colcannon. Joggers panting past the windows prompt temperance but there are unusual desserts to tempt – try mango and cinnamon crème brûlée or chocolate and prune tart (both £4.50). A solid establishment with fine service – all it needs now are customers.

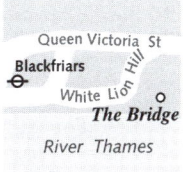

starter £4.50-£8
main £10.50-£14.50
dessert £4-£5
wine £12-£43.50

JCB MC V; SW

Open: Mon-Fri noon-10.30pm (summer only Sat & Sun noon-6pm); reservations advisable in summer; licensed, no BYO

CITY

Tube: Tower Hill (400m),
DLR: Tower Gateway

Smoking throughout

starter £3.95-£5.95
main £6.50-£14.75
dessert £3.75-£4.50
Set menu £22 or £40
wine £11.90-£23.90

AC DC JCB MC V; SW

Cafe Spice Namaste
Indian

☎ 7488 9242
16 Prescot St E1

This is a restaurant big and brash enough for its City clientele. The interior heralds the colours of India; the walls of the 150-year-old building were painted using traditional methods. The starters are as memorable as the décor. Bhel poori (£4.25) is a flavoursome terrine of nuts and herbs; just as good is the lip-burning empadao de espinafre (£4.50), a spinach pastry awash in a rich coriander sauce. High expectations are lowered when mains arrive plated-up, with rice in microwaveable containers. The only flavour in the rice and seafood ullathiyad (£14.75) came from the garnish of coconut shavings. Ordered in disbelief, black pepper ice cream (£3.75) has a creamy vanilla flavour that is pleasantly sharpened by coarse pepper. Our meal may not have been flawless, but the interesting menu and convivial atmosphere demand a revisit. *Also at 247 Lavender Hill, Battersea, SW11* ☎ *7738 1717.*

Open: Mon-Fri noon-3pm, 6.15pm-10.30pm, Sat 6.30pm-10.30pm; reservations advisable; licensed, no BYO

Map 6 B1
Tube: Chancery Lane (300m)
Wheelchair access
Smoking throughout

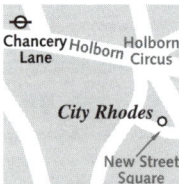

starter £7.50-£18.50
main £14.50-£23
dessert £7.50
wine £16.50-£300

AE DC MC V; SW

City Rhodes
Modern British

☎ 7583 1313
1 New Street Square EC4A

Gary Rhodes and the excellent reputation of modern British cooking are inseparable. Indeed, this TV celebrity chef has brought flair and imagination to traditional British fare, making it light, delicate and sophisticated. The pressed tomato cake with peppered goat's cheese (£8.50) is a perfect combination. The roast loin of lamb (£24) on a bed of leeks with caramelised onion gravy of lingering sweetness epitomises Gary's concept of modern comfort food. The spacious, minimalist dining room, in soothing shades of grey with gentle mauve lighting, provides the perfect backdrop for such dazzling culinary creations. Sadly, we were too full to try the famous Rhodes bread-and-butter pudding (£7.50), although we did manage to squeeze in several delectable baby chocolate sponge cakes with our coffee (£2.50). Be prepared for an unconventional menu (great for fans of foie gras, veal and pig) and exorbitantly priced vegetables (£3 a portion), but otherwise an undeniably impressive dining experience.

Open: Mon-Fri noon-2.30pm, 6pm-9pm; reservations essential; licensed, no BYO

CITY

The Don Restaurant and Bistro
Modern European

☎ 7626 2606
The Courtyard, 20 St Swithin's Lane EC4

Housed in the old Sandeman port bottling cellar, The Don upholds a tradition of vinous excellence begun in 1798, and the food's not bad either. The restaurant upstairs is more popular (especially with suits) but try ducking into the cellar bistro – if the sympathetic conversion (candles throwing shadows over the arched brick roof, a huge frieze depicting the building's past) doesn't draw you in, the personable staff will. The food gets off to an inauspicious start, with bland goat's cheese and plum tomato tatin (£5.50) and vinegary seared peppered beef (£6.75). The mains, though, are superb: beautifully flaky smoked haddock (£8.95) complemented by a subtle gruyere sauce, and perfectly cooked rump steak (£12.95) vying for attention with the chunkiest of chips. The proof here is not in the pudding so skip dessert and call over the sommelier – a bottle of vintage port is decanted daily for your delectation.

Open: Mon-Fri noon-3pm, 6pm-10.30pm; reservations accepted; licensed, no BYO

Map 6 C4
Tube/rail: Cannon Street (80m) or tube: Bank or Monument

 Smoking throughout

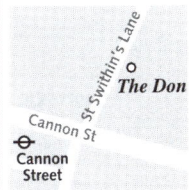

starter £4.50-£6.95
main £8.75-£12.95
dessert £5-£7.75
wine £14.95-£850

AE MC V; SW

Futures Café-Bar
International Vegetarian

☎ 7638 6341
2 Exchange Square EC2A
www.1e.btwebworld.com/futures1/

Slap bang in the centre of the action, Futures offers a refuge from the cut and thrust of the working day (the palm tree growing in the conservatory suggests a certain awareness of this oasis appeal). The cafe is a blithe yellow and the walls display undemanding art (for sale). To kickstart your taste buds, you can email them (futures.restaurant@btinternet.com) and ask them to send a copy of the daily vegetarian menu – and if time is tight then takeaway is available. A plate piled high with combination salad (£5.50) included spoonfuls of rice with a lemongrass and chilli dressing. Good service became memorable when our query regarding an elusive flavour in the chasseur (fresh vegetables in a wine and herb sauce; £6.50) was answered with a handwritten recipe. Dessert came in huge slices but we still wanted more of the lemon meringue pie (£2.95). *Also at 8 Botolph Alley, City, EC3R* ☎ *7623 4529 for takeaway only.*

Open: Mon-Fri 7.30am-3pm (bar until 10pm); reservations not accepted; licensed, no BYO

Map 6 A5
Tube/rail: Liverpool Street (100m)

Wheelchair access

 No smoking at lunch; nonsmoking tables available otherwise

 Terrace tables

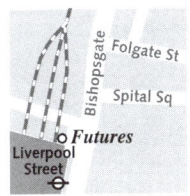

main £2.95-£6.50
dessert £2.95
wine £9.95-£25.50

AE JCB MC V; SW

CITY

Map 6 C2
Tube: St Paul's (250m)
Wheelchair access
Smoking throughout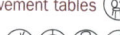
Pavement tables

Perc%nto
Italian

☎ 7778 0010
26 Ludgate Hill EC4M
www.etruscagroup.co.uk

Perc%nto is an attempt to make a corporate hotel restaurant funky and modern but, hard as the design and staff try, there's no getting away from its unatmospheric sterility. However, it does offer a wonderfully varied menu, thanks to its famed chef, Valentino Bosch, who creates some unique and innovative Italian dishes. Tender carpaccio with rocket and parmesan (£8) is enhanced by a sweet fruit dressing, while tangy, fresh marinated seabass (£8.50) is deliciously light. Creative mains include rich barbery duck (£13.75), which is beautifully presented on a tower of aubergine, sundried tomatoes and fondant potatoes. Complementing the food is a extensive wine list, including some exceptional vintages. Perc%nto has responded to the needs of its City clientele: if you want a table over lunch you'll need to book in advance. In the evenings, however, the place is almost deserted save a few solitary business travellers.

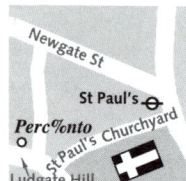

starter £6.50-£8.50
main £7-£17.50
dessert £4.50-£5
wine £12.50-£260

AE DC MC V: SW

Open: Mon-Fri noon-3pm, 6.30pm-10pm; reservations advisable; licensed, no BYO

Map 6 C3
Tube: Mansion House (200m)
Courtyard tables

The Place Below
Modern British Vegetarian

☎ 7329 0789
St Mary-le-Bow Church Cheapside, EC2V
www.theplacebelow.co.uk

Buried in a church crypt, The Place Below is a vegetarian haven for the masses. Full of fresh, imaginative ideas, Bill Sewell's crew are experts at blending and incorporating flavours on the daily changing menu. Try the hearty soups (£2.90) or a hot dish of the day such as chunky field mushroom and lentil casserole (£7). There's also a quiche of the day (£6.50) and a range of interesting sandwiches (£5). Another sure bet is the healthbowl (£5.50), wholegrain rice and puy lentils in tangy soy balsamic dressing; served with a varying selection of vegetables and nori (dried seaweed), it's a vibrant combination of colour and flavour. Don't leave without trying one of the delicious desserts (£2.80), the juicy apple and raspberry crumble was the best we'd ever tasted. Wash it all down with one of their crisp cordials (£1.40) or some of the best coffee (£1.15) in the City.

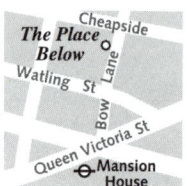

starter £2.90
main £5-£7.50
dessert £2.80

MC V; SW

Open: Mon-Fri 7.30am-4pm; reservations not accepted; BYO (no corkage)

CITY

Singapura
South-East Asian

☎ 7329 1133
1-2 Limeburner Lane EC4M
www.singapura-restaurants.co.uk

Map 6 C2
Tube: St Paul's (400m)
Wheelchair access

 Smoking throughout

Singapura is a buzzy lunchtime favourite for the suits and a quieter dinner destination in the evening. The traditional Indonesian outfits worn by the staff add authenticity to this large, comfortable and stylish South-East Asian restaurant. A complimentary dish of prawn crackers with spicy sauce is served as you peruse the difficult-to-choose-from dozen starters. Siput (£5.95), a dish of stir-fried mussels with lemongrass, lime leaves, ginger and chilli in sherry sauce, assaults the taste buds with flavours, and few Thai fishcakes (£5.75) offered in London are as good as these, served with spices and lime leaves. Features of the mains include itek sio (£11), braised magret duck in soya sauce flavoured with galangal and star anise, and ayam goreng (£7.50), crispy chicken marinated in sesame oil and soy sauce. With rice dishes at £3 and vegetables £4.95, Singapura is a little pricey but worth the extra outlay.

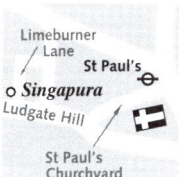

starter £4.50-£9.50
main £7.50-£12.50
dessert £6
set menu £18, £25 or £30
wine £9.95-£39

AE JCB MC V; SW

Open: Mon-Fri 11.30am-10pm; reservations advisable; licensed, no BYO

Sweetings
Seafood

☎ 7248 3062
39 Queen Victoria St EC4

Map 6 C3
Tube: Mansion House (100m)

 Smoking throughout

With almost 100 years on the same premises Sweetings is an institution and, like the décor, the no-frills menu and clientele hasn't changed in 50 years. Seating is at communal tables or on stools at one of the four counters lorded over by the young and effortlessly casual staff. We tried the very generous prawn salad (£8.75) and followed with the daily special, in this case moist baked hake with a tomato and vegetable sauce (£17.50). Otherwise, grilled salmon (£12.75) was just that, perfectly cooked but utterly forlorn on its plate. Desserts (£3.25) were dry and uninspiring old favourites. Food at Sweetings is a bit hit and miss but, if you're willing to pay for an old-world atmosphere, this is your chance to sip a glass of vintage port and belly up to the bar with some hard-core traditionalists.

starter £3.25-£16.75
main £8.25-£19.95
dessert £3.25
wine £11.50-£26.50

cash or cheque only

Open: Mon-Fri 11.30am-3pm; reservations not accepted; licensed, no BYO

CITY

Map 6 A4
Tube/rail: Liverpool Street (200m)
Smoking throughout

starter £3.50-£9.80
main £15-£35
set lunch £28-£43, £40-£80
wine £15-£132
AE DC JCB MC V; SW

Tatsuso
Japanese

☎ 7638 5863
32 Broadgate Circle EC2M

A favourite with the City business crowd, Tatsuso offers expensive but high-quality versions of two very different kinds of Japanese cuisine. Upstairs it's teppanyaki with the chefs staging cookery performances as they fry up beef, lobster and the like on steel griddles inches from diners' plates. Downstairs there's the less theatrical traditional dining room, where kimono-robed waitresses proffer warm, scented hot towels and cups of green tea. It's possible to sit at the counter watching the sushi chefs, but if you have a small party, go the whole hog and book one of the private tatami mat rooms and enjoy your meal in appropriate surroundings. The Tekago set lunch (£38) includes fine sashimi and tempura, but the highlights are the melt-in-the-mouth deep-fried fig appetiser and the savoury egg custard – as good as we've ever had.

Open: Mon-Fri 11.30am-2.30pm, 6pm-9.45pm; reservations advisable; licensed, no BYO

Map 15 A5
Tube: Tower Hill (350m)
Wheelchair access
Smoking throughout
Terrace tables

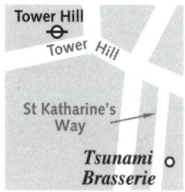

starter £3.50-£6.95
main £6.50-£10.80
dessert £3.75-£5.50
wine £12-£130
set lunch £10
AE DC JCB MC V; SW

Tsunami Brasserie & Waterside Terrace
International

☎ 7481 0972
**International House,
1 St Katharine's Way E1**
www.tsunami-events.com

Tsunami's neon-framed entrance leads into a marine-coloured, pop-art interior, replete with tropical fish tank. Catering to the rich seam of suited booted locals, it's a fine venue for a business lunch – with widely spaced tables overlooking a cluster of yachts in St Katherine's Dock – though not an ideal evening haunt unless you cherish your own space. Uptight food involves sauces daintily scattered across large white plates and dishes piled precipitously at their centres. Starters are rich and punchy – try aubergine with pesto and parmesan (£3.50) and cockles, winkles and whelks in fragrant Thai broth (£4.50). Monkfish wrapped in ham on wasabi mash with tomato and papaya salsa (£9.95) and cod on sag aloo with chermoula sauce (£9.50) try too hard, and could do with simplification. But buttery apple tarte tatin with Calvados cream (£5.50) or voluptuous white chocolate brownie (£5.50) are superlative ways to close the deal.

Open: Mon-Fri noon-2.30pm, Mon-Sat 6pm-10pm; reservations advisable; licensed, no BYO

CITY

Vertigo 42
Seafood

☎ **7877 7842**
Tower 42, Old Broad St EC2N
www.vertigo42.co.uk

Map 6 B5
Tube: Liverpool Street (350m) or Bank
Wheelchair access
 Smoking throughout

For amazing views, forget the BA London Eye and visit Vertigo 42. But for amazing food, forget Vertigo 42 and visit anywhere else. Vertigo boasts an awesome panorama and truly awful seafood, at prices that'll have you wishing you'd eaten at the sandwich bar downstairs. We'd planned on oysters (£20 for a dozen), but after our canapes starter (£15) we decided fresh produce wasn't Vertigo's strength. The rank potted shrimp (£12.75) came as no surprise, and the sludgy smoked haddock risotto (£9.95) lived up to our by then low expectations. But the folk at *wallpaper** would still adore Vertigo's rounded hallways and astounding views, best just before sundown. Vertigo's an apt name: peering out the thin glass windows is stomach-churning at first but soon you'll be spotting Big Ben like everyone else.

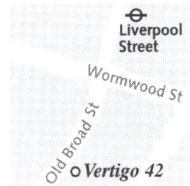

starter £12-£15
main £10-£30
dessert £6.50
wine £22-£56

AE DC MC V; SW

Open: Mon-Fri noon-3pm, 5pm-11pm; reservations essential; licensed, no BYO

Asia de Cuba (Carl Drury)

COVENT GARDEN

Map 2 E1
Tube: Leicester Square (300m)
Wheelchair access
Smoking throughout

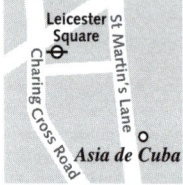

starter £8.50-£14.50
main £14.50-£39
dessert £7.50-£13.00
wine £26-£180

AE DC JCB MC V; SW

Asia de Cuba
Asian/Cuban

☎ 7300 5500
45 St Martin's Lane WC2N

Giant chess pieces and gold molar seats in the lobby of the St Martin's Lane Hotel set the Dali-esque tone for Asia de Cuba. Dragging our attention from the Starck-designed interior, the matey waiter informed us the menu is a 'share concept' and that two starters and one main is ideal. At these prices it'd have to be. The fusion of tropical and oriental was immediately apparent in dishes such as the tunapica (£10.50), spicy, fruity tuna tartare on wonton crisps, and the calamari salad (£12.50), teaming slightly rubbery squid with a zesty salad including banana and heart of palm. Another unlikely combo of five-spiced sirloin steak with a pink grapefruit salad and black bean croquettes (£22.50) worked well and was nicely presented, just like our dessert (a knockout tequila and lime sorbet with pineapple and strawberries; £7.50), which looked so fetching we didn't know whether to eat it or wear it.

Open: Mon-Fri noon-2.30pm, Mon-Wed 5.30pm-midnight, Thurs-Sat 5.30pm-1am, Sun 5.30pm-10.30pm; reservations essential; licensed, no BYO

Map 2 D1
Tube: Covent Garden (180m)
Smoking throughout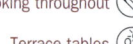
Terrace tables

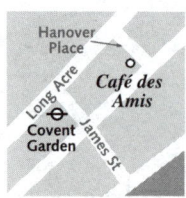

starter £5.50-£8.50
main £8.50-£16.95
dessert £4.75-£7.50
pre- & post-theatre menu £12.50 or £15
wine £10.95-£39

AE DC JCB MC V; SW

Café des Amis
Modern French

☎ 7379 3444
11-14 Hanover Place WC2E

Tucked down a narrow Covent Garden alley, sleek Café des Amis calls itself French, but that description fades right after the French subheadings on the menu. 'Les Pains' include a nice oily ciabatta (£1.95) and 'Les Entrées' feature a mozzarella salad with rocket and delectable aubergine croutons (£5.75). 'Les Petits ou Grands Plats' comprise an array of variably sized dishes such as a rich, three-onion risotto (£5.85/9.95), and 'Les Plats' offer a range of meat and fish dishes including a crispy but moist roasted halibut (£16.95) atop tasty garlic mashed potato. We left the wine choice to the server who rewarded our faith with an excellent tasting, well-priced Spanish Lorinõn Crianza 1996 Rioja (£9.60). The pre- and post-theatre menu served before 7pm and after 10pm is an excellent deal at £12.50/15.00 for two/three courses. We told the staff we had a 7.30pm curtain and we finished right on time.

Open: Mon-Sat 11.30am-11.30pm; reservations advisable; licensed, no BYO

COVENT GARDEN

Calabash
African

☎ 7836 1976
38 King St WC2E

Map 2 E1
Tube: Covent Garden (180m)
 Smoking throughout

Pass through the Africa Centre to get to Calabash, where a magnificent flurry of spices and flavours await in the form of generously portioned, inexpensive and delicious dishes from all over Africa. The atmosphere is relaxed, the decorations authentic; note the injera (bread) holder, the screen-printed tablecloths and the African landscapes. The vegetarian sambusa (£2.95), a stuffed pastry, makes an inspired starter; likewise the aloco (fried plantain in hot tomato sauce; £2.30), an African classic that comes sweet but not too sweet. The Nigerian egusi (£6.95), a main featuring chunks of fish in a rich, musky sauce, can be delightfully accompanied by a baked yam sponge. For dessert, the pineapple and rum fritter (£2.50), which the waiter expertly sets alight, is easily enough for two. The sole disappointment is that the full slate of African beers and wines – which can be tasted by the glass – is not always available.

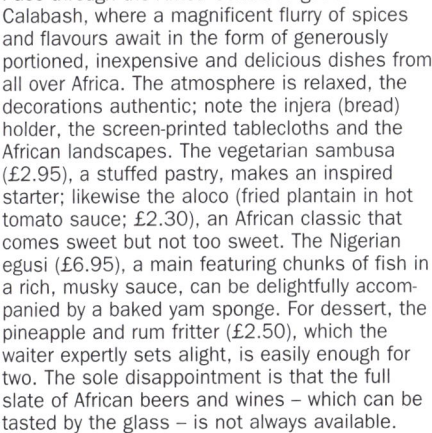

starter £2-£2.95
main £4.75-£7.75
dessert £1.80-£2.50
wine £6.95

MC V

Open: Mon-Fri noon-3pm, Mon-Sat 6pm-midnight; reservations accepted (advisable at weekends); licensed, no BYO

Christopher's American Grill
American

☎ 7240 4222
18 Wellington St WC2E
www.christophersgrill.com

Map 2 E2
Tube: Temple (600m)
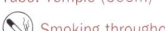 Smoking throughout

This high-ceilinged restaurant, founded to bring Londoners traditional American fare, inhabits a grand old building that was once, variously, a casino and (allegedly) a brothel. The food is classy and good, and the clientele comprises theatre-goers and other tranquil types. Attentive, efficient staff weave between tables carrying trays laden with fresh bread. The ample pear salad (£7) is threaded with soft chunks of blue cheese and hard caramelised walnuts. The fishcake main (£12) comes as thick, flavourful twin patties resting on a foamy bed of basil cream, and the grilled chicken breast (£14.50) with borlotti beans is pleasantly tender. The cappuccino brownie (£7.50) is moistened by a smooth dollop of chocolate-chip ice cream. Those resisting a full bottle of wine will find plenty of choice by the glass – but be sure to specify whether you want a full glass or a taster. *Also at Thistle Victoria, Buckingham Palace Road, Victoria, SW1W ☎ 7976 5522.*

starter £4.50-£9.50
main £12-£28
dessert £5.50-£7.50
pre-theatre menu
£14.50/£18.50
wine £14.50-£480

AE DC JCB MC V; SW

Open: Mon-Fri noon-3pm, 5pm-midnight, Sat 11.30am-4pm, 5pm-midnight, Sun 11.30am-4pm; reservations advisable (especially weekday lunches); licensed, no BYO

COVENT GARDEN

Map 2 D1
Tube: Covent Garden (100m)
Entertainment: DJ Thurs-Sat
Smoking throughout

starter £4-£5.80
main £10-£13.75
dessert £4
wine £12.75-£20
AE DC MC V; SW

Detroit
International

☎ 7240 2662
35 Earlham St WC2H
www.detroit-bar.com

For the hipper London socialites, the basement bar and restaurant Detroit is certainly a place to be seen. The cavernous interior, sandstone walls and circular designs adorning the ceiling are reminiscent of a 1960s sci-fi film set. The bar is the venue's focal point and boasts a superb cocktail list. Off to the side, a small dining area provides sustenance to soak up any alcohol intake. The generous platter of Scotch smoked salmon with anchovies in oil and vinegar (£5.80) receives well-earned praise, and the vegetarian lasagne stefano (£10) is full of interesting flavours – Jerusalem artichokes, aubergines and mushrooms layered between sheets of pasta and topped with freshly grated parmesan. A side portion of fries (£3) seems pricey but is more than enough to feed two hungry people. The service is relaxed and unpretentious, making it a good place to chill.

Open: Mon-Fri 5pm-midnight, Sat 6pm-midnight; reservations advisable; licensed, no BYO

Map 2 E1
Tube: Leicester Square (150m)

starter £5.50-£10
main £7.50-£21
dessert £3.50-£5.50
wine £13.50-£250
AE DC JCB MC V; SW

Giovanni's
Italian

☎ 7240 2877
10 Goodwin's Court,
off 55 St Martin's Lane WC2N

Hidden away down an 18th-century alleyway, this small Italian restaurant is popular with the stars who appear at Covent Garden and the English National Opera. Roberto Alagna and Angela Gheorghiu, still the current darlings of the opera scene, had their first date at Giovanni's and they continue to make frequent visits. The atmosphere of romance is almost palpable – in fact, young Chilean tenor Tito Beltran, a regular, has been known to belt out a few arias for the assembled diners. If he's not in town you can try his favourite dish, rosetta alla Tito Beltran: rolled breast of chicken with spinach, tomato and pecorino cheese (£9.50). The menu has a distinct Sicilian influence, with spicy pasta sauces and wines which are deep, flavourful and pricey (few choices under £20 a bottle).

Open: Mon-Fri noon-3pm, Mon-Sat 5.45pm-11.30pm; reservations essential; licensed, no BYO

COVENT GARDEN

The Ivy
Modern European

☎ 7836 4751
1 West St WC2H

For the grand central of London luvviedom, The Ivy is surprisingly unpretentious. The snappy service is friendly and unobtrusive, and the menu as ready to dabble in world cuisine – such as sashimi (£11.50) or Thai-baked sea bass (£21.75) – as British standards. We pass from the neat bar to the panelled dining room – a place where Celia Johnson might have had a tryst with Trevor Howard in another age – to tuck into starters of crisp asparagus and artichoke (£8.75), fresh and liberally truffled, and a creamy onion and cider soup (£5.75). The shepherd's pie (£10.75) is a classic round of mince and potato in a sea of glistening gravy, while the kedgeree (£10.25) features mushrooms and salmon and a touch too much curry powder. Round it all off with more comfort foods, such as the spot-on sticky toffee pudding (£6.25). Scoring a table is the trickiest part.

Open: Mon-Sat noon-3pm, Sun noon-3.30pm, daily 5.30pm-midnight; reservations essential; licensed, no BYO

Map 2 D1
Tube: Leicester Square (150m)

 Smoking throughout

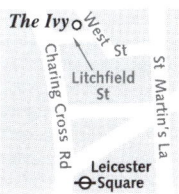

starter £5.75-£23
main £9.50-£30
dessert £5.75-£6.75
set lunch (weekends) £16.50
wine £11.50-£500

AE DC MC V; SW

Mon Plaisir
French

☎ 7836 7243
21 Monmouth St WC2H
www.monplaisir.co.uk

Mon Plaisir, one of the oldest French restaurants in London, is a delightfully intimate series of low-lit rooms with exposed brickwork and expressionist canvases. Couples, business types – even genuine French people – are waited on by polite French staff. Bargain set meals abound, but the most interesting choices are kept for the imaginative à la carte. Who wouldn't be intrigued by venison with bitter chocolate and girotte sauce (£15), livery meat surprisingly well matched with chocolate and cherries? Whatever your order, crispy pommes allumettes (£1.95) are a must. Earlier, the starter menu had paired perfect scallops with pumpkin and Parmesan purée and an aromatic sage pesto (£7.95), and produced an onion soup (£5.95) that was big and beefy. Crème brûlée (£5.50) has lots of lovely caramel topping, but we failed to spot the promised orange flavour. The fondant chocolate (£5.50) is a soft-centred sponge pudding. The pleasure was all ours.

Open: Mon-Fri noon-2.15pm, Mon-Sat 5.45pm-11.15pm; reservations advisable; licensed, no BYO

Map 2 D1
Tube: Covent Garden (250m)

 Nonsmoking tables available

starter £5.20-£11.50
main £13.75-£15
dessert £5.50
set dinner £23.50/person (min 2 people), pre-theatre menu £11.95 or £14.95
wine £14.50-£75

AE DC JCB MC V; SW

COVENT GARDEN

Map 2 E1
Tube: Charing Cross (400m)
Wheelchair access
Entertainment: traditional Irish music Sun afternoon, DJs Thurs-Sat evening
Smoking throughout

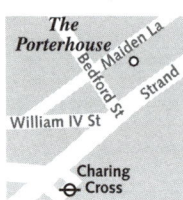

starter £2.50
main £4.95-£13.50
dessert £2.95-£4.95
wine £10.95-£22.50
MC V; SW

The Porterhouse Stout & Oyster Bar
Irish/Thai

☎ 7379 7917
20/22 Maiden Lane WC2E
www.porterhousebrewco.com

The Porterhouse succeeds neither as gastropub nor as novelty act, given the slew of Irish theme bars across London. The labyrinthine interior is soulless and poorly designed around a central atrium with lost rooms spun off at random, and the service is indifferent. Foodwise, however, it fares better. The menu initially looks like a standard pub-fodder roll call of steaks (£11.95) and burgers (£5.75). Scratch beneath the veneer, however, and the beer and stout served with mashed potatoes (£6.95) offers tender meat in a tasty stout-tinged sauce, while the Thai Irish stew (£7.95) is a real winter warmer – hunks of meat and vegetables with a gentle pinch of chilli-inspired spice. It's satisfying pub grub, but more impressive are the huge range of world beers and delicious speciality brews on tap. A place where the beer is definitely first and the food is an afterthought.

Mon-Fri noon-3pm, 5pm-9pm, Sat noon-9pm, Sun noon-5pm; reservations accepted; licensed, no BYO

Map 2 D1
Tube: Covent Garden (350m)
Smoking throughout
Pavement tables

starter £1.50-£3
main £3-£12
dessert £2
wine £7-£10
MC V; SW

The Rock & Sole Plaice
British/Fish

☎ 7836 3785
47 Endell St WC2H

One of London's oldest fish-and-chip shops (est. 1871), the Rock & Sole Plaice is a Covent Garden institution, enjoying a constant stream of customers at both its takeaway and restaurant. Its reputation is certainly well deserved. The succulent cod (£7) is crisply battered and garnished with lemon and parsley, while the thick chips (£2) are freshly made and not at all greasy. For the more adventurous fish-eater, the range of specialities includes dover sole (£11), Scotch salmon (8.50) and tuna steak (£8). Vegetarians can have a pastie (£4), plus a host of extras such as baked beans (£1) and, of course, mushy peas (£1). You can sit upstairs and lap up the atmosphere or relax downstairs amid the aquarium mosaics that adorn the walls – wherever, you can be sure of quick, friendly service and top-quality fish and chips.

Open Mon-Sat 11.30am-11.30pm, Sun noon-10pm; reservations accepted; licensed, no BYO

The Rock & Sole Plaice (Simon Bracken)

Rules
British

☎ **7836 5314**
35 Maiden Lane WC2
www.rules.co.uk

Map 2 E1
Tube/rail: Charing Cross (350m)

The dark mahogany booths, heavy curtains, extensive wine list and monied hush of the business clientele all whisper that, yes, you are in 'London's Oldest Restaurant' (est. 1798). So it was a shock when the waiter took out a computer hand pad to electronically send the order to the kitchen; the high prices are another reminder that you're in the 21st century. Still, you are dining in a place that welcomed Charles Dickens and countless other luminaries, and the service is of a high standard. As you would expect from an establishment steeped in such history, the menu offers traditionally prepared fish (salmon and brill with vermouth sauce for £17.95) along with classic game cookery (foie gras, deer, pigeon, grouse), much of the latter bred for the restaurant on Scottish ranges. Traditionalists will love it, but sensitive vegetarians should probably keep walking.

Open: daily noon-midnight; reservations advisable; licensed, no BYO

starter £6.95-£13.50
main £16.95-£22.50
dessert £6.75
wine £13.95-£36.95
set menu Mon-Fri (3pm-5pm) £19.95
AE DC JCB MC V

COVENT GARDEN 37

COVENT GARDEN

Map 2 D2
Tube: Holborn (450m)
Wheelchair access
Entertainment: opera Sun & Mon
Nonsmoking tables available

Sarastro
Mediterranean

☎ 7836 0101
126 Drury Lane WC2B
www.sarastro-restaurant.com

An Aladdin's cave of theatrical memorabilia, Ottoman artefacts, gilded stucco and plush velvet drapery, Sarastro is a treat for the senses. The flamboyant interior was created by renowned Turkish designer Richard Sleeman, who has maximised space by mimicking the layout of a theatre – there are stall, balcony and dress circle seats as well as a royal opera box. Meze is served on arrival as you select from the tempting Mediterranean menu. Anatolian-style lamb (£11) was slightly overcooked, but it comes in a tasty, rich sauce, while the salmon (£8.50) is a fresh, light alternative. The atmosphere is unique and on Sunday and Monday evening singers entertain diners with well-known arias. For the best views and some privacy, ask for one of the opera boxes. Sarastro is a visual sensation, a great night out and an interesting (and cheaper) alternative to an evening at the Royal Opera House.

starter £4-£8.50
main £8.50-£14.50
dessert £3.50-£4.50
set lunch £10
set dinner £19.50
wine £10.75-£35

AE DC MC V; SW

Open: Mon-Sun noon-midnight; reservations advisable; licensed, no BYO

Map 2 D1
Tube: Covent Garden (250m)

World Food Cafe
Global Vegetarian

☎/fax 7379 0298
1st Floor, 14 Neal's Yard
WC2H

Overlooking one of London's prettiest courtyards, the World Food Cafe has a vegetarian menu spanning three continents. Huge windows and travel photographs ensure your meal comes with a serving of wanderlust. When the communal tables are full, there are seats at the counter framing the kitchen (a cafe that washes its dirty plates in public has nothing to hide). You can feast on traditional Mexican, Indian, Turkish or African dishes (£7.95) while sipping on fresh lime juice or a banana lassi. If your hunger isn't of global proportions opt for one of the light meals (£5.95), smaller portions but with similar ingredients. Simple desserts include fruit compote (£3.25) and an indulgent chocolate cake (£3.45). The dishes are unpretentious and true to their origins, and the easygoing atmosphere is a relief from all the manic shopping outside. You'll wonder what the previous residents (see the plaque outside) think of such wholesome pursuits.

main £5.95-£7.95
dessert £3.25-£3.45
MC V; SW

Open: Mon-Fri 11.30am-4.30pm, Sat 11.30am-5pm; reservations not accepted; BYO (corkage 95p/bottle)

EDGWARE ROAD

Abu Ali
Lebanese

☎ 7724 6338
136-138 George St W1H

Map 4 D2
Tube: Marble Arch (550m)
Nonsmoking tables available
Pavement tables

Many Middle Eastern restaurants try to conjure up the romance of Arabia, but Abu Ali is more like what you find when you get there. Lebanese regulars congregate in this unpretentious kebab house for a taste of home, be it coffee with cardamom, home-style Lebanese food or a leisurely afternoon with some friends and a bubbling hookah pipe (£5). Expect no frills though – the tables are formica, the clientele is mostly male and a large-screen television belts out non-stop Arabic hits on cable TV. To start, try the warak inab (£3), tasty pickled vine leaves stuffed with chickpeas, rice and herbs, or salty grilled halloumi cheese (£3). Wholesome kebabs such as the minced-lamb kafta halabiyeh (£6) are served simply with rice, Turkish pickles and tomatoes. Top it all off with a Turkish coffee (£2) and nutty baklava (£1.75). Simple but satisfying.

Open: daily 9am-11pm; reservations not accepted; unlicensed

starter £2.50-£4.50
main £6-£7
dessert £1.75-£3
cash or cheque only

Al Dar
Lebanese

☎ 7402 2541
61-63 Edgware Rd W2

Map 4 D2
Tube: Marble Arch (500m)
Smoking throughout
Pavement tables

Lively, dependable and friendly, Al Dar offers an extensive menu that includes all the usual Middle Eastern standards (houmous, tabbouleh, grilled halloumi – £3.50) as well as some less familiar choices. The best bet is to order a range of dishes and mix and match while you sip on one of the stunning freshly squeezed juices (£2.50). Try loubiah bizeit, a spicy combo of French beans with tomato, onion, garlic and oil (£3.50) or the generous and tasty mixed grill (£8.50). Or there's kibbeh bessineyeh (£8.50), an unusual dish of fried minced meat and pine kernels, oven baked in a crushed-wheat casing. Alternatively, wolf down one of the excellent sandwiches (£2.50-£3) or some sweet and sticky baklava (£3.50). Choose the brightly lit cafe section where eating is a no-nonsense affair or the more relaxed and comfy bistro where regulars smoke a sheesha (£6) or two and watch the world go by.

Open: daily 8am-1am; reservations not accepted at the weekend; unlicensed

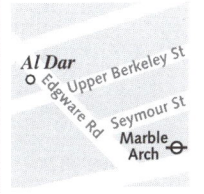

starter £2.50-£4.50
main £7.50-£8.50
dessert £3-£4
AE MC V

EDGWARE ROAD

Tube: Edgware Road (300m) or Warwick Avenue

Entertainment: musician evenings

Smoking throughout

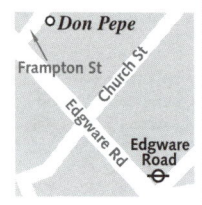

Don Pepe
Spanish

☎ 7262 3834/7723 9749
99 Frampton St NW8
www.don-pepe.com

Grab your castanets for a trip to Edgware Road's slice of Spain, where tapas, fish, pork and more pork are served up to lulling melodies on an electric keyboard. Established in 1974, this tapas bar prides itself on being London's first, winning a host of awards in the '80s. Little has changed since the glory days: the food is *excelente*, the waiters are hospitable and it's the closest thing to Spain in the big smoke. Gape in awe as waiters chip blocks of salt from Don Pepe's favourite dish, lubina a la sal (£15.00), a floorshow for the moist, surprisingly unsalty seabass hidden inside. If you hanker for meat, try juicy layers of Serrano ham (£6.00) or mouth-tingling pork fillets (£7.50). Top it off with syrupy flan de huevo (crème caramel; £2.50) and you're one of the family – like the chappy with the bagpipes, Gallgo, the Galician mascot.

starter £3-£14.50
main £7.50-£16.50
dessert £2.25-£3.00
set dinner £13.95
wine £8.50-£29

AE DC JCB MC V; SW

Open: Mon-Sat noon-3pm, 7pm-1am (tapas bar from 6pm); reservations advisable; licensed, no BYO

Tube: Edgware Road (250m)

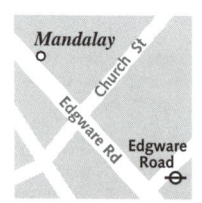

Mandalay
Burmese

☎/fax 7258 3696
444 Edgware Rd W2

Mandalay looks like a solicitors' office from the street. Inside, it feels like a caff run by a faith-healer. Somehow, the plastic tablecloths, Burmese bric-a-brac and avuncular service soothe the spirit. We couldn't resist the price of the three-course set lunch (£5.50) and weren't disappointed. Tamarind and ginger dipping sauces lifted succulent spring rolls – a simple thing rarely done this well – and hints of coriander added complexity to a coconut chicken curry. The full menu offers salads, noodle and vegetarian dishes, most liberally spiced with chillies, dried shrimp and lemongrass. The sauce accompanying crisp fried fish (£5.90) needed more of these flavours, but mokhingar (£5.50) is a showcase of the cuisine, shrimp paste and fish sauce giving an intense, sinus-clearing zing to a magnificent hot soup with rice noodles. Like everything else here, banana fritters (£1.90), served in a pool of light molasses sauce, are unbelievable value.

starter £1.20-£5
main £3.90-£6.90
dessert £1.50-£2.50
set lunch £3.70 or £5.90
wine £7.90-£8.90

AE DC JCB MC V; SW

Open: Mon-Sat noon-2.30pm, 6pm-10.30pm; reservations essential; licensed, no BYO

EDGWARE ROAD

Patogh
Iranian

☎ 7262 4015
8 Crawford Place W1

Map 4 C2
Tube: Edgware Road (250m)

Smoking throughout

Londoners would rather you didn't know about this inexpensive and deeply authentic Persian restaurant. For one thing you might take their seat – Patogh has just a handful of tables in its tiny dining room-cum-kitchen. The food is superb, and the subtle lighting and earthy décor make it feel surprisingly intimate. The highlight of the menu is the Persian bread (£1.50), a vast oversized pitta topped with sesame and poppy seed, served hot from the oven. Get primal and rip it up to dip in your houmous (£2) or masto moosir (£2), a creamy mix of yoghurt and minced shallots. Kebabs are the mainstay of Persian cuisine, and Patogh doesn't disappoint. The chenjeh kebab (£8) is mouth-watering – perfectly cooked lamb marinated in lemon and olive oil, served with bread, salad or rice. Come early if you want to beat the locals to a seat.

Open: daily noon-midnight; reservations accepted; BYO (no corkage)

starter £2-£4.50
main £5-£9.50

cash or cheque only

CENTRAL

Patogh (Carl Drury)

EUSTON

Diwana Bhel Poori House
Indian Vegetarian

☎ 7387 5556
121-123 Drummond St NW1

Map 3 A1
Tube: Warren Street (100m) or tube/rail: Euston
Nonsmoking tables available

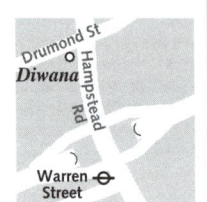

Diwana's reputation as top dog among the doyens of Drummond St has been formed over years of dishing up superb vegetarian food. Tear into the enormous lentil and rice deluxe dosa (£4.60) and you'll see why: the spiced potato filling with coconut chutney and hot lentil and vegetable sambhar is well worth savouring. The chewy cheese and vegetable kofta malai (£4.95) offers a bit more substance and has a rich but mild sauce. For the really ravenous, the Diwana thali (£6.20) is a full meal, comprising a range of vegetable dishes and lentil dhal, as well as rice, breads, a starter and shrikhand – a syrupy dessert of cheese, spices and sugar. If the heat leaves your tongue tingling, try a sweet yoghurt lassi (£1.50) – the best oral fire extinguisher this side of Bombay (or Brick Lane, at least).

starter £2.30-£3
main £2.80-£6.20
dessert £1.50-£1.75
buffet lunch £5.10
AE DC JCB MC V; SW

Open: daily noon-midnight; reservations advisable; BYO (no corkage)

Ravi Shankar
Indian

☎ 7388 6458
133 Drummond St NW1

Map 3 A2
Tube: Euston Square (250m) or tube/rail: Euston

Sister restaurant of nearby Chutneys, at Ravi Shankar you'll eat with the satisfaction of knowing you're getting the same food at cheaper prices. The furniture's simple and the dining room is bright, airy and spotless. There's the standard over-abundance of waiters serving, none of whom seem happy to be doing so, but does it matter at these prices? Take the Mysore thali (£5.70) – how they produce something this tasty, this fresh and this quickly is beyond us. The bhindi du plaza (lady fingers in tomato and onion sauce; £2.80) is a telling dish – at dodgy curry houses it's mush but Ravi Shankar passes the test admirably. For dessert, dry gulab jamun (fried milk balls in syrup; £1.25) is a mistake, though tasty kulfi (Indian ice-cream; £1.45) makes up for it. If you're stuck at Euston, for little more than that miserable sandwich you're eyeing up, consider Ravi Shankar instead.

starter £1.95-£2.75
main £2.80-£6.95
dessert £1.25-£3
wine £6.95-£13.95
MC V

Open: daily noon-11pm; reservations accepted; licensed, no BYO

FITZROVIA

CENTRAL

Bam-Bou
French-Vietnamese

☎ **7323 9130**
1 Percy St W1P
www.bam-bou.co.uk

Map 3 B2
Tube: Tottenham Court Road (350m) or Goodge Street

Smoking throughout

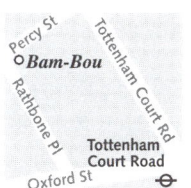

Terrace tables

Trendy, chic and full of beautiful people, Bam-Bou attracts media darlings from Fitzrovia. This listed Georgian townhouse has been transformed into a 'Colonial French-Vietnamese' restaurant and exclusive club, with food as sophisticated as the clientele and as original as the venue. To start, a disappointing selection of bland Bam-Bou rolls (£6.25) was compensated for by delicious sesame prawns (£6.25). Mains were excellent – pan-fried duck (£11.80) melted in the mouth and spice-rubbed swordfish (£9.50) was a taste sensation. Servings weren't generous, though mango and ginger sponge cake (£4.25) proved a tasty gap-filler and a perfect end to the meal.

starter £5-£7
main £9-£12
dessert £5-£6
set lunch & pre-theatre menu £12.50
wine £13-£80

AE DC MC SW; V

Open: Mon-Fri noon-3pm, Mon-Sat 6pm-11.15pm; reservations advisable; licensed, no BYO

Bam-Bou (Carl Drury)

FITZROVIA

Map 3 B2
Tube: Goodge Street (250m)
Smoking throughout

starter £1.50-£4.50
main £6.50-£13.50
dessert £3.50-£4
wine £11.50-£32

AE MC V; SW

Dish Dash
Anglo-Persian

☎ 7637 7474
57-59 Goodge St W1P
www.dish-dash.com

Dish Dash sets out to educate its clientele about the origins and extents of Persian cuisine via the place mats on its centrally sub-lit tables. A dim yet cheery interior is kitted out with chunky box-like stools, the odd hookah, and other Persian paraphernalia placed in vaguely Middle Eastern arches. Prompt but rough-edged service delivers diminutive meze portions (£3.50 each) to start, outflanked by the flavoursome native breads (£1.20). The tender braised Iraqi lamb shank (£10) was marginally bettered by lightly spiced honey and chilli swordfish kebab (£12.80). Desserts were also on the small side, but rich enough to sate the appetite. Some of the exotic sorbets (£4) were questionable, others were great – flavours change regularly. Baklava (£4.50), accompanied by honey ice cream, pleases the sweeter toothed. Try out the lively bar downstairs afterwards.

Open: Mon-Fri noon-4pm, 6pm-midnight, Sat & Sun 6pm-midnight; reservations advisable; licensed, no BYO

Map 3 B2
Tube: Goodge Street (20m)
No smoking at the counter

starter £1.10-£10.30
main £3.10-£13
dessert £2.30-£3
set menu £6.50-£8.30
wine £10-£11

AE DC MC V

Ikkyu
Japanese

☎ 7636 9280
67a Tottenham Court Rd W1T

Subterranean Ikkyu is a bustling, slightly frantic robatayaki (Japanese restaurant serving grilled food), with chefs working feverishly behind the main counter. The extensive menu includes standards as well as a number of pleasant surprises. The assorted sushi selection (£12.50) – six pieces of sushi and three pieces of tuna maki-sushi (with sesame seeds around the rice instead of nori) – uses good-quality fish, although our rice was somewhat dry. The kani-tama roll (£5) – maki-sushi with crab, egg, avocado and cucumber, an unusual but effective combination – is even better. Best of all, though, are succulent rolls of fresh asparagus, cucumber and sweetened bamboo and shitake mushrooms wrapped in fried egg (£8.20); the tender agedashidofu (fried tofu with ginger and daikon; £3.30) is a fine complement. Service is polite and efficient, and the food reasonably priced – it's easy to see why Ikkyu is one of London's most popular Japanese restaurants.

Open: Mon-Fri noon-2.30pm, 6pm-10.30pm, Sun 6pm-10pm; reservations advisable; licensed, no BYO

FITZROVIA

Navarro's
Spanish

☎ 7637 7713
67 Charlotte St W1P

Map 3 B2
Tube: Goodge Street (50m)
Smoking throughout
Pavement tables

Think Spanish farmhouse circa the 1950s and you will have mentally glimpsed Navarro's, where wooden floors and an indoor trellis-like fixture create a homey feel. The name connotes not Spain's Navarra region but the owner's last name; the food is Andalucian, as are the agreeable staff. The array of exotic tapas, such as the stuffed baby squid with pine kernels (£4.95), was promising, but several of our dishes lost heat quickly, as if they had been hurriedly warmed up. The quick-cooling, pimenton-sprinkled octopus (£4.95) was chewy and a bit smoky, but the peppers (£4.50) – warm, excellent and soothingly tinged with seafood – showed Navarro's potential. Desserts, at £2.95 each, were worthwhile – our shapely flan, drizzled with raspberry sauce, had just the right level of sweetness. The rare-wine catalogue includes, among others, a £300 Rioja, but a more reasonable investment is a half-bottle of Manzanita sherry (£9.50), dry but tart.

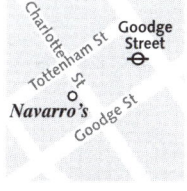

main £2.95-£12.50
dessert £2.95
wine £8.95-£600
AE DC JCB MC V; SW

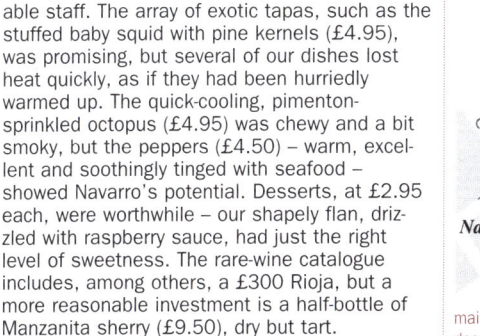

Open: Mon-Fri noon-3pm, 6pm-10pm, Sat 6pm-10pm; reservations advisable; licensed, no BYO

Oscar
Modern British

☎ 7907 4005
15 Charlotte St W1T
www.charlottestreethotel.com

Map 3 B2
Tube: Goodge Street (100m)
Wheelchair access
Nonsmoking tables available
Pavement tables

The young, confident kitchen at Charlotte Street Hotel's restaurant, Oscar, sits exposed at the end of a sepia-toned dining room. Such an arrangement shows your dish from conception to delivery but forces chefs to keep a lid on it. Top-notch brasserie food is served with aplomb. Herbed canon of lamb (£17.50) was lean, mild and tender, its bed a bundled conglomerate of lightly fried vegetables. The ensemble of sautéed calves liver with warm chervil potatoes in truffle oil (£14.50) radiated a fresh, sweet and still earthy aroma. Starters were great: a sweet and creamy risotto (£7.50) daringly blended gorgonzola with pumpkin to brilliant effect. Elsewhere, the softly nutty fragrance of the sesame-seed dressing compensated for the slender serving of tuna carpaccio (£7). Only caesar salad (£11.50) was ho-hum. Desserts were pleasurable, the rum and raisin parfait's (£6.50) cylindrical chocolate bucket bearing a boozy ice-cream load.

starter £5.50-£9
main £10.50-£19.50
dessert £6.50
wine £16.50-£100
AE MC V; SW

Open: daily noon-11.30pm; reservations advisable; licensed, no BYO

FITZROVIA

Pied à Terre
Contemporary French

☎ 7636 1178
34 Charlotte St W1P
www.pied.a.terre.co.uk

Map 3 B2
Tube: Goodge Street (100m)
Smoking throughout

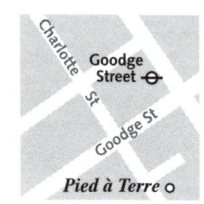

Pied à Terre scales heights of culinary ecstasy that other restaurants only dream about. An audacious platter of amuse-gueule – including a caramelised quail's egg and a shot glass of carrot purée with a frothy anise foam – set the tone for a spectacular meal. The boudin of guinea fowl with French beans, drizzled in cep vinaigrette and topped with a nob of foie gras, is a triumph of taste and texture. The pot-au-feu of lamb, which came with a spoon to sup up all the good juices, is an event in itself. We were almost too delirious with the memory of it all to mention the succulent venison with juniper, never mind the raspberry sablé or the exquisite petits fours. The only thing that disappoints is the restaurant's plain and windowless décor and cramped setup. The thing is, if we're going to squeal with delight, we want to do so without alarming our fellow diners.

set lunch £19.50
set dinner £39.50
dessert £3.50 (lunch),
£10.50 (dinner)
menu degustation £55
wine £18-£1200

AE DC JCB MC V; SW

Open: Mon-Fri 12.15pm-2.30pm, Mon-Sat 7pm-10.45pm; reservations advisable; licensed & BYO (corkage £25/bottle)

Rasa Samudra
South Indian

☎ 7637 0222
5 Charlotte St W1P
www.rasarestaurants.com

Map 3 B2
Tube: Tottenham Court Road (350m)
Nonsmoking tables available

If you thought South Indian cuisine was all about lentils and potatoes, think again. Rasa Samudra is out to make you re-examine everything you thought you knew about Indian food. Behind its shocking pink façade, this excellent restaurant showcases the little-known seafood cuisine of Kerala, backed by an ambitious menu of more conventional vegetarian delights. Forget pappadams and mango chutney; let Rasa tempt you with pappadavadai (pappadams dipped in rice flour and cumin) and travancore (a flower-shaped confection of rice and coconut flour) to dip in your shrimp or kingfish pickle (£4 for mixed snacks; £3.50 for pickles). Our main dish, kappayum meenum (a complex kingfish curry with perfectly-judged chilli and spices; £12.50) and aromatic lemon rice (£3.75), was almost a religious experience. Intriguing vegetarian curries such as mango and green banana (£6.25) were also expertly prepared. Worth a visit just for the side dishes.

starter £4.25-£7.50
main £6-£12.95
dessert £2.75-£3.50
set menu £22.50 or £30
wine £10.50-£45

AE DC JCB MC V; SW

Open: Mon-Sat noon-3pm, daily 6pm-11pm; reservations accepted; licensed, no BYO

FITZROVIA

Sardo
Italian

☎ **7387 2521**
45 Grafton Way W1P

Map 3 A2
Tube: Warren Street (150m)

Nonsmoking tables available

Pavement tables

With worn timber floors, wall-mounted lighting and earthy walls, Sardo manages to feel cosy and authentic at the same time. Terrific food helps. As well as Sardinian specialities, the menu offers the usual salads, pizzas and pastas with a regional twist. We tried bottargo (dried grey mullet roe grated over spaghetti; £7.50) and a moreish ravioli stuffed with ricotta, hazelnuts and aubergine (£7.25). Simple preparation makes the most of seasonal ingredients in dishes such as calamari ripieni (£5.90), six tiny squid stuffed with a meaty mix of squid and aromatic herbs in tomato sauce, and juicily rich and smoky sausages (salsiccia Sarda; £7.90). A thoughtful wine list offers a range of Italian regionals at fair prices, though a glass of dessert wine was served sacrilegiously warm. It was the only blip in otherwise excellent service; great coffee (£1.50) and delicate profiteroles (£3.95) stuffed with a light chocolate mousse helped us forget.

starter £2-£7.50
main £6.90-£12.75
dessert £3.95
wine £10-£119

AE DC JCB MC V; SW

Open: Mon-Fri noon-3pm, 6pm-11pm, Sat 6pm-11pm; reservations advisable (essential lunch); licensed, no BYO

HOLBORN

Cigala
Spanish

☎ **7405 1717**
54 Lamb's Conduit St WC1N

Map 2 B2
Tube: Russell Square (250m)

Smoking throughout

Pavement tables

Very fresh, very fashionable and very sleek, Cigala is full of media moguls and arty types. The décor is crisp and minimalist (all wooden floors and bare walls), the menu simple and strong. The only frill seems to be the extensive wine list. A small herd of helpful staff roam between the closely spaced tables and deliver such delicacies as tender and perfectly flavoured grilled langoustine (£10) or succulent clams (£5.50) in a wine broth so potent it almost drowns all other flavours. We followed with thick, juicy lamb chops with roasted vegetables (£13), the meat falling from the bone with just a touch of the fork. The token vegetarian main, an aubergine and potato casserole with braised spinach (£9), was hearty but a little unadventurous. Desserts were disappointing too with a rather blackened tarta de naranja (orange cake; £4) delivered to the table without a qualm.

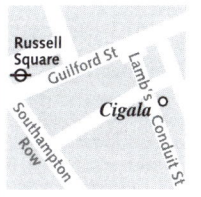

starter £4.50-£10
main £9-£14.50
dessert £4
set lunch £15-£18
wine £12-£164

AE MC V; SW

Open: Mon-Sat noon-3pm, 6pm-10.45pm, Sun noon-3pm; reservations essential; licensed, no BYO

FITZROVIA & HOLBORN

HOLBORN

Map 2 D3
Tube: Holborn (300m)
Smoking throughout

Coopers
Modern European

☎ 7831 6211
49a Lincoln's Inn Fields WC2A

A firm favourite with local legal eagles, the restaurant at Coopers hits all the right 'business lunch' notes. The unusual décor of red brick walls, dark wooden floorboards, high-backed chairs and large plants – all gently illuminated with subtle spotlights – is simple and unassuming, carefully designed to create a relaxed yet elegant ambience. The service is smooth and unquestionably efficient, the portions are perfectly sized and the presentation immaculate. A warm tian (stack) of delicately grilled vegetables and creamy mozzarella is a good start (£5.50); the beef (£14.95) is a little tough but the accompanying herb risotto is beautifully flavoured and the roast parsnips are sweet and crisp. Though the daily menu is not particularly inventive, there is something for everyone. Everything at Coopers is thoughtfully calculated not to offend, and it certainly works: both the restaurant and the brasserie below enjoy a steady stream of diners.

starter £3.95-£7.25
main £8.95-£14.95
dessert £4.25-£5.00
wine £10.95-£60
AE JCB MC V; SW

Open: Mon-Fri 11am-10.30pm; reservations essential; licensed, no BYO

Map 2 C2
Tube: Holborn (100m)
Wheelchair access
Dress code: Collar & tie
Smoking throughout

High Holborn
Modern French

☎ 7404 3338
95-96 High Holborn WC1V
www.highholborn.com

The applause for this recent arrival isn't exactly deafening: our Tuesday evening visit to High Holborn saw a nearly 1:1 ratio of staff to guests. The décor is frankly baffling: while the cavernous expanse of spotless tables clearly caters to the business crowd, a bizarre medley of lighting fixtures, including several monstrous glowing Easter eggs, gives the interior a Bohemian air. Still, service is meticulous while the food, a steeply priced assortment of haute cuisine (£18 for roast rabbit with linguini, for example), is superb. Seafood dishes revel in rich, luxuriant sauces: the red mullet starter (£10) sits in a sunburst of tomatoes, while the tender sea bass main (£16) swims in decadent musk. For dessert, the apple royale (£7) – a fruit-infused crème brûlée complete with a mini-pitcher of apple syrup – delivers airy indulgence. The wine list is extensive; elaborate cocktails (£7) at the lounge-bar downstairs offer supplementary pleasures.

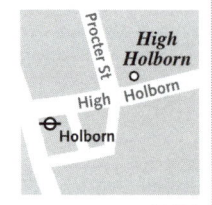

starter £6-£20
main £13-£25
dessert £7
wine £19-£963
AE JCB MC V; SW

Open: Mon-Fri noon-2.30pm, 7pm-9.30pm; reservations advisable; licensed, no BYO

LEICESTER SQUARE

Incognico
French

☎ 7836 8866
117 Shaftesbury Ave WC2H

You could almost dine incognito in the cultured, discrete, sober surrounds of award-winning Incognico (a punning reference to owner and semi-retired chef Nico), if not for the fact that some tables are simply too close together for comfort. Service was as attentive as you would expect, and the food beautifully presented. The fresh pasta starter in creamy truffle sauce (£12.50) was fabulously rich but not heavy. Vegetables and garnishes (£2.50) are offered separately from main courses, though our very successful juicy breast of guinea fowl (£11.50) did sit on a bed of lentils. We felt the crispy salmon (£11.50) lacked subtlety – the ginger didn't blend well with the fish and the plum sauce was too dominating. Similarly, the lovely champagne jelly (£5.50) was overpowered by the sourness of the grapefruit. Yet overall the many tastes to savour made for an enjoyable meal. Definitely worth a visit.

Open: Mon-Sat noon-3pm, 5.30pm-midnight; reservations essential; licensed, no BYO

Map 1 B6
Tube: Leicester Square (400m)

Smoking throughout

starter £8-£16.50
main £11.50-£16
dessert £5.50
set lunch & pre-theatre menu £12.50
wine £15-£450
AE DC MC V; SW

Seven
Modern British

☎ 7909 1177
1 Leicester Square WC2H
www.homecorp.com

Named after the floor it occupies, Seven has panoramas over Leicester Square to Westminster, the BA London Eye and beyond. Unfortunately the food doesn't quite meet these heights. Starters and mains are not particularly inventive; you can't fault the cooking but it lacks that something extra. An adequate choice is the lemon sole (£17): crispy tender fish, precision-cooked vegetables, fresh Hollandaise sauce. Better, however, are the desserts. Try the peanut ice cream with mousse (£6) – a smooth fusion of nuts and chocolate given a fiery crunch by the pepper tuile (biscuit). With its minimal décor – white walls, pristine tablecloths and tiled floor – Seven certainly has a 'trendy' feel (the building does house the club Home after all), but the subdued lighting (ceiling spotlights and tiny candles), unobtrusive music and delicate table adornments also give it the elegant edge required of a restaurant with such great views.

Open: Mon-Fri noon-3pm, 6pm-midnight, Sat 6pm-midnight; reservations advisable; licensed, no BYO

Map 1 D5
Tube: Leicester Square (180m)

Wheelchair access

Smoking throughout

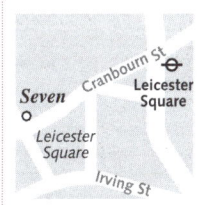

Balcony tables

starter £5.50-£16
main £13-£36
dessert £6
wine £14-£650
set lunch & pre-theatre menu £14.95 or £17.95
AE MC V; SW

Tea Time

Given the important role that tea has always played in English culture, it should be no surprise that going out for 'afternoon tea' is something dear to the heart of many Londoners. These days, however, it's more of a special occasion than a daily ritual. A traditional tea includes a selection of delicate sandwiches, scones with jam and cream, and rich desserts. Oh, and lots and lots of tea. You may also find it comes with a spot of old-fashioned 'tea dancing' – dancing to light waltzes played by a band. The following are some of the best places to go for afternoon tea:

Brown's Hotel (map 5 A1)
30 Albemarle St, Mayfair W1S ☎ 7493 6020 www.brownshotel.com
Brown's dispenses tea in the Drawing Room daily from 3pm to 6pm (from 2.30pm at the weekend), with a pianist to soothe away any lingering stress. A sizable tea will set you back £23 per person (£33 with a glass of champagne).

Claridge's Hotel (map 4 5E)
Brook St, Mayfair, W1A ☎ 7629 8860 www.savoy-group.co.uk
This landmark hotel serves tea in its grand 18th-century foyer daily from 3pm to 5.30pm. There's a string quartet or a pianist and violinist playing each day. It'll cost you £22 per person (£30 with champagne). Dress is smart casual (gentlemen must wear a tie before 6pm). It's recommended to book in advance.

Fortnum & Mason (map 1 3E)
181 Piccadilly, W1 ☎ 7734 8040 www.fortnumandmason.com
The celebrated Fortnum & Mason serves afternoon tea in its fourth-floor restaurant from Monday to Saturday between 3pm and 5pm. Afternoon tea costs £17.50 or £19.50 while high tea (more of everything) costs £19.50 or £21.50.

Orangery (map 20 E5)
Kensington Palace, Kensington Gardens, W8 ☎ 7376 0239
The graceful Orangery in Kensington Gardens is a superb place to have a relatively affordable set tea; prices range from £7.95 to £12.95. It opens daily from 10am to 6pm (until 5pm November to February).

The Ritz (map 5 B6)
150 Piccadilly, W1J ☎ 7493 8181 www.ritzhotel.co.uk
Probably the best-known place to take tea, The Ritz requires booking at least six weeks in advance. Tea costs £27 and is served daily at two sittings (3.30pm and 5pm) in the Palm Court; a strict dress code applies.

Savoy (map 2 E2)
Strand, Aldwych WC2R ☎ 7836 4343 www.savoy-group.co.uk
The Savoy serves tea in its enormous Thames Foyer daily between 3pm and 5.30pm. From Monday to Saturday there's a resident pianist but on Sunday the famous tea dance takes place (£28). Tea costs £22 from Monday to Friday and £25 on Saturday (£9.50 for children). The dress code is smart casual.

Waldorf Meridien (map 4 D2)
Aldwych, WC2 ☎ 7836 2400
Tea at the Waldorf is served in the splendidly restored Palm Court on weekdays between 3pm and 5.30pm for £18 (£21 with champagne). If you book ahead, you can also take part in a tea-dance (Sat 2.30pm-5.30pm, Sun 4pm-6.30pm) for £25.

Ryan Ver Berkmoes & Steve Fallon

MARBLE ARCH

La Porte des Indes
Indian

☎ 7224 0055
32 Bryanston St W1H
www.la-porte-des-indes.com

Map 4 D3
Tube: Marble Arch (100m)
Entertainment: jazz Sun
Smoking throughout

The British may think they once had the run of India, but an outing to La Porte will put them straight. The menu centres on recipes gleaned by chef Mehernosh Mody from the *grand dames* of Pondichèry, a French stronghold until 1954. A cocktail in the basement Jungle Bar sets the colonial tone. Sister to Fulham's Blue Elephant, this restaurant boasts extravagant leafy décor. Under glass-dome ceilings, staff flit between businessmen and couples while water discreetly slips down a marble wall. The menu maison (£32) provided a smorgasbord of quality delights. Nothing more so than the rasoul, chock-full of warmly spiced lamb and peas. Of the mains, only one disappointed: the rogan josh was a tad chewy. Good naan bread proved useful in soaking up the delicious coconut sauce of the crevettes assadh in which prawns, mango, ginger and chilli all vied for attention.

starter £4-£9
main £9.80-£21
dessert £3.50-£6.50
vegetarian menu £30 or £32, set menu £32 or £34, buffet lunch Mon-Fri £16.75, Sun £17.50
wine £10.50-£99.75
AE DC JCB MC V; SW

Open: Mon-Fri noon-2.30pm, Sun noon-3pm, Mon-Sat 7pm-11.30pm, Sun 6.30pm-10.30pm; reservations advisable; licensed & BYO (corkage £10.50/bottle)

MARYLEBONE

The Ard-Ri Dining Room
Modern European/Irish

☎ 7696 8994
88 Marylebone Lane W1U

Map 4 D5
Tube: Bond Street (300m)
Smoking throughout

The family-run Ard Ri (Gaelic for 'high king') has a regal air. Considering it sits atop a pub, it's surprisingly elegant with high ceilings and a grand fireplace. Tables don't crowd and the room is alive with chatter. The short menu offers the best of Irish plus international dishes that still manage to satisfy the Irish obsession with carbohydrates, hence Thai fishcakes (£8.75) with great big chips. We started well with a warm salad of lardons, avocado and croutons (£3.90) and a moist smoked-chicken salad (£4.25). But the night's hit was the beef and Guinness casserole with mash (£9.95), a rich stew through which the black stuff sang. Cream had found its way into our bowl of 'Irish mussels (Moules Mariniere)' for £8.80, and it worked. Neither sticky toffee pudding nor the chocolate brownie (both £3.95) were sinful enough, but the Irish coffee (£3.30) would certainly send a nun scurrying to confession.

starter £3.50-£6.95
main £7.95-£15.95
dessert £2.75-£4.95
wine £10.75-£50
(£10 min) AE MC V; SW

Open: Mon-Fri noon-2.30pm, 6pm-10pm, Sat & Sun private bookings only; reservations advisable; licensed, no BYO

MARYLEBONE

Map 4 C4
Tube: Bond Street (350m)
Smoking throughout

Fairuz
Lebanese/Mediterranean

☎ 7486 8108
3 Blandford St W1H

Urbane hosts in dark suits welcome you into this expertly authentic Lebanese world, aptly named after the fine Middle Eastern songstress. Like this lady, Fairuz deserves an ovation – for its tantalising medleys of lamb, rice, pulses and olive oil which, as the waiter assures us, hail from villages throughout the Lebanon. Dunk thick bread into the Fairuz special houmous (£3.95) and lick the earthenware clean before starting on the sumptuous mjadara (lentil salad; £8.95) and undoing a notch in your belt. The moreish kharouf mahshi (£9.95) could be translated as lamb meets rice in gigantic proportions. Portions are achingly generous, so dessert can be shelved in favour of a little baklava and a stiff drink. The cardamom-infused (and highly viscous) Lebanese coffee (£2), served in a gold coffee pot, will keep you wide-eyed for days ... or until you come back for more.

starter £3.95-£4.75
main £9.95-£10.95
dessert £3.50
set menu £16.95 or £24.95
wine £1.50-£35
AE DC MC V; SW

Open: daily noon-11.30pm; reservations advisable; licensed, no BYO

Map 4 C2
Tube: Edgware Road (250m)
Nonsmoking tables available

Garbo's
Swedish

☎/fax 7262 6582
42 Crawford St W1H

With its bright, candle-lit dining room and windowsills bearing wooden horses and other native accoutrements, Garbo's – allegedly central London's only Swedish restaurant – is welcoming. The food is prepared traditionally, and our Scandinavian guest consistently voiced his approval of the mains. Try the classic raw-salmon gravadlax (£5.75) with its distinctive accompanying mustard or the pretty toast skagen (£6.50), with its contrasting texture of prawns, roe and crunchy toast. Staples such as kåldolmar (£5.75), cabbage leaves stuffed with beef and pork, and beef rydberg (£7.95), basically a fancy fry-up, were served in the proper style. The whopping planksteak garni (£10.95), beautifully presented on a charred wooden platter with a decorative potato edging, was delicious. Crêpe Garbo (£4.25), a pancake crammed with rich ice cream, was our favourite dessert. Service on our visit was a very capable one-woman show.

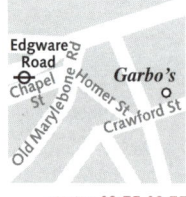

starter £2.75-£6.75
main £5.75-£13.25
dessert £4.25-£4.65
wine £9.75-£16.50
AE MC V

Open: Mon-Fri noon-3pm, 6pm-11pm, Sat 6pm-11pm, Sun noon-3pm; reservations advisable; licensed, no BYO

MARYLEBONE

Levant
Lebanese

☎ 7224 1111
Jason Court, 76 Wigmore St W1H

An incense-scented stairwell descends to a bustling basement, where trance-inducing North African music plays and waiters weave in and out, platters held high. Have a drink in the bar area under the seductive glow of lanterns. The menu's an impressive array of meze, grills and fish, plus desserts awash with nuts, orange blossom and rose water. With a day's notice why not treat 15 of your friends to a whole roast lamb (£170)? Alternatively, go for a set meal (£16 or £24) – they offer a fine introduction to Lebanese cuisine. Meze, particularly the meaty sfeeha 'pizza', the fatayer (spinach-filled pastry) and the jawaneh (juicy chicken wings) were great and came with a gutsy garlic dip. Grilled lamb and chicken featured in the mains, either minced (kafta) or cubed (shish) – each pleasantly spicy and moist. The only disappointment was the treacly, chewy baklava, and the mint tea – neither dazzled.

Open: Mon-Fri noon-midnight, Sat 5pm-midnight; reservations advisable Thurs-Sat evening; licensed, no BYO

Map 4 D5
Tube: Bond Street (150m)
Entertainment: belly dancer Fri & Sat evening
Nonsmoking tables available

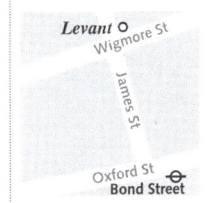

starter £3.75-£5.50
main £8-£15.50
dessert £4.50
set lunch £6.50, set menu £16 or £24
wine £12.50-£70

AE DC JCB MC V; SW

RIBA Cafe
Modern British

☎ 7631 0467
66 Portland Place W1B

The RIBA (Royal Institute of British Architects) is an imposing 1930s building full of architectural enthusiasts, attracted by the many exhibitions, specialist bookshop and the fantastic cafe in the Florence Hall. The focal point of the second floor, the cafe's high ceilings give a wonderful feeling of space and enormous windows flood the room with light. A moveable exhibition space in the centre of the room can also be visited amid the background noise of chattering voices and clinking cutlery. From the breakfast menu, smoked salmon and perfectly cooked scrambled eggs (£6.25) are served on buttery brioche while the full lunch menu boasts cured Cumbrian ham with ripe figs and rocket (£5.75) and a delicious warm goat's cheese salad (£7.95) with a complementary black olive dressing. In summer head for the sun-trapping roof terrace, a tranquil location for a relaxing lunch.

Open: Mon-Fri 8am-6pm, Sat 9pm-5pm; reservations essential; licensed, no BYO

Tube: Regent's Park (150m)
Wheelchair access
Entertainment: pianist
Roof-terrace tables

starter £3.75-£5.75
main £7.20-£11.75
dessert £4.50-£4.95
wine £12.95-£29.50

AE DC MC V; SW

MARYLEBONE

Six-13
Kosher

☎ 7629 6133
19 Wigmore St W1H
www.six13.com

Map 4 D5
Tube: Bond Street (250m) or Oxford Circus

Wheelchair access
Nonsmoking tables available

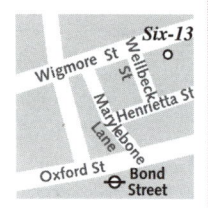

starter £5-£15.50
main £10-£24.50
dessert £5-£5.75
set lunch & pre-theatre menu £15 or £18.50
wine £16-£40

AE DC MC V; SW

London's dearth of classy kosher restaurants prompted Six-13's arrival, and for those keeping kosher it's a blessing. But blessings this classy aren't cheap. Named after the 613 rules the observant Jew must follow, some posh clientele frequent this fine dinery, where you'll find top-notch chicken and matzo ball soup (£5). Not unexpectedly, there's a preponderance of fish on the menu but if our excellent sea bream (£14) is anything to go by, that's a great thing. Pay a visit to the glitzy toilets and you'll see where the £24.50 you might have spent on that mediocre steak and *mountain* of chips is being reinvested – if anyone can find more expensive paper hand towels, let us know. But it's these little touches, as well as big touches such as fine china, ultra-comfortable leather seating and outstanding service, that'll have you schlepping back for more.

Open: Sun-Thurs noon-3.30pm, Fri 11.30am-4pm (2pm in winter), Sun-Fri 5.30pm-10.45pm; reservations advisable; licensed, no BYO

Villandry
Modern European

☎ 7631 3131
170 Great Portland St W1W

Map 3 B1
Tube: Great Portland Street (150m)

starter £5.25-£8.50
main £11.50-£17.25
dessert £4.50-£5.50
wine £11-£42.50

AE DC MC V; SW

For a foodie, the short stroll from the hip bar past the groaning baskets of the foodstore and on into Villandry's austere dining room has to be one of the great London walks, especially at night when the dining room's sheer surfaces are softened by cosy candlelight. The salad of anchovy, pickled cucumber, potato and egg (£7.25) is typical of Villandry's non-interference with fresh quality ingredients, and the cooking is complemented by efficient service and a terrific wine list. Winter truffles and white beans (£8.50) are rustic perfection, shavings of black truffle infusing a light bean stew. From seven mains we chose pan-fried duck breast a l'orange (£14.75) – tender, sweet thigh meat but served on soggy potato rosti – and pungent goat's cheese empanadas (£11.50), golden half-moon pastries balanced with a light vinaigrette. Finish with a heavenly orb of frozen lime parfait (£5.50), tart and unctuous at the same time.

Open: Mon-Sat noon-3pm, 7pm-11pm, Sun noon-3pm; reservations advisable; licensed, no BYO

MAYFAIR

The Avenue
Modern European

☎ 7321 2111
7-9 St James's St SW1A

Map 5 B6
Tube: Green Park (600m)
Wheelchair access
Dress code: collared shirt
Entertainment: piano daily from 8pm

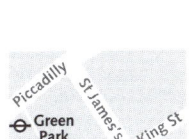

Smoking throughout

Designed by American architect Rick Mather, this slick bar-restaurant – with its huge glass front – definitely has a transatlantic feel. Dramatic high ceilings and white walls frame a stylish crowd munching on Dean Carr's (The Ivy, Langan's Brasserie) ambitious concoctions and drinking wines from affordable to sublime. Artichoke, feta and beetroot salad (£5.95) looked and tasted good, but duck pancakes (£6.25) were damp and tepid. Simpler stuff, such as hearty rib-eye steak with celeriac and potato (£15.25), super-sweet cherry tomato salad (£2.50) and French green beans with Parmesan (£2.95), succeeds well. It's a bit uneven: service vacillates between charming and abrupt, mango parfait (£5.75) doesn't quite do its name justice, and rhubarb cheesecake with hazelnut crumble (£5.75) was a mistake. But The Avenue's style is enough to leave you content (at a price) and the glamorous pianist hammering out impassioned 1980s pop is the perfect accompaniment to your exit.

starter £4.75-£8.95
main £13.25-£17.25
dessert £4-£5.75
wine £14.50-£260

AE DC MC V; SW

Open: daily noon-3pm, Mon-Thurs 5.45pm-midnight, Fri & Sat 5.45pm-12.30am, Sun 6.30pm-10pm; reservations advisable; licensed, no BYO

---

cheznico
Classical French

☎ 7409 1290
90 Park Lane W1A

Map 4 E4
Tube: Marble Arch (250m)
Wheelchair access

Smoking throughout

At cheznico you instantly sense the wealth in the sumptuous décor, the well-heeled clientele and the superfluity of staff whisking silver trays hither and thither. It's easy to see why starters, such as the exemplary parmesan risotto (£10.50), are firm fixtures on the menu. We were more than happy with the silky chicken liver parfait (£11), teaming with neat dollops of tart grape chutney. The iceberg white fillet of cod (£15), on a bed of upmarket puréed peas, worked a treat. Cheznico might be famous for its classical French cuisine but, cream-heavy desserts apart, many dishes have a lightness of touch that's very appealing, especially if you want to go the full nine courses at dinner for £62. Given the quality of the cooking, the final bill is good value and caused us to overlook the ailing flowering plant on the table and, at times, over-intrusive service.

starter £10.50-£26
main £13.50-£26
dessert £8
set dinner £58, gastronomic lunch & dinner £62
wine £20-£2000

AE DC MC V; SW

Open: Mon-Fri noon-2pm, Mon-Sat 7pm-11pm; reservations advisable (essential for dinner); licensed, no BYO

MAYFAIR

Map 4 E5
Tube: Green Park (650m) or Bond Street
Dress code: jacket & tie
Smoking throughout

The Connaught
Classic French/Traditional British

☎ 7499 7070
16 Carlos Place W1K
www.savoy-group.co.uk

The Connaught, with its hushed mahogany-panelled dining room and tail-coated waiters, is caught in a glorious time warp. Grand Gallic fare and traditional British cooking sum up the menu and dishes are delivered with a certain sense of occasion. From the set lunch (£28.50), we chose the excellent smoked trout, served with a good squeeze of lemon and a dollop of horseradish, and a dish of warm artichoke and asparagus for starters. The rendez-vous du pecheur, a sumptuous medley of fish and seafood served with a mushroom sauce, and filet mignon followed. What really tickled us, however, was when a French waiter announced that among other dessert offerings, 'we have zee roly-poly pudding'. It was a tough choice, but we finally opted for a sublime sherry trifle that had just the right amount of fruit, boozy sponge, gooey custard and two deliciously thick inches of whipped cream.

starter £5-£120
main £6.50-£90
dessert £6.50-£15
set lunch £28.50
wine £15-£750

AE DC JCB MC V; SW

Open: daily 7.30am-10am, 12.30pm-2.30pm, 6.30pm-10.45pm; reservations advisable (essential at weekends); licensed, no BYO

Map 4 E5
Tube: Bond Street (100m)
Wheelchair access
Smoking throughout
Courtyard tables

hush
Modern French

☎ 7659 1500
8 Lancashire Court, Brook St W1S
www.hush.co.uk

Forget everything you may have heard about hush. This exclusive hang-out for London's young, rich and hip is actually rather good. Lesser mortals than the Beckhams may swoon slightly at the sight of the bill, but hush has haute cuisine to match the haute prices. In fact, there are two restaurants: the downstairs brasserie known as hush down, and the more refined dining at hush up upstairs. When we visited hush up, the standard was set by a beautifully-presented black crab and horseradish salad with lobster oil (£13.50), though the raw smoked haddock with avocado (£9) came a close second. After such strong flavours, the chicken paillard (a thin rolled fillet) with artichoke, potato and lemon hash (£17) was refreshingly light on the palate, smoothed off perfectly by the exquisite vanilla yoghurt bavarois (cold egg custard; £5.50).

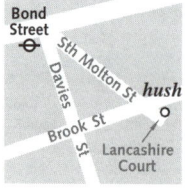

starter £8.50-£13.50
main £17-£26.50
dessert £5.50-£7
set lunch £22 or £25 (hush up)
wine £13-£275

AE DC MC V; SW

Open: hush down Mon-Sat noon-10.30pm, hush up Mon-Fri noon-3pm, 7pm-10.30pm, Sat 7pm-10.30pm; reservations advisable; licensed, no BYO

MAYFAIR

L'Artiste Muscle
French

☎ 7493 6150
1 Shepherd Market W1G

Map 5 B4

Tube: Green Park (200m)

Smoking throughout

Punters were packed in tight over two cosy levels when we arrived, but our waiter managed to find us a rickety table among smoochy couples and posters of sparring heavyweights. Good-value bistro standards are mostly well done: a starter of snails in garlic butter (£4.50) was succulent and garlicky, and rich flavours oozed from a pungent leek and cheese tart (£4.50). Gambas flambées au Ricard (£10.90) were six fat and sweetly juicy king prawns, but a mean portion of dreary beef bourguignon (£8.90) was more than enough. It's tempting to linger over the list of inexpensive French wines and savour the Gitanes smoke and Left Bank atmosphere, but you'd be better off at one of the nearby cafes for coffee and dessert: our gluey tarte tartin (£4.50) had spent too long in the microwave, and the supermarket truffle ice cream (£4.50) not long enough in the freezer.

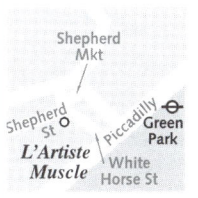

starter £4.50-£5.50
main £9.50-£12.50
dessert £4.50
wine £12.90-£35

AE MC V; SW

Open: Mon-Sun 10.30am-11.30pm; reservations advisable; licensed, no BYO

L'Autre
Polish/Mexican

☎ 7499 4680
5b Shepherd St W1J

Map 5 B4

Tube: Green Park (200m)

Smoking throughout

Pavement tables

How this small restaurant came to serve dishes as incongruous as borscht and burritos is a complex tale, but both the food and the atmosphere in this charming mock-Tudor corner of Mayfair work very well together. Salt herring in a lightly soured cream with apple and dill (£3.50) shows how flavours can blend rather than do battle on the palate, and the refreshingly tangy borscht with mushroom-filled piroshki (£2.95) is as Polish as the polka. Beneath the taut skin of the kielbasa (Polish smoked sausage; £7.95) lurk the tastes of garlic, herbs and smoke, but we found that a plate of mixed piroshki (£9.95) can prove a bit much for a lunchtime main course, as these heavy, almost gluey 'ravioli' can get rather tiresome after three or four. And the Mexican element? Well, it's all here, but we stayed east – not south – of the border.

starter £3-£5
main £8-£12.50
dessert £3.50
wine £9.95-£29.50

AE MC V; SW

Open: Mon-Sat noon-2pm, 6pm-10.30pm, Sun 6pm-10.30pm; reservations advisable; licensed, no BYO

MAYFAIR

Map 4 E4
Tube: Marble Arch (250m)
Dress code: jacket
Smoking throughout

starter £18.20-£26.90
main £26.80-£64
dessert £11.80-£28
set lunch £38.50,
set dinner £78
wine £18-£1900

AE DC JCB MC V; SW

Le Gavroche
French

☎ 7499 1826
43 Upper Brook St W1Y
www.le-gavroche.com

When Albert Roux opened his haute cuisine restaurant in 1967, he cheekily named it after the street urchin in *Les Miserables*. If only the kid could have dined so elaborately. Guests are received in the opulent upstairs sitting room; downstairs, in the formal but easy dining room, debonair French waiters spring to your every need and then melt magically away. Amid the breathtaking array of delicacies, gold-leaf consistently features: it brushed our crystalline chocolate and praline dessert tart (£18.90), and even the sole vegetarian main – spokes of petite stuffed vegetables and truffle sauce (£26.80) – came with gold-leaf risotto. Seafood (be it lobster, tiger prawns or luscious red mullet) is essential for at least one course – the accompanying sauces and broths are gorgeous. Every little touch is unstintingly attended and, with a 38-page wine list, there is no danger of running short.

Open: Mon-Fri noon-2pm, 7pm-11pm; reservations essential; licensed, no BYO

Map 5 B6
Tube: Green Park (650m) or Piccadilly Circus
Dress code: no jeans or trainers
Smoking throughout
Terrace tables

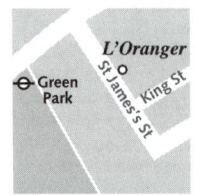

set lunch £20 or £24, set dinner £35 or £39.50
wine £24-£890

AE DC JCB MC V; SW

L'Oranger
French Provençal

☎ 7839 3774
5 St James's St SW1H

With its gracious, salon-like atmosphere and a wine list that reads like a Christie's fine-wine auction, L'Oranger is firmly up the haute end of London cuisine. When we visited, the staff were obliging and unpretentious, and the food every bit as good as you'd expect. Raw oysters made an odd addition to a starter of three plump pan-fried scallops, but this was our only quibble with a night of glorious dishes. A few stood out: beautifully cooked potato salad with caviar (£8 supplement), pigeon d'Anjou (a neat shield of gamey, part-confit meat in a rich jus) and a hazelnut soufflé – a house speciality – with a delicately puffed head and heart-breaking flavour. This luxurious experience comes at corresponding prices, so have one of the staff guide you through the minefield of steep supplements before you order, or end up washing dishes for a very long time.

Open: Mon-Fri noon-2pm, Mon-Sat 6.30pm-11pm; reservations essential for dinner; licensed & BYO (corkage £25/bottle)

MAYFAIR

Mirabelle
French

☎ 7499 4636
56 Curzon St W1J
www.whitestarline.org.uk

Marco Pierre White has relinquished his chef's hat, but not the reins of this stylish restaurant. Start with an aperitif in the 1930s-style piano bar, then move on to the clean, white dining room with its regimented tables and huge floral displays. The à la carte menu is larger than life, literally and figuratively, a fascinating read of sophisticated ingredients and French culinary terms. Alternatively, the set lunch is a great way to see Mirabelle in all its glory. Smoked haddock vichyssoise was warm and buttery, and a perfect rosette of smoked salmon was generous. A main of seared salmon flaked to perfection, resting on a creamy bed of cauliflower purée. Rump of lamb was similarly stacked – this time over a delicious mass of caramelised turnips. To follow was a soupy fruit gratin and a poire belle Hélène that fanned out when cut and whose basket snapped into delicious splinters.

Open: Mon-Fri noon-2.30pm, Sat & Sun noon-3pm, Mon-Sat 6pm-11.30pm, Sun 6pm-10.30pm; reservations advisable (essential Sat dinner); licensed & BYO (corkage varies, max £50/bottle)

Map 5 A5
Tube: Green Park (100m)
Entertainment: pianist/singer in bar Tues-Sat

Smoking throughout
Terrace tables (lunch only)

starter £7.50-£40
main £14.95-£28.50
dessert £7.95
set lunch Mon-Sat £16.50 & £19.95, Sun lunch £19.50
wine £18-£455
AE DC MC V; SW

Mô tea-room
Moroccan

☎ 7734 3999
23 Heddon St W1B

Set back from Regent St, this intimate Moroccan tearoom will revive the weariest of shoppers. Multicoloured glass lights hang from the wooden ceiling, and smoking pipes, copper urns and all manner of North African artefacts (some for sale) make it a paradise for anyone who was a magpie in a former life. The first decision is where to sit, with leather cushions, wooden benches covered in mirrored throws and authentic camel saddles to choose from. Tea is the drink to go for: mint tea (£1.50) is strong and sweet, and wild blackberry and apple iced tea (£1.95) can only be described as lovely. Make up your own sandwich: olive bread with le méchoui (tomato and pepper dressing) and houmous (£4.05) is a succulent combination. There's also a good range of salads and traditional pastries. Customers will either feel energised to continue shopping or be inspired to get on the next flight to Marrakesh.

Open: Mon-Wed noon-11pm, Thurs-Sat noon-midnight; reservations not accepted; licensed, no BYO

Map 1 D2
Tube: Piccadilly Circus (400m)

Smoking throughout
Pavement tables

main £5-£5.95
dessert £3.50
set menu £22.95 or £20.55 (for 4 people)
wine £13.50-£26.50
AE JCB MC V; SW

Mô tea-room (Carl Drury)

Map 1 D2
Tube: Piccadilly Circus (400m)

Smoking throughout
Terrace tables

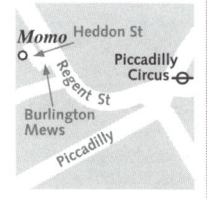

Momo Heddon St
Piccadilly Circus
Regent St
Burlington Mews
Piccadilly

starter £6-£10
main £9.75-£17
dessert £5.50-£6
set lunch £17-£20
wine £11.50-£75
AE DC MC V; SW

Momo Restaurant Familial
North African

☎ 7434 4040
25 Heddon St W1B

Not the greatest place for herbivores, or haute cuisine, Momo is packed nonetheless. Overlook the annoying two-sitting system, the inflated prices and the third degree from staff in the fabulous basement Kemia Bar (members only, unless you're eating upstairs in which case you're allowed an aperitif) and focus instead on the outstanding Moorish décor, the party vibe and the scent of the orange-blossom water they wash your hands with. The menu includes fish, meats, tajines and couscous, but starters and desserts stand out. A lamb, apricot and almond samosa starter (£6.50) was delicious and came with a rich balsamic reduction. Tajine of chicken, olives and preserved lemons (£14.50) was fine, but better was the couscous Momo (£15.50), with excellent Merguez sausage and lamb, and the duck tajine (£15.50) with prunes and poached pears. A sweet, refreshing spearmint tea was the ideal partner to a plate of dainty Maghrebi pastries (£5.50).

Open: daily noon-2.30pm, Mon-Sat 7pm-11pm, Sun 6.30pm-10.30pm; reservations advisable (essential for dinner); licensed, no BYO

LONELY PLANET OUT TO EAT

MAYFAIR

Nobu
Japanese

☎ 7447 4747
19 Old Park Lane W1Y

Map 5 B4
Tube: Hyde Park Corner (300m)
Wheelchair access
Nonsmoking tables available

Much has been made of California-based chef Matsuhisa Nobuyuki's fusion-style Japanese cuisine and, although his London operation is a tad pretentious, it's difficult to fault on any other level. Trust in the chef's judgement was amply rewarded by the omakase menu (£40), a banquet of seven kaiseki-influenced dishes on steroids, kicked off in style with an ice-cooled bowl of salmon in wasabi sauce. The seared tuna sashimi salad, a signature dish, was lifted by a zesty soy sauce, and although the pan-fried halibut took a while to arrive, the fish looked fantastic and burst with flavour. An elegant platter of sushi led to the spectacular finale of a strawberry chawan-mushi – a creamy, heavenly dessert supported by an intriguing cast of tropical fruit. On a democratic note, it's first come, first served if you want to sit at the sushi bar.

starter £5-£14
main £12.75-£22.50
dessert £7-£9
wine £14.50-£55
set lunch £23.50, set menu £25, £40 or £60

AE DC JCB MC V; SW

Open: Mon-Fri noon-2.15pm, 6pm-10.15pm, Sat 6pm-11.15pm, Sun 6pm-9.45pm; reservations essential; licensed, no BYO

Sotheby's Café
Modern British

☎ 7293 5000
34-35 New Bond St W1A

Map 4 E6
Tube: Bond Street (250m)

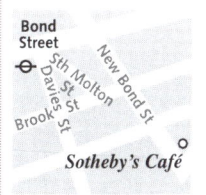

This elegant oasis of tranquillity in the heart of the West End is the place to have luncheon with mother or to glimpse how the other half lives. Style and simplicity are the keynotes, from the crisp white linen, silver service and mirrored walls hung with Cecil Beaton photographs to the daily changing menu of good modern British cuisine. The signature dish is a generously proportioned lobster club sandwich (£12.50), but the succulent char-grilled tuna with puréed aubergine, slow-roasted tomatoes and crunchy green beans (£14.50) is recommended for its textural variety. Leave room for temptations such as the chocolate, quince and almond tart with clotted cream (£4.95). As expected, the wine list is impeccable, selected by Sotheby's wine expert. The cafe is also good for breakfast (salmon and eggs rather than bacon and eggs, of course) and for proper English afternoon tea.

starter £4.95-£6.95
main £10.50-£14.50
dessert £4.95-£5.50
wine £12.50-£42.50

AE DC MC V; SW

Open: Mon-Fri 9.30am-11.30am, noon-4.45pm; reservations advisable; licensed, no BYO

MAYFAIR

Map 4 E6
Tube: Green Park (550m)
Wheelchair access
Smoking throughout

The Square
Modern French

☎ 7495 7100
6-10 Bruton St W1J

We expected the food to be seriously good at Philip Howard's two-star Michelin restaurant, but we didn't think we'd be treated to such a culinary happening. Delightful amuse-gueule started dinner and left us in mouth-watering anticipation of the courses to come – layers of paper-thin lasagne stuffed with crab, a creamy mousseline of scallops and salmon, and a playful medley of John Dory, plump gnocchi and chanterelle mushrooms. The menu offers plenty of meatier dishes too, including saddle of lamb and roast pigeon, and a curtain call of devilish desserts. All this in an airy, modern dining room, beautifully appointed with well-spaced tables decked in crisp linen. The only niggle we had was that the service, while gracious and friendly, was a mite slow. You might not be doing your wallet any favours but rest assured your taste buds will be doing cartwheels.

set lunch £20 or £25,
set dinner £50 or £65
wine £18.50-£10,000

AE DC JCB MC V; SW

Open: Mon-Fri noon-2.45pm, Mon-Sat 6.30pm-10.45pm, Sun 6.30pm-10pm; reservations essential; licensed & BYO (corkage £25/bottle)

Map 5 A4
Tube: Green Park (200m)
Dress code: collared shirt & jacket, no trainers
Nonsmoking tables available

Tamarind
Modern North Indian

☎ 7629 3561
20 Queen St, W1X
www.tamarindrestaurant.com

Tamarind may appear rather stiff at first sight but its charm soon reveals itself. Despite the formal setting with its cocktail bar and pristine table settings, dining is a relaxed affair. Service is impeccable but friendly, and dishes are authentically spiced with a wink to European influences yet without sacrificing genuine flavour. The bhalla papri chaat (£4.95) coats tasty lentil dumplings in a minty yoghurt sauce, while the subj purdha (£6.50) sealed spicy vegetables under a crisp pastry hat. We stuck to ordering a selection of vegetarian side dishes for mains (eschewing the meat- or fish-based options). Baigan muttar ka bharta (£5.80), smoked aubergine pulp with green peas and spices, had enough hues and textures to match its firey flavour while the pindi chana (chickpeas and cottage cheese in onion and tamarind sauce, £5.80) had a smooth, creamy texture. Finish up with a mango lassi (£3.50) – it's fruity and freshly made.

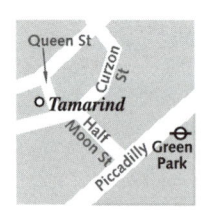

starter £3.50-£17.50
main £15.50-£32
dessert £4.50
set lunch £12.50 or £14.50
wine £14.50-£142

AE DC MC V; SW

Open: Sun-Fri noon-3pm, Mon-Sat 6pm-11.30pm, Sun 6pm-10.30pm; reservations advisable; licensed, no BYO

MAYFAIR

Truc Vert
French/Modern European

☎ 7491 9988
42 North Audley St W1K

Map 4 E4
Tube: Marble Arch (250m)

You can as easily picnic as dine here – diners are encouraged to assemble their own feast from the deli and shelves groaning with wine, bread and condiments. Unfortunately, to judge from the problems we witnessed, the restaurant operation is still a little under-baked. A small menu proved too small – only one main was still available at 8pm. But the leftovers were terrific: a starter of organic chicken liver (£6.75) expanded to a main-size serving of succulent braised livers on a beautifully textured bed of herb polenta; buffalo mozzarella (£6.50) were juicy quivering lugs drizzled in fine olive oil; and a tangy carrot and orange soup (£3.80) was light and perfectly seasoned. Thinnish but fine grilled tuna steaks (£11.95) gave way to superb Phillippe Olivier cheeses, sadly without bread. Fine food makes Truc Vert worth a visit – just make sure you arrive before the lunchtime locusts strip the cupboard bare.

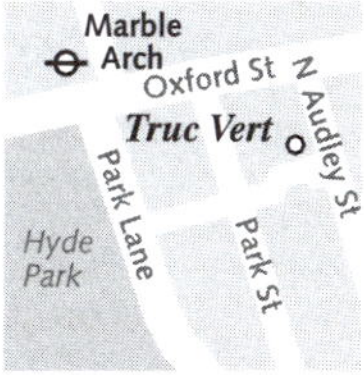

starter £3.80-£6.75
main £11.95-£13.50
dessert £3.35-£4.50
wine £7.80-£31
AE JCB MC V; SW

Open: Mon-Sat 7.30am-10pm, Sun noon-5pm; reservations advisable; licensed & BYO (corkage £4.50/bottle)

Zinc Bar & Grill
Modern European/Pacific Rim

☎ 7255 8899
21 Heddon St W1R
www.conran.com

Map 1 D2
Tube: Piccadilly Circus (400m)
Wheelchair access

Smoking throughout

Terrace tables

Conran's classy Zinc Bar & Grill, popular with suits and showgoers, nestles in a secluded courtyard five minutes' walk from Piccadilly. Felt banquettes line the walls and marble tables dot the convivial dining room, separated from the bar by glass panelling. From the unadventurous, sturdy menu we chose carrot and coriander soup (£4.50), with marbled texture and Indian resonance, and smoked salmon with crème fraîche (£7.50), delectably crisp. Entrecôte béarnaise (£14.95) and peppered rib of beef (£13.20), though succulent, didn't quite maintain the standard – both cuts could have been leaner. Commanding form returned with dessert – super-concentrated, pristine dark chocolate mousse (£4.50) and superb mixed berries with Jersey cream (£4.50), the fruit fresh and flavourful as if plucked straight from the bush. Decent service, stylishly presented classics, a central location – this brasserie delivers.

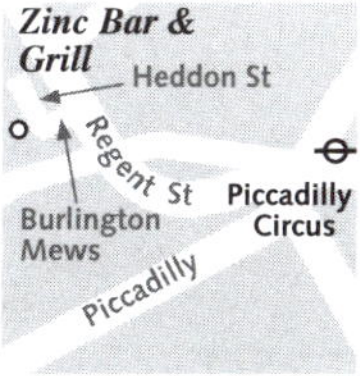

starter £4.50-£7.50
main £8.50-£14.95
dessert £4.50
set lunch & pre-theatre menu £11.50 or £14
wine £11.50-£27.50
AE DC JCB MC V; SW

Open: Mon-Wed noon-11pm, Thurs-Sat noon-midnight; reservations advisable; licensed, no BYO

OXFORD CIRCUS

Map 3 B1
Tube: Oxford Circus (350m)
Wheelchair access
Dress code: collared shirt at lunch
Nonsmoking tables available
Pavement tables

starter £4-£9
main £7.50-£17.50
dessert £3.50-£5
meze menu £10, introductory menu £8 (max 6 people)
wine £14-£200
AE DC JCB MC V; SW

Ozer ☎ 7323 0505
Modern Ottoman
2-5 Langham Place W1B

Quality 'Modern Ottoman' is the secret behind this success story. French chef Jérôme Tauvron delivers polished, beautiful food to a dining room whose seductive crimson walls and sumptuous cushions belie the fact that it's seen many a business lunch. The less formal bar area is a great spot to flirt over a platter of probably the best meze in town. The börek (£4.50) – feta and spinach in filo pastry – shouldn't be missed. İçli köfte (£4.50), a crisp lamb and pine nuts parcel, maintained the standard but sucuk (grilled garlic sausage; £4.50) was unexceptional. Mains see exotic spices and fruits paired with fish, plus some familiar Turkish fare. Lamb shish (£8.50) came char-grilled yet tender and iskender (£9.50), with grilled chicken, lamb and köfte (seasoned mince meat) sitting atop crispy bread and yoghurt, was surprisingly moreish. Shortbread-like baklava (£3.50) with rose ice cream and muddy, sweet Turkish coffee (£1.50), were a lovely way to finish.

Open: daily noon-midnight; reservations essential; licensed, no BYO

Map 4 C6
Tube: Oxford Circus (350m)
Wheelchair access
Nonsmoking tables available

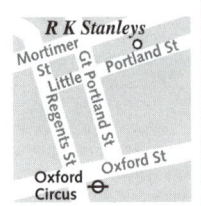

starter £3.95-£5.95
main £6.95-£10.95
dessert £4.50
wine £11.25-£22
AE MC V; SW

RK Stanleys ☎ 7462 0099
British
6 Little Portland St W1W

Any place that can combine diner booths with a sleek metallic bar and 1970s futurism and still end up with something quintessentially British deserves an audience, but the key to RK Stanley's popularity is superb, hand-crafted sausages. Starters such as a huge bowl of lightly fried whitebait (£4.95) or a melting tranche of whiskey-cured salmon (£4.95) are fine, but really just a teaser for the main event: obscenely long bangers and creamy mash. Will it be the game sausage (£9.95), a moist blend of rabbit and venison? Or a hot Caribbean (£8.95) jerky-style snag? Perhaps the classic lamb (£8.95), subtly spiced to show off the superb flavour of the meat? If sausages don't light your fire, there are plenty of other options too and desserts continue the theme of irresistible nursery food. Try the spotted dick (£4.50), a fruit scone sunk into a light and glossy custard your grandma would be proud of.

Open: Mon-Fri noon-3.30pm, 5.30pm-11.30pm, Sat 6pm-midnight; reservations advisable; licensed, no BYO

PICCADILLY

Benihana
Japanese

☎ 7494 2525
37 Sackville St W1X
www.benihana.com

Map 1 E3

Tube: Piccadilly Circus (250m)

Smoking throughout

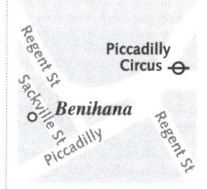

This spry, modern teppanyaki joint delivers a range of Japanese favourites with panache. Perched around a dapper communal table, you watch the affable, talented chefs sizzle the meal in a masterful whirl of chopping knives, salt-shaker juggling and prawn-flipping. Service is decorous and attentive, and the food is excellent. Robust sashimi slabs (£6.50) are just right for an appetiser. Mains seem pricey, but include soup, prawn nibbles, lettuce salad delectably topped with a syrupy ginger and mustard dressing, and more. The hibachi prawns (£18.50) are chunky and delicious, and the vegetarian plate (£19.50) is an artful profusion of tasty vegetables. Whatever your dish, a serving of warm, strong saki (£3.50) is a shrewd accompaniment. Prices are lower at lunch – bento boxes cost a reasonable £8.50. *Also at 77 King's Rd, Chelsea SW3 ☎ 7376 7799 and 100 Avenue Rd, Swiss Cottage NW3 ☎ 7586 9508.*

Open: daily noon-2.30pm, 6pm-10.30pm; reservations advisable; licensed, no BYO

starter £3.20-£6.50
main £14-£40
dessert £4-£5.50
set menu £14-£60
wine £12

AE DC JCB MC V; SW

Dot.com Dining

Though few are comprehensive in their coverage of London's restaurants, there's a plethora of Web sites designed to help you chose a restaurant, locate it on a map and even book a last-minute table. Here are some that we recommend:

www.5pm.co.uk – this handy site lists where you can get a good deal on a last-minute booking

www.taste.co.uk – a food Web site with a section on restaurants that allows you to search by name, cuisine or area

www.squaremeal.co.uk – has suggestions based on price range, cuisine and area, plus a list of every possible 'best of' you can think of

www.toptable.co.uk – a free online booking and advisory service; check out tabletalk for the latest news, views and gossip

www.menumaster.co.uk – a search engine covering the whole gamut of restaurants, pubs, cafes *and* takeaways

www.dineline.co.uk – another search engine from people who've been providing similar information over the phone since 1998

www.menu2menu.co.uk – the site to visit if you're after ethnic restaurants or information on ethnic cuisine, there's a search engine by cuisine and then area plus recipes, chef's tips and cultural information

Imogen Franks

PICCADILLY

Map 5 A6
Tube: Green Park (150m)
Wheelchair access
Nonsmoking tables available

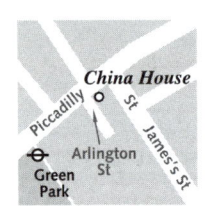

China House map: Piccadilly, St James's St, Arlington St, Green Park

starter £3.75-£4.75
main £7.75-£14.95
dessert £3.50-£4.50
wine £12.50-£25.50

AE DC MC V; SW

China House
Chinese

☎ 7499 6996
160 Piccadilly W1J
www.chinahouse.co.uk

Next door to The Ritz, China House boasts two bars, two restaurants and a shop to fulfil your every China-House need. All this in a Feng Shui-friendly ex-bank. There's fine dining upstairs but groundlings can stretch out in the huge street-level restaurant. Expensive-looking gold-and-lacquer designs strike a pleasing contrast with the favourably priced ground-floor menu. Confusingly laid out – watch those price supplements – the menu offers rice and noodle dishes (come at the weekend for dim sum; minimum £6.50 per person). The 'combo' starter (£13.95 for three people) harmonises Chinese spices and sweet sauces. Gingery lobster (£14.95) shares its bed of crispy noodles with pak choy. Generously portioned rice dishes include the flavoursome risotto-like jai pai (£9.95) with seafood, beef and chicken. Not priding itself on authenticity, desserts are unashamedly Western (chocolate brownies for £3.50) and unquestionably good. Teetering on the edge of tourist territory, China House remains remarkably good value.

Open: Mon-Sat noon-11.00pm, Sun noon-10.00pm; reservations essential for groups; licensed, no BYO

Map 1 D4
Tube: Piccadilly Circus (100m)
Wheelchair access
Entertainment: magicians on weekend evenings
Smoking throughout

The Criterion map: Piccadilly Circus, Coventry St, Regent St, Piccadilly

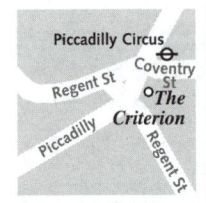

starter £8.95-£18.50
main £14.95-£23.50
dessert £7.50
set menu £14.95 or £17.95
wine £15-£225

AE DC JCB MC V; SW

The Criterion
Modern French

☎ 7930 0488
224 Piccadilly W1J

The transition from the tawdry neon lights of Piccadilly to Marco Pierre White's opulent haven couldn't be more marked. The lavish interior has an Ottoman feel, with marble walls, potted palms and an ornate gilded mosaic ceiling. The food is equally sumptuous, with a light fresh starter of terrine of salmon rillette (£9.75) followed by roast lamb (£14.95) with a rosemary and tomato jus, perfectly cooked and beautifully presented. The roast tuna (£14.95) is rich in flavour and complemented by a lemon and sage sauce. To complete this eating extravaganza there's a range of international delights for dessert (£7.50), and a dauntingly extensive and expensive wine list which the attentive staff are happy to decipher. For the quality of the food, the crispness of the service and the unusually decadent location, The Criterion experience is sensibly priced.

Open: Mon-Sat noon-2.30pm, 5.30pm-11.30pm, Sun 5.30pm-10.30pm; reservations advisable; licensed & BYO (at restaurant's discretion)

PICCADILLY

Marco Pierre White
The Oak Room
French

☎ 7437 0202
**Le Meridien Hotel,
21 Piccadilly W1V**

Map 1 E3

Tube: Piccadilly Circus (150m)

Wheelchair access

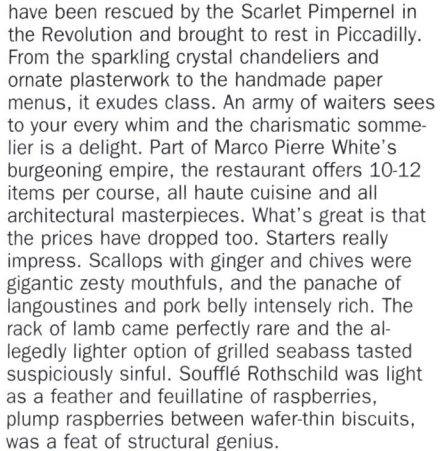

Smoking throughout

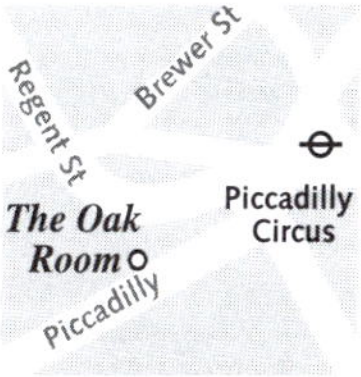

The Oak Room, like French aristocrats, must have been rescued by the Scarlet Pimpernel in the Revolution and brought to rest in Piccadilly. From the sparkling crystal chandeliers and ornate plasterwork to the handmade paper menus, it exudes class. An army of waiters sees to your every whim and the charismatic sommelier is a delight. Part of Marco Pierre White's burgeoning empire, the restaurant offers 10-12 items per course, all haute cuisine and all architectural masterpieces. What's great is that the prices have dropped too. Starters really impress. Scallops with ginger and chives were gigantic zesty mouthfuls, and the panache of langoustines and pork belly intensely rich. The rack of lamb came perfectly rare and the allegedly lighter option of grilled seabass tasted suspiciously sinful. Soufflé Rothschild was light as a feather and feuillatine of raspberries, plump raspberries between wafer-thin biscuits, was a feat of structural genius.

Open: Mon-Fri noon-2.30pm, Mon-Sat 7pm-11.15pm; reservations advisable (essential Fri & Sat evenings); licensed & BYO (corkage £30/bottle)

set lunch £27.50, set dinner £38, menu gourmand £48
wine £24-£30,000

AE DC MC V; SW

Woodlands
South Indian Vegetarian

☎ 7839 7258
37 Panton St SW1Y

Map 1 D5

Tube: Piccadilly Circus (300m)

Nonsmoking tables available

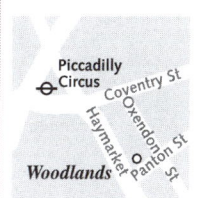

A lively place, attractively decorated with colourful abstract designs, Woodlands sets out to prove that South Indian vegetarian cuisine can offer enormous variety – and does a pretty convincing job. Our favourites are the spicy and perfectly textured paneer dosa (£5.50), a savoury pancake with home-made cottage cheese, and an outstanding version of that perennial stand-by, vegetable korma (£4.50), made with deliciously fresh vegetables, thickened with roasted cashew nuts and complemented by wonderfully light coconut rice (£3.95). The cool flavours of the desserts provide the perfect end to the meal: mango ice cream (£2.95) oozes flavour and the badam halwa (a sugary mix of almonds, ghee and saffron; £4.25) is utterly sublime. Even the often uninterested and careless service can't detract from the admirably high quality of the food, but watch out for the service charge surreptitiously hidden in the middle of the bill.

Open: Mon-Sat noon-3.20pm, 5.30pm-11.20pm, Sun noon-3pm, 6pm-11pm; reservations advisable; licensed, no BYO

starter £2.95-£3.75
main £3.95-£13.50
dessert £2.95-£4.25
set menu £12.50-£13.50
wine £11-£13

AE DC MC V; SW

PICCADILLY

Map 1 E3
Tube: Piccadilly Circus (200m)
Nonsmoking tables available

Yoshino
Japanese

☎ 7287 6622
3 Piccadilly Place W1V

With a discreet entrance off Piccadilly, stark contemporary interior design, classical music in the background and an almost all Japanese clientele, Yoshino could be an exclusive club. The friendly staff and low prices immediately soften the effect. Menus change regularly but always feature home-made items, including excellent tofu (£4.90), ice cream (£2.80) and natto (fermented soy beans; £2.80). This is also one of the few Japanese restaurants we've found that often serves oden (a popular stew of vegetables and fish dumplings), a dish that tastes much better than it looks. The Yoshino no Zen (£9.80) course, beautifully presented, includes three tasty appetisers, grilled mackerel, fresh pink tuna sashimi, a hearty miso soup flavoured with aubergine and a bowl of rice. The flickering lights of hibachi (mini ceramic stoves) on the tables and cool jazz music create a sophisticated atmosphere at dinner, but Yoshino gets our vote any time of day.

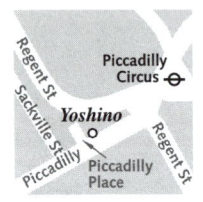

starter £2.50-£5
main £10-£15
dessert £2.80
set menu £19.80-£35.90
wine £12.80-£35

AE DC JCB MC V; SW

Open: Mon-Fri noon-2pm, Sat noon-2.30pm, Mon-Sat 6pm-10pm; reservations advisable; licensed, no BYO

PIMLICO

Map 7 B1
Tube: Sloane Square (200m)
Dress code: collared shirt
Smoking throughout

Hunan
Chinese

☎ 7730 5712
51 Pimlico Road SW1W

Earthy and aromatic, Hunan cuisine is zealous in its commitment to the red chilli. Beaming chef and proprietor Mr Peng shows a real passion for what he's producing, and oversees its consumption with care – ask for the soya sauce at your peril. He knows what he's doing, so relinquish control and plump for the mysterious banquet (£24). You can select some dishes from the menu and sample a myriad of others besides. Griddle-fried, lettuce-wrapped dumplings (£5.50) express Hunan's characteristics – fresh, hearty, spicy and fragrant – with style. Duck smoked in camphor wood tea (£18) is soaked in a fiery sweet sauce with ginger and conversation-stalling chillies (you can specify how spicy you like it). The interior's all peach and plants, unusually intimate for a Chinese restaurant, and the staff an efficient back-up to Mr Peng's star turn.

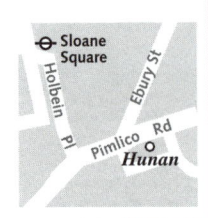

starter £3.50-£10
main £4.80-£33
dessert £2-£3
set menu £24 (min 2 people)
wine £10-£95

AE MC V

Open: Mon-Sat noon-2.30pm, 6pm-11.30pm; reservations essential; licensed, no BYO

PIMLICO

La Poule au Pot
French

☎ 7730 7763
231 Ebury St SW1W

Map 7 B1
Tube: Sloane Square (200m)

Smoking throughout

Terrace tables

An exquisite dining experience awaits in this snug French farmhouse-style restaurant, which features baskets of dried flowers, wooden floors, chivalrous waiters and hearty yet gourmet French fare. The cascade of enticing specials – partridge, rabbit, fish – is the best place to start; our rabbit in mustard sauce (£15.50) came tender and delicious. On the à la carte menu, the caper-seasoned raei (skate; £14.75), which flaked smoothly off the bone, is a more exciting dish than the signature poule au pot (creamy chicken; £13.50). Recommendable starters include the crisp roquette salad (£6.75), topped by splinters of fresh parmesan, and the hot, colourful ratatouille (£5.75). Desserts are nothing short of divine, from the warm apple crumble (tarte maison; £4.50) to the decadent chocolate mousse (£4.50). Not surprisingly, La Poule au Pot's exceptional cuisine and fine collection of French wines have enticed celebs – the model Claudia Schiffer was among our fellow diners on our visit.

starter £5.50-£8.50
main £13.75-£19
dessert £4.50
wine £14.50-£165
set lunch £14.50 or £16.50

AE DC MC V; SW

Open: daily 12.30pm-3.30pm, Mon-Sat 7pm-11.15pm, Sun 7pm-10.15pm; reservations essential; licensed, no BYO

Roussillon
Modern French

☎ 7730 5550
16 Barnabas St SW1W
www.roussillon.co.uk

Map 7 B2
Tube: Sloane Square (200m)

Smoking throughout

Roussillon's interior – soothing, refined, clean-cut – is matched by informed and confident service. Cuisine, which could loosely be described as modern European (despite its name and given cuisine, influences are not discernibly more French than British), is superbly prepared and presented: smoked salmon moist without being over-oily, steamed halibut that remains intact just long enough to be deposited on the tongue (where, of course, it promptly melts) and tender, gamey, hearty venison. A highpoint of our visit, surprisingly, was the offering of pot-roasted vegetables, not on the menu but provided unquestioningly when requested. Roussillon is a fine dining experience, in all senses of the phrase; location, price and, hence, clientele dictate this. We could ask for little more, short of that quality that separates the expert from the exceptional.

set menu £29-£42, garden menu £35, winter menu £50
wine £13-£250

AE DC MC V; SW

Open: Mon-Fri noon-2.30pm, 6.30pm-10.30pm, Sat 6.30pm-10.30pm; reservations advisable; fully licensed, no BYO

CENTRAL

ST JAMES'S

Map 5 B6
Tube: Green Park (500m)
Wheelchair access
Smoking throughout

Che
Modern British

☎ **7747 9380**
23 St James's St SW1A

Che boasts eight Warhol Marilyns and a huge Lichtenstein in a former banking hall with creamy mosaic walls, lofty ceilings and views onto swanky St James's. We started with well-seasoned salmon tartare with crème fraîche (£8) and pappardelle with asparagus and a buttery chervil sauce (£9). The steak (£16.50) and seared yellow fin tuna (£16) were done competently. Skip the comforting desserts (sticky toffee pudding and the like; £6.50) and move right onto the cigar course. This is where Che excels, with a choice of over 80 Havanas for its cosmopolitan clientele. The smoking lounge is at the back of the achingly hip and noisy downstairs bar, where there's even a photograph of Señor Guevara.

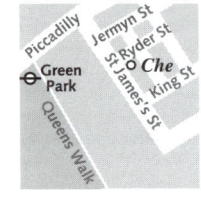

starter £8.50-£18
main £11.50-£40
dessert £6.50
wine £15-£7000

AE DC JCB MC V; SW

Open: Mon-Fri noon-3pm, Mon-Sat 6pm-11pm; reservations essential; licensed, no BYO

Quilon (Carl Drury)

ST JAMES'S

Quilon
South Indian

☎ **7821 1899**
41 Buckingham Gate SW1E

The Queen's local Indian, Quilon serves superior Goan and Keralan cuisine. While the spacious dining area, muted colours and suited clientele won't evoke memories of India, the food will. The slither of masala dosa (stuffed rice and lentil pancake; £4.95) was filled with lightly curried potatoes. Disappointingly flavourless crab cakes (£5.95) were followed by firm pieces of mango served in a florid yoghurt-based curry (£7.00). Zingy lemon rice (£2.95) battled with the curry but added flavour to the fresh and beautifully presented masala-fried stuffed squid (£11.00). Bibinka (layered pancake; £4.95) had the texture of marzipan and a subtle caramelised flavour. A subdued atmosphere, swift service and award-winning food make Quilon an ideal venue for entertaining, whether your business is the search for good food or something more official.

Open: Mon-Fri noon-2.30pm, Mon-Sat 6pm-11pm; reservations accepted; licensed & BYO (corkage £10/bottle)

Map 7 3A
Tube: St James's Park (200m)
Nonsmoking tables available

starter £4.50-£7.75
main £7-£18.25
dessert £2.75-£4.95
wine £15-£78
AE DC V

Wiltons
Traditional English

☎ **7629 9955**
55 Jermyn St SW1Y
www.wiltons.co.uk

When visiting Wiltons, you enter an Olde England time warp. A long-standing hangout for Tory MPs and hereditary peers, it is the classic spot for both fresh seafood and political intrigue. As expected, the club-like setting comes at a high cost. But while other restaurants serve pre-made prawn cocktails, Wiltons offers fresh langoustines (£20.25), which are shelled and cooked to order to preserve their sweetness. Dover sole, a speciality of the house, is prepared in several ways, all of which will set you back about £20. Wiltons provides its own unique form of entertainment (beyond spotting celebrities and office workers plotting their discreet affairs). The waiters seem to have come straight from a West End theatre – portly, vested men who can convey approval or disapproval of your choice for dinner with a slightly raised eyebrow. Go ahead – give your credit card a workout and order a bottle of champagne.

Open: Mon-Fri noon-2.30pm, 6pm-10.30pm, Sun noon-2.30pm, 6pm-10pm; reservations essential; licensed, no BYO

Map 1 E3
Tube: Green Park (200m) or Piccadilly Circus
Dress code: jacket & tie
Smoking throughout

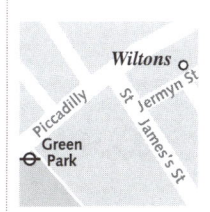

starter £4-£99
main £7.75-£29
dessert £5.25
Sun lunch £19.75
wine £17.50-£4000
AE MC V; SW

A Taste of History

People have gone out to eat and drink in London for centuries, so it's no surprise that some places have long and unusual histories behind them. To find out about the favourite drinking holes of Samuel Pepys, Samuel Johnson, Charles Dickens and others, turn to A Tipple by the Thames (page 197). Restaurants in this book with past lives include:

The Admiralty (page 15) Built in the late 18th century to house government departments, Somerset House was home to, among others, the Inland Revenue offices and the national registry of births, deaths and marriages. It now contains three museums, a cafe and a restaurant, The Admiralty (which opened in 2000), situated in what were once the offices of the Royal Navy.

Bleeding Heart Bistro (page 130) Though there's only been a restaurant on the site since 1983, the building and adjoining courtyard date from Elizabethan times. Its name comes from the gruesome murder in 1626 of a nubile aristocrat by a jilted ex-lover. Apparently her dismembered body was found the following morning, with her heart still pumping blood onto the courtyard's cobblestones.

The County Hall Restaurant (page 172) Opened in 1922 by King George V and Queen Mary, the County Hall was home to the London County Council and its successor, the Greater London Council (GLC), until the GLC was abolished in 1986 under the Thatcher Government. After lying empty for several years, the site now houses two of London's top tourist attractions (the London Aquarium and the BA London Eye), as well as residential flats, restaurants and a hotel.

The Don Restaurant and Bistro (page 27) In 1798 George Sandeman bought the current site of The Don for his port- and sherry-bottling company. The wine, shipped from Oporto and Jerez, was lowered into the bottling cellar (now the bistro) by a handturned crane, which can still be seen today. The sign outside the restaurant entrance, showing a don in a black sombrero, is the original Sandeman port sign.

Kettners (page 80) This restaurant was founded by chef Auguste Kettner in 1867, after he got fed up feeding up Napoleon III. Regular diners have included Edward VII and Oscar Wilde, and Bing Crosby once serenaded a crowd from an upstairs window.

Quo Vadis (page 84) This stylish restaurant is sited in one of Soho's oldest buildings (dating from the mid-17th century); Karl Marx lived in upstairs rooms in 1851 and 1856.

Rules (page 37) London's oldest restaurant (est. 1798), Rules has supplied victuals down the years to notables such as Charles Dickens, HG Wells, John Betjeman, Charlie Chaplin and Laurence Olivier. It has also been mentioned in novels by (among others) Graham Greene, Evelyn Waugh and John Le Carré.

Mark Honan

SOHO

Alastair Little
Modern British

☎ 7734 5183
49 Frith St W1D

It's easy to like Little's low-key restaurant – an oasis of calm amid the bustle of Soho – which has been serving up reliably good nosh since 1986. Starters are spot on, with lots of robust flavours – smoked eel, pancetta and horseradish top a fluffy potato pancake, and a delicious fruity mouthful of tomato chutney rounds off a tasty terrine maison. Mains, roast halibut and spring lamb among them, are well-cooked, simple and satisfying – so satisfying, in fact, that we were tempted to call it a night. A glance at the desserts, however, convinced us to forge ahead: the apple and amaretto tart with crème fraîche is sensational. Lunchtime is for media types, evenings more convivial and relaxed, which is just as well given the laid-back service. By the way, the ceiling lighting is a work of art.
Also at 136a Lancaster Rd, Ladbroke Grove W11 ☎ *7243 2220.*

Open: Mon-Fri noon-3pm, Mon-Sat 6pm-11pm; reservations advisable; licensed, no BYO

Map 1 B5
Tube: Tottenham Court Road (300m)

Smoking throughout

set lunch £27,
set dinner £35
wine £14-£80

AE DC JCB MC V; SW

Andrew Edmunds
Modern European

☎ 7437 5708
46 Lexington St W1R

Modern European cuisine is all the rage in London, but Andrew Edmunds is one place among the dozens serving up new takes on wood pigeon and duck that hasn't forgotten its old English roots. The décor in this attractive old pub harks back to Pepys' time, with wild flowers and linen cloths on the tables, satirical etchings on the walls and simple wooden pews for seats. When we visited, the starters outdid the mains: try the winning combination of harissa mackerel, couscous and mint, topped with yoghurt (£4.25). Predictably, game meats feature heavily on the menu, but servings are generous and well-prepared. We opted for a flavoursome braised rabbit with warm black bean salad (£12) and a robust red from Andrew Edmund's extensive cellar, with sticky toffee pudding to finish (£4). You'll need to book well in advance for one of the cosy tables downstairs.

Open: Mon-Fri 12.30pm-3pm, Sat & Sun 1pm-3pm, Mon-Sat 6pm-10.45pm, Sun 6pm-10.30pm; reservations essential; licensed, no BYO

Map 1 C3
Tube: Piccadilly Circus (300m)

Smoking throughout

starter £2.95-£4.75
main £8-£12
dessert £3.50-£5.25
wine £10.50-£190

AE DC MC V; SW

CENTRAL

SOHO

Map 1 C3
Tube: Oxford Circus (250m) or Piccadilly Circus

Smoking throughout

Aperitivo
Italian

☎ 7287 2057
41-45 Beak St W1F
www.massivepub.com

At Aperitivo, you're presented with a menu of *carne* (meat), *verdure* (vegetables) and *pesce* (fish), from which you pick and mix. The idea may be novel to London (essentially this is Italian tapas) but the décor isn't: frosted glass and pine floors reign. Refreshing, though, are the cheerful staff, who skim between tables of mainly young, unpretentious parties. The food is solid rather than revolutionary, consisting of well-prepared ingredients served simply – and in pastry. Best is fagottino (£3.75), sweet, runny poached egg enveloped in tomato and light carasatu bread. Other plates – sausage and red onion (£5.50), prosciutto and salami (£4.95), and vegetables with soft cheese in, um, pastry (£5.50) – are agreeable if inconspicuous. For those not entirely undone by dough, desserts consist of standard favourites (£3.50) – ice cream, panna cotta and so on. In all, Aperitivo makes for a pleasant pitstop, but go elsewhere for more adventurous dining.

◉ Oxford Circus
Gt Marlborough St
Regent St
Carnaby St
Aperitivo
Beak St

main £3.75-£6.75
dessert £3.50
wine £9.50-£31.50
MC V; SW

Open: Mon-Sat noon-11pm; reservations accepted (advisable Fri & Sat); licensed, no BYO

(Simon Bracken)

SOHO

Aurora
Modern European

☎ 7494 0514
49 Lexington St W1R

Bohemian but chic Soho lurks behind Aurora's inconspicuous doorway. The exposed floorboards, low ceilings, comfortable sofas and solid candlelit tables packed closely together create an aura of intimacy in which to peruse the modern European menu. Ease into the cosy twilight warmth by trying the roasted red onion and butternut squash soup (£3.95). Tantalise your taste buds with spicy Thai potato cakes and tomato salsa (£6.25), followed by delicate sea bass fillets (£12.50) with roasted potatoes and peppers. As you choose from a selection of ephemeral cakes (£3.95) to wash down with coffee, Aurora will seduce you, encouraging you to chill out and forget the time – but the two sittings in the evening mean that you may be hurried back onto the streets when you'd rather snuggle in for the night.

Open: Mon-Sat 12.30pm-3pm, 6pm-10.30pm; reservations advisable; licensed, no BYO

Map 1 C4
Tube: Piccadilly Circus (250m)

Smoking throughout (nonsmoking areas upon request)

Garden tables

starter £2.50-£6.50
main £10.50-£13.95
dessert £3.95
wine £11.90-£28

MC V; SW

Blues Bistro & Bar
International

☎ 7494 1966
42-43 Dean St W1V
www.bluesbistro.com

Blues does a good job of plying the jabbering Soho masses with a range of global dishes from tempura soft shell crab with Thai curried vegetables (£11.95) to Maryland chicken with corn fritter and bacon (£10.95). The caesar salad (£4.95) is lavished with huge anchovies and lots of garlic croutons. Linguini with prawns (£12.50) is spicy and has a rich coriander flavour, and the New York steak (£13.95) comes with some fine herb mash that may attract the unwanted attentions of neighbouring forks. The pecan tart with banana ice cream (£4.25) yields a dreamy 'wow'. By 9pm the open dining room is heaving with diners and spillovers from the small bar. Service is untroubled by the mobs.

Open: Mon-Thurs noon-11.30pm, Fri noon-1am, Sat 5pm-1am, Sun 5pm-11.30pm; reservations advisable; licensed, no BYO

Map 1 B5
Tube: Leicester Square (500m)

Wheelchair access

Smoking throughout

starter £4.50-£10.25
main £7.50-£15.95
dessert £4.95
pre-theatre menu £10, set menu £23.50-£38.50
wine £10.95-£80

AE JCB MC V; SW

SOHO

Café Emm
International

☎ 7437 0723
17 Frith St W1V
www.cafeemm.com

Map 1 B5
Tube: Tottenham Court Road (300m)
Smoking throughout

Tucked away from the heady sights and sounds of Soho Square and its lavish counterparts on Frith St, Café Emm is a frugal haven for trendy but unpretentious diners in the know. The clientele varies from huddled clusters of gossiping friends to party revellers burning the candle at both ends. Go for the gargantuan portions of Cumberland sausages with char-grilled tomatoes and mash or the delectable stuffed red bell peppers with wild rice, mushrooms and cheese heaped with salad on the side – both are £5.50 and both look a million dollars. If you can manage a dessert, the pecan cheesecake (£4.20) is delicious. Do as the waiters do at brash, boisterous and bohemian Café Emm – dress down to impress.

starter £3.40-£5.40
main £5.50-£7.20
dessert £4-£4.50
wine £9.80-£17.80
MC V; SW

Open: Mon-Fri noon-3pm, 5.30pm-10.30pm, Sat 4.30pm-12.30am, Sun 5.30pm-10.30pm; reservations not accepted; licensed, no BYO

Café Espana
Spanish/Continental

☎ 7494 1271
63 Old Compton St W1V

Map 1 C5
Tube: Piccadilly Circus (600m)
Smoking throughout

If you can snag one of the front tables by the window, there are few better places than Café Espana for a lazy afternoon feed, lingering over a spread of small picky dishes and a bottle of the quite decent Spanish wine. Favourites among the starters include the spicy albóndigas (spicy meatball soup; £3.95), patatas bravas (spicy potatoes with tomato; £1.95) and gorgeous calamares fritos (fried calamari; £4.50) with pleasing restraint on the batter. Order plenty to share and forget the main courses, which are not a highlight. An exception is the show-stopping paella (£19.50), which is described as being for two but kept four happy on our last outing. Café Espana is always packed, and there are no reservations – but the staff will give you a time to come back if you want to wait it out in the pub.

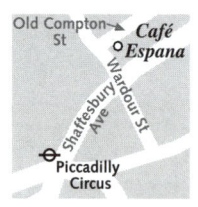

starter £2.50-£5.95
main £6.95-£10.95
dessert £2.50
wine £9.95-£25
MC V; SW

Open: Mon-Sat noon-midnight, Sun noon-11pm; reservations not accepted; licensed, no BYO

SOHO

Centrale
Italian

☎ 7437 5513
16 Moor St W1D

We've been eating at Centrale since university days, when its cheap eats and big helpings were invaluable. Times have changed, but Centrale hasn't – it still has that shabby Soho feel of the 1950s. Patrons are crammed onto banquette seating at Formica-topped tables and you'll probably end up sharing table space. Although the menu contains plenty of meat and potato dishes such as steaks (£7), escalopes (£4.50-£6.50) and grilled chicken (£3.75-£5.50), most regulars come for the pasta. Rigatoni alfredo (£4) with a creamy garlic and tomato sauce and plenty of mushrooms is our personal favourite, and the vongole (£4.20), a slippery mound of garlicky clams entwined in spaghetti, is also good. Go easy on your BYO wine – there are no toilets. Portions are still huge and rarely do we manage to clear our plates. Perhaps that's why the choice of desserts is so shabby – nobody ever gets that far.

Open: Mon-Sat noon-9.30pm; reservations accepted; BYO (corkage 50p/bottle)

Map 1 B6
Tube: Leicester Square (400m) or Tottenham Court Road

Smoking throughout

starter £2-£3.50
main £5-£7
dessert £1.50
cash or cheque only

Circus Restaurant & Bar
Modern European

☎ 7534 4000
1 Upper James St W1R
www.circusbar.co.uk

The setting is sleekly minimalist but there's maximum attitude among the clientele at Circus. This is one of Soho's 'buzziest' venues – and proud of it. The good news is that the food's pleasing, and the three-course pre-theatre menu is a winner at £12.50. Stick to the (high-class) basics: salads feature mustard greens and potatoes or pan-fried foie gras, while mains such as Dover sole and wild rabbit with roast pumpkin are expertly prepared and presented. You'll spot many a media type dining on an expense account here, and if you like to taste what you're eating, be forewarned: Circus virtually encourages diners to light up post-prandial cigars. You can experience some of this heady atmosphere at a discount by checking out the popular basement bar scene.

Open: Mon-Fri noon-3pm, 5.40pm-midnight, Sat 6pm-midnight; reservations advisable; licensed, no BYO

Map 1 C3
Tube: Piccadilly Circus (300m)
Entertainment: DJ Thurs, Fri & Sat

Smoking throughout

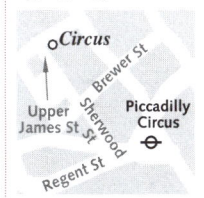

starter £6-£50
main £11.50-£19
dessert £5.75
set lunch, pre- & post-theatre menu £10.50 or £12.50, à la carte lunch £17.50 or £19.50
wine £11.50-£100
AE DC MC V; SW

SOHO

Map 1 D3
Tube: Piccadilly Circus (250m)

Country Life
Vegan

☎ 7434 2922
3-4 Warwick St W1B
www.countrylife-restaurant.co.uk

Anyone doubting the appeal of vegan food will have their assumptions thoroughly challenged at Country Life. It's a bright, well-presented place, tasteful botanical prints lining its pastel-coloured walls. The avocado pomadora (£2.70) is a typical starter – succulent organic avocado baked with tomato sauce and soya cream. The main courses are impressively inventive: the stroganoff with basmati rice (£11.25) is a long-standing favourite, with strips of gluten roast (wheat-derived protein) sautéed with onion, mushroom and red peppers and served in a gravy with paprika and cashew cream. It would be a stubborn carnivore indeed who was not seduced by its luscious flavours. The desserts are the icing on the cake: try the raspberry tarte (£2.30), the berries bursting with juicy flavour. Some may find the dietary leaflets on each table a little evangelical, but the wholesomeness of the food is hard to resist.

starter £2.30-£2.70
main £10.05-£11.25
dessert £1.95-£2.65
set menu £7.95-£10.95

MC V; SW

Open: Sun-Thurs 11.30am-5.30pm, Fri 11.30am-3.30pm (2.30pm in winter), Sun-Fri 6pm-10.30pm; reservations accepted; unlicensed

---

Map 1 C5
Tube: Leicester Square (500m) or Covent Garden

Smoking throughout

French House Dining Room
Modern British

☎ 7437 2477
First Floor, 49 Dean St W1D

This tiny-but-plush eatery is a charmer. With only 30 seats, a meal here feels like eating at a friend's cosy, warm house. Chef and owner Fergus Henderson believes in 'nose to tail eating' – that to not use the entire beast after you've gone to the trouble of killing it is disingenuous. You might not have thought of using, say, an ox in the way Henderson does – in the excellent oxtail stew (£10.50) – but you'll leave thinking it's crazy to do anything else. As well as the more dramatic items such as calves liver (£11.50) or teal (wild duck; £11), the menu has some classics: fried squid (£5.50), which was fresh and crispy, and goat's curd tart (£10), a studied perfection in fine pastry. Desserts were less pleasing – the crème fraîche tart (£5.20) was a minor disaster. But then friends are allowed some mistakes.

starter £5-7.50
main £10-13
dessert £5.20
wine £11.25-£70

AE DC MC V; SW

Open: Mon-Sat noon-3.15pm, 6pm-11.15pm; reservations advisable; licensed & BYO (corkage £10/bottle)

SOHO

Gay Hussar
Hungarian

☎ 7437 0973
2 Greek St W1D

Map 1 B5
Tube: Tottenham Court Road (250m)

Smoking throughout

If you're after the Soho of the early 1950s, this is your destination: an old-style Hungarian eatery where the walls are covered in sepia-toned hunting scenes and there's meat, meat and more meat on the menu. For a starter, try the chilled wild cherry soup (£3.80) or the házi pástétom (£3.90), a grainy, home-made pâté; unfortunately our mushroom soup (£3.40) suffered from a lack of forest mushrooms. The kacsa sült (£16.50) is a crispy though somewhat dry roast duck with all the trimmings, and cigány gyors tál (£13.90) a 'Gypsy quick dish' of pork medallions, onions and green peppers. For dessert there's dobos torta (£3.60), cream layer cake, and somlói galuska (£4.50), a mountainous sponge with chocolate and whipped cream. The wine list includes a decent Villányi merlot (£13) and a top-rated Tokaji Aszu (£5.50 a glass), an amber nectar fit for the gods.

Open: Mon-Sat 12.15pm-2.30pm, 5.30pm-10.45pm; reservations advisable; licensed, no BYO

starter £3.70-£6.85
main £11.50-£17.50
dessert £3.50-£4.50
set lunch £15.50 or £18.50
wine £10.50-£57.50

AE DC JCB MC V; SW

SOHO

Map 1 C4
Tube: Oxford Circus (300m)
Smoking throughout

Hujo's
Mediterranean

☎ 7734 5144
11 Berwick St W1F

Hujo's stands apart from the current crop of olive-oil-toting restaurants thanks to its low-key, friendly service and the part-familiar, part-original and frequently changing menu. The vibe is both hip and relaxed; warm yellow walls act as a shop window for up-and-coming artists, and there's a truly international drinks list (New Zealand and Chilean whites, Argentinean and Italian reds, German and English beers). Start with the warm salad of marinated wild mushrooms with walnuts and new potatoes (£5.25), or deep-fried potato skins with sour cream and onions (£5.25) – light enough to stimulate rather than spoil the appetite. Salmon fishcakes (£7.25) are less inspired, though the accompanying sautéed greens are a succulent delight. Seared tuna steak (£9.95), pan-fried to perfection, is matched by lightly herbed corn fritters. Opt for the two-course matinee menu (£9.95), and enjoy.

starter £3.45-£5.25
main £6.95-£11.25
dessert £2.95-£3.95
matinee menu (noon-7.30pm) £9.95 or £11.25
wine £8.95-£24.95
AE DC MC V; SW

Open: Mon-Sat noon-midnight; reservations advisable; licensed, no BYO

Map 1 C5
Tube: Leicester Square (350m) or Piccadilly Circus
Entertainment: piano daily, jambalawa and quartet Sun
Smoking throughout

Kettners
International

☎ 7734 6112
29 Romilly St W1V

Having sated the culinary cravings of Napoleon III, Auguste Kettner moved to London and founded his eponymous hotel in 1867. Many years have passed and Pizza Express mogul Peter Boizot is now in charge, but customers keep returning to the beautifully decorated establishment. A Soho institution, Kettners retains the feel of a decadent hotel. Considering there are over 50 varieties of champagne on offer, as well as a pianist accompaniment, the menu may come as something of a surprise: pizza is the speciality, and salads and burgers make up the rest. The leek, rosemary, mozzarella and tomato pizza (£8.10) is light and very tasty, while the mozzarella and tomato salad comes with delicious dough balls (£1.95). The desserts range from home-made apple pie (£4.25) to a Kettners knickerbocker glory (£4.25). A great find if you're looking for atmosphere rather than adventurous cuisine.

starter £2.50-£3.90
main £7.95-£16.75
dessert £3.95-£4.70
wine £11.75-£34
AE DC JCB MC V; SW

Open: daily 9am-midnight; reservations not accepted (essential for groups); licensed, no BYO

SOHO

L'Escargot
(Ground Floor Restaurant)
French

☎ 7437 6828
48 Greek St W1D
www.whitestarline.org.uk

Map 1 B5
Tube: Tottenham Court Road (300m)

Dress code: smart dress

Smoking throughout

The Ground Floor Restaurant at L'Escargot may not be quite as sumptuous – or expensive – as the Picasso Dining Room upstairs, but it's still a classy dining experience. Everything from the Chagall prints to the prim napery and the 40-page wine list speaks of measured opulence. This theme continues on the menu, a classically Gallic selection displaying all the passion for rich flavours – and disdain for vegetarianism – you'd expect. The signature escargot en coquille (£6.75) sets each snail atop a smear of savoury mash, but there are originals as well: smoked haddock and curry soup (£6.75) is an inventive triumph of textures and spices. The caramelised skate and potato salad (£6.75) is flavoured beautifully, and fans of hearty cooking will swoon over the indecently rich roast breast and confit leg of duck (£12.95) or the slow-cooked confit shoulder of lamb (£12.95).

Open: Mon-Fri 12.15pm-2.15pm, Mon-Sat 6pm-11.30pm; reservations advisable; licensed, no BYO

starter £6.95
main £12.95
dessert £6.50
set lunch & pre-theatre menu £14.95 or £17.95
wine £14-£1175

AE DC JCB MC V; SW

Mezzo (Carl Drury)

SOHO

Mezzo
Modern European

☎ 7314 4000
100 Wardour St W1F
www.mezzo.co.uk

Map 1 C4
Tube: Piccadilly Circus (350m)
Wheelchair access
Entertainment: live jazz trio Mon-Sat evenings
Smoking throughout

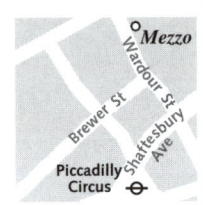

starter £5-£13.50
main £12.50-£29.50
dessert £4.50-£8.50
set lunch & pre-theatre menu £12.50 or £15.50
wine £13.50-£105

AE DC JCB MC V; SW

The grand success of Terence Conran's Soho baby is largely down to its something-for-everyone concept. On entering there's the hopping bar cheek by jowl with Mezzonine, the palatable, affordable Asian-fusion brasserie. Next door is Mezzo Café, serving tempting pastries and snacks to the cappuccino crowd. We're here for the main event – the glam, modern jazz, 350-seater dining room, with its sweeping staircase, crustacean bar and army of efficient waiters. Once the crowds arrive, the place starts to swing to good live music. The food? Well, it's uneven. A Tuscan bean soup with lardon (£5.50) is hearty and satisfying; the pigeon on a corn pancake (£11) is pretty but insipid. Our mains, scallops (£16.50) and red mullet (£15.50), were both generous and proficient, but lack pizzazz, while the dessert – vanilla and blueberry brûlée (£5.75) – was a lush, delicious partnership. Come for the atmosphere, the variety and just to say you've been.

Open: Wed-Sun noon-3pm, Sun-Thurs 6pm-10.30pm, Fri & Sat 6pm-midnight; reservations accepted; licensed, no BYO

Mildreds
Wholefood Vegetarian

☎/fax 7494 1634
58 Greek St W1V

Map 1 B5
Tube: Tottenham Court Road (250m)
Pavement tables

starter £2.50-£3.75
main £4-£6.50
dessert £2.20-£3.30
wine £9-£13

cash only

Clichéd perhaps, but Mildreds really is an institution. More art-college canteen than school-dinner hall (décor: art and photography showcases), it's long been packing 'em in – literally – with hearty vegetarian fare. So what's fresh? Well, ingredients, ideas and presentation. Spring rolls (£3.50) are not smothered but – yes – drizzled with warm chilli jam. Quark, caramelised onion, mushroom and sage dumplings with sour cream (£3.75) are another departure, subtle flavours rather masked by a bland olive-oil dressing; celeriac and parsnip fritters (£6.50), redolent with winter warmth, top a mound of smoked cheese and leek mash. A daily special burger (£5.40), with the crispest of salads and jacket chips (too fat-free to be called fries), is the epitome of healthy gluttony. The rich aroma of the double chocolate pudding with mocha sauce (£3.30) signals a moist, crumbling mass that lives up to its olfactory promise.

Open: daily noon-11pm; reservations not accepted; licensed, no BYO

SOHO

Nam Dae Moon
Korean

☎ 7836 7235
56 St Giles High St WC2H

Don't panic! This may be a karaoke venue but you're not required to sing for your supper. In fact, with its scruffy décor and muted atmosphere, you could dine unaware of what lies beneath. The focus of the extensive menu (a little confusing, with side dishes pricier than noodle/rice mains) are dishes destined for individual table barbecues. Our choice of cuttlefish (£7.50), ox rib (£10.00) and vegetables (£4.00) proves that timing can be tricky: delicately flavoured wafer-thin ox cooks immediately, leaving fresh cuttlefish, in a mildly spicy marinade, to curl a little later, and rather bland vegetables to finish last. Presentation and spice vary alongside value and price: Chinese leaves (£2.00) are fiery while spicy noodles (£7.00) come chilled with cleansing slices of pear. Unlikely to be detained by pudding (fruit for £3.50), you can always invest in a muse (Bell's whiskey £50) and complete the evening singing Korean style.

Open: Mon-Fri 6pm-11pm; reservations accepted; licensed & BYO (pre-arranged only)

Map 1 A6

Tube: Tottenham Court Road (150m)

Entertainment: karaoke Mon-Fri evenings

Smoking throughout

main £6.50-£25
dessert £3.50
wine £12
set menu £20 or £25
JCB MC V; SW

Opium
Vietnamese/French

☎ 7287 9608
1a Dean St W1D

Classy, dreamy and fun: dining at Opium is, perhaps, all that the name suggests. A latticed wooden canopy sheathes part of the dining room, which features Vietnamese lanterns, low ceilings and seating on velvet bariquettes or low, cushioned stools (Opium's designer was Miguel Cancio Martin, of Parisian Buddha Bar fame). The brief but creative menu includes stunning appetisers – gui cuon (rice pancakes; £5.50) are sleek, cool and minty compressions of Asian vegetables, while the warming and wonderful cha gio (fried dumplings; £7.50) come filled with scallops and lobster. Mains are less distinguished – the marinated lamb in black-bean sauce (£19.50) was monotonous, though the palm garlic poussin with taro leaf (£14.50) musters some zest. Desserts, while stylishly presented, can be tame to taste: the toasted banana mousse (£5.50) wrapped in a banana leaf suffered this failing. The service is genial, and Opium becomes a dance club late in the evenings.

Open: Mon-Fri noon-3.30pm, 6.30pm-11.30pm, Sat 7.30pm-11.30pm (bar open to 3.30am Mon-Sat); reservations essential; licensed, no BYO

Map 1 A4

Tube: Tottenham Court Road (180m)

Dress code: collared shirt

Entertainment: cabaret some evenings

Smoking throughout

starter £5-£7.50
main £12.50-£29
dessert £5.50-£9.50
lunch & pre-theatre menu £16 or £20
wine £14.50-£120
AE JCB MC V; SW

SOHO

Quo Vadis
Modern European

☎ 7437 9585
26-29 Dean St W1V
www.whitestarline.org.uk

Map 1 B5
Tube: Tottenham Court Road (350m)
Wheelchair access
Smoking throughout

starter £6.50-£16.50
main £8.50-£32
dessert £7.50
set lunch £14.50 or £17.50
wine £13.50-£990
AE DC JCB MC V; W

Originally set up by Marco Pierre White, Damien Hirst and Matthew Freud, Quo Vadis was best known for its display of Hirst's art. Times have changed. Despite the Pierre White spin paintings and lizard skeletons on the ceiling, the atmosphere is comfortable with mellow lighting, leather banquettes, a parquet floor and tables with crisp, white cloths. Quo Vadis offers modern European food with a good choice of fish and roasts, daily specials and a separate vegetarian menu. Beautifully presented, the baked cod (£14.50) is topped with pastry, moist and flaky inside, and surrounded by tasty mouthfuls of courgette fritter, fennel and cherry tomato. The creamy nougatine quo vadis (£7.50), with its raspberry coulis, is gorgeous. Service is impeccable and the lack of music welcome.

Open: Mon-Fri noon-2.30pm, Mon-Sat 5.30pm-11.30pm; reservations advisable; licensed, no BYO

Ramen Seto
Japanese

☎ 7434 0309
19 Kingly St W1B

Map 1 C2
Tube: Oxford Circus (180m)
Smoking throughout

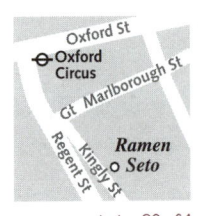

starter 80p-£4
main £4.20-£7
wine £8-£9.50
JCB MC V; SW

London diners can't get enough of Japanese food these days but Ramen Seto (confusingly marked 'Harry's' above the door with 'ramen' legible only to Japanese readers) transcends any food fad. This is a place packed with Japanese regulars. The attraction? Excellent quality authentic food at budget prices, an unpretentious canteen environment with shared tables and welcoming Japanese staff. The chunky slabs of salmon sashimi (£4.50) are so fresh they practically taste of the sea. Fried udon (£5.30) are a bit on the greasy side so best stick to the house speciality, ramen – noodles served in simmering broth with meat and vegetables (from £4.50-£6). The chasu men (£5.00) is particularly superb, topped with tasty hunks of roasted pork. In Japan, the preparation of ramen is regarded as a fine art with hot competition for the annual Ramen Olympics. Should such a contest ever come to London, Ramen Seto would be assured of gold.

Open: Mon-Sat noon-3pm, 6pm-10pm; reservations accepted; licensed, no BYO

SOHO

Randall & Aubin
International

☎ **7287 4447**
16 Brewer St W1R

Map 1 C4
Tube: Piccadilly Circus (500m)

Smoking throughout

This trendy 'champagne and oyster express food bar' is packed to the gills each night, its even trendier clientele sampling the delights of an incongruous mix of seafood- and rotisserie-orientated dishes that blend the venue's present with its past. This was once a butcher's shop, as the white tiles and high counter (behind which the food is prepared) won't let you forget. Randall & Aubin have added subdued lighting, black-and-white images and dark wooden blinds, but the real atmosphere comes from the bustle of a constant stream of diners (and the fast service they receive), loud music and the feeling that everything's happening at once. Eat up while the high (and not very comfortable) stools are yours: calamari frites (£7.75) are thick, chunky and served with a sweet chilli sauce; the sea bass (£12.75) fresh and flavoursome, and served with the excellent R & A sauce. Simply delightful, darling. *Also at 329 Fulham Rd, Chelsea, SW10* ☎ *7823 3515.*

Open: Mon-Sat noon-11pm, Sun 4pm-10.30pm; reservations not accepted; licensed, no BYO

Randall & Aubin

starter £3-£9
main £7-£24
dessert £4.95
wine £12-£72

AE DC MC V; SW

Richard Corrigan at Lindsay House
Modern British

☎ **7439 0450**
21 Romilly St W1V
www.lindsayhouse.co.uk

Map 1 C5
Tube: Leicester Square (300m)

Smoking throughout

One ring of the door bell and we were lead into a world of indulgence: fabulous home-made nibbles were followed by an amusette of creamy celeriac soup and, later, a sublime pre-dessert of Amaretto-soaked figs. The dining rooms have an elegant front-parlour feel but Corrigan challenges tradition with his cuisine – vegetables on the dessert menu and brûléed starters – which demonstrates global influences and a real creative flair. Sautéed veal kidneys were served with aubergine and North African spices. 'Native scallops (returned from India)' were gigantic, fantastic and sun-tanned, and came with a remarkable citrus-spicy sauce. Closer to home, a fillet of Irish beef with snail butter and mash was faultless. Puddings are equally special – we loved the poached pear, quince and Sauternes jelly with blue cheese bavarois (cold egg custard), and the 'orange & orange' – tart, brûlée, sorbet and jelly all on one plate. Do push on to coffee (£3.50) – it comes with superb petits fours.

Open: Mon-Fri noon-2.30pm, Mon-Sat 6pm-11pm; reservations essential; licensed, no BYO

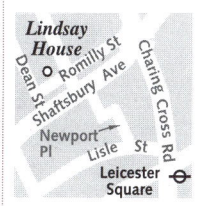

Lindsay House

starter £10-£14 (lunch only)
main £16-24 (lunch only)
dessert £8 (lunch only)
set lunch £23, set dinner £44, menu gourmand £65
wine £18-£600

AE DC JCB MC V; SW

SOHO

Map 1 C4
Tube: Piccadilly Circus (300m) or Leicester Square
Wheelchair access

satsuma
Japanese

☎ **7437 8338**
56 Wardour St W1V

Falling into line with the now-familiar model of long wooden benches, chic décor and hi-tech ordering, satsuma concentrates on providing excellent Japanese food with speedy efficiency. The tasty and filling yaki udon (£5.50) – fried noodles with chicken and fresh vegetables – is excellent value, and the sashimi salad (£9.90) superbly presented, with succulent cuts of salmon, tuna and surf clam arranged round a fresh green salad and sprinkled with soy sauce dressing, so good that the wasabi is hardly necessary. The vegetable maki-sushi (£3.60 for six pieces) with avocado, okra, red ginger and cucumber is near-perfect, and the side dish of steaming-hot edamame (soy beans; £2.90) has superb texture and flavour. Perhaps best of all, however, are the desserts – try the absolutely divine ice-cream tempura (£4.50): two scoops of ice cream in light batter, one covered in chocolate sauce, the other in mango; a superlative finale.

main £3.50-£9.90
dessert £3.30-£4.50
set menu £9.50-£15.50
wine £10.90-£14.50
AE DC JCB MC V; SW

Open: Mon-Thurs noon-11pm, Fri & Sat noon-11.45pm, Sun noon-10.30pm; reservations not accepted; licensed, no BYO

satsuma (Carl Drury)

SOHO

Sugar Club
Asian Fusion

☎ 7437 7776
21 Warwick St W1R

When chef Peter Gordon opened the Sugar Club in a townhouse in Notting Hill, he offered London something rare and new: a menu that reflected the influence of both his native New Zealand and the more subtle flavours of Australasia. This wild mix, dubbed 'Asian fusion' in the food press, attracted worldwide attention, and the fuss continued when Gordon moved the Sugar Club to these stylish premises in Soho. Traditional choices such as rump steak, duck and lamb are cooked to absolute perfection, and fish dishes are laced with chilli, ginger or soy sauces. Where else in London can you get smoked kangaroo salad with peanuts and coriander (£8.10)? It's nearly impossible to pass up dessert, as the daily tarts and cheese choices practically beg you to take the plunge. The Sugar Club doesn't come cheap, but you're paying the price not only for fame, but also for perfection.

Open: Mon-Fri noon-3pm, Sat & Sun 12.30pm-3pm, daily 6pm-10.30pm; reservations essential; licensed, no BYO

Map 1 C3

Tube: Piccadilly Circus (300m)

Nonsmoking tables available

starter £6-£12
main £12-£20
dessert £6.50
wine £12.50-£250

AE DC JCB MC V; SW

Sugar Reef
Pan American

☎ 7851 0800
42-44 Great Windmill St W1V
www.sugarreef.co.uk

From the street, it's possible to mistake Sugar Reef for one of its more risqué neighbours, with its dark tinted-glass doors, cheeky leather-clad bouncer and enormous disco glitter ball. The glitter-ball theme is continued inside but provides comforting dappled lighting and, together with a polite welcome from staff, customers are safe to assume they have indeed entered a restaurant. Bubble-gum pink walls hung with movie-star portraits complete the dream-zone décor. In fact, the only subtle thing about Sugar Reef is the cuisine. The roast cod with herb crust and olive mash (£12.95) melts on the tongue, and the mushroom and asparagus risotto (£9.95) uses jumbo mushrooms yet flavours are carefully balanced to avoid mushroom overkill. There's a very extensive wine list, and if you're watching your weight have a cigar for pudding – there are 20 varieties to choose from.

Open: Mon-Sat 6pm-1am; reservations advisable; licensed, no BYO

Map 1 D4

Tube: Piccadilly Circus (100m)

Wheelchair access

Dress code: no jeans or trainers

Smoking throughout

starter £4.90-£12
main £9.95-£24.95
dessert £5.50
set lunch & pre-theatre menu £14.95 or £17.95
wine £14-£90

AE DC MC V; SW

SOHO

Map 1 D3
Tube: Piccadilly Circus (200m)
Wheelchair access
Dress code: no trainers
Entertainment: DJ Thurs-Sat evening
Smoking throughout

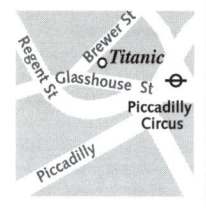

starter £5.95-£8.95
main £9.50-£16.75
dessert £6.50
wine £15-£84

AE DC JCB MC V; SW

Titanic
Modern European

☎ 7437 1912
81 Brewer St W1F

Titanic doesn't know whether it wants to be a nightclub or a restaurant, and ends up being neither to any great degree of success. Modelled on the ballroom of a certain accident-prone vessel, it's all glitter balls, brusque service and fashion-victim clientele. The menu sounds intriguing, with the likes of bang bang chicken (£7.75) and steak haché à la McDonalds (£9.50), but the flavours reveal themselves to be little more than disappointing – only the sea bream (£13.95), simply cooked and presented, was tender and tasty. Besides, it's hard enough to enjoy a moribund scallop risotto with a measly three scallops at £9.95 at the best of times. Harder still when the nightclub across the partition is blasting Kylie down your ear at volume 11. Titanic is a place to see and be seen – the feeling is that diners are aspiring to a certain social scene rather than seeking out genuinely good food.

Open: Tues-Sat 5.30pm-11pm; reservations advisable (especially Fri & Sat); licensed, no BYO

Map 1 B4
Tube: Tottenham Court Road (250m)
Entertainment: occasional Irish bands
Smoking throughout

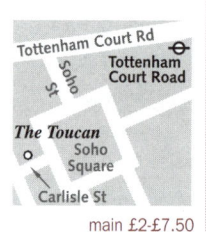

main £2-£7.50
wine £10
MC V; SW

The Toucan
Irish

☎ 7437 4123
19 Carlisle St W1D
www.thetoucan.co.uk

Unusually for an Irish theme bar in London, the *craic* wins out at The Toucan, a diminutive bar located in the thick of Soho. There's a great lunchtime menu (available until 10pm) featuring simple dishes such as Irish stew and mushroom risotto for around £5.50. The few tables are squeezed into the cellar section of the bar – a warmly lit comfort zone. Friendly, prompt service brought us half-a-dozen Galway Bay oysters (£7) – they didn't squirm but were a sensational taste of sea and metal nevertheless. Less fishy folk might like the meaty, mushroomy, gravy-rich Guinness pie (£5.50), which comes with creamy mashed potato – comfort food par excellence. There are no desserts on the menu, but you can always make do with a perfectly poured Guinness or one of the 38 Irish whiskies (from £2.50 to £50 per shot) on offer. *Also at 94 Wimpole St, Marylebone, W1G ☎ 7499 2440.*

Open: Mon-Sat 11am-11pm; reservations not accepted; licensed, no BYO

SOHO

Vasco & Piero's Pavilion Restaurant
Italian

☎ 7437 8774
15 Poland St W1V
www.vascosfood.com

Map 1 B3
Tube: Oxford Circus (180m)
Smoking throughout

With over 30 years' experience, Vasco & Piero's knows to keep the ingredients simple and the ideas fresh. Calamari and borlotti beans is rather a rich combination with which to whet the appetite but the altogether lighter salmon and caper fishcakes lift the palate. Served with a creamy avocado salsa and crunchy sautéed potatoes, this smooth blend of fish and seed works very well. Last up from the set menu (£21.50) is baked plums, nothing out-of-this-world but just the right light, fruity finish. And the polish is there with the staff. An all-male entourage glide effortlessly around this elegant establishment, catering to your every need without ever becoming overbearing. With its plain décor and subtle lighting, Vasco & Piero's is gentle on the senses, but its popularity ensures that it's a lively little joint. It's a fine art, both in food and design, and it's clear that here experience definitely pays.

starter £6.50 (lunch only)
main £14.50-£17 (lunch only)
dessert £5.50 (lunch only)
set dinner £17.50 or £21.50
wine £11.50-£49

AE, DC, MC, V; W

Open: Mon-Fri noon-3pm, 6pm-11pm, Sat 6pm-11pm; reservations accepted (essential during the day); licensed, no BYO

Zilli Fish
Italian Seafood

☎ 7734 8649
36-40 Brewer St W1R
www.zillialdo.com

Map 1 C4
Tube: Piccadilly Circus (300m)
Smoking throughout

This bright noisy restaurant is always full of media hounds and wannabes living large at the funky bar and tightly packed tables. When we visited, a wordless waiter squeezed us onto a grimy wave-shaped velour banquette at the back. Reports had led us to expect great food, but the promise of the long and interesting menu didn't always translate to our plates. Buffalo mozzarella (£6.90) was fluffy and delicious, but juicy pieces of monkfish were an endangered species in an undercooked risotto (£15). There were superb flavours in the wild salmon stuffed with crab meat (£15) but the dish was too heavy to finish, and tiramisù (£5) lacked richness. Still, you can't fault the rocking atmosphere: maybe you don't notice the prices when you can slap a bottle of superb Jermann Pinot Bianco (£26.50) or the enormous seafood platter (£60) onto your expense account.

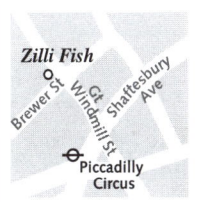

starter £6.90-£10.90
main £11.90-£22
dessert £5
wine £10-£29

AE DC JCB MC V; SW

Open: Mon-Sat noon-3pm, 5.30pm-midnight; reservations advisable; licensed, no BYO

TRAFALGAR SQUARE

Map 2 E1
Tube/rail: Charing Cross (100m)
Nonsmoking tables available

The Café in the Crypt
British

☎ 7839 4342
St Martin-in-the-Fields, Duncannon St WC2N
www.stmartin-in-the-fields.org

Sitting beneath one of London's most well-known churches is a unique experience; unfortunately the food here isn't. Tough too-long-under-the-hot-light turkey (£6.50) came with cold carrots and no potatoes, watery vegetable curry (£3.00) lacked rice but you can have those carrots – if you wish. Skip dessert in favour of the excellent cakes (£1-£3.50); tuck yourself behind a pillar, grab a coffee and indulge. The tables are placed to make the most of the crypt's nooks and crannies, and blue uplights illuminate the vaulted ceiling. Service is canteen-style by amiable staff and the tables are cleared so fast you know they're used to a steady stream of people – a mixture of tired tourists, struggling students and gassing grannies. Certainly not recommended if you're after hearty lunchtime fare, the friendly and functional Café in the Crypt is perfect for that afternoon cuppa.

The Café in the Crypt
Duncannon St
Trafalgar Sq — The Strand — Charing Cross

main £2.25-£6.50
dessert £2.50
wine £9.50

cash or cheque only

Open: Mon-Wed 10am-8pm, Thurs-Sat 10am-11pm, Sun noon-8pm; reservations not accepted; licensed, no BYO

Map 2 E1
Tube/rail: Charing Cross (200m)

Wheelchair access
Smoking at the bar only

The Portrait Restaurant
Modern British

☎ 7312 2490
National Portrait Gallery, St Martin's Place WC2H
www.searcys.co.uk

After looking at the extensive collection of portraits in the Gallery, head to the top floor for some real-life people-spotting. One wall of this long chic restaurant is glass, giving diners breathtaking views over Trafalgar Square, Westminster and the BA London Eye. The menu is varied, with innovative combinations creating an interesting eating experience. Goat's cheese fritters (£6.50) contrast well with the accompanying rocket and sweet balsamic dressing, and are a generous starter. The char-grilled tuna niçoise (£13.50) main is delicious but the tartlet of leeks and Caerphilly (£12.50) disappointingly bland. The desserts all look tempting; iced raspberry parfait (£4.75) is served with a sweet gooseberry jam and sour redcurrants, making for an interesting opposition of flavours. Presentation makes each dish a masterpiece, competing with the artworks on display downstairs. It's unfortunate that the restaurant's opening hours are restricted to those of the Gallery.

The Portrait Restaurant
Charing Cross Rd — The Strand
Trafalgar Sq — Charing Cross

starter £5.25-£8.50
main £12.50-£19
dessert £4-£5.75
wine £12.50-£28.50

AE MC V; SW

Open: Mon-Fri 11.45am-2.45pm, Thurs-Fri 5.30pm-8.30pm, Sat-Sun 11.30am-3pm; reservations advisable; licensed, no BYO

VICTORIA

The Goring Dining Room ☎ **7396 9000**
Traditional British **Beeston Place,**
Grosvenor Gdns SW1W
www.goringhotel.co.uk

This is proper British cuisine, just like it used to be, though the elegant Edwardian dining room represents a piece of England you may be forgiven for thinking existed only in Merchant-Ivory flicks. Savour the white tablecloths, florid complexions, bone china and doilies while casting your eye over the list of more than 480 wines; then make vigorous work of some lightly curried parsnip soup or a knuckle of ham terrine with piccalilli. Perhaps, old chap, follow it with a grilled rib-eye steak from the Scottish Buccleuch Estate, cooked to perfection by ex-Claridges man Derek Quelch. The Sunday lunch is a fine option, with the estate supplying roast beef that the deferential, cheery staff carve by your table. And how else to finish than by mulling over the sweet trolley, which wheels about a few old favourites from fruit salad to steamed pudding.

Open: Mon-Fri & Sun 6.30am-10am, 12.30pm-2.30pm, 6pm-10pm, Sat 6.30am-10am, 6pm-10pm; reservations advisable (essential for lunch); licensed, no BYO

Map 7 A2
Tube/rail: Victoria (100m)
Wheelchair access
Dress code: collar & tie
Entertainment: piano evenings

Smoking throughout

set lunch £25 or £29
set dinner £38
wine £20-£500

AE DC JCB MC V; SW

VICTORIA

Map 7 B2
Tube/rail: Victoria (100m)

Smoking throughout

Pavement & garden tables

main £5-£7.50
dessert £2.95
wine £9.50

cash or cheque only

Jenny Lo's Tea House ☎ 7259 0399
Chinese 14 Eccleston St SW1W

Despite its name, Jenny Lo's Tea House is a noodle bar where patrons sit communally and tuck in to some fast Chinese food with a difference. Jenny's late father, the famous Chinese chef Ken Lo, once operated his cookery school from this site. Now it's a restaurant with a vibrant interior, cheery staff and a menu so healthy it's almost therapeutic. Loyal customers come here for dishes such as gong bao chicken with pine nuts (£6.95) or one of the several types of noodles on offer. Chilli beef soup hofun (£6.95) is a mammoth bowl of marinated beef, flat ribbon noodles, Chinese mushrooms and an enthusiastic dose of chilli and coriander. Crispy 'seaweed' (£2.50), actually made from greens, is a sugary melt-in-your-mouth accompaniment. Those still in need of a tonic should order a cup of 'long life' or 'cleansing' tea (both £1.85). Takeaway and home-delivery services are available.

Open: Mon-Fri 11.30am-3pm, Sat noon-3pm, Mon-Sat 6pm-10pm; reservations not accepted; licensed, no BYO

WESTMINSTER

Map 7 A3
Tube: St James's Park (450m), tube/rail: Victoria

Entertainment: jazz Sun noon onwards

Smoking throughout

Courtyard tables

starter £4.50-£10.50
main £9.50-£18.50
dessert £5.90-£13
wine £12.50-£350
set menu £13.90-£17.50

AE DC JCB MC V; SW

Bank Westminster & ☎ 7379 9797
Zander Bar 45 Buckingham Gate SW1E
Modern English/European www.bankrestaurants.com

Moon lamps dangle from the high ceiling of this sophisticated eatery, where treats are topped by glam touches. Sit by the huge window at night and look out on the private courtyard with its fairylight-illuminated trees, bright fountain and the imposing red-brick Bank Hotel. A courteous bunch are on hand and you'll be drooling over the menu before you know it. Top marks go to the Bank fish and chips, mushy peas and tartare sauce (£13.50) – a deliciously hip (and large) version of the English classic, with thin crispy batter, flaky cod and a portion of chunky-chip heaven. The corn-fed chicken with caramelised vegetables and thyme nage (£16.50) was supremely taste-bud friendly. Share white-chocolate cheesecake with blueberry compote (£6.00) and slip into a sensory delirium. This is a special place where trendiness doesn't outweigh dining experience. They're even planning on children's cutlery.

Open: Mon-Sat noon-3pm, 5.30pm-11.30pm, Sun noon-3pm, 5.30pm-10pm; reservations advisable; licensed & BYO (corkage £10/bottle)

WESTMINSTER

Cinnamon Club
Indian

☎ 7222 2555
The Old Westminster Library, 30 Great Smith St SW1P
www.cinnamonclub.com

The Old Westminster Library has bequeathed to the Cinnamon Club a setting fit for an anglophile rajah: a book-lined mezzanine, a grand dining room and a studious hush in which eager-to-please waiters hover like anxious footmen. The design is echoed in a highly original menu that combines Indian ingredients with modern European style. A starter of char-grilled sea-bream fillet (£6.50) is moist and infused with fragrant pomegranate, Goan spiced duck (£12.70) has complex curry flavours – though ours was marred by tough meat – and curry-house regulars will barely recognise tubes of breast meat stuffed with spinach and apricot as a unique and superb chicken korma (£13.50). The fusion ethos is most obvious and least successful in some remarkable desserts: delicate semolina and almond fritters (£4.50) are inventive and delicious, but a dropped pancake (£4.50), spicy and served with ice cream sprinkled with fennel seeds, is merely odd.

Open: Mon-Fri noon-3pm, 6pm-11pm, Sat 6pm-11pm, Sun noon-4pm; reservations advisable; licensed, no BYO

Tube: St James's Park (350m)
Wheelchair access
Smoking throughout

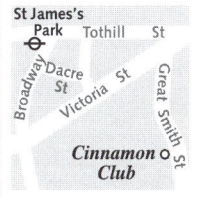

starter £5.25-£7.50
main £9-£17.50
dessert £4.50-£6.50
set lunch £15 or £18
wine £13-£130

AE DC JCB MC V; SW

Texas Embassy Cantina
Tex-Mex

☎ 7925 0077
1 Cockspur St SW1Y
www.texasembassy.com

There's nothing bashful about Texas – and indeed the cavernous 'Embassy', a salute to the Texas Republic of yore, exults in the giddy spirit of its homeland – from the Texas license plates hanging on the walls and a sign pointing towards Dallas (4747 miles away), to the brassy margaritas (£4.35-£6.50), which can also be sipped at the saloon. Bring a Texas-sized appetite too, since the Embassy's tasty tex-mex standbys command gargantuan portions. A fresh basket of tortillas and salsa comes free; the platter of nachos (£6.50), a starter rich with cheese and guacamole, could have fed the entire Alamo (ditto the build-your-own fajitas, £11-£12.50). As a slightly lighter touch, the ensalada de espadas (£7.75) features lettuce, fresh grilled vegetables and soft goat's cheese, all cascading down a mammoth tortilla shell. The warm, bulky apple pie drizzled with caramel (£4.50) makes an excellent dessert – but only for those with room.

Open: Mon-Wed noon-11pm, Thurs-Sat noon-midnight, Sun noon-10.30pm; reservations advisable; licensed, no BYO

Map 1 E5
Tube/rail: Charing Cross (350m)
Wheelchair access
Smoking throughout
Patio tables

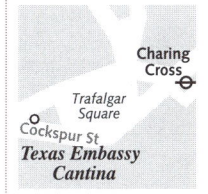

starter £2.30-£7.25
main £3.75-£23.95
dessert £4-£5.50
wine £9.50

AE DC MC V

Food with A View

Sometimes the food looks great on the plate, and often the restaurant décor is equally appealing, but what happens if you glance outside? Most people lose their appetite when confronted by grimy alleyways heaving with rubbish bins, car parks shrouded in an exhaust-fume haze or parades of derelict shops bearing graffiti-scarred window boards.

Fortunately, it doesn't have to be that way. Some restaurants can offer a backdrop of boats on the river, harmonious adjoining architecture, or even a panorama of the whole city. If the scenery is more important to you than the food, towering views (literally) are presented as an entrée at **Vertigo 42 (page 31)**. However, if you would rather that the eyes and the palate are given equal stimulation, then consider a visit to the following places:

Bank Westminster & Zander Bar (page 92) Digest quality British fare while enjoying the adjacent Victorian courtyard that's both tranquil and romantic. There's a fountain, gorgeous building façades and colourful flowers.

The Bridge Brasserie & Bar (page 25) Situated by the river across from Tate Modern, the raised terrace offers enviable views of the former power station turned art gallery and the visually appealing, structurally suspect Millennium Bridge.

The Depôt (page 218) A former horse depot and wheat warehouse, The Depôt offers a fine perspective of a scenic stretch of the river near Barnes Bridge – watch the Oxford-Cambridge boat race swish past in late March.

Le Pont de la Tour (page 157) This Conran restaurant serves up wonderful views of Tower Bridge and the Thames, particularly resplendent at night, to accompany its modern European menu.

Oxo Tower Restaurant (page 174) For a sweeping panorama of London to the east, west and north, you can't do better than ascend this tower.

The Portrait Restaurant (page 90) Sitting pretty on the top floor of the National Portrait Gallery, this restaurant allows you to enjoy creative cuisine while staring at Nelson atop his column.

The Putney Bridge Restaurant (page 226) Panoramic views of the Thames by, you've guessed it, Putney Bridge, are fine enough to draw the eye away from the £3 million restaurant building, nominated for a couple of awards for design and architectural excellence.

Seven (page 49) Take in a different view of Leicester Square and the West End, beyond tourists and tat, from this seventh-floor restaurant. Other landmarks to spy are the BA London Eye and Big Ben.

'Smiths' of Smithfields (page 138) From its outside terrace, this restaurant offers fine vistas above the rooftops – buildings in view include St Paul's and the Old Bailey.

Mark Honan

Archway
Barnsbury
Belsize Park
Camden

NORTH

Crouch End
East Finchley
Finchley
Finsbury Park
Golders Green
Hampstead
Highbury
Highgate
Islington
Maida Vale
Muswell Hill
Primrose Hill
St John's Wood
Stoke Newington
Tufnell Park
Turnpike Lane
West Hampstead

FAVOURITE

- **British**
  Frederick's (p116)

- **French**
  L'Aventure (p122)

- **Gastropub**
  The Engineer (p119)

- **Indian**
  Jashan (p124)

- **Italian**
  Artigiano (p98)

- **Modern European**
  Mesclun (p122)

- **South-East Asian**
  O's Thai Café (p104)

- **Vegetarian**
  Manna (p120)

North

Whoever said that London is a 'collection of villages' must have had the northern boroughs in mind; nowhere is that old chestnut more applicable than to such disparate neighbourhoods as Stoke Newington and Islington, Camden and Highgate. There are few villages anywhere without a pub, and north London is no exception; it counts them in spades. Many of them have cleaned up their acts (and their lavatories), hired a chef and are now turning out food that ranges from acceptable to exceptional. The gastropub may not have been born in north London, but it reigns supreme here. The indisputable king of north London's eating zones is Islington. At last count there were more than 60 restaurants and cafes between Angel and Highbury Corner alone. If the truth be known, many of these places are third-rate or branches of chains (or both) and cater to a youngish but not very trendy crowd in search of a bit of blotter before or after a pub crawl. Stoke Newington Church St, never too hip for hops and lined with pubs, is also a thoroughly cosmopolitan area and boasts several ethnic restaurants well worth the effort of reaching this tube-challenged enclave. Multi-ethnic Camden is another kettle of different fish, with a pride of Greek restaurants that does no one proud but some tasty offerings of Caribbean, South-Asian and Lebanese cuisine. Nearby Primrose Hill, the closest London gets to Paris, has some good vegetarian and modern European options, perfect for this well-travelled and health-conscious crowd. Similar options abound in Hampstead, the well-to-do 'village' nestling to the south-west of Hampstead Heath, and in even more affluent Highgate to the north. Farther north again, there's a diverse selection of good-value cuisine to choose from. Try Spanish in Crouch End or Japanese in Golders Green.

ARCHWAY

Paris London Café
French

☎/fax 7561 0330
5 Junction Rd N19

Tube: Archway (50m)

Smoking throughout

There's something undeniably sexy about a French bistro in London – it oozes the flavour of the Continent and sets the taste buds tingling with the unfamiliar. With its deep red walls, low lighting and closely packed tables, intimate Paris London Café knows that the secret to the bistro lies not only in creating a certain ambience but also in serving good French cuisine. A huge slab of crunchy broccoli quiche (£2.25) could be a main in itself; the more modest serving of salmon (£9.75) was slightly overdone but the creamy basil sauce gives it the necessary lift, and the gratin dauphinois (£1.95), packed with herbs and garlic, is the perfect complement. And what really makes this place worth a visit is the service – it's fast, friendly and very French – where else would a waitress threaten to chase you out the door with her baguette? Ooh la la madame …

Open: Mon-Sat 8am-3pm, 7pm-11pm; reservations accepted; licensed, no BYO

starter £1.95-£5.75
main £5.95-£9.75
dessert £2.75-£3.75
set menu £9.95/£15.95
wine £9.95-£18

cash only

BARNSBURY

The Dining Room
Country European

☎ 7609 3009
169 Hemingford Rd N1

Map 9 C1

Rail: Caledonian Road & Barnsbury (100m), tube/rail: Highbury & Islington

Smoking throughout

Garden tables

The Dining Room is as close to a Parisian *restaurant du quartier* as we've found in London, with well-prepared, simple yet imaginative dishes at very affordable prices. Seating just 22 diners in the front room of a terraced house, with a large shop-like window, low lighting and deep blue walls, this charming place might just as well be called The Living Room. Portions are unusually generous. After enjoying a large plate of complimentary bread and olives, the delightful pappardelle (£5) with hare sauce and salt-cod cakes (£4) bound with a titch too much egg white, we soldiered on, slowly battling through sea bass (£10) on spinach and caramelised fennel and enough braised pork (£11), white beans and pumpkin to feed a battalion. We managed to polish off a dish of plums and quince stewed in red wine (£3.50) but were finally defeated by the organic ice cream (£3.50).

Open: Tues-Sat 7pm-10.30pm, Sun 1pm-4pm; reservations advisable; licensed, no BYO

starter £3.50-£6.50
main £7.50-£15
dessert £3.50
wine £10-£20

cash or cheque only

BELSIZE PARK

Map 8 B2
Tube: Belsize Park (350m)
Smoking throughout
Pavement tables

Artigiano
Modern Italian

☎ 7794 4288
12a Belsize Terrace NW3
www.etruscagroup.co.uk

Tucked away down a warren of residential streets in leafy Belsize Park you'll find Artigiano, a fantastic modern Italian. The comprehensive menu is varied and the accommodating chef, Carlo, will even adapt dishes for the fussy diner. Italian cured beef is served with rich creamy goat's cheese (£7.25) in a delicious starter. Imaginative mains and top-quality ingredients create tempting, beautifully presented dishes. Tuna steak with rocket (£14.50) is incredibly fresh, while the home-made pasta with fresh tomato, marjoram and smoked mozzarella (£6.75) is a perfect combination of subtle flavours. The extensive wine list appeals to every pocket and the helpful staff can direct you to the right choice. Artigiano is a haven for affluent media and city types who come here to forget about their hectic lives, and the proof is there to be seen – a genuine Oscar is on display, given by one of the regulars.

starter £5.25-£8.50
main £6.75-£15.50
dessert £4.50-£5.50
set lunch £12.50 or £14.50
wine £13-£230
AE DC MC V; SW

Open: Tues-Sun noon-3pm, Mon-Fri 6.45pm-11pm, Sat 6.45pm-11.30pm, Sun 6.45pm-10pm; reservations advisable; licensed, no BYO

CAMDEN

Map 10 A4
Tube: Camden Town (250m)
Smoking throughout
Garden tables

Café Bintang
South-East Asian

☎ 7428 9603
93 Kentish Town Rd NW1

Bintang's food draws on diverse flavours from South-East Asia, eschewing the standard array of green curries common in eateries of this genre. The bamboo-strewn interior recalls Indonesian warungs or maybe a Thai beach cafe, an impression reinforced by smiling, youthful service. Yes, coconut milk and chillies are prominent, but a competent gado gado (tofu salad with peanut sauce; £2.75) and mouth-tingling ayam narikal (chicken with basil, coriander and lemongrass; £4.50) lean towards Malaysia and Indonesia. We were less impressed by the native vegetables (£3.99), awash with a rather muddied sauce, but were mollified by pla tod (£5.50) – the tender fish, cooked to perfection in tamarind, lemongrass and basil, fell off the bone and melted on the tongue. You can eat more refined Asian cuisine in London, but it won't be as much fun.

starter £2.50-£5.95
main £3.99-£6.50
pre-theatre menu £5 or £6.50, set menu £10.95
wine £6.95
MC V; SW

Open: Mon-Thur 5.30pm-11.45pm, Fri & Sat 5.30pm-midnight, Sun 3pm-11pm; reservations advisable; licensed & BYO (corkage £2/bottle)

CAMDEN

The Crown & Goose
Modern European

☎ 7485 8008
100 Arlington Rd NW1

Yes, it's another trendy gastropub, but The Crown & Goose is refreshingly different. Much more 'pub' than 'gastro', the menu is a mix of old favourites and tasty specials. The huge plate of nachos (£3.25) were excellent value, baked salmon (£7.95) was accompanied by creamy mash and generous helpings of pesto, and the tender lamb (£8.20) was served with lashings of ratatouille. But while you could probably create the dishes yourself, you couldn't cook up this atmosphere. This is a small, friendly local. Diners share space with chattering drinkers and ensconce themselves for the night, happily welcomed by the fun-loving hard-working and very accommodating staff. Homely touches such as fresh flowers and logo-printed napkins complement the candle-lit minimalistic décor of green walls, huge mirrors and wooden tables. Enjoy the cheap, cheerful food for being just that and make the most of that most British of institutions: the local pub.

Open: Mon-Sat 11am-11pm, Sun noon-10.30pm; reservations advisable at weekends; licensed, no BYO

Map 10 C4
Tube: Camden Town (150m)

Smoking throughout
Pavement tables

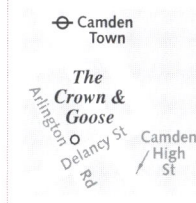

starter £3-£5
main £6-£12
dessert £3.50-£4
wine £10.50-£22
MC V; SW

El Parador
Spanish

☎ 7387 2789
245 Eversholt St NW1

In winter, El Parador is just another convivial restaurant serving a wide selection of tapas, but in summer it moves into that elusive category of London eateries where you can dine alfresco. On a balmy night, after a glass or two of Spanish wine, shielded from the sound of the traffic and with a table full of tapas in front of you, you begin to feel you're somewhere much farther south. Our favourite dishes include the roast fennel (£3.70), the fleshy and lime-doused grilled swordfish (£4.90) and the tender grilled marinated lamb (£4.50). Book well ahead if you're hoping to grab a seat in the garden – open from around 1 May to the onset of colder weather, usually sometime in September.

Open: Mon-Fri noon-3pm, Mon-Thurs 6pm-11pm, Fri & Sat 6pm-11.30pm, Sun 7pm-10.30pm; reservations advisable; licensed, no BYO

Map 10 C5
Tube: Mornington Crescent (100m)

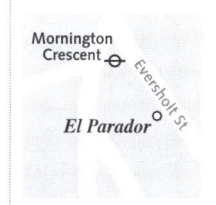

Smoking throughout
Garden tables

main £3.30-£4.90
dessert £3-£4
wine £10-£20
MC V; SW

CAMDEN

Map 10 C4
Tube: Camden Town (250m)
Smoking throughout
Pavement tables

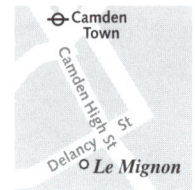

Le Mignon
Lebanese

☎ 7387 0600
9a Delancey St NW1

This cosy restaurant off Camden High St is a regular haunt for Camdenites in the know. Owner/chef Hussein Dekmak has kept the French name and warm Mediterranean décor but drastically changed the menu to his native Lebanese cuisine. Mains such as farrouge moussahab (grilled chicken; £7.80) and stuffed lamb (£8) are enticing, but a meal of meze dishes is definitely the authentic way to go. You can't beat the golden felafel served with tahini (£3.25), the spicy fattoush (mixed vegetable salad; £2.90), the aromatic hummus snoubar (with pine nuts; £4.50), any of the sambouseks (stuffed pastries; £3.25) and the arayes Le Mignon (pitta bread stuffed with meat; £4.75). Try one of the imported Chateau Kefraya wines, finish with some sugary baklava and a glass of arak, and you won't be disappointed.

starter £3-£4.75
main £7.95-£14
wine £11.75
dessert £3
MC V; SW

Open: Tues-Sun noon-midnight; reservations advisable (essential evenings); licensed, no BYO

Lemongrass (Carl Drury)

CAMDEN

Lemongrass
South-East Asian

☎/fax 7284 1116
243 Royal College St NW1

Map 10 B5
Tube: Camden Town (350m),
rail: Camden Road

It's good Lemongrass has a mere 28 seats because chef Thomas Tan can only just keep up with demand. From his woks behind the small partition he creates a range of wonderful South-East Asian dishes, focusing on Cambodia. The aptly named 'treats' (£8.30 for two, £12.60 for three or £16.30 for four) include bite-sized prawn toasts, leek cakes and crispy king prawns. Set 'feasts' gather items from across the menu. Vegetarian features include the delicately spiced Khmer Buddhist cabbage (£4.30), infused with coriander, while the spring chilli chicken (£4.95), loaded with chilli and lemon, is the star of the meaty mélange. Save room for the banana cake (£3.60), a tasty pudding in a banana leaf that you'll want to lick. Items arrive sporadically from the woks, so ordering the treats and feasts means that there will always be something new showing up.

starter £2.60-£3.90
main £4.80-£7.90
dessert £3-£3.90
set feast £13.90 or £15.90
wine £10.30-£19.80

MC V; SW

Open: daily 6.30pm-11pm; reservations advisable; licensed, no BYO

Mango Room
Traditional & Modern Caribbean

☎ 7482 5065
10-12 Kentish Town Rd NW1

Map 10 B4
Tube: Camden Town (15m)

Smoking throughout

Stretched over three smallish rooms, Mango Room – with its deep red walls, large pieces of colourful modern art and jazzy music – is funky. And it's busy, each and every table groaning with the delights of the delectable cuisine on offer here. The menu is largely made up of specials, although there are some permanent fixtures too. Fat green-lip mussels (£4.75) come with a creamy coconut sauce, and flavoursome Creole snapper (£9.00) is served on the bone with a sweet, fiery mango and green peppercorn sauce. Side dishes include garlicky white- and sweet-potato mash (£2.50) and dessert is another experience altogether. Mango (is there a theme here?) and banana brûlée (£3.50) is incredible. Perfect crème, perfect fusion of fruit, perfect brûlée. Unfortunately our 'dining slot' finished just as we did, and the staff made sure we knew it. Relax and enjoy the excellent food, while you can.

starter £3.70-£4.75
main £8.50-£11.50
dessert £4-£5.50
set menu £18 or £22
wine £10.50-£29

AE MC V; SW

Open: Tues-Sun noon-3pm, 6pm-midnight, Mon 6pm-midnight; reservations essential; licensed, no BYO

CAMDEN

Map 10 B5
Tube: Camden Town (200m)
Smoking throughout

Pescador
Portuguese

☎/fax 7482 7008
33 Pratt St NW1

There is nothing quite like a Portuguese restaurant that works magic on fish, and this cosy, family-run venue rates as a sterling find. Even the walls are dotted with reminders of the sea – a colourful lobster net hangs here, a ship's wheel there. The menu runs the gamut of simple, inexpensive but filling seafood dishes, from grilled squid and prawns to a striking assortment of fish. The chunky seafood soup (£2.50), packed with goodies, makes a hot, tasty starter; the grilled sea-bass (£10.50), so huge it overshoots the plate, comes tender and meaty. Do stick to the seafood, though: the house-style grilled chicken was lacklustre compared to the sea-bass. Molotof (Portuguese flan; £2.50), the most intriguing dessert choice, is pleasantly sweet and airy. Pescador's tasty cooking is complemented by obliging, friendly service, which ensures the continued regard of Portuguese patrons and others in the know.

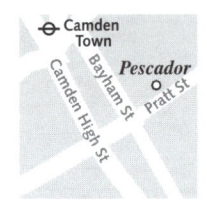

starter £2.50-£4.90
main £6.50-£25
dessert £2.50-£4
wine £7
cash or cheque only

Open: Tues-Fri 6pm-11.30pm, Sat 1pm-11.30pm, Sun 1pm-10pm; reservations advisable; licensed, no BYO

Map 10 B4
Tube: Camden Town (100m)
Certified Organic
Smoking throughout

SauCe
Modern British

☎ 7482 0777
214 Camden High St NW1

Soft, filling organic food is the main draw of this friendly downstairs restaurant. The décor is modern without being overbearingly trendy, and the gas fireplace adds a pleasing touch. SauCe's offerings are varied and consistently tasty, including burgers, tofu, salads and seafood. Brunch is available all day. Most of, though not all, the food is organic; any rogue ingredients are noted at the bottom of the menu. The drinks list, which can also be indulged at the small bar, includes colourful smoothies, exotic cocktails and organic wine and beer (including the mild, irresistibly named hemp brew). The supple corn-fritter starter (£4.75) is a speciality – it comes brushed with spinach, squash and crème fraîche. The build-your-own salad (from £3) is mammoth, and the sizeable veggie-burger (£6.50) – accompanied by a saucer of tasty potato wedges – is spongy and healthful. Recommendable desserts include the deliciously crumbly wedge of pecan pie (£3.95).

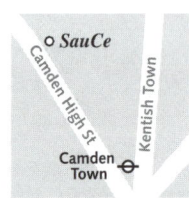

starter £2.50-£4.95
main £5.75-£12.25
dessert £2.95-£3.95
set menu (noon-7pm) £7.50
wine £10.95
JCB MC V

Open: Mon-Thurs noon-10.30pm, Fri-Sat noon-11pm, Sun noon-4.30pm; reservations accepted (advisable at weekends); licensed, no BYO

CROUCH END

Fiction
Vegetarian

☎ 8340 3403
60 Crouch End Hill N8
www.crouchendhill.demon.co.uk

Opening its doors to the chattering classes of Crouch End four years ago, Fiction has been touted as a Great White Hope of vegetarian dining. An elegant, relaxed space in what was previously a bookshop, décor, music and service are warm and stylish, leaning towards boho. Less over-ambitious than in some similar ventures, dishes utilise fresh, locally bought ingredients and demonstrate the culinary nous of chef Fiona Cowen. Black truffle pâté (£4.95) is a fine example: piquant lemon-stuffed olives and crisp three-seed crostini provide ideal counterpoints to the musky desirability of the fungus. Dig into the good gamekeeper's pie (chef's adjective; £9.85) and a steaming whiff of wine-rich marinade is released; inside, mock duck, leeks and ceps vie for the palate's attention. Special mention goes to the tart of darkness (£3.95), strawberries pan-fried in balsamic vinegar and pepper, served in a filo nest with a drizzle of enticing fruit coulis.

Open: Wed-Sun 6.30pm-11.30pm; reservations advisable; licensed, no BYO

Tube: Archway, then bus 41 (bus stop: 25m)

Separate smoke-free dining available

Garden tables

starter £3.95-£4.95
main £8.95-£9.85
dessert £3.95-£4.25
wine £8.75-£16.75

AE MC V; SW

La Bota
Spanish

☎ 8340 3082
31 Broadway Parade (Tottenham Lane) N8

Everything at La Bota is full on, from the small army of frantically busy waiters to the dizzying choice of tapas on the menu. Try the generous portion of fried whitebait (£3), sprinkled with paprika, or the delicious peppers stuffed with rice and topped with cheese (£3). It's not all tapas, however – the excellent main courses include tender lemon sole in a rich wine sauce (£9.50) and succulent monkfish with giant prawns and mussels (£10.75). Unfortunately the tempting paella choices (from £8 per person) are available only for two or more people. The handful of not-so-Spanish desserts includes moreish lemon and sultana cheesecake (£2.50). The main problem is La Bota's size; as the evening unwinds the already cramped gangways get completely blocked by those negotiating a table for later. A relaxed eating experience it isn't, but the generous portions of excellent food are a good reason to persevere.

Open: Mon-Fri noon-3pm, 6pm-11.30pm, Sat noon-3.30pm, 6pm-11.30pm, Sun noon-3.30pm, 6pm-11pm; reservations advisable; licensed, no BYO

Tube: Archway, then bus 41 (bus stop: 50m)

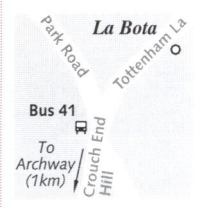

Smoking throughout

starter £1.80-£6
main £6.50-£10.75
dessert £2.50
wine £7.60-£21.90

AE MC V; SW

CROUCH END

Tube: Archway, then bus 41 (bus stop: 50m)
Nonsmoking tables available

O's Thai Café
Thai

☎ 8348 6898
10 Topsfield Parade N8

O's Thai Café is warm and inviting. The décor is minimalist but bright: wooden tables, cream walls, blackboards on one wall, funky colourful squares on another, nothing but a simple lily on the tables. The staff are friendly and the service is quick, and it's easy to see why it's become a Crouch-End favourite. And that's without sampling the food. The extensive menu covers both old Thai favourites and new alternatives – there's something for everyone and decision-making is hard. We eventually went for Thai fishcakes (£3.50): the perfect fusion of fish is given a wonderful piquant by the sweet and sour sauce. Next is gueyteow lad na (£5.50), thick noodles with generous amounts of mild tangy sauce, crunchy stir-fried vegetables and just a few king prawns. Authentic food from O's homeland and a relaxed welcoming ambience are a winning combination – no wonder they've opened nearby O's Thai Bar as well.

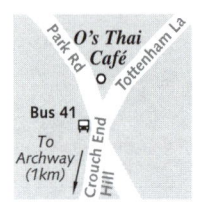

starter £1.95-£7.95
main £5.50-£6.50
dessert £1.95-£2.50
set menu £13.95
wine £8.95-£15.95

MC V; SW

Open: Tues-Sun noon-3pm, Mon-Sat 6.30pm-11.30pm, Sun 6.30pm-10.30pm; reservations advisable; licensed, no BYO

EAST FINCHLEY

Tube: East Finchley (200m)
Entertainment: live Gypsy music Thurs evening (£2)
Nonsmoking tables available

The Old Europeans
Hungarian

☎ 8883 3964
106 High Rd N2
www.oldeuropeans.com

With its wood-panelled walls lined with prints of old Budapest and Gypsy music drifting out of the speakers, eating at The Old Europeans is like an evening in Central Europe, an effect compounded by the many Hungarian-speaking customers. The food is similarly evocative and authentic. The vegetable soup (£2.60) is a particularly good starter – creamy, gently seasoned and with deliciously fresh vegetables. Hortobagy pancakes (£7.95), filled with tasty minced chicken and served with a mild paprika sauce, are filling without being stodgy, while the deep-fried Hungarian mushrooms (£8.25) come in a perfectly grease-free batter. The dobos gateau (£2.95) – alternate layers of sponge and rich chocolate cream topped with crunchy caramel – is a monumental finish. The high-quality food and extremely friendly service ensure that The Old Europeans is consistently packed at the weekend – book ahead to try this north London gem.

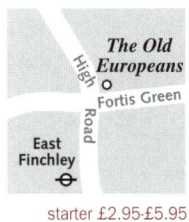

starter £2.95-£5.95
main £7.95-£10.25
dessert £1.95-£3.35
wine £8.50-£11

MC V; SW

Open: Tues-Sun noon-11pm; reservations advisable; licensed, no BYO

FINCHLEY

Rani
Indian Vegetarian

☎ 8349 4386
7 Long Lane N3

Tube: Finchley Central (400m)

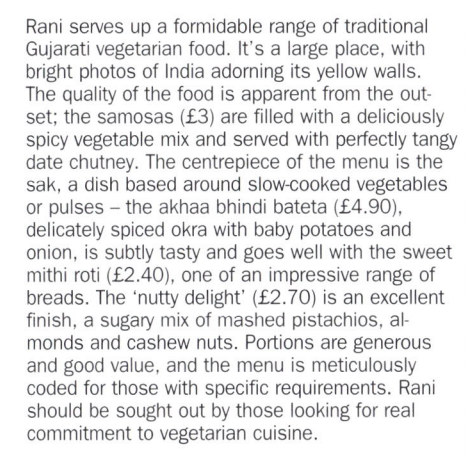

Rani serves up a formidable range of traditional Gujarati vegetarian food. It's a large place, with bright photos of India adorning its yellow walls. The quality of the food is apparent from the outset; the samosas (£3) are filled with a deliciously spicy vegetable mix and served with perfectly tangy date chutney. The centrepiece of the menu is the sak, a dish based around slow-cooked vegetables or pulses – the akhaa bhindi bateta (£4.90), delicately spiced okra with baby potatoes and onion, is subtly tasty and goes well with the sweet mithi roti (£2.40), one of an impressive range of breads. The 'nutty delight' (£2.70) is an excellent finish, a sugary mix of mashed pistachios, almonds and cashew nuts. Portions are generous and good value, and the menu is meticulously coded for those with specific requirements. Rani should be sought out by those looking for real commitment to vegetarian cuisine.

Open: daily 6pm-10pm, Sun 12.15pm-2.30pm; reservations accepted; licensed, no BYO

starter £2.50-£3.30
main £4.10-£4.90
dessert £2.40-£2.90
set menu £7.40-£12.45
wine £9.70

AE MC V; SW

FINSBURY PARK

La Porchetta
Italian

☎ 7281 2892
147 Stroud Green Rd N4

Tube: Finsbury Park (450m)
Nonsmoking tables available

First thing to hit you at La Porchetta is the appalling pop music. Next are the heavenly pizza aromas. Then the wave of enthusiastic young staff surround you and escort you to your table. Meals arrive within seconds and, if you're lucky, you'll be treated to some grated parmesan via a four-foot-long grater. Stick to pizzas (£4-£6), as starters are usually ordinary – the tuna salad (£3.70) little more than a can of tuna dumped onto lettuce. And don't get us started about the over-sweet tiramisù (£3.50). But you're here for pizza, and it's always unforgettably good, absolutely mammoth and shockingly cheap. You forgive the well-worn checked white-and-green floors, become fond of the Italian soccer flags adorning the walls, and admire the staff's bravura. Don't change a thing, La Porchetta, not even that awful pop. *Also at 265 Muswell Hill Broadway, Muswell Hill, N10* ☎ *8883 1500 and 141 Upper St, Islington, N1* ☎ *7288 2488.*

Open: daily noon-midnight; reservations accepted; licensed & BYO (corkage £5/bottle)

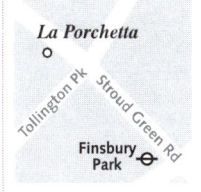

starter £2.10-£4.70
main £4-£8
dessert £3-£5
wine £7.90-£22.50

MC V

Part of the Food Chain

Until recently, the word 'chain' conjured up images of burger joints and pizza parlours, but now a new breed is infiltrating the capital. Restaurateurs have set their cap at wooing the capital's cash-rich, time-poor twenty- and thirty-somethings. With their clear style statements, interesting food and sexy vibe, these places are irresistibly convenient for the text-messaging generation looking for a post-work rendezvous. And the sheer speed at which they operate is ideally suited to their fast-paced lives. Below are some of the best around, with a few of the more traditional chains whose formulae still work well.

Belgo www.belgo-restaurants.co.uk
Diners share communal tables in post-industrial surroundings and devour hefty portions of Belgian classics such as moules and frites (£10.95) and stoemp (mash with bits in; £2.95) served by waiters dressed as monks. The legendary beer list has over 100 entries – some nicer than others. Chic sister bar Bierodrome offers pretty much the same deal.

Browns www.browns-restaurants.com
An awfully English experience: elegant, colonial décor with parlour palms and ceiling fans provides a classy backdrop for good value (around £18 per head) British soul food such as bangers and mash, steak and Guinness pie and nursery puds. A great place to bring the folks or conduct a first date.

Chez Gérard www.santeonline.co.uk
Popular with business lunchers and the pre-theatre crowd, Chez Gérard is a reliable, smart brasserie chain serving French food. As well as steak (from £9), the restaurant menu includes classics such as bœuf bourguignon and tarte tatin. The cafe-bar serves sandwiches and light dishes from £4.

Gaucho Grill
These are sexy-looking low-lit Argentinean restaurants in earthy hues, where no bit of the cow goes to waste. The seating is the last word in designer skewbald hide and the fabulous, fat, juicy steaks come in all sizes and cuts. There's lighter fare too and even the odd token vegetarian dish. Around £24 per head (without drinks).

Giraffe
Eclectic international menu (curries, fishcakes, salads) from a hippy-happy, child-friendly, brightly-coloured chain. Open for breakfast (blueberry and banana pancakes!), lunch and dinner (about £15 per head) at communal tables. Desserts are a must.

Jamies www.jamiesbars.co.uk
Classy wine bar popular with business lunchers and after-work drinkers. Menus (around £24 per head) range from sandwiches to inventive modern global mains and simple desserts. Not surprisingly, the wine and champagne lists are lengthy. Foodies should beat a path to the slightly pricier Bank branch, where the cooking excels.

New Culture Revolution www.newculturerevolution.co.uk
Fast food Chinese-style in minimalist, blond wood surrounds. Fresh noodles and dumplings dominate a menu inspired by cuisine from northern China where the weather's cold and portions are hearty. Dishes range from warming chicken soup (£2) to a traditional casserole (£7.50). An additive-free zone, but flavour can be lacking.

PizzaExpress www.pizzaexpress.co.uk
PizzaExpress has a knack of snapping up architecturally impressive buildings for its branches. Interiors are tastefully modern, with polished metal chairs and open kitchens where glass bowls of pizza toppings are displayed for inspection. Pizzas are the wood-fired variety and come in at around £7. The house wine is very drinkable and there's live jazz in some venues.

Stockpot
A London institution and one of the few places in town where you can get three courses for well under a tenner. European and British staples (pasta, meat and two veg, pudding and custard, jelly and cream) of varying quality are available in functional surrounds. Profits must made by the sheer volume of punters.

Tiger Lil's www.tigerlils.com
Inspired by roadside foodstalls in northern China, Tiger Lil's flaming woks are cunning. You choose ingredients from a £12.50 all-you-can-eat buffet, then queue for a chef to cook them in your sauce of preference (teriyaki, satay and so on), so you can't blame them if it tastes rotten.

Wagamama www.wagamama.com
Frenetic Japanese canteen chain, specialising in noodles, with electronic-order-pad-wielding staff. The hard wooden benches and the communal tables are not designed for dawdling, but at around £5 to £7 for a steaming bowl of ramen noodles, few complain. And there's a decent choice for vegetarians too.

wok wok www.wokwok.co.uk
Stylish, modern restaurant with ceiling spotlights, funky chairs and an open kitchen frying up good-value noodles, stir-fries and curries from South-East Asia, China and Japan. As well as children's menus, some branches offer family entertainment on Sunday afternoons. Expect to pay around £16 per head, plus drinks. Also on offer is wok.box, a home-delivery service.

Yo! Sushi www.yosushi.co.uk
Hi-tech conveyor-belt dining with robotic drinks trolleys in some outlets. Over 100 different colour-coded sushi plates circulate at prices between £1.50 and £3.50. The Yo! Below bars feature personal beer taps on the table, sunken seating, Manga videos and free massages. Big on merchandise – you've been to the restaurant, now buy the T-shirt.

Susan Grimshaw

GOLDERS GREEN

Tube: Golders Green (25m)
No smoking at the counter

Café Japan
Japanese

☎ 8455 6854
626 Finchley Rd NW11

Regularly packed to bursting, Café Japan is fast becoming an institution, serving up a formidable range of sushi, yakitori (grilled chicken on skewers) and other Japanese standards. The excellent starters include tender deep-fried aubergine with sweet miso (£5) and shumai (£4.50), tasty prawn dumplings coated with crispy noodles and served with a wonderful sesame-seed sauce. The top-flight maki-sushi include spider roll (£7.90), crammed with succulent crab, avocado, cucumber, asparagus, flying-fish roe and mayonnaise. For delicious noodles, try the soba with sweetly cooked tofu (£8). There's an ample selection of inventive specials and although the range of desserts may seem a little half-hearted, the quality will not disappoint. The dorayaki (sweet pancake with adzuki beans; £1.50) has the perfect degree of sponginess, and the various ice creams (£1 per scoop) brim with satisfying flavour. Café Japan may be uncomfortably cramped and conspicuously free of Japanese customers but its food is seriously good.

starter £3-£7
main £8-£12.50
dessert £1-£3
set menu £12-£19.50
wine £8.50-£12
MC V; SW

Open: Tues 5.30pm-10.30pm (sushi only), Wed-Sun noon-2pm, 5.30pm-10.30pm; reservations essential; licensed & BYO (corkage £5/bottle)

Tube: Golders Green, then bus 13/82 (bus stop: 15m)
Smoking throughout

Laurent
North African

☎ 7794 3603
428 Finchley Rd NW2

Although Laurent brings a welcome splash of colour to one of the more unprepossessing stretches of Finchley Rd, the atmosphere in this small, intimate restaurant is resolutely no-frills. The menu itself is an essay in minimalism, with only one starter on offer: basic but tasty brique à l'oeuf (£2.70), an egg wrapped in thin pastry and deep-fried. There are a number of fish and meat choices, as well as one simple but delicious vegetable option (£7), whose rich sauce is spicy without being overpowering, but it's the couscous – perfectly textured and delicately flavoured with cumin seeds – that's the main attraction. The portions are generous, so you may not feel like dessert, but the pleasantly tangy crêpe Suzette (£3.80) is well-worth trying. Convivial service and a steady stream of regulars contributes to the familiar, informal ambience, but it's the selection of couscous dishes that will entice you back for more.

starter £2.70
main £7-£11.50
dessert £3-£3.80
wine £9.50-£22
AE MC V

Open: daily 11am-2.30pm, 6pm-11pm; reservations accepted; licensed, no BYO

108 LONELY PLANET OUT TO EAT

HAMPSTEAD

Cucina
Modern European

☎ 7435 7814
45a South End Rd NW3

Cucina has a brilliantly cosmopolitan selection of dishes. There's a colourfully presented starter to everyone's taste, but we were tempted by the egg, vermicelli, mango, vegetable and peanut roll in hot and sweet sauce (£5.50) – as mouth-watering and appetite-whetting as it sounds. The confit of duck with baked ginger plums and sesame-fried courgettes (£12.95) was also a success, the perfect mix of fruity and savoury. The dessert menu held an unusual surprise in the warm chocolate and beetroot cake (£5), which turned out to be delicious, the beetroot playing down the richness of the chocolate. While the well-heeled Hampstead clientele chattered in pleasant but unimaginative surroundings – tangerine walls and asymmetric furniture – what really stood out for us at Cucina was the exceptionally friendly and cheerful staff, who behaved as if it were their only joy to fulfil difficult requests (of which we, of course, had none!).

Open: daily noon-2.30pm, Mon-Thurs 7pm-10.30pm, Fri & Sat 7pm-11pm; reservations essential; licensed, no BYO

Map 8 A3

Tube: Belsize Park (300m), rail: Hampstead Heath

Smoking not encouraged

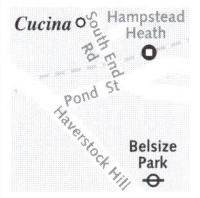

starter £3.95-£5.50
main £9.95-£13
dessert £5
wine £11.95-£65

AE MC V; SW

The House
Modern European

☎ 7435 8037
34 Rosslyn Hill NW3

In one long room, with photographs of the famous on the walls and Egyptian-esque banners hanging from the ceilings, The House is an interesting mishmash of styles – and that goes for the cuisine too. Although light on starters – sweet, fiery, tender BBQ chicken wings (£4.25) are recommended – the menu is an extensive list of British favourites, traditional Mediterranean dishes and even has a hint of Asia (stir-fry – we did say just a hint). With such an eclectic mix, it's no wonder it falls down occasionally: chicken mozzarella (£10.95), served with a watery, flavourless avocado sauce, was dry with only the merest hint of mozzarella. Creamy chicken risotto (£9.95) proved much better. Perhaps slightly over-priced, what makes The House worth a visit is the friendly service and the live entertainment – the staff have a sense of humour and it's not often you get serenaded as you tuck in.

Open: Mon-Fri 11am-midnight, Sat 10am-midnight, Sun 10am-11.30pm; reservations advisable; licensed, no BYO

Map 8 A2

Tube: Hampstead (400m)

Wheelchair access

Entertainment: singers Tues & Fri evening, disco Sat evening

Smoking throughout

Garden tables

starter £3.75-£6.95
main £7.95-£19.95
dessert £4.95
wine £12.75-£36

AE MC V; SW

HAMPSTEAD

Map 8 A1
Tube: Hampstead (150m)
Wheelchair access
Separate smoke-free dining available

PJ's Restaurant
Modern European

☎ 7435 3608
82 Hampstead High St NW3

Wood-panelled PJ's includes a bar and upstairs private room. Slick service complements the creatively assembled and well-presented meals. Wild mushroom soup with truffle oil (£3.50) and salmon tartare with onion cream (£6), chosen from the interesting range of starters, opened affairs. Several dishes weren't available on the night we dined but mains of honey-roast duck with bubble and squeak (£12.95) and grilled salmon fillet (£9.95) didn't disappoint. The dessert menu includes standards such as crème brûlée (£5.50), although the addition of raspberries lifted it beyond the ordinary. The adequate wine list includes half bottles at fair prices. Treat yourself to an enjoyable lunch or dinner in this restaurant that makes an obvious effort to please.

starter £5-£6
main £9-£13
dessert £5.50
set lunch £8.95
wine £10.50-£25
AE DC JCB MC V; SW

Open: daily 11.30am-11.30pm; reservations advisable; licensed, no BYO

PJ's Restaurant (Carl Drury)

Zamoyski (Carl Drury)

Zamoyski
Eastern European

☎ 7794 4792
85 Fleet Rd NW3

Map 8 A3
Tube: Belsize Park (500m), rail: Hampstead Heath
Entertainment: live Polish/Russian music Fri & Sat evening
Nonsmoking tables available

Ever had an inexplicable craving for egg-flavoured vodka? No? You surprise me. In this diminutive hideaway, Eastern Europe is authentically explored with Slavic staff, bare brick walls, candlelight and terracotta floor tiles, but Western Europe is represented by suited sorts, pseudo-designer platters and quirky vodka flavours. Inaugurate the experience with klops (£3.95). Never was onomatopoeia so misguided – this delicious meatloaf arrives with a crimson side serving of swikla (beetroot and horseradish relish). Try placki po wegiersku (£8.65), tender lamb goulash served with a crispy onion and potato pancake, red sauerkraut and juicy vegetables. If you're not a linguistic type, we're sure your pronunciation of the dishes will improve immeasurably after you tuck into the barrels of bisongrass vodka from the bar. *Smacznego* (enjoy your meal)!

Open: Tues-Sun 5.30pm-11pm; reservations advisable; licensed & BYO (corkage £3/bottle)

starter £2.30-£4.75
main £6.95-£9.95
dessert £3.15
Polski menu £7.55
wine £9.95-£20

AE MC V; SW

HIGHBURY

Map 9 A1
Tube: Arsenal (750m),
tube/rail: Highbury &
Islington
Nonsmoking tables
available

Galiano's
Italian

☎ 7359 9042
104 Highbury Park N5

The huge plastic menus at Galiano's don't bode well. Relax: they're the only thing this friendly, efficient trattoria does badly. Rustic Galiano's offers simple, cheap food prepared without pretension. There's a long specials list we suspect changes rarely, but if they can deliver the goods – as they did with our light, tasty asparagus soup (£3.50) – who cares? Our veal (£7.50) was well prepared, tender and tasty, and the creamy tortellini alla panna (£6.50) equally good; both were mammoth serves and quality produce was used. Tiramisù (£3) was exceptional, and predictably fantastic coffee (£1.20) rounded it all off. And if the adage that a kitchen's cleanliness can be judged by that of the front windows holds true, Galiano's is Europe's cleanest restaurant. Galiano's has been quietly serving Highbury for the last three years. Here's to nothing changing. Even the menus.

starter £3-£5
main £5-£10
dessert £4
wine £8.50-£21.50

AE MC V

Open: Tues-Fri noon-3pm, Mon-Sat 6pm-11pm; reservations accepted; licensed, no BYO

HIGHGATE

Tube: Highgate (300m)
Wheelchair access
Smoking throughout
Terrace tables

Idaho
Contemporary South-West American

☎ 8341 6633
13 North Hill N6
www.idahofood.co.uk

Open-plan Idaho merges bar into restaurant smoothly; there are huge mirrors creating an illusion of space, and light shines through wooden planks on the walls to illuminate your dinner, which is served on brown paper tablecloths. But while the décor is simple, the imaginative dishes can verge on the fussy. Any flavour left in the tasteless roast cod (£14) was masked by the sharp, cold tang of artichoke salsa; the plain steak (£16) is, however, cooked to tender perfection. The use of different flavours works well in dessert, with cinnamon ice cream and passion fruit complementing the apple and pecan cake (£5) very nicely. The service is slow but incredibly polite; the clientele, on a mid-week night, a mixture of families and the Highgate 'darling' set. Idaho is not quite as different as it wants to be but its little quirks and easy ambience ensure it's a firm favourite.

starter £4-£7
main £10-£16
dessert £4-£6
wine £12-£50

AE MC V; SW

Open: Mon-Fri noon-3pm, 6.30pm-11pm, Sat 11.30am-4pm, 6.30pm-11pm, Sun 11.30am-4pm; reservations advisable; licensed, no BYO

HIGHGATE

Oshobasho Café
Vegetarian

☎ 8444 1505
Highgate Wood, Muswell Hill Road N10

This little cafe in the middle of the woods, doing a roaring trade on a winter Sunday, is a firm summer favourite – as the number of garden seats testifies. Inside are beige walls, gentle lights and closely packed tables which, along with the jovial nature of the staff, create a warm and welcoming ambience. Choose from soup, sandwich and pasta options: incredibly fresh ciabatta (£ 2.90) is filled with the ever-popular mozzarella, tomato and basil combination and heated so that everything mingles together just as it should. But make sure you try the cakes as well. The carrot cake (£2.50), with a wonderful creamy frosting and a hint of orange, is better than anything we've tasted before. Relax alongside family outings and courting couples and let your taste buds enjoy themselves; you can even exercise your mind as well as your palate with the Japanese existentialist art on the walls.

Open: Tues-Sun 8.30am to half an hour before dusk; reservations not accepted; licensed, no BYO

Tube: Highgate (400m)
Wheelchair access
Entertainment: classical musicians in summer
No smoking inside
Garden tables

main £2.90-£6
dessert £2.50 (cakes)
wine £9
cash or cheque only

ISLINGTON

Afghan Kitchen
Afghan

☎ 7359 8019
35 Islington Green N1

Space maximisation is the name of the game in funky Afghan Kitchen – even the coat hooks snap back against the wall when not in use. In the midst of this chic establishment, Habib cooks up Afghan delights. The menu is as understated as the décor and dishes are displayed under the counter to help you choose. Yoghurt is ubiquitous, appearing in half the dishes and mixed with mint for a glass of dogh (£1.50). It makes a subtle companion to enormous chunks of pumpkin (£6), while tender lamb comes with spiced spinach (£6). Portions are restrained but freshly baked flat-bread (£2), coated in sesame seeds, will satisfy any lingering hunger. The dessert decision is easily made as bite-sized syrupy sweet baklava pastries (£1) are the only option. Popularity ensures a buzzing atmosphere and communal tables a friendly air. For a tiny place this leaves a big impression.

Open: Tues-Sat noon-3.30pm, 5.30pm-11pm; reservations advisable in the evenings; licensed, no BYO

Map 9 E2
Tube: Angel (350m)
Smoking throughout

main £4.50-£6
dessert £1
wine £9.50-£12.50
cash or cheque only

ISLINGTON

Map 9 D3
Tube: Angel (400m)
Smoking throughout

Bar and Dining House
Modern European

☎ 7704 8789
2 Essex Rd N1

To lure punters away from Upper St these days you have to offer exceptional ambience and top-notch nosh – happily Bar and Dining House has both by the bucket-load. Primarily a stylishly retro drinking den, the 'dining' part of the establishment draws an eclectic mix to its leather couchettes and plastic chairs – families and trendy couples chomped side by squashed side on our visit. The menu is short but all-encompassing. Starters of fresh asparagus tortellini (£4), enlivened by crisp minted beans, and wonderfully tender stuffed squid (£4.25) are almost too generous. The gargantuan theme continues with a huge, juicy rib-eyed steak (£10.50) accompanied by a mountain of fluffy fries. The chicken breast (£9.55) is refreshingly succulent but its parma-ham and spinach cape adds little flavour. If lard-laden desserts (knickerbocker glory, banoffi pie; all £4.75) don't tempt, we can recommend examination of the 'bar' part of the concern.

Open: Mon-Sat noon-3pm, 5pm-10pm, Sun 1pm-6pm; reservations accepted; licensed, no BYO

starter £3.50-£8.00
main £9.25-£11.95
dessert £4.75
wine £10.50-£18.00
JCB MC V; SW

Map 9 C2
Tube/rail: Highbury & Islington (200m)
Nonsmoking tables available

Cantina Italia
Italian

☎ 7226 9791
19 Canonbury Lane N1

You can love your flat, but what really makes the neighbourhood? A good pub? Probably. A good market? Sure. But having a great local restaurant when the thought of your kitchen turns your feet to stone is essential. Cantina Italia, an unprepossessing Italian joint off hopping Upper St, fits the bill just fine. There's good food and no frills on two levels, the no-nonsense point carried through right down to the sturdy but comfy chairs. A long list of thin and crispy pizzas – with just the right hint of fresh tomato in their sauce – leads the left side of the menu. The more serious right side has a fine char-grilled filetto alla griglia (grilled steak fillet; £14.90), and fresh gnocchi (£5.80) which is warming and comes bathed in a zesty tomato basil sauce. The affable service delivers and the wine list has many numbers that won't strain a mid-week budget.

Open: daily 6.30pm-11.30pm; reservations advisable; licensed, no BYO

starter £4-£8.50
main £9.90-£14
dessert £3
wine £10.90-£110
MC V; SW

ISLINGTON

The Crown
Modern British

☎ **7837 7107**
116 Cloudesley Rd N1

Map 9 D2
Tube: Angel (550m)

Smoking throughout

Pavement tables

The Crown looks like the perfect pub. Etched glass windows, high ceilings and moody lighting give it a bordello-cum-sophisticated-boozer charm. Our starters – tasteless swordfish and tiger prawns (£6) and rocket salad (£4.50) drenched in mediocre olive oil – came on huge white platters and looked superb, but tasted nowhere near as good. For mains, the veggie sausages and mash (£6.95) made your mouth water to look at and your lips curl to taste: dry and over-stuffed with herbs. Only the rump steak (£10.95) looked *and* tasted amazing. The lemon tart (£3.50) was again a joy for the eye, not the mouth, to behold. And ice cream (£3.50) was perfectly serviceable, nothing more. Perhaps this good-lookin' but soulless food is an analogy for contemporary Islington? Full marks to the ultra-professional staff: they knocked several pounds off our incorrect bill to keep us happy, which we were. Or maybe we just looked happy.

Open: Mon-Sat noon-3pm, 6.30pm-10pm, Sun noon-3.30pm; reservations advisable; licensed, no BYO

starter £4.50-£6.50
main £7-£9
dessert £3.50
wine £11-£30

AE MC V; SW

The Crown (Carl Drury)

ISLINGTON

Map 9 E3
Tube: Angel (600m)
Certified Organic
Courtyard tables

The Duke of Cambridge
Modern British

☎ 7359 9450
30 St Peter's St N1
www.singhboulton.co.uk

The UK's first organic pub energetically attempts the improbable: to meld 100% organic food – and even lifestyle – with pub-like comfort. The Duke eschews music and television (just good conversation, please), recycles whenever possible, and keeps organic babyfood on hand. Does it work? Well, yes – though the food is inconsistent. While most food writers swoon over the Duke's daily changing fare, our meal was unspectacular. Plaice accompanied by limp potato slices came bland and a bit slippery (£12.50), while an immense roast guinea fowl with red wine jus (£11.50) fell short of its expected allure. Dessert, bakewell tart (£5), was firm and filling – but unexciting. However, the wine list boasts organics from across the globe, and organic beers aplenty are on tap. While the Duke's prices outpace typical pub grub, the £6 lunch special, which includes half a pint of beer or a glass of wine, is a good deal.

starter £4-£5
main £7.50-£14
dessert £5-£6
set lunch Tues-Fri £6
wine £11-£45
AE DC JCB MC V; SW

Open: Mon 7pm-10.30pm, Tues-Fri 12.30pm-3pm, 6.30pm-10.30pm, Sat & Sun 12.30pm-3.30pm, Sat 6.30pm-10.30pm, Sun 6.30pm-10pm; reservations advisable; licensed, no BYO

Map 9 E2
Tube: Angel (300m)
Nonsmoking tables available
Courtyard tables

Frederick's
Modern British

☎ 7359 2888
Camden Passage N1

The expense-account brigade who flock to Frederick's aren't often disappointed. Of course, at these prices they (or their employers) shouldn't be. Frederick's bright, leafy atrium-style dining room could feel like a restaurant plonked in the middle of a high-school basketball court, but somehow the posh furniture and table linen convey infinite class. Surrounded by Islington's finely tailored businessmen and their Mont Blancs, we tucked in. For starters, cos and mint salad (£6.50) was extraordinarily fresh, and luscious crab and prawn tabbouleh (£8) was beautifully presented in a crab shell. The artichoke raviolo with truffles (£12) was amazing (no skimping on truffle shavings here) and the pepper-roasted duck (£16) equally magnificent, the crispy skin sending us into delight so enraptured as to disrupt the mobile-phone conversation of the besuited chap next to us. For dessert, the dry, unexceptional bakewell tart (£5) was but a minor glitch in an unforgettable meal. Bravo, Fred.

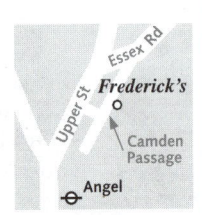

starter £6.50-£11.50
main £9.50-£18.50
dessert £5
set lunch & pre-theatre menu £12.50 or £15.50
wine £10.95-£105
AE DC JCB MC V; SW

Open: Mon-Sat noon-2.30pm, 5.45pm-11.30pm; reservations advisable; licensed, no BYO

ISLINGTON

Kam-Pai!
Japanese/Mediterranean

☎ 7833 1380
26 Penton St N1

In what's surely a first, Kam-Pai! ('Cheers!' in Japanese) offers dishes from both Japanese and Mediterranean cuisine, and meals seem to lurch between breathtaking and miserable. While the carrot soup (£1.80) could have been richer, the miso soup (£1) was a great victory for humankind. Our tiger prawns (£3.50) sufficed, but the tofu steak (£3.80) was delicious. The vegetarian moussaka (£5) was proof the Mediterranean side of the menu is a wonder, while the ultra-cheap sushi platter (£9) did nothing for the Japanese element – it looked dishevelled and tasted none too fresh. The apple crumble (£2.75) was scrumptious while the cheesecake (£2.75) was hardly fit for consumption. We think the food will come good, and the great prices and vibrant, beautifully lit interior make Kam-Pai! a place worth a visit. We hope the affable owners succeed – somewhere this interesting deserves to.

Open: Mon-Fri noon-2.30pm, Mon-Sat 6.30-11pm; reservations advisable; licensed, no BYO

Map 9 E1

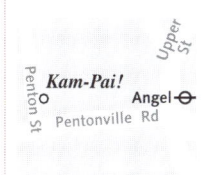

Tube: Angel (300m)

Nonsmoking tables available

starter £1.80-£4.50
main £4.50-£9
dessert £2.75
wine £11-£29

cash only

Le Mercury
French

☎ 7354 4088
140a Upper St N1

Le Mercury is one of the more romantic corners of fashionable Upper St, with candles, plenty of gilt mirrors and tables for two positioned beneath reproductions of glorious old masterpieces. Starters (all £3.25) include ever-popular mussels cooked in wine and shallots, garlic mushrooms (two large succulent discs that almost ruin you for what's to come) or choux de crabe – profiteroles with crab meat and Hollandaise sauce. Mains (all £5.95) are along the lines of pork medallions with cream of mushroom sauce, poached salmon mousse with lobster sauce or perhaps a well-executed dish of fishcakes – two large balls with crispy thin skin served with fresh herb sauce. Desserts (all £2.95) such as coconut mousse with raspberry coulis, and apple and forest fruit crumble are a bit of a hit-and-miss affair, but Sunday lunch by the upstairs fire is one meal not to be missed.

Open: Mon-Sat noon-1am, Sun noon-11.30pm; reservations advisable (essential weekends); licensed, no BYO

Map 9 D2

Tube/rail: Highbury & Islington (500m), tube: Angel

Smoking throughout

starter £3.25
main £5.95
dessert £2.95
set lunch Mon-Sat £5.45 or £6.95, Sun lunch £6.95
wine £8.95-£19.95

DC MC V; SW

ISLINGTON

Map 9 D2
Tube: Angel (700m)
Nonsmoking tables available
Pavement tables

Monitor
Australian

☎ 7607 7710
201 Liverpool Rd N1

If food quality is to be judged by the happiness of a restaurant's staff, you'll find food no better than Monitor's: these folk seem tremendously pleased to have their jobs, and it comes through in the cuisine of this bright, high-ceilinged eatery. Our Thai fish cakes (£5.95) were delectable, and the perfect, ultra-fresh caesar salad (£3.95) was not drenched in dressing. Mains are shockingly big: the splendid mishmash of the socca (chick-pea-flour pancake; £9.95) rolled with basil was a hearty, tasty meal. Though pricey, the Moreton Bay bug (£17.95) with squid, shark and tagine was almost as fresh as you'll find in Brisbane; twice weekly the restaurant flies in the bugs, which resemble lobster in size, shape and taste. Notable in the desserts was that Australian favourite, the pavlova (£4.95). It, like every other course, was presented beautifully and delivered cheerfully. Like we said, these guys are happy.

starter £3.75-£5.95
main £7.95-£16.95
dessert £3.50-£4.95
wine £10.50-£30
MC V; SW

Open: Tue-Fri noon-3pm, Sat & Sun 10.30am-3.15pm, daily 6pm-10pm; reservations advisable; licensed, no BYO

MAIDA VALE

Tube: Warwick Avenue (200m)
Wheelchair access
Smoking throughout
Canal-side tables

Jason's Wharf
Mauritian Fish & Seafood

☎ 7286 6752
**Jason's Wharf,
opposite 60 Blomfield Rd W9**
www.jasons.co.uk

When the sun shines on the canal-side tables at Jason's you can taste the Mauritian influence in more than just the food. Happily, the food is more reliable than the weather, and the restaurant's glass wall and terracotta floor can give the illusion of dining alfresco. Seafood is the speciality and the menu ranges (availability allowing) from starters of simple Scottish salmon (£7.75) and Irish oysters (£7.50) to roasted sea bass (£19.50) with a spicy Creole sauce. Red snapper (£15.50) comes bathed in a rich ginger and spring onion sauce and a mound of cream-filled profiteroles (£4.25) make a perfect end to an indulgent evening. Those at Jason's know the value of location and high prices reflect this, but generous portions and informed, friendly service leave you content.

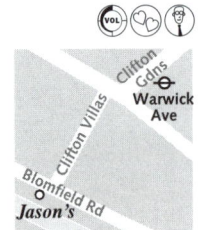

starter £3.95-£8.25
main £8.75-£24.75
dessert £4.25
Mauritian fish meal £17.95 or £21.50
wine £11.50-£45
AE DC MC V; SW

Open: daily 9.30am-10.30pm; reservations advisable (essential at weekends); licensed, no BYO

MUSWELL HILL

Toff's
British/Fish

☎ 8883 8656
38 Muswell Hill Broadway N10

Tube: East Finchley, then bus 102/234 (bus stop: 50m)

Smoking throughout

Once you've squeezed past the jam-packed takeaway counter, you'll find yourself in the calmer dining area of this award-winning, traditional fish restaurant, old photos of Muswell Hill lining the wood-panelled walls. Toff's refuses to rest on its laurels, and before you contemplate the excellent selection of fresh fish you should definitely try one of the fine starters: the deep-fried Camembert in redcurrant sauce (£2.95) simply oozes flavour. It's difficult to choose which fish to go for but the grilled dover sole (£17.50) can be recommended, the delicious, tender white flesh coming effortlessly away from the bone. Aficionados of classic English desserts will find it hard to resist Toff's selection – the spotted dick (£3) is magnificent. The quality of the food at Toff's cannot be faulted, and the service is friendly and knowledgeable; it won't be long before this restaurant entices you back for more of what it does so exceptionally well.

Open: Tues-Sat 11.30am-10pm; reservations not accepted; licensed & BYO (corkage £2.50/bottle)

starter £2.50-£3.95
main £5-£17.50
dessert £1.50-£3
set menu £5-£7.50
wine £9.50-£16.95

AE MC V; SW

PRIMROSE HILL

The Engineer
Modern British

☎ 7722 0950
65 Gloucester Ave NW1
www.the-engineer.com

Map 10 B3
Tube: Chalk Farm (500m)
Wheelchair access

Smoking throughout

Courtyard tables

Many a Sunday afternoon has been whiled away at The Engineer. In winter the candle-lit bar is the perfect snug to glug red wine, while in summer the garden is positively blooming with trendy twenty- and thirty-somethings primed on Pimms. You can eat in the bar, restaurant or garden, but it pays to book for the restaurant. The downstairs dining room is fresh and white, making first-daters and regulars alike feel comfortable and relaxed. The menu has the modern British staples of mash and mixed leaves in predictable abundance but changes regularly and offers a balanced choice. The lamb chump (£15) is a regular favourite, always served rare and with a wonderful rosemary Madeira jus. If the day's fish is salmon (£15) you're on to a winner – poached and very simply garnished, it's light enough to leave room for an indulgent chocolate cake (£4.50) with berries and cream.

Open: Mon-Sat 9am-11pm, Sun 9am-10.30pm; reservations advisable; licensed, no BYO

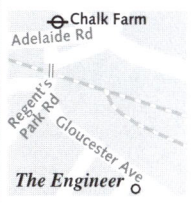

starter £3.75-£8
main £8.75-£16
dessert £4.50
wine £11.25-£70

MC V; SW

PRIMROSE HILL

Map 10 B2
Tube: Chalk Farm (300m)
Pavement tables

Manna
Vegetarian

☎ 7722 8028
4 Erskine Rd NW3
www.manna-veg.com

Opening over 30 years and four owners ago, Manna retains a certain 1960s vibe in terms of attitude and unpretentious decor (plain wooden tables and chairs, low-key art). However, the location, prices and ambitious menu speak of a sophistication apart. Polenta-crusted stuffed chilli with salsa verde, salsa roja and chocolate mole (£5.95) risked disaster (polenta? chocolate? chilli?) but resulted in triumph. Steamed pudding filled with fennel, carrot, parsnip, pea and celeriac (£11.50), warming but a tad bland, was rescued by the sweetest, crispest of snow peas, a hint of truffle oil and exemplary presentation. Organic sticky date and maple syrup pudding (£5.95), amid a lake of toffee sauce and cream, is all that a pudding should be: rich, luxurious and gone all too quickly. Leaving, we took with us a warm glow. Excellent organic Italian Merlot (£11.75), delightful service or simply Zen? We'll be back to find out.

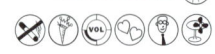

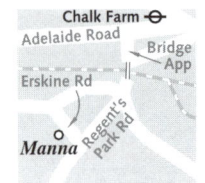

starter £3.95-£6.50
main £8.50-£11.95
dessert £2.95-£5.95
organic brunch Sat & Sun £6.95, pre-theatre menu £11.95
wine £10.50-£25.75

AE MC V; SW

Open: Sat & Sun 12.30pm-3pm (brunch only), daily 6.30pm-11pm; reservations advisable; licensed, no BYO

Map 10 B2
Tube: Chalk Farm (400m)
Smoking throughout
Pavement tables

Odette's
Modern European

☎ 7586 5486
130 Regent's Park Rd NW1

Although it's called a 'wine bar', Odette's is really the best restaurant in trendy Primrose Hill. The romantic upstairs dining room is lined with mirrors, and has no doubt seen more than one marriage proposal. There's a refined, continental menu on offer. From the set lunch, simple starters such as oysters or a warm asparagus salad can be paired with heartier mains such as roast Gressingham duck or rump of lamb on a goat's cheese cream. Predictably, the wine list is spectacular, with hard-to-find selections such as Chinon and Vorvrays from the Loire available at reasonable prices. If Odette's has a flaw, it's the standard selection of puddings: there's nothing exactly exciting about crème caramel or chocolate mousse, though both are well prepared. A lower-priced menu is available in the wine cellar, offering lighter fare such as grilled steak for around £10.

starter £4.50-£11
main £10.50-£19.50
dessert £4.75
set lunch £12.50
wine £11.95-£168

AE DC MC V; SW

Open: Mon-Fri & Sun 12.30pm-2.30pm, Mon-Sun 7pm-11pm; reservations advisable (essential weekends); licensed, no BYO

PRIMROSE HILL

Troika
Russian/Eastern European ☎ 7483 3765
101 Regent's Park Rd NW1

Although Troika bills itself as a Russian tea-room, its menu embraces a whole swathe of Eastern and Central Europe right down to Vienna (schnitzel, of course). The Poles are well represented by a hunters' stew (£6), heavy with sauerkraut and smoked sausage, while Hungary is done credit by a rich Gypsy latke (£6.50) – chunks of beef in a red wine sauce served with potato pancakes and smetana. We usually can't resist the pelmeni (£6) – little doughy packets stuffed with meat and smothered in butter and smetana (cream). There are lighter dishes, especially on the lunch menu, plus plenty for vegetarians. And the restaurant itself is anything but stodgy, with large windows, light wooden floors and bright walls. The one letdown is in the limited choice of vodkas. No matter, the Ukrainian 'zhiguli' beer goes down just fine.

Open: daily 9am-10.30pm; reservations advisable; licensed & BYO (corkage £3/bottle)

Map 10 B3
Tube: Chalk Farm (300m)
Entertainment: live Russian music Fri & Sat evening
Nonsmoking tables available
Pavement tables

Chalk Farm ⊖
Adelaide Rd

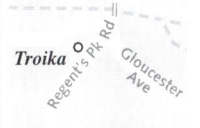

Troika

NORTH

starter £2.50-£3.70
main £5.50-£8.50
dessert £3-£3.50
wine £7.95-£16
set lunch Mon-Fri £6.95

AE DC MC V; SW

(Simon Bracken)

ST JOHN'S WOOD

Tube: St John's Wood (500m)

Smoking throughout

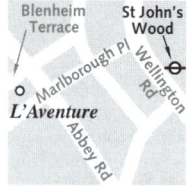

Terrace tables

set lunch £18.50
set dinner £27.50
wine £15.25-£118.50

AE MC V; SW

L'Aventure
Traditional French

☎ 7624 6232
3 Blenheim Terrace NW8

The well-to-do of NW8 flock to L'Aventure, and it's not hard to see why: this tiny restaurant with its fairy-lit exterior offers possibly the best food in north London for the price. With its densely packed tables swathed in white linen and jumbled pictures and pot-pourri baskets, the dining room is part French bistro, part English tearoom. The emphasis on the food, though, is definitely *français* (you might consider taking a language course before booking). Starters of finely seasoned winter vegetables topping delicate pastry and a choice duck-liver salad have the tastebuds in somersaults. The mains effect higher levels of gastronomic ecstasy, with the mute flavours of baked fruit the perfect foil for rich, plump duck breast, and pink lamb soothed by puréed potatoes. Delectable orange crème brûlée and just-so apple tart serve as apt peaks to the meal. Our only complaint: service is leisurely to the extreme (and we're not *that* continental).

Open: Mon-Fri & Sun 12.30pm-2.30pm, daily 7.30pm-11pm; reservations advisable; licensed, no BYO

STOKE NEWINGTON

Rail: Stoke Newington (250m)

Smoking throughout

starter £3.95-£5.40
main £7.95-£13.95
dessert £3.95
wine £10.95-£27.95

MC V; SW

Mesclun
Modern British/ European

☎ 7249 5029
24 Stoke Newington Church St N16
www.mesclun.co.uk

Confronted by a brazen blue frontage you'll soon see why trendies are attracted to this classy joint in their droves. Awarded for its exceptional value, you can expect smiley service and a menu that tangles an assortment of lip-licking European flavours. Despite being packed, the pale wooden floors and lights, wired across the ceiling, create an airiness that enables you to swoon over your divine bresaola (air-dried cured Italian beef), baby spinach and pecorino cheese (£5.50) with impunity. The bulky smoked haddock and salmon fishcake (£5), caught in a smooth rémoulade sauce, was chased by a fine full-bodied Bourgogne Chardonnay (£3.75), and heavenly fish dishes, fresh from the market, included juicy seabass (£13.95). Mesclun, named after the green-salad mélange, blends a wildly flavoursome band of dishes with a top atmosphere – yes, this is a place to crow about.

Open: Mon-Sun 6pm-11pm; reservations advisable; licensed, no BYO

TUFNELL PARK

Lalibela
Ethiopian

☎ 7284 0600
137 Fortess Rd NW5

Tube: Tufnell Park (100m)

Smoking throughout

Decorated with Ethiopian artefacts and memorabilia and run by an Ethiopian family, Lalibela is an authentic introduction to Ethiopian cuisine. Diners sit at low stools and eat without cutlery, using the spongy sour doughbread injera (£1.50) instead. The spring rolls (£3.50) were perhaps overcrisp and short on filling but Lalibela tibs (£6.85) – hunks of tasty lamb seasoned with chunky onions and juicy tomatoes – are delicious, and the minced beef minchet abish (£6.25) is rich, thick and fiery. It's hearty fare which won't leave you wanting. Service is courteous and very, very leisurely; with its gentle lighting, quiet Ethiopian melodies and benevolent murmur of conversation, Lalibela is certainly relaxed. With your eye catching something different every time you look around and your palate discovering new tastes, a visit to Lalibela is more than just an unusual meal out – it's a unique and interesting dining experience.

Open: daily 6pm-midnight; reservations essential; licensed, no BYO

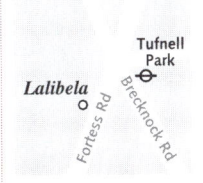

starter £3.50
main £5.95-£12
dessert £2-£3.50
wine £10

AE DC MC V; SW

Posh Nosh
Caribbean

☎ 7916 1047
135 Fortess Rd NW5

Tube: Tufnell Park (100m)
Entertainment: occasional DJs

Smoking throughout

In need of a lick of paint, Posh Nosh may be slightly rough around the edges but that's its charm. The setting – unpolished wooden furniture, posters displayed ad hoc and tiny candles barely lighting your food – is basic and unpretentious. The staff are characters, the service is light-hearted and relaxed (you'll never be kept waiting though) and the food as colourful as Caribbean cuisine should be. Chewy doughbread doubles (£2.25) come with deliciously spicy chickpeas; the mild Jamaican favourite of ackee fruit and saltfish (£9.75) is perhaps over-oiled but the vegetables are fresh and the saffron rice flavoursome. And desert is no rum deal: Auntie Miris Tropical Caribbean Explosions (£2.95) are certainly a blast. Watch out for the secret ingredient in this seemingly simple combination of tart peaches, chunky bananas and lashings of custard. If you don't have a smile on your face already, you certainly will do now.

Open: Tues-Fri 6pm-11pm, Sat 6pm-midnight, Sun 6pm-10.30pm; reservations accepted; licensed, no BYO

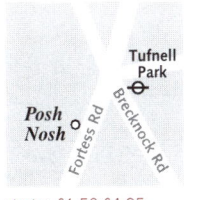

starter £1.50-£4.95
main £4.75-£9.95
dessert £2.95
wine £9.95-£14.95

JCB MC V; SW

TURNPIKE LANE

Tube: Turnpike Lane (200m)

Smoking throughout

Jashan
Indian

☎ 8340 9880
19 Turnpike Lane N8
www.jashanrestaurants.com

Refreshingly simple décor, with just the occasional Asian touch, is the first sign that Jashan is different to the ubiquitous curry house. Then there's the menu, which eschews lists of well-known dishes for wildly colourful photographs of the more unusual options available. And there's the food. Jashan blends fresh spices to draw out the full flavours of dishes and the results set it apart. Sukha macchi (£3.95) has the perfect amount of chilli to give a bite to the succulent crispy fried fish, and the mustard and coconut blend in the irachi mulagu (£6.50) gives the lamb madras a spicy kick. Food arrives in small brass-pots, wheeled out by friendly, efficient waiters to tables on either side of one long well-lit room. Jashan keeps things simple and focuses on what it does best. For once this really is a genuine 'authentic' Indian restaurant. *Also at 1-2 Coronet Parade, Ealing Rd, Wembley, HA0 ☎ 8900 9800.*

starter £2.75-£3.50
main £5.95-£10.95
dessert £2.95-£3.50
wine £8.95-£29
set menu £16
AE DC MC V; SW

Open: Tues-Sun 6pm-11.30pm; reservations advisable; licensed, no BYO

WEST HAMPSTEAD

Tube: West Hampstead (400m)

Entertainment: jazz Thurs evening

Smoking throughout

Patio tables

La Brocca
Italian

☎ 7433 1989
273 West End Lane NW6

West-Hampstead-dwellers can rest assured of a fun, buzzy local. La Brocca features brick walls, invitingly laid tidy tables, and a conservatory to catch any fleeting sunlight. Portions are gargantuan, even if the food – assorted pastas and pizzas – is only average. Our marinated seafood salad starter (£4.95) – a mini-mountain of oysters, shrimp and more – was overwhelmed by vinegar, likewise the roasted red peppers with goat's cheese (£5.45). Blanca pizza (without tomato; £7.95) was too big for the plate and had too much cheese, though black-crab ravioli (£8.95) appeared with a warm, rich sauce. True to form our banana-split dessert (£4.25) was resolutely average, and the house wines sang 'cheap-o'. But unless you're a snooty gourmet, La Brocca is a reasonably priced, lively spot to enjoy pizza and wine – and the genial service ensures packed tables and repeat visitors.

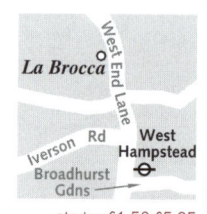

starter £1.50-£5.95
main £5.45-£8.95
dessert £3.50-£4.25
wine £9-£25.95
AE JCB MC V; SW

Open: Mon-Sat noon-11pm, Sun noon-10.30pm; reservations essential; licensed, no BYO

Aldgate
Bethnal Green
Brick Lane
EAST
Clerkenwell
Docklands
Farringdon
Hackney
Haggerston
Hoxton
Shoreditch
Spitalfields
Wapping
Whitechapel

FAVOURITE

- **British**
  'Smiths' of Smithfield (p138)

- **French**
  Les Trois Garçons (p142)

- **Gastropub**
  The Crown Organic Pub (p140)

- **Italian**
  Great Eastern Dining Room (p141)

- **Modern European**
  291 (p127)

- **Pakistani**
  New Tayyab's (p145)

- **South-East Asian**
  Viet Hoa Café (p144)

- **Vegetarian**
  Carnevale (p141)

East London

In the not so distant past, a culinary quest eastward promised little in the way of return. In essence, the choices amounted to a curry along Brick Lane or traditional British fodder in a Bethnal Green caff. But what a difference just a few years make in this organic city. Skyrocketing property prices began to shift people (and businesses) out of central London to the more affordable east. The first areas to undergo major transformations were Clerkenwell and Farringdon, both just north of the City. Within a short time, these working-class areas could offer cuisines as diverse as designer French, gastropub Mediterranean and the previously unknown Moorish. This sea change continued eastward, sweeping through less-than-salubrious Hoxton and Shoreditch and depositing in its wake enough trendy modern British and European restaurants to feed a medium-sized developing nation on roast cod and mashed parsnips for a year. The loft-dwelling YBAs (Young British Artists) in residence here provided a suitable backdrop to these chilled-out, distressed-decorated establishments, but once design mogul Terence Conran turned the shabby old Great Eastern Hotel into a must-have address, the flight east was on again. Who would have imagined that grimy Bethnal Green Rd would become home to a veritable palace of fine cuisine *française* or that an organic gastropub would find its way to Bow? Even poor Hackney – now championed as the new Islington – has got a piece of the action. But it hasn't been all change in these parts. Despite the advent of a restaurant in the unlikely setting of a hydraulic power station, Wapping remains by and large a culinary desert, and the Docklands is still the land of expense accounts and quick lunches. But the opening of the two new Canary Wharf Towers could see quality restaurants sprouting up like mushrooms after rain and eventually pushing things eastward again. Who's to say?

ALDGATE

Parco's
Modern Italian

☎ 7488 2817
**Aldgate Barrs, Marsh Centre,
1 Whitechapel High St E1**

If, like Tarzan, you fancy some tree-top business then dine on the mezzanine level of this swish joint. The spiral staircase leads you to the restaurant where you can look down on the brasserie and 35-foot foliage. The City clientele and efficient staff give it a slick, highly polished feel. Don't strain your neck looking at the dessert trolley gliding round the room; instead, focus your attention on the menu. Commence deals with zuppa d'aragosta (£4.25), a fine lobster, brandy and cream soup, or the filling roasted vegetables (£6.95). If the powerful starters leave space for mains, pollo Gennaro (escalopes of chicken; £11.75) with pungent mascarpone, chive and mustard sauce will finish the job. You'll decide to say no to pudding but wait till that trolley is wheeled under your nose. Pecan pie and cream (£4.25) clinched it – we couldn't refuse.

Open: Mon-Fri noon-3pm; reservations advisable; licensed, no BYO

Map 11 D4
Tube: Aldgate East (75m) or Aldgate
Dress code: collared shirt
Entertainment: pianist
Smoking throughout

Algate East ⊖
Whitechapel High St
Mansell St
○ *Parco's*

starter £6.50-£8.50
main £11.50-£17.50
dessert £4.25-£4.50
wine £11.95-£101
AE DC MC V; SW

BETHNAL GREEN

291
Modern European

☎ 7613 5675
291 Hackney Rd E2

In a converted church off Hackney Rd, 291's nave hosts modern art shows while off the lobby is a bustling bar filled with loud jazz and locals drinking cappuccino while reading the Sunday papers. The small restaurant is tucked upstairs in a dormered space that feels like a chapel or meeting room. Starters include a tangy borscht (£4.25) laced with vodka, traditional Ukrainian potato cake (£4.50) and a filling toasted brioche with chorizo and bacon (£4.95). The salmon (£11.25), presented with a 'quenelle of tagliatelle verde and finely latticed vegetables' topped with caviar Romanov, seemed a bit overwrought but the braised duck-leg bourguignon (£10.95) is a creative take on the classic, served with cranberries and shallots. Round things off with the deliciously rich white and dark chocolate pistachio mousse (£3.25). The staff had a few kinks to iron out when we were there, but they cheerfully dealt with the glitches.

Open: Tues-Sat 7pm-midnight, Sun noon-6pm; reservations advisable; licensed, no BYO

Map 12 B1
Rail: Cambridge Heath (750m), tube: Old Street
Wheelchair access
Entertainment: bands, DJs and performing arts (varies daily)
Smoking throughout
Garden tables

Yorkton St
○ Hackney Rd ○
291   Cambridge Heath

starter £3.95-£5.50
main £8.50-£12.50
dessert £3.25
wine £9.95-£102.50
DC MC V; SW

BRICK LANE

Café Naz
Contemporary Bangladeshi

☎ 7247 0234
46-48 Brick Lane E1
www.cafenaz.co.uk

Map 11 C5
Tube: Aldgate East (600m)
Smoking throughout

The menu blurb at this cut-above Brick Lane joint boasts of a 'unique east-west marriage', a claim somewhat negated by the many baltis and kormas on offer. A proliferation of frosted glass and incongruous statuary strain to give the interior a contemporary feel; however, though neither as stylish nor unique as it would have you believe, Café Naz has a lot of saving graces. High points include starters, such as deep-fried, moist lentil-stuffed kachori balls (£1.95) and Bombay-style snacks such as bhel puri (crisp puffed rice, onion, garlic and sweet-sour sauce; £2.95). The cuisine peaks with the traditional Bengali fish dishes: rashun machli (£5.95), diced fish with onion, tomato and garlic sauce, is lush with spices. In fairness to the more standard dishes, prawn biryani (£6.95) is far from pedestrian, lush vegetable sauce complementing plentiful plump prawns. Choose unfamiliar dishes and anticipate a treat. *Also at 7 Middlesex St, Algate, E1 ☎ 7247 6461.*

starter £1.95-£4.95
main £3.95-£8.95
dessert £1.75-£2.95
set buffet noon-5pm £7.95
wine £7.50-£23.95

AE DC MC V; SW

Open: Sun-Wed noon-midnight, Thurs-Sat noon-1am; reservations advisable; licensed, no BYO

Le Taj
Indian

☎ 7247 4210
134 Brick Lane E1
www.letaj.co.uk

Map 11 C5
Tube/rail: Liverpool Street (900m)
Smoking throughout

Without a doubt, Le Taj is one of Brick Lane's better restaurants – at least as far as the food is concerned. The brusque service, unfortunately, leaves something to be desired. But don't let this put you off. Le Taj boasts authentic Indian dishes (as well as the more commonly experienced Bengali fare) and while we can't verify that claim, the food is definitely different to anything we've had before. Free of the usual ghee, the chicken tikka (£2.10) starter is tender and wonderfully fiery. Lamb byrani (£4.95) is simply superb: the lamb perfectly cooked, the spices blended precisely and the saffron rice crunchy. Le Taj is modestly decorated with figurines painted on the walls, colour-coded table settings and its name printed elegantly on the crockery. Perhaps the tables are a little too close for intimacy but this encourages a convivial atmosphere. It's a pity the waiters don't do the same.

starter 50p-£3.95
main £3.50-£7.95
dessert £1.50 (kulfi only)
set lunch £7.25

AE MC V; SW

Open: daily noon-2.30pm, 5.30pm-midnight; reservations advisable; BYO (no corkage)

BRICK LANE

Shampan
Bangladeshi/Indian

☎ **7375 0475**
79 Brick Lane E1
www.shampan.co.uk

Map 11 C5
Tube/rail: Liverpool Street (900m)

Smoking throughout

Embodying the Indian restaurant stereotype, Shampan has all the garish décor (tasteless carpets, flock wallpaper, tacky photographs), all the tinkling music and all the ultra-efficient male waiters one would expect. The lights are bright, the tables closely packed and the food is wheeled out on slightly ramshackle-looking trolleys. The speciality rejeshwari (£4.95) lacks the chillies it promises but the chicken is tasty and the herbs, coriander and capsicum blend smoothly together. The chicken balti jalfrezi (£4.95) has the fire but definitely more chunky onions than meaty hunks. Desserts are the usual array of kulfi and pre-packaged ice creams and have little to recommend them. Whether or not Shampan does, as it claims, really offer authentic Bangladeshi we couldn't say. Don't come here for something different, come here because you want to experience what the English 'Indian' has to offer.

Open: Sun-Wed noon-12.30am, Thurs & Sat noon-1am, Fri noon-2am; reservations advisable at weekends; licensed & BYO (corkage £1/person)

⊖ Liverpool St

starter £1.80-£3.75
main £3.45-£11.95
dessert £1.75-£2.50
set lunch £6.95
wine £7.95

AE MC V; SW

(Simon Bracken)

CLERKENWELL

Bleeding Heart Bistro
French

☎ 7242 8238
**Bleeding Heart Yard,
off Greville St, Hatton Garden EC1**
www.bleedingheart.co.uk

Map 13 B2
Tube/rail: Farringdon (200m), tube: Chancery Lane
Smoking throughout
Terrace tables

The courtyard may be named after a particularly gruesome Elizabethan murder, but the Bleeding Heart Bistro is one of the city's most romantic outdoor dining venues – in the warmer months at least. The square is secluded, the ground underfoot is cobbled and the delicious food is light French. The kitchen is best known for its country salad with bacon and its salmon fishcakes. Standard meat fare is also expertly handled, with juicy lamb burgers available at lunch. If you want to make a night of it, you can repair to the nearby Bleeding Heart Tavern or simply stay put in the wine bar on the restaurant's ground floor, where you can quaff selections from the reasonably priced wine list (most bottles are in the £15 range).

Bleeding Heart Bistro

starter £4.95-£6.50
main £7.95-£11.95
dessert £3.95
wine £12.95-£525
AE DC JCB MC V; SW

Open: Mon-Fri noon-3pm, 6pm-10.30pm; reservations essential; licensed, no BYO

The Eagle
Mediterranean

☎ 7837 1353
159 Farringdon Rd EC1R

Map 13 A1
Tube/rail: Farringdon (600m)
Smoking throughout
Pavement tables

It's one for all and all for one at this small but very popular gastropub, where diners battle with drinkers for tables and the friendly staff prepare your meal in full view of everyone in the bar. Written on blackboards above the kitchen, the daily menu is original, fresh and enticing. We opted for perfectly seared, wonderfully seasoned tuna (£11.50), which is served with crunchy, creamy sautéed potatoes and a plain green-leaf salad, and the steak sandwich (£8.50) – thin strips of succulent steak, marinated, peppered and served with the freshest of bread. Desserts are little to speak of (Portuguese tartlets at £1, for example) but they'll satisfy the sweet tooth. And you'll like the ambience too. The Eagle has a slightly rustic feel with its rough wooden tables and earthenware crockery, but the funky music, subdued lighting and buzz of conversations take this pub firmly into the trendy category.

The Eagle

main £4.50-£12
dessert £1
wine £10-£14.50
SW

Open: Mon-Fri 12.30pm-2.30pm, Sat 12.30pm-3.30pm, Mon-Sat 6.30pm-10.30pm, Sun 12.30pm-3.30pm; reservations not accepted; licensed, no BYO

CLERKENWELL

Gaudi
Modern Spanish

☎ **7608 3220**
63b Clerkenwell Rd EC1M
www.turnmills.co.uk

Serve good food and they will come: you'd best book well ahead if you want to sample Gaudi's fine, sophisticated Spanish cuisine. The fantastically twisting iron and colourful tiles owe their inspiration to the restaurant's namesake. However, the real appeal is provided by Nacho Jiménez, the inventive Castilian chef. Typical of his efforts is the alcachofas con jamon (£11.50) which seamlessly melds baby artichokes with Spanish ham and truffles. The gazpacho (£10) is a sensation of fresh flavours and is accompanied by lobster. The mains are equally stellar, such as the roast duck (£15) with a foie gras stuffing and a surprising sauce redolent with spices that include sesame and cinnamon. Desserts change regularly – the manchego cheese mousse (£6) is divine. Service is smooth and knowledgeable – a help with the unusual menu – and the wine list would do the Spanish wine board proud.

Open: Mon-Fri noon-2.30pm, 7pm-10.30pm; reservations advisable; licensed, no BYO

Map 13 A2
Tube/rail: Farringdon (250m)
Nonsmoking tables available

starter £10-£13
main £16-£17.50
dessert £6.00
set lunch £15
wine £11.50-£257
AE DC MC V; SW

Maison Novelli
Modern French

☎ **7251 6606**
29-30 Clerkenwell Green EC1R

This is the only kitchen in which Jean-Christophe turns his culinary cartwheels for the Novelli group. Sadly, he wasn't in evidence on our visit, which could explain the slight hiccups in an otherwise top-drawer meal. A cêpe powder intended for one dish turned up on another, our mains arrived too quickly and service was a little over-attentive. Glitches aside, these classy, blue dining rooms have much to recommend them. The menu is short but high maintenance: dishes are splashed with fancy reductions and are visually stunning. Glazed beef (£23) came with a translucent potato flower; a delicious, if over-peppery, wild mushroom starter (£11.50) enveloped by a pancake was offset by lacy Parmesan crackling; and some slightly chewy venison and plump scallops (£21.50) were skewered by a stem of sage. The flawless bread-and-butter pudding (£4.95) had a plate-glass caramel ceiling and the crème brûlée (£4.95) was textbook stuff.

Open: Mon-Fri noon-3pm, Mon-Sat 6pm-11pm; reservations advisable; licensed, no BYO

Map 13 A2
Tube/rail: Farringdon (400m)
Smoking throughout
Pavement tables

starter £5-£11.50
main £15-£24
dessert £4.95-£8
wine £15-£500
AE DC MC V; SW

CLERKENWELL

Moro
Spanish/North African

☎ 7833 8336
34-36 Exmouth Market EC1R

Map 13 A1
Tube: Angel (900m), tube/rail: Farringdon
Wheelchair access
Smoking throughout
Pavement tables

starter £4.50-£6.50
main £9.50-£14.50
dessert £4
wine £9.50-£42.50

AE DC MC V; SW

Sexy low-slung Moro offers minimalist chic in earthy hues. The lack of soft furnishings makes for noisy dining, but that doesn't phase the arty crowd. Service is friendly and informed, and personal touches include excellent sourdough bread and cruets crafted by the owner's brother-in-law. There are six or so choices per course on a Spanish menu peppered with North African elements such as harissa and rosewater. Our flatbread starter (£5) was spread with a wonderful paste of lamb, leek and yoghurt; and crab brik with harissa (£7) was Tunisian-style fried filo pastry generously stuffed with shredded crab. Puddings also shone. Treacly biscuits complemented zesty Seville orange ice cream (£4), and walnut and cardamom cake (£4) was delightfully crumbly. Mains were an interesting read, but roast suckling pig (£14.50), cotton-wool pink in colour and texture, didn't sit well with sweet quince jelly and a walnut stuffing with the mackerel (£13) was bitter.

Open: Mon-Fri 12.30pm-10.30pm, Sat 6.30pm-10.30pm; reservations essential; licensed, no BYO

Quality Chop House
British

☎ 7837 5093
92-94 Farringdon Rd EC1R

Map 13 A1
Tube/rail: Farringdon (600m)
Separate smoke-free dining available

starter £4.75-£40
main £6.75-£22
dessert £4.50
wine £11-£70

MC V; SW

When the Quality Chop House expanded into the building next door, the extension was dubbed the 'Quality Fish House' – a symbol of trends in modern British cooking. By any name, this upmarket workman's cafe is a top media hangout (in fact, the restaurant serves as a virtual canteen for the *Guardian* newspaper, which is located across the street). The menu offers a winning mixture of old and new – red meat perennials such as grilled rump steak (£12.50) and Toulouse sausages, mash and onion gravy (£9) coexist with a raw bar and daily seafood specials. Unusually for this business-oriented part of town, the QCH is open for Sunday brunch – more than a few hangovers have been fed by a big plate of eggs, bacon and chips (£6.95) or beef hash (£12). Those who haven't overindulged will appreciate the wine list, with house bottles starting at around £11.

Open: Mon-Fri noon-3pm, Mon-Sat 6.30pm-11.30pm, Sun noon-4pm, 7.30pm-11.30pm; reservations advisable; licensed, no BYO

CLERKENWELL

St John
British

☎ **7251 0848**
26 St John St EC1M
www.stjohnrestaurant.co.uk

Map 13 B3
Tube/rail: Farringdon (400m), tube: Barbican
Wheelchair access
Smoking throughout

When we first visited St John in mid-2000, we found Clerkenwell's dot.com brigade basking amid the glory of its high-ceilinged, stark white dining room. Six months and millions of venture capital dollars later, they'd been replaced by more standard business-lunch types. The excellent but unforgiving food (pigs trotters, smoked eel and the like) hadn't changed. The staff, unfailingly polite in explaining the more challenging items such as the outstanding entrée-sized grilled ox heart (£5), are used to a bit of diner reluctance. Don't be afraid though – you'll remember that excellent cured pork belly (£4.80) for years. Dessert was a letdown, with the burnt cream's (£5) hard topping impossible to crack and the apple pancake (£5.40) dry and lukewarm. But otherwise it's a fascinating romp through Ye Olde English cuisine. The WAP-toting new-meeja types might be gone, but we suspect St John will still be indulging meat lovers for years to come.

Open: Mon-Fri noon-3pm, Mon-Sat 6-11pm; reservations advisable; licensed, no BYO

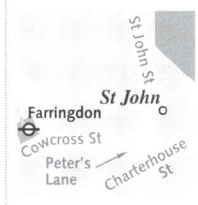

starter £4.80-£9
main £8.60-£15
dessert £5-£6.50
wine £11-£157.50

AE DC MC V; SW

Stream Bubble & Shell
Seafood

☎ **7796 0070**
52-54 Long Lane EC1A

Map 13 B3
Tube: Barbican (150m)
Nonsmoking tables available

Worried your partner's bald patch is on the move? Take them to Stream Bubble & Shell: the huge angled mirrors make for excellent follicular research. It's hard to take the mirrors too seriously, or anything else in this over-designed cavern. But the seafood is the equal of any in the land, and cooked by the most industrious kitchen we've seen: the three-man team slave over meals as if lives depend on it. We had their mushroom salad (£4.25), a dish to make the toughest fungophile drool, and the perfect risotto nero (black risotto; £4.95). The cod (£9.80) was glorious, the scallops (£10.95) just as good. Desserts – lemon tart and a chocolate pot (both £3.95) – were also delectable. If you forgive the designer's ego and concentrate on the food, Stream Bubble & Shell can look itself in any mirror (even these mirrors) proudly.

Open: Mon-Fri noon-midnight, Sat 6pm-midnight; reservations advisable; licensed, no BYO

starter £3.75-£5.50
main £7.80-£16.50
dessert £3.95
wine £9.95-£33

AE DC JCB MC V; SW

CLERKENWELL

Map 13 A2
Tube: Farringdon (700m)
Smoking throughout
Pavement tables

The Well
Mediterranean

☎ 7251 9363
180 St John St EC1
www.downthewell.com

The Well can't seem to make up its mind if it's a pub or a wine bar or a restaurant, but it does a pretty good job of all three. This converted public house features a trendy basement bar and an earthy, relaxed upstairs dining area full of warm natural wood tones. Complementing the ambience is an intelligent wine list and a classy selection of dishes. Start as you mean to go on with the generous portion of mussels (£5.95) with coriander, white wine and cream. Main courses are slightly overwhelmed by the huge plates, but are certainly tasty; try the robust chump of lamb (£11.95) with rosemary and gratin dauphinois or the salmon fishcake (£9.95) drizzled with sweet chilli oil. Leave room for dessert, the sublime banoffee pie (£3.95) is almost indescribably good. A great choice for a little after-work high living.

starter £4.25-£5.95
main £7.95-£13.85
dessert £3.95
wine £9.95-£350
AE DC MC V; SW

Open: Mon-Sat 11am-11pm, Sun noon-10.30pm; reservations advisable; licensed, no BYO

DOCKLANDS

DLR: Crossharbour & London Arena (50m)
Wheelchair access
Nonsmoking tables available
Terrace tables

Baradero
Spanish

☎ 7321 2111
Turnberry Quay, off Pepper St E14

In barren, office-beset Docklands lurks a particularly fine Spanish restaurant. Close your eyes and you can imagine yourself dappled in sunlight, near the Mediterranean rather than Millwall docks, as you sample chunky patatas bravas (spicy potatoes in tomato; £2.75) with a thick, decadent sauce or tasty berenjena jardinera (stuffed aubergine covered in melted cheese; £4.15). Chef Olegario Martin offers twists on the staples with the tempting tapas of the week; try pescado encebollado – divine marinated red snapper (£3.95), to which a mixed salad (£3.95) soaked in simple oil and vinegar dressing is the ideal accompaniment. And leave room for the sumptuous Catalan custard (£5.75), subtly flavoured with lemon zest and cinnamon and with a crisp burnt sugar topping. Admittedly the tacky décor may be more Costa del Sol than costly, but the formidable flavours, friendly staff and mighty Spanish wine list more than make up for it.

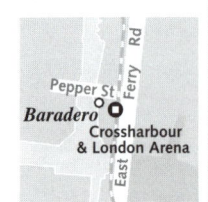

starter £3.75-£6.95
main £10.50-£16.50
dessert £5.75
set menu £16.50, £19.50 or £22.50 (min 2 people)
wine £8.95-£160
AE DC JCB MC V; SW

Open: Mon-Fri 11am-11pm, Sat 6pm-11pm; reservations essential at weekends; licensed, no BYO

DOCKLANDS

First Edition Restaurant and Wine Bar
International

☎ 7513 0300
25 Cabot Square E14

Tube/DLR: Canary Wharf (100m)

Nonsmoking tables available

Courtyard tables

Light streams through First Edition's giant windows during the lunchtime rush, illuminating vibrantly coloured artwork on stark white walls. Later the lights go down and the work crowd pours in again to sample something from the excellent wine list or a quiet meal in one of the curtained booths. The wide and varied menu roams the globe and is a lively mixture of traditional and modern favourites. Salmon sashimi (£5.95) was light, tasty and beautifully presented, but the ravioli of king scallops and mango (£5.95) turned out to be a doubtful order, deep fried until only the remnants of flavour remained. Much better was the generous braised shank of Scottish lamb (£13.95), tender, juicy and well seasoned, and the piquant Thai fish cakes and stir-fried vegetables in lemon-grass sauce (£12.95). Two courses may leave you feeling overstuffed but the ostentatious dessert menu will still be tempting.

First Edition Restaurant and Wine Bar

starter £2.95-£11.95
main £7.97-£16.95
dessert £5.95
wine £10.95-£26.95
AE DC MC V; SW

Open: Mon-Fri 9am-10pm; reservations advisable for lunch; licensed, no BYO

Tabla
Indian

☎ 7345 0345
The Dockmaster's House, West India Dock Gate, Hertsmere Rd E14
www.tablarestaurant.com

DLR: West India Quay (100m) or Westferry

Separate smoke-free dining available

Garden tables

Tabla puts an upmarket contemporary spin on Indian food with a strong range of vegetarian options and fish-based curries using produce fresh from nearby Billingsgate. What's more, it doesn't sacrifice authentic flavours for mass appeal. The hot and sour haddock (£11.50) is spiced without being obtrusive and the Kashmiri-style lamb (£9.50) has a real kick to the tomato-based sauce. Starters and deserts are less impressive, however, with the spinach and potato cake (£4.25) about as interesting as a wet weekend in Walsall and the sorbet (£4) not so much cleansing the palate as giving it a sickly sweet coating. Although highly professional when the wrong starters arrived, service was mixed. Overall, Tabla scores well for quality and presentation but loses points for a dearth of atmosphere despite the smart interior. A place best reserved for when you want to impress with a true taste of Indian cuisine.

Tabla

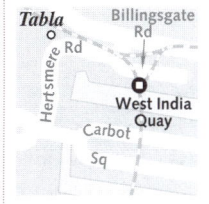

starter £3.95-£6.95
main £7.95-£15.95
dessert £4
wine £11.50-£43
AE DC MC V; SW

Open: Mon-Fri 11am-3pm, 6pm-11pm, Sat 6pm-11pm; reservations essential; licensed, no BYO

Eat, Drink and Dance the Night Away...

Rather than move from pub or bar to your chosen restaurant and then on to a club, how about trying one of these hybrids that allow you to enjoy a drink, great food and a decent dance, all under one roof. Nearly all of these restaurants are heaving on Friday and Saturday nights, so it's important to book a table or get there early to ensure a seat. Late licenses are the norm so be prepared for a long session.

a.k.a bar & restaurant (map 2 C1)
18 West Central St, Bloomsbury, WC1A ☎ 7836 0110 www.akalondon.com
Open: Tues-Fri 6pm-3am
This huge post-office sorting house has been converted into one of the coolest venues in town. The music is mainly house and techno with the popular club night 'Mistermeaners' on Thursdays hosted by renowned DJ Lottie. The mezzanine-floor restaurant offers an eclectic global menu (mains around £13) and views of the packed bar area below. On Saturday nights the restaurant closes as a.k.a merges with the neighbouring club The End (entrance £12).

Boardwalk (map 1 B5)
18 Greek St, Soho, WC1V ☎ 7287 2051 www.latenightlondon.co.uk
Open: Mon-Sat 5pm-3am
Based in the heart of Soho, Broadwalk's bar prices reflect the location, so get here early to make the most of happy hour (5pm-7pm). Ceiling fans, cane furniture and palm trees give the place a colonial feel, while downstairs the nightclub plays mainstream popular music. Bar food ranges from chips (£2.50) to burgers (£7.95) or the restaurant offers an enticing three-course global menu (£21.95).

Cafe Sol (map 16 A5)
56 Clapham High St, Clapham, SW4 ☎ 7498 8558
Open: Mon-Thurs 12.30pm-1am, Fri & Sat 12.30pm-2am, Sun 12.30pm-1am
This fun, brightly coloured Mexican restaurant is extremely popular – especially when the pubs close. There's a relaxed atmosphere and after 11pm the friendly staff act as DJs for the night, playing a mix of salsa and 1970s and '80s classics. The Mexican menu offers traditional dishes of sizzling fajitas (£8.95) and tasty burritos (£7.50).

Cargo (map 11 A3)
83 Rivington St, Shoreditch EC2A ☎ 7739 3440 www.cargo-london.com
Open: Mon-Fri noon-1am, Sat 6pm-1am, Sun noon-midnight
These former railway arches have been transformed into a young, trendy music venue for the East End. Live bands play nightly, so you'll need to check for the latest line-up. There's a global bar menu offering tempting tapas (£2.25-£5.50) and unless you come in a group of 10 or more you'll need to share your table.

Cuba Libra (map 9 D2)
72 Upper St, Islington N1 ☎ 7354 9998
Open: Mon-Sat 10.30am-2am, Sun 10.30am-10.30pm
Cuba Libra looks more like a restaurant than a club, but at 11pm tables are moved to the side and the salsa and merengue is turned up. The brightly coloured interior has a truly Latin feel and the menu has some tempting Cuban specialities (mains around £10).

Jerusalem (map 1 A4)
33-34 Rathbone Place, Soho, W1P ☎ 7255 1120
Open: Mon-Fri noon-11pm, Sat 7pm-11pm
This basement restaurant boasts a delicious modern British menu at reasonable prices (mains around £9). The deep red walls and candle-lit interior give it a warm, friendly ambience, while the long tables in the bar area encourage you to be sociable. DJs play funky Latin jazz and reggae on Wednesday and Thursday nights while at weekends the music is predominately low house. The fantastic bar serves draught beer – a rare treat for this type of venue.

Red Cube Bar & Grill (map 1 D6)
1 St Annes House, Leicester Place, Leicester Square, WC1H ☎ 7287 0101
www.redcubebarandgrill.com
Open: Tues-Sat 6pm-1am
After the success of **Sugar Reef (page 87)**, Marco Pierre White and colleagues have opened a sister venue in the heart of Leicester Square. The lavish interior boasts fantastic views over central London and is *the* place to be seen. Chef Garry Hollihead (two Michelin stars) is at the helm with modern British bar/grill food ranging from burgers (£10.50) to surf'n'turf (lobster and steak; £24.95).

Sara Yorke

(Simon Bracken)

EAT, DRINK AND DANCE THE NIGHT AWAY...

FARRINGDON

Map 13 B3
Tube: Barbican (200m)
Dress code: collared shirt
Entertainment: jazz Thurs evening twice monthly
Smoking throughout

Le Café du Marché
French

☎ 7608 1609
22 Charterhouse Square,
Charterhouse Mews EC1M

Tucked away in an alley near the Smithfield meat market, hip Le Café du Marché is well worth seeking out for a business lunch, a romantic tryst or polish off an evening after a visit to the Barbican Centre just across the way. Indeed, with its exposed brick walls, bustling open kitchen and jazz combo on the first floor, it's the perfect place to while away those cold winter hours. Vegetarians are offered several choices on the daily menu (£24.95 for three courses), but the restaurant is justifiably proud of its delicious porterhouse steak and game dishes, such as roast pigeon and quail. Crème caramel and chocolate mousse, accompanied by a drop from the wine list (starting at £12.50 per bottle), continue the no-nonsense theme.

set menu £24.95
wine £12.50-£49
MC V; SW

Open: Mon-Fri noon-2.30pm, Mon-Sat 6pm-10pm; reservations advisable; licensed & BYO (corkage £9.50/bottle)

Map 13 B3
Tube/rail: Farringdon (250m)
Wheelchair access
Smoking throughout
Terrace tables

'Smiths' of Smithfield
Modern British

☎ 7236 6666
Top Floor,
67-77 Charterhouse St EC1M
www.smithsofsmithfield.co.uk

Appropriately situated opposite the famous meat market, the rooftop restaurant at 'Smiths' of Smithfields specialises in the best of British fine meats. A mixed clientele surveyed the Cityscape through sliding glass walls this Sunday lunchtime – though you can imagine a weekday pinstriped invasion. Meats include Islay Rump, Shorthorn Sirloin and roast leg of lamb with inspirational goat's cheese mash. Vegetarians aren't ostracised completely: buffalo mozzarella, sweet peppers and fresh herb salad is one starter. With an expansive wine list and generous portions, three courses (Sunday brunch; £25) is a lot to get through. If tempted though, desserts include poached apricots, pears, quinces, figs and dates on wafer-thin shortbread, with homemade ice cream. The menu changes daily, so visit often to see what other wizardry they concoct.

starter £6-£12
main £14-£25
dessert £5.50-£6.50
Sun brunch £25
wine £12.50-£300
AE DC MC V; SW

Open: Mon-Fri noon-3pm, 7pm-10.30pm, Sat 7pm-10.30pm, Sun noon-3.30pm, 7pm-10.30pm; reservations advisable; licensed, no BYO

FARRINGDON

Vic Naylor
Eccentric British

☎ **7608 2181**
38-40 St John St EC1M

Vic Naylor led the renaissance of Clerkenwell and Farringdon in the 1980s, and the exposed brick walls now almost give it a historical look. But there's nothing historical about the atmosphere, which heaves with twenty-somethings from the City. The lively bar action can spill into the dining room so don't be surprised if plans for an assignation are negotiated right over your shoulder. Somehow the staff fjord the sea of bodies and deliver good modern British fare. The changing menu leans toward simple meat and fish. The large roast pork fillet (£14) is flavoured with fennel and served with creamy mashed potato and garlic. A char-grilled sirloin steak (£17.50) was cooked as ordered and gets a nice punch from sun-dried tomato relish. The passion fruit tart (£5) has plenty of passion and a great flaky crust. The wine list is long, with many good choices by the glass.

Open: Mon-Wed noon-midnight, Thurs-Sat noon-1am; reservations advisable; licensed, no BYO

Map 13 A3
Tube/rail: Farringdon (200m)
Smoking throughout

starter £4.50-£8.50
main £11-£18
dessert £5
wine £12-£35
AE MC V; SW

HACKNEY

Tube: Bethnal Green (950m)
Wheelchair access
Certified Organic
Balcony tables

The Crown Organic Pub
Modern British

☎ 8981 9998
223 Grove Rd E3
www.singhboulton.co.uk

Bright on a summer's evening and snug on a winter's afternoon, with a daily changing organic menu reflecting the season, The Crown sets a standard to which all gastropubs should aspire. Large windows flood the upstairs restaurant with natural light, adding further charm to the mismatched furniture, tall ceilings and bare boards. The anti-pasti plate (£7.50) of radish, parma ham, fried rice balls, mozzarella and sweet potatoes with white beans proves an irresistible starter, though rabbit and pork terrine (£6.50) was jeopardised by its dry texture. This minor hiccup is soon forgotten with robust pork loin (£12) atop creamy mash and apple sauce and risotto (£9) with perky asparagus and parmesan. Enormous portions generally thwart plans for puds but ample choices revolve around themes of chocolate, pears and figs. With an impressive wine list and great views over Victoria Park, there's good reason to linger when plates are cleared away.

starter £4.50-£7.50
main £8.50-£12.50
dessert £5-£6
wine £11-£40
AE DC JCB MC V; SW

Open: Mon 6.30pm-10.30pm, Tues-Fri 10.30am-3pm, 6.30pm-10.30pm, Sat 10.30am-3.30pm, 6.30pm-10.30pm, Sun 10.30am-9pm; reservations advisable Fri-Sun; licensed, no BYO

HAGGERSTON

Map 12 A2
Rail: Cambridge Heath (450m), tube: Bethnal Green
Smoking throughout
Pavement tables

Little Georgia
Georgian

☎ 7249 9070
2 Broadway Market E8

Set in a spacious room with windows on two sides, wooden floors and Georgian folk costumes on the walls, Little Georgia is immediately inviting. And the restaurant's appeal increases as the food starts to arrive. Unable to choose from the wide selection of starters, we opted for the mixed vegetarian meze (£12.50). We used bread to scoop up fresh-flavoured pastes made of various combinations of crushed walnuts, herbs and spices with leek, beetroot, spinach and aubergine. We continued with satsivi chicken (£8.50), in a strongly flavoured garlic and walnut sauce, and chakinzuli (£8.50), an aromatic lamb stew prepared with abundant fresh coriander. With eight Georgian wines to choose from, it seemed churlish to drink anything else: we quaffed the eminently drinkable Balanchine. The service was charming and relaxed yet we were never kept waiting.

starter £3-£4.50
main £8-£12
dessert £2.50-£3.50
wine £10-£30
MC V; SW

Open: Tues-Sat 6.30pm-midnight, Sun 1pm-4pm; reservations advisable; licensed, no BYO

HOXTON

Carnevale
Vegetarian

☎ **7250 3452**
135 Whitecross St EC1Y
www.carnevalerestaurant.co.uk

Little more than the tiny back room of a just-as-bijou deli, Carnevale is the kind of restaurant you think twice about recommending – it should be everyone's favourite secret. Décor, wine list and service speak of modest confidence, a humility not merited by the menu, which offers a Mediterranean slant on global dishes. Celeriac and horseradish spring rolls (£4.75) effortlessly blend orient and occident. Tagliatelle with morels and tarragon (£6.00) is outrageously accomplished, the upfront cream sauce still retaining the delicate essence of the fungus. There's light, fragrant courgette and goat's cheese risotto (£9.00), and felafel with spicy roast vegetables (£8.50) boasts a gorgeous lemon tahini to leaven the slightly dry chickpea balls, while back across the Straits of Gibraltar a fine manchego cheese with Catalan quince jelly and oatcakes (£4.25) completes the tour in style. Come try yourself – but don't tell a soul.

Open: Mon-Fri 10am-10.30pm; Sat 5.30pm-10.30pm; reservations advisable; licensed, no BYO

Map 11 B1
Tube: Barbican (600m) or Old Street

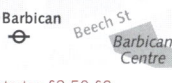

Smoking throughout

starter £3.50-£6
main £7-£9
dessert £4.25
lunch & pre-theatre menu £10.50
wine £9.75-£18.50

debit cards only

SHOREDITCH

Great Eastern Dining Room
Modern Italian

☎ **7613 4545**
54-56 Great Eastern St EC2A

Sinking into a squishy brown sofa with a glass of wine at the Great Eastern Dining Room is a just reward after a hard day's work. The staff are as trendy as the punters but the atmosphere is easy and relaxed. The dining room is nicely lit and the dark brown wooden walls give the room an ocean-liner air. Bread sticks and olive oil start the proceedings, soaked up by the very good house red (£10). The linguine primavera (£8) tastes fresh but definitely needs a good flirt with the seasonings. The roast halibut (£10) is crowned with a zealous tapenade and pesto sauce, making it a better choice than the whole grilled sea bream (£10) cooked in lemon and fennel – although a generous-sized fish, the dish needs a bit more lemon and fennel to warrant its title. A unanimous decision voted the olive oil mash (£2.50) comfort-food king.

Open: Mon-Sat 12.30pm-midnight; reservations essential; licensed, no BYO

Map 11 B3
Tube: Old Street (550m)

Smoking throughout

starter £4.50-£6
main £7.75-£11
dessert £3-£5
set menu £18 or £22.50
wine £10-£60

AE DC JCB MC V; SW

SHOREDITCH

Map 11 B3
Tube: Old Street (550m)
Wheelchair access
Smoking throughout

Home
International

☎ 7684 8618
100-106 Leonard St EC2A
www.homebar.co.uk

After the success of the bar, Home has now expanded to open a restaurant immediately above. Spacious and funky, it combines great food with a relaxed, young atmosphere. An open kitchen enables you to watch the flamboyant chefs who create an array of unusual, unfussy dishes for the monthly changing menu. Starters are varied and include roast Jerusalem artichokes, pancetta, poached egg and truffle oil (£6), a delicious mix of flavours, and beautifully presented roasted vegetables (£5) with parmesan grissini, a simple healthy option. Rich and creamy risotto (£11) with butternut squash, goat's cheese and rocket is served in generous portions and is incredibly filling yet moreish. A lighter option is the chargrilled salmon filet (£13.25), served with clams which complement the subtler flavours of the salmon. Home is a trendy, designer restaurant that avoids the pretentiousness of many of the neighbouring bars – making you feel very much at home!

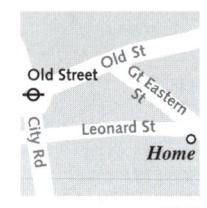

starter £4-£6
main £11-£14
dessert £4.50
wine £12.50-£42
AE MC V; SW

Open: Mon-Fri 12.30pm-3pm, Mon-Sun 7pm-10pm; reservations advisable; licensed, no BYO

Map 11 B4
Tube: Shoreditch (400m)
Smoking throughout

Les Trois Garçons
French

☎ 7613 1924
1 Club Row E1
www.lestroisgarcons.com

Les Trois Garçons glitters, shimmers and intrigues, like some camp *Tales of the Unexpected*. A bulldog with fairy wings and a tiara stands guard by a crocodile waving a parasol while enormous jewel-bedecked flies hover on the bar. The menu is exuberantly theatrical too (pheasant with pigs trotters, anyone?) but got off to a mediocre start. Winter salad with Roquefort (£8) translated as mixed leaves with two smidgens of cheese; the duck giblet and chicken liver confit (£9.50) was perfectly realised though dull. The mains are the principal act – exquisitely presented asparagus mousse (£12.50) is gentle on the palate, its soft flavours drawn out by rich Vermouth and truffle sauce and its smooth texture teased by crispy asparagus heads. The venison in port wine (£19.00) is superbly cooked and flamboyantly presented. Zesty grapefruit and champagne sorbet (£7) refreshes the palate after this most extravagant of performances. Cue encore.

starter £7.50-£14
main £12.50-£19
dessert £7-£8.50
wine £20-£195
AE JCB MC V; SW

Open: Mon-Sat noon-2pm, Mon-Thurs 7pm-10pm, Fri-Sat 7pm-10.30pm; reservations advisable; licensed, no BYO

SHOREDITCH

The Real Greek
Greek

☎ **7739 8212**
15 Hoxton Market N1
www.therealgreek.co.uk

Map 11 A3
Tube: Old Street (350m)

Smoking throughout

With its voguishly neutral décor and characterful chandeliers, The Real Greek courts the boho crowd. So named to distinguish itself from the moussaka brigade, it ships specialist ingredients from the homeland and chef-owner Theodore 'Livebait' Kyrikou consults his mother about recipes. Prices are high and tables cramped, but dishes are imaginative and elegantly presented. Service is jolly and knows its way around the Greek wine list. Mezade starters are made for sharing. Red pepper and feta salad, cured beef and preserved chicken (£8.20 each) are bold and spicy. A simple hotpot of kid (£16.70) comes with dandelion and leek fricassée which, despite its pondweed appearance, tasted amazing. Tournedos (£15.90) are pink-centred and partnered with rich sweet potato, chestnut and celeriac. Desserts are fruity – even chocolate bread-and-butter pudding (£4.90) comes with raspberry sauce – but reassuringly calorific. The fruit-free galaktobouriko (£4.90) is a wonderful syrup-drenched filo-pastry custard tart.

Open: Mon-Sat noon-3pm, 5.30pm-10.30pm; reservations essential; licensed & BYO (corkage £10/bottle)

starter £7.20-£9.30
main £15-£16.90
dessert £4.90
set lunch £14.50
wine £12.50-£38.75

MC V; SW

SHOREDITCH

Map 11 A4
Tube: Old Street (900m)
Smoking throughout

Viet Hoa Café
Vietnamese

☎/fax 7729 8293
70-72 Kingsland Rd E2

Viet Hoa, from its school-canteen ambience to its retro plastic tablecloths, has no pretensions. And more power to it. Superlative freshness of ingredients, a varied menu and friendly service puts it at the vanguard of London's budget diners. What's more, it attracts the trendy Shoreditch set yet seats them at shared tables with old Vietnamese couples seeking a nostalgic taste of Saigon. The food is completely authentic: bun xa (£4.50) scatters meat, crisp salad and lemon grass across a bed of rice vermicelli while the shaking beef (£6.70) positively convulses with chilli-fired flavour. Surprisingly, the national dish pho bo (beef noodle soup; £3.50) was a little lacklustre. However, the crispy duck pancake was very tasty. Sink a cold Tiger beer (£2.50), skip desert and round off with a pot of Jasmine tea (65p). Viet Hoa is a little gem indeed.

starter £2.50-£12.50
main £4.80-£6.90
dessert £2-£2.50
wine £7.99-£16
JCB MC V; SW

Open: Mon-Sat noon-3.30pm, 5.30pm-11.30pm, Sun 12.30pm-4pm, 5.30pm-11.30pm; reservations advisable; licensed, no BYO

SPITALFIELDS

Map 11 C4
Tube/rail: Liverpool Street (650m)
Nonsmoking tables available
Marketplace tables

Arkansas Café
American Barbecue

☎ 7377 6999
Unit 12,
Old Spitalfields Market E1

The test of any cuisine served far from its origins is whether locals with the same roots will eat it. Thus the number of American expats chowing down at Arkansas Café is really recommendation enough. Bubba Helberg has created an American barbecue outpost in Spitalfields Market which is better than you'll find in most US cities. The menu is short and to the point: lots of meat grilled to perfection and slathered with Bubba's own-recipe barbecue sauce (another good sign since no self-respecting barbecue chef would ever use anyone else's recipe). The char-grilled US rib-eye steak (£12.25) was cooked right to the medium we'd requested and the beefburger (£3.95) is one of the best in London, especially if you add cheddar cheese (50p). However, Bubba really delivers with his classic BBQ platter (£10.50) of ribs, chicken and sausage. With a little sunshine, you could almost think you're in the American south.

main £4-£12.50
dessert £2.25
wine £8.95-£17.50
MC V; SW

Open: Mon-Fri noon-2.30pm, Sun noon-4pm; reservations advisable; licensed, no BYO

WAPPING

Wapping Food
Modern British

☎ 7680 2080
Wapping Hydraulic Power Station, Wapping Wall E1
www.wapping-wpt.com

Word spread quick when Wapping Food opened in October 2000 but, happily, it's passed its ultra-chic stage and progressed to eatery-for-all. This is a dramatic dining room: the cathedra-lesque proportions of the former turbine hall – still scattered with dormant machinery – make it feel almost spiritual. The divinity falls down with the food though: flawless it ain't. Certainly it's quality produce prepared simply – our starters of tomato and oregano soup (£4.50) and crab (£6.75) are tasty, but our beyeldi with couscous (£11) took simplicity to a strange level. Served with nothing else, the first few mouthfuls were delicious; a whole plateful became dreary. Similarly, the trifle (£4.50) would've been better from a supermarket freezer. The bill brought a pleasant surprise: three courses with wine for £50 – a remarkable achievement in so beautiful a restaurant, even if the food can't compete with the stunning surrounds.

Open: daily 10am-4pm, Mon-Sat 7pm-10.30pm; reservations advisable; licensed, no BYO

Map 14 A2
Tube: Wapping (475m)
Wheelchair access
Nonsmoking tables available

starter £4-£7
main £9-£16
dessert £4-£6
wine £12.50-£45
AE DC MC V; SW

WHITECHAPEL

New Tayyab's
Pakistani

☎ 7247 9543
83-89 Fieldgate St E1
www.tayyabs.co.uk

A safe distance from the heavily frequented Brick Lane curry houses, New Tayyab's comprises a string of adjacent addresses: a lunch restaurant, an evening dining room and sweet shops, under the same management, between the two. Giant urns and brass tableware add character to the humble, tightly packed dining rooms. From start to finish, the superb meal kept our taste buds busy. Complimentary thick-sliced vegetables came with a zingy raita. Pakora (onion bhaji; £1) was airy and not the least bit oily, indicating an unusual lightness of touch in the kitchen, confirmed by the fluffy nan (60p) and discretely grained 'pillow' rice (£1.50). Bhindi gosht (£4.50), lamb with sliced okra, was bursting with spices. Deliciously soothing, rich yoghurt-based banana and mango lassis (£2) were absolute necessities. Unbeatable grub for under a tenner awaits you at New Tayyab's.

Open: daily noon-midnight; reservations accepted; BYO (no corkage)

Map 11 D6
Tube: Aldgate East (550m) or Whitechapel
Smoking throughout

starter £1-£4
main £3-£6.50
dessert £2-£3.50
cash or cheque only

Farmers Markets

Remember when apples really tasted like apples, when sausages had flavour, when bread bore little resemblance to cotton wool? You may have thought those days were long gone, but they're back – with a vengeance. And if you want to taste the difference, we suggest heading off to one of the increasing number of farmers markets in London. Prices may not always be the cheapest but the advantages the farmers' foodstuffs have over anodyne pre-packaged produce are soon apparent.

The main concept behind a farmers market is that sellers are not permitted to sell anybody else's produce. Their produce may not necessarily be organic or free-range, but what's on sale must have been personally sown, grown or reared by the individual concerned. This guarantees you fresh produce – at London's farmers markets everything is grown or reared at farms within 100 miles of the M25, which means it can be delivered straight to market. And, perhaps more importantly in an age when concerns over food production are never long out of the headlines, it enables you to check exactly where the food you eat comes from and exactly what went into producing it. The latest outbreak of foot and mouth disease, coming hot on the tail of worries over GM (genetically modified) foods, salmonella and BSE/CJD, has reinforced fears that high-turnover, big-business farming may be cutting corners and endangering the consumer as a result. At farmers markets, the consumer can talk directly to the producer – farmers are only to happy to discuss their production processes – and walk away with fresh, tasty produce and peace of mind.

First introduced to London by Nina Planck – an American farmer's daughter who moved to London and brought with her a trend that's been popular in the States for years – in Islington in June 1999, the concept of farmers markets was immediately successful and Planck soon opened other markets. The number across Britain now exceeds 250, and looks likely to rise. They are sociable places – the personal interaction is a world away from shopping in monolithic modern supermarkets – and well worth wandering around to catch a flavour of agricultural Britain without ever leaving the cosseting concrete of the city. London's farmers markets include:

Blackheath (rail station car park) Sun 10am-2pm

Islington (Essex Rd) Sun 10am-2pm – the original market, which sells organic produce

Notting Hill (Kensington Place) Sat 9am-1pm

Palmers Green (rail station car park) Sun 10am-2pm

Peckham (Peckham Square) Sun 9.30am-1.30pm

Swiss Cottage (next to Camden Library) Wed 10am-4pm

Wimbledon Park (Havana Rd) Sat 9am-1pm

And you can check out the farmers markets online at www.londonfarmersmarkets.com.

Mark Honan

Balham

Battersea

SOUTH

Bermondsey

Blackheath

Brixton

Camberwell

Clapham

Dulwich

Greenwich

Kennington

New Cross

South Bank

Southwark

Stockwell

Tooting

Wandsworth

Wimbledon

FAVOURITE

- **British**
  Butlers Wharf Chop House (p155)

- **French**
  Chez Bruce (p180)

- **Gastropub**
  Sun & Doves (p163)

- **Indian**
  Bombay Bicycle Club (p164)

- **Italian**
  Eco (p166)

- **Modern European**
  Ransome's Dock (p152)

- **Portuguese**
  Café Portugal (p178)

- **South-East Asian**
  Thailand (p171)

- **Vegetarian**
  Kastoori (p180)

South

Old Man River, the Thames, has for centuries been south London's lifeline – and its noose. The gulf between north and south London is today as wide psychologically as it was physically in the Middle Ages, and a common question in Londoner-to-Londoner interviews is 'When was the last time you crossed the river?' Most 'northerners' refuse to believe that there's anything of importance down here, but how ignorant they are: the choice of restaurants may not be as extensive as it is north of the river but what places do exist are often stellar. The revitalised South Bank, Southwark and Bermondsey offer an array of restaurants unimaginable a few short years ago. Many, including Terence Conran's gastronomic palaces at Shad Thames, take full advantage of their riverine locations, offering a titbit of romance as a prelude to the main course. Brixton, a focus of Caribbean immigration after WWII, can still serve up the best of jerk chicken, curried goat and savoury ackee fruit but has now set its sights farther afield, with a variety of global cuisines on offer. Lying just north of Brixton, Stockwell is where to head if you fancy a dish of bacalhau and a bottle of vinho verde. This is Portuguese country. Bourgeois Battersea, a leafy borough hard by a great park to the west, can almost feel country-like at times. This is where denizens dine discreetly on new cuisine (modern Scottish, progressive Italian and so on) and savour some of the freshest and most thoughtfully prepared modern British food available. Farther south is Clapham, boasting both an enormous green and one of the busiest railway crossings in the city. In the vicinity of this ill-matched pair are Lavender Hill and Battersea Rise, two 'strips' positively bursting with eateries and offering everything from Italian and French to meatier-than-meaty Argentinean.

BALHAM

Tabaq
Pakistani

☎ 8673 7820
47 Balham Hill SW12

Map 16 D4
Tube: Clapham South (125m)
Nonsmoking tables available

It wasn't so long ago that English chefs were picking up all the awards for South-Asian cooking, but that was before Tabaq put all the newcomers firmly in their place: the Ahmed brothers have received a string of accolades for their Pakistani creations. If you fancy expanding your curry repertoire, try the succulent seekh kebabs (£6.25), minced lamb with a rich palate of spices straight from the clay oven. Award-winning house specialities include the complex zaikidaar haandi gosht (£8.50), cooked in a metal *haandi* pot with a smooth blend of spices and plenty of yoghurt. Uncoloured 'pulao' rice (£3) is the logical accompaniment. If you book in advance, Tabaq even can rustle up a whole steam-roast leg of lamb (£38). The restaurant produces a range of fresh cooking sauces if you feel like trying this at home.

starter £2.95-£7.25
main £7.25-£13
dessert £2.75-£3.25
wine £8.50-£35
AE DC JCB MC V; SW

Open: Mon-Sat noon-2.45pm, 6pm-midnight; reservations advisable Fri & Sat evenings; licensed, no BYO

BATTERSEA

Antipasto & Pasta
Traditional Italian

☎ 7223 9765
511 Battersea Park Rd SW11

Tube/rail: Clapham Junction (900m)
Smoking throughout
Pavement tables

Half-price food (starters and mains Mon, Thurs & Sun; full prices given here) in cheerful Antipasto means two things: popularity and precipitous service. The lighting is subtle, the colours warm and the menu traditional. Parma ham, rocket and smoked mozzarella (£7.50) are deliciously unfussy, as are the fresh grilled sardines (£5.50). Penne with aubergines (£7.50) has only the briefest flirtation with aubergine but the goat's cheese sauce is satisfyingly rich. Similarly, spaghetti with clams, mussels and saffron (£8.00) is flavourful but light on shellfish. Presentation and dessert seem to be the casualties of the high-speed half-price meal. Tartufo (£3.00) had the consistency of a chocolate-covered cricket ball and the nuts appeared to have gone missing somewhere between the menu and the table, and the tiramasù (£3.00) lacked the kick and lift of coffee and alcohol. Still, with fantastic value at half price, Antipasto & Pasta would be a prudent choice any day of the week.

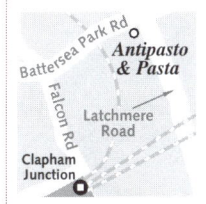

starter £4.00-£7.50
main £6.40-£13.00
dessert £3.00
wine £10.50-£19
AC DC JCB MC V; SW (debit cards only Mon, Thurs & Sun)

Open: Mon-Sat noon-2.45pm, 6.30pm-11.30pm, Sun noon-11.00pm; reservations essential; licensed, no BYO

BATTERSEA

Map 19 E5
Tube: Sloane Square, then bus 19 (bus stop: 15m)
Smoking throughout
Pavement tables

To Sloane Square (2km)
Battersea Bridge Rd
Bus 19
Buchan's
Westbridge Rd

starter £4.50-£6.25
main £10.95-£16.95
dessert £4.50
set menu £9.50
wine £10.50-£55
AE DC JCB MC V; SW

Buchan's
Modern Scottish

☎ 7228 0888
62-64 Battersea Bridge Rd SW11
www.buchansrestaurant.com

If you fancy a Caledonian fling in the nosh department, skip along to Buchan's where beef steak meets duck with more than a cheeky wink. Beyond the bar, you'll find snug-fitting wall rugs hemming in the neatly arranged diners. It's all quite formal, with dazzling tablecloths and buffed cutlery, till the wee dram o' single malt whisky takes effect – then you'll be giggling into your haggis, neeps and tatties (£4.95) along with the rest. The herb-crusted rack of lamb (£14.95) is chunky enough to get your chops round and the roast duck (£13.75) a pretty bird to say the least. Kilts aside, the menu (which changes monthly) knots together other British treats, such as smouldering smoked haddock soup with Welsh rarebit toasties (£4.50). Puds to make you podgy include the sugar-happy meringue-infused banoffee Eton mess (£4.45). But if you want it all, watch for swift plate-swiping.

Open: Mon-Sat noon-2.45pm, 7pm-10.45pm, Sun 12.30pm-3.30pm; reservations advisable; licensed, no BYO

The Pepper Tree (Carl Drury)

BATTERSEA

Jack's Place
British

☎ 7228 8519
12 York Rd SW11

Rail: Clapham Junction (600m)

Smoking throughout

A visit to Jack's Place feels very much like being invited to … Jack's place. Jack himself awaits, and his visage appears among the photographs and curios on the walls. Many of these displays have a US connection – apparently Jack's used to be a discrete haven for US secret-service staff. What attracted them is probably the warm welcome and solid British ambience, as the food alone – though not bad – wouldn't entice anyone halfway across the world, or even halfway across London. You get competent if unremarkable British fare, served up in huge portions. Sunday lunch (£14.50) is three-courses, including a main of roast meat with a groaning platter of ten (!) assorted vegetables. The weekday menu contains few surprises: starters include the cockney favourite of jellied eels (£5.10) and mains are dominated by various preparations of Scotch steaks (£14.85). 'Arfters' (their tongue-in-cheek spelling) include a good, not-too-sweet crème caramel.

Open: Tues-Sat 5pm-11pm, Sun noon-3pm; reservations advisable; licensed, no BYO

starter £1.95-£7.95
main £10.50-£17.50
dessert £2.25-£3.50
set Sunday lunch £14.50
wine £8.25-£25.50

MC V; SW (except Fri-Sun)

Metrogusto
Progressive Italian

☎ 7720 0204
153 Battersea Park Rd SW8

Map 19 E6
Rail: Battersea Park (250m)

Nonsmoking tables available

Metrogusto opened in summer 1999, and quickly built up a loyal following for its authentic Italian cuisine. A converted pub, with elongated lampshades dangling from the high ceiling and primitivist art hanging on the walls, it attracts a youngish, casual crowd. The calamari (£6.50) is a delicious starter – tender, and steeped in a reduced onion and sultana sauce. Tasty pizzas (around £7) are sizable, with generous toppings and a light, crispy base. Most other mains are on the small side, but they are creatively conceived and presented. Lamb with garlic and spinach (£12.50) includes a whole bulb of roasted garlic, with the cloves bursting out of their peeling skins. Desserts include a delectable pear-and-almond tart (£4), served with a strange yet memorable pecorino cheese ice cream. We'll be back for more. *Also at 13 Therbeton St, Islington, N1* ☎ *7226 9400.*

Open: Mon-Fri noon-2.30pm, 6.30pm-10.30pm, Sat noon-3pm, 6.30pm-11pm; reservations advisable; licensed, no BYO

starter £6-£7.50
main £9.50-£14.50
dessert £4-£5.50
wine £12.50-£65

MC V; SW

BATTERSEA

Map 19 E5
Tube: Sloane Square, then bus No 19, 49, 239, 319 or 345 (bus stop 350m)

Wheelchair access
Smoking throughout
Terrace tables

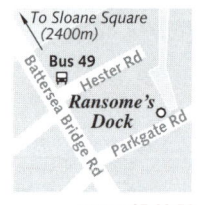

Ransome's Dock
Modern European

☎ 7223 1611
35-37 Parkgate Rd SW11
www.ransomesdock.co.uk

Diners flock to this restaurant for some of the freshest and most thoughtfully prepared food in London. Crab cakes (£6.25) with lamb's lettuce and Romanesco sauce (a 'pesto' of sun-dried tomatoes, olive oil and pinenuts) and smoked Norfolk eel (£7.50) served with little buckwheat pancakes and crème fraîche will have you rewriting your next dinner-party menu. For main courses try solid British fare: noisette of English lamb (£15) done to pink perfection and served with roast root vegetables or melt-in-your-mouth calf's liver (£13.50) with pancetta and field mushrooms. The hot prune and Armagnac soufflé (£6) is the lightest, fluffiest soufflé you'll ever spoon your way through, with jewels of brandy-soaked fruit along the way, and the baked banana with rum, orange, cream and cardamom (£5.75) is wonderfully rich, dark and sweet. And as if all that weren't enough, the wine list is among the best in London.

starter £5-£9.50
main £10-£18.50
dessert £4.25-£6
set lunch Mon-Fri £13.50
wine £13.50-£350

AE DC JCB MC V; SW

Open: Mon-Fri noon-11pm, Sat noon-midnight, Sun noon-3.30pm; reservations essential; licensed & BYO (corkage £9/bottle)

Map 16 A3
Rail: Queenstown Road (500m)
Nonsmoking tables available

Stepping Stone
Modern British

☎ 7622 0555
123 Queenstown Rd SW8

Think Stepping Stone and think subtle sophistication. This tasteful restaurant offers fine modern British cuisine (read plenty of game meats and unusual fish dishes) in a stylish dining room that resembles a three-dimensional Mondrian painting. The menu changes regularly, encouraging repeat visits. Our attention was caught by the zesty potted mackerel and crab with lemongrass jelly (£6) to start. For the main courses, it was a close thing between diver-caught scallops (£13) and the lean haunch of venison (£13.50) with beetroot and garlic mash, and it was back to basics for dessert – a velvety chocolate pudding filled with hot chocolate sauce (£5). The mature and varied wine list would be the envy of many more self-consciously chic places and consistent high quality has earned Stepping Stone a dedicated following – book ahead!

starter £4-£6
main £9.50-£13.50
dessert £4-£5
set lunch £12.50 or £17.50
wine £10.25-£34

MC V; SW

Open: Mon-Fri noon-2.30pm, Sun 12.30pm-3pm, Mon 7pm-10.30pm, Tues-Sat 7pm-11pm; reservations advisable; licensed, no BYO

BERMONDSEY

The Apprentice
Modern British

☎ **7234 0254**
**Cardamon Building,
31 Shad Thames SE1**
www.chef-school.co.uk

Map 15 B3

Tube/rail: London Birdge (550m)

Wheelchair access

Nonsmoking tables available

If you're looking for gastronomic glory without the designer damage try The Apprentice, the restaurant wing of the Butlers Wharf Chef School. Bright, modern and clutter-free, everything from food preparation to table settings is treated with incredible care and attention to detail. The menu is stylish but restrained, and offers four to six choices for each course. Go for the tangy snapper, orange and beetroot salad or the chunky terrine of guinea fowl to begin. Follow with a thoughtfully seasoned grilled pork entrecôte with braised red cabbage in Calvados jus. Meaty mains may be the best choice as the creamed sweetcorn and Thai asparagus risotto was a little uninspired and starchy. Every dish is beautifully presented, and the desserts are works of art. Mouthwatering chocolate blinis (Russian pancakes) and a heavenly almond and amaretto cheesecake were simply irresistible. On our visit, the apprentices seemed to have outshone their masters.

Open: Mon-Fri noon-1.30pm, 6.30pm-8.30pm; reservations advisable; licensed, no BYO

set lunch £12.50-£14.50
set dinner £16.50-£18.50
wine £11.25-£32.85

AE DC MC V;SW

BERMONDSEY

Tube: Bermondsey (1000m)
Smoking throughout

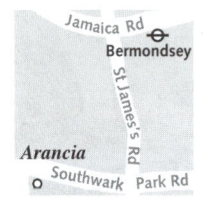

Arancia
Italian

☎ 7394 1751
52 Southwark Park Rd SE16

Tucked away in a former corner shop in south Bermondsey, Arancia is a pleasant surprise, making up for its rather obscure location with some extremely classy but unpretentious food at great prices. Squeeze into your seat beside the warm orange walls, sip a regional Italian wine and deliberate over the seasonally inspired menu. Begin with creamy home-cured crab meat tartlets (£4.50) or a stunning roast marinated quail (£5) before moving on to thick and juicy lamb fillets served with couscous, mint and salsa verde (£9.50) or the succulent poached chicken (£9) wrapped in parma ham with a porcini sauce – just the right blend of flavours. Portions are generous so consider skipping starters to leave room for one of Arancia's wickedly indulgent desserts: smooth, rich chocolate semifreddo (chilled cream dessert; £3) or light and creamy rhubarb fool (£3.40) – nothing short of divine.

starter £3-£5
main £8.90-£9.50
dessert £3-£4
set lunch £7.50-£10.50
wine £8-£17

MC V

Open: Wed-Sun 12.30pm-2.30pm, daily 7pm-11pm; reservations advisable; licensed, no BYO

Map 15 B5
Tube/rail: London Bridge (550m), tube: Tower Hill
Entertainment: piano Tues-Sat evening
Nonsmoking tables available

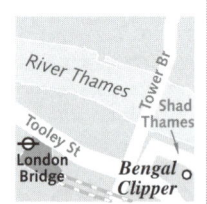

Bengal Clipper
Indian

☎ 7357 9001
31 Shad Thames SE1
www.bengalrestaurant.com

Large and pleasant, this clipper is more of a cruise-liner with wood, brass, oceans of blue carpet and splashy modern canvasses. By day it hosts a hundred expense accounts, by night tourists who've escaped from the Tower of London. Chefs Azam Khan and Raj Kumar offer unusual regional specialities, such as Bengal tiger fish hara massala (river fish with coriander and ginger; £13.95) or spicy Bangladeshi vegetables (milijui shobji; £3.50). Service can be offhand, although there's a real flourish to the production of golda chiagri pardanashin (prawns cooked in a coconut shell; £15.50). The lavish menu descriptions are a hard act to follow but Azam Khan has, among other accolades, won the title of Spinach Master Chef (1998) – so do top up your iron intake with one of his many delicious takes on the green stuff. Try crispy dry roshoon palook with aniseed and garlic for £3.50.

starter £3.15-£7.95
main £8.15-£15.50
dessert £2-£5
set menu £28
Sun buffet £7.75
wine £10.95-£95

AE DC MC V; SW

Open: Mon-Sat noon-2.30pm, 6pm-11.30pm, Sun noon-4.30pm, 6pm-11pm; reservations advisable; licensed, no BYO

Bengal Clipper (Carl Drury)

Butlers Wharf Chop House
Traditional British

☎ 7403 3403
The Butlers Wharf Building, 36e Shad Thames SE1
www.conran.com

Map 15 B5
Tube/rail: London Bridge (550m), tube: Tower Hill
Wheelchair access
Smoking throughout
Terrace tables

Reminiscent of a cricket pavilion or boathouse, this light-flooded, wood-lined restaurant is situated under the south-east rampart of Tower Bridge, and is part of Conran's 'gastrodome' complex. We arrived for a memorable Sunday lunch to the sound of sizzling beef and the aroma of home-made sausages. The potato pancake with smoked eel (£8.50) is an inventive starter, while the roasts are delectably tender: try roast rump of lamb (£17), accompanied by delicately minted parsley potatoes, or juicy roast beef (£17), served with a massive gravy-topped Yorkshire pudding. There's also an excellent selection of fresh fish. The desserts are outstanding – the beautifully presented bread-and-butter pudding (£4.75) and mouthwatering mocha fudge and walnut tart (£4.75) stand out. There's no doubt about it: the Chop House is a first-class standard bearer for British cuisine.

Open: Mon-Fri noon-3pm, 6pm-11pm, Sat 6pm-11pm, Sun noon-3pm; reservations advisable; licensed, no BYO

starter £5.50-£22
main £12.50-£25
dessert £4.75-£5.75
set lunch £19.75 or £23.75
wine £13.50-£3000

AE DC JCB MC V; SW

SOUTH

BERMONDSEY 155

BERMONDSEY

Map 15 B5
Tube/rail: London Bridge (550m), tube: Tower Hill

Smoking throughout
Terrace tables

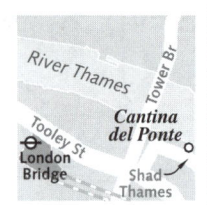

Cantina del Ponte
Italian

☎ 7403 5403
The Butlers Wharf Building, 36c Shad Thames SE1
www.conran.com

The sleek lines of Cantina's interior are typically Conran but there are Mediterranean elements here too: warm Italian staff, a terrace fronting the Thames, splashes of colour in quarry tiles and a huge, bustling mural. The chef has considerable artistic flair but beauty of presentation is not at the expense of flavour nor portion. The mackerel starter (£6.95), on a bed of tomato salsa, is as tasty as it is simple; the spinach and parmesan frittata (£6.75) is delicate and soothing. While mains consist of familiar faces (steak, seabass, pork loin), the scallop and crab lasagne (£14.50) stands out as most promising newcomer: plump scallops, sharply seared, complement warm crab wrapped in a smooth pasta shawl. With a rich cream sauce and tender orange flesh, pumpkin cannelloni (£8.95) is a reliable co-star. The dessert list is thoughtful rather than expansive, with bread-and-butter pudding (£5.95) capping a confident culinary performance.

starter £4.50-£6.95
main £8.95-£14.75
dessert £5.95
wine £12.50-£38

AE DC JCB MC V; SW

Open: daily noon-3pm, Mon-Sat 6pm-11pm, Sun 6pm-10pm; reservations advisable; licensed, no BYO

Map 15 B4
Tube/rail: London Bridge (550m), tube: Tower Hill

Wheelchair access
Smoking throughout

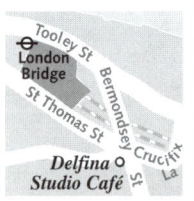

Delfina Studio Café
Global

☎ 7357 0244
50 Bermondsey St SE1
www.delfina.org.uk

Delfina showcases both art and the art of food. The restaurant, housed in a converted chocolate factory, displays works by members of its charitable trust, and the same lucky artists can lunch for £1. But it is the food that takes centre stage. Our cauliflower soup (£3.95), sprinkled with pecorino cheese, parsley and pine nuts, was creamy and warm with just the right hint of cheese, and the juicy slow-roasted shank of lamb (£13.25) rubbed with tarragon and mustard fell off the bone. The chocolate tart with cardamom ice cream (£4.25) was sublime, the crisp pastry filled with smooth chocolate. It's such a shame that Delfina is only open for lunch on weekdays (the restaurant is hired for private parties for the balance of the time).

starter £3.95-£5.50
main £9.95-£13.50
dessert £4.25
wine £12.50-£36

AE DC MC V; SW

Open: Mon-Fri noon-3pm; reservations advisable; licensed, no BYO

BERMONDSEY

Honest Cabbage
Modern British

☎ 7234 0080
99 Bermondsey St SE1

True to its name, the Honest Cabbage serves up good, honest food. The portions are generous, the ingredients are fresh and the atmosphere is bohemian. The menu, which changes daily, is posted on a series of blackboards on the restaurant's main wall. With the option of 10 main dishes, you're bound to find something that appeals. Our choices ranged from carrot and wild rice soup (£4) to pan-fried monkfish with star anise and sweet chilli (£13). The pasta offering for the day, spinach and ricotta ravioli with a wild mushroom cream sauce (£5 small, £8 large), was fresh and delightful, and the fresh meat dish of ostrich sausages in red wine jus (£10) was inventive and interesting. The restaurant is just a few blocks from London's legendary Bermondsey flea market – in Honest Cabbage you'll find a treasure indeed.

Open: Mon-Fri noon-3pm, Sat & Sun noon-4pm, Mon-Wed 6.30pm-10pm, Thurs & Fri 6.30pm-11pm, Sat 7pm-11pm; reservations advisable; licensed, no BYO

Map 15 B4
Tube/rail: London Bridge (650m)
Wheelchair access
Smoking throughout

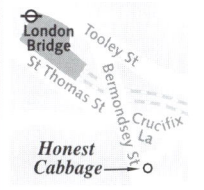

starter £4-£6
main £7-£14
dessert £5
wine £11-£23
DC MC V; SW

Le Pont de la Tour
Modern European

☎ 7403 8403
Butlers Wharf Building, 36d Shad Thames SE1
www.conran.com

Favoured haven of high-powered wheeler-dealers, Le Pont de la Tour hosted the christening of the Blair-Clinton alliance on its riverbank perch downstream from namesake Tower Bridge. Conran's impeccably assiduous staff excel themselves here: empty plates vanish, swiftly replaced by studied gems such as the Dorset crab (£12.50) and the milk-white roast veal sweetbreads (£12.50). Alabaster roast fillet of hake (£17.50) left the oven on time to the second, exquisitely flavoured and properly moist. Gressingham duck (£18.50), specially bred for its gamier taste, created an unexpectedly tender portion of the classic with orange and thyme. A rich, lazy slab of chocolate marquise (£7.50) failed to divert; lively orange and cardamom parfait (£7) reigned victorious. Check out the walk-in wine room bristling with bottles.

Open: Mon-Fri & Sun noon-3pm, Mon-Sat 6pm-11.30pm, Sun 6pm-11pm; reservations essential; licensed, no BYO

Map 15 B5
Tube/rail: London Bridge (550m), tube: Tower Hill
Smoking throughout
Courtyard tables

starter £8-£18.95
main £17.50-£27.50
dessert £6.50-£8.50
set lunch £28.50, pre- & post-theatre menu £19.50
wine £15-£800
AE DC MC V; SW

SOUTH

BLACKHEATH

Rail: Blackheath (100m)

Smoking throughout

starter £1-£5.50
main £2.50-£15
dessert £3.95-£4.95
set menu £12.50-£19.50
wine £8-£30
MC V; SW

Laughing Buddha
Chinese

☎/fax 8852 4161
41 Montpelier Vale SE3

Three courses at this mid-market restaurant and you'll be on your way to resembling its eponymous mascot. The food is extremely filling, albeit a bit glutinous. Laughing Buddha is popular with couples, its romantic reputation enhanced by the its location on the edge of the village green. Bright yellow dining rooms are further enlivened by floral arrangements and water features. Try seafood gourmet mixed hors d'oeuvres (£11 for two), a varied selection of shellfish, calamari and shredded seaweed. Imaginatively titled mains such as tiger's whiskers (a stodgy vegetarian dish with super-fine noodles; £5) and scallops in a crunchy fried potato 'bird's nest' (£6.50) often sound better than they taste. To survive (and enjoy) a full meal here, shy away from the fried offerings. Drunken fish (£5), for example, is cooked in wine and leaves room for more. The Chinese staff do their best but falter at complex requests.

Open: Mon-Sat noon-2.30pm, 6pm-11.30pm, Sun 2pm-11pm; reservations advisable at weekends; licensed, no BYO

BLACKHEATH

Thyme
Modern European

☎ **8293 9183**
1a Station Crescent SE3

This intimate, serene restaurant is simply decorated, with parquet floors and Venetian blinds. It appears to be a labour of love, from Neil Salter's small menu of carefully presented food to the quietly attentive, rather formal staff. Recommended is a substantial salmon fishcake (£4.75), whose soft creamy centre forms a delightful textural contrast with its crisp outer layer, or bruschetta with fragrant, marinated red peppers (£4.25). A couple of dishes seem to have ideas above their station, lacking sufficient complexity of flavour; the bacon-wrapped scallops with noodles and spinach (£12.95) combine good, fresh ingredients but the lovely meaty scallops are overwhelmed by the bacon. This isn't true, however, of the delicious peach and plum crumble (£4.25) in which the fruit offsets the crumble perfectly, complemented by a pale wash of vanilla custard. It's a good, reliable choice in one of London's quieter corners.

Open: Tues-Sat 6pm-10.30pm, Sun noon-2.30pm; reservations advisable (essential at weekends); licensed, no BYO

Rail: Westcombe Park (75m)
Nonsmoking tables available
Garden tables

starter £3.95-£5.24
main £10.95-£12.95
dessert £3.95-£5.25
wine £9.95-£30

MC V; SW

BRIXTON

Asmara
Eritrean

☎ **7737 4144**
386 Coldharbour Lane SW9

With its pots of burning frankincense, comfy wicker chairs and goat-skin trinkets, this homely little restaurant manages to summon the spirit of East Africa to the incongruous surrounds of downtown Brixton. Alongside Eritrean classics, the menu lists pasta dishes introduced to Abyssinia by the Italians. Anyone who knows Eritrea will find themselves transported back by the wonderfully aromatic zelzel tibssi (£7.50), tender pieces of lamb sizzling with green chilli and onion on a clay brazier, and a dish of spinach and ricotta (£5) perfumed with spicy butter. The motherly waitress regularly parades fragrant pan-roasted coffee beans around the room: you can opt for a clay thimble of the Eritrean coffee with cloves (£4.50) or the more well-known Italian version (£1). After a cooling dessert of yoghurt, sultanas and honey (£2), the brave can go for the fully authentic experience and try a shot of firewater zibib.

Open: Mon-Sun 5pm-1am; reservations advisable; licensed, no BYO

Map 17 D3
Tube/rail: Brixton (100m)
Smoking throughout

starter £2.50-£4
main £4-£7.50
dessert £2
wine £6-£12.50
set menu £22 or £25
(min 2 people)

AE DC JCB MC V; SW

SOUTH

BLACKHEATH & BRIXTON 159

BRIXTON

Map 17 E2
Tube/rail: Brixton (350m)
Wheelchair access
Entertainment: jazz monthly
Smoking throughout
Garden tables

starter £3.50-£4.70
main £7.30-£12.70
dessert £4.50
wine £9.90-£20
JCB MC V; SW

Bah Humbug
Modern British

☎ 7738 3184
**The Crypt,
St Matthew's Church SW2**
www.bahhumbug.co.uk

Set in a church crypt, Bah Humbug buzzes at night and relaxes in style during the day at weekends. Huge lounging sofas beckon, tables of all shapes and sizes are moulded into nooks and crannies and the occasional bronze hangs on the wall, all adding to the place's individuality. We opted for the Sunday brunch, or 'mood food'. The totus porcus (£10.70) vegetarian organic fry up was pure indulgence, as was the aptly named sybaryte (£14.50). It kicked off with a truly fruity smoothie, swiftly followed by fluffy scrambled eggs with slivers of smoked salmon, and wild and oyster mushrooms. Then came maple syrup pancakes with fresh lemon to give a tang to the sweet, and a frothy cappuccino to finish. Oh, and not forgetting the glass of Champagnoise. What a brunch, perfect for the hungry and the hungover. Bah Humbug oozes personality – go and lap it up!

Open: Mon-Thurs 5pm-11.30pm, Fri & Sat 5pm-midnight, Sun 11am-11pm; reservations advisable at weekends; licensed, no BYO

Bah Humbug (Carl Drury)

BRIXTON

Brixtonian Havana Club
West Indian

☎ 7924 9262
11 Beehive Place SW9
www.brixtonian.co.uk

This first-floor bar/restaurant, tucked away on a narrow street, resounds with tropical colours and exuberant blasts of salsa. The exotic menu blends Caribbean, French, British and African influences in dishes such as roast pepper and ginger soup (£4.50), sensational baked ham with sweet sorrel sauce (£14) and subtly flavoured chicken breast stuffed with spinach and dates (£14). Scene of many packed-out, cocktail-toting evenings, the loud, funky décor – like the clientele – seems to have had a few too many late nights. It's bright yet bleary, like a drag artist who's slept in his makeup, but white tablecloths against the red leatherette seating lend a spicy glamour to the nightclub pallor. And the sun-splashed menu – offering balmy desserts such as coconut tart with rum cream (£4.50) – helps keep that Caribbean dream alive, as does the sublime array of over 300 rums (£3-£100 per shot) – enough to warm any aficionado's cockles.

Open: Tues-Sun noon-6pm, Tues & Wed 7pm-10.30pm, Thurs-Sun 7pm-11pm (bar until 2am); reservations advisable; licensed, no BYO

Map 17 D3
Tube/rail: Brixton (100m)
Entertainment: 'ramjam' Tues evening, comedy Wed evening, live gospel music Sun evening

Smoking throughout

Terrace tables

starter £4.50
main £14
dessert £4.50
wine £14.95

DC JCB MC V; SW

Fujiyama
Japanese

☎ 7737 2369
5-7 Vining St SW9

One of Brixton's best-kept secrets, Fujiyama is an intimate canteen-style Japanese noodle bar. The décor is much more congenial and cocoon-like than its central London counterparts, with a deep-red colour scheme and bench seating. The main offerings on the menu are ramen noodles (£4.95-£5.95) and fried noodle dishes (£4.50-£5.50). Ginger, lemongrass, chilli and spring onions figure prominently, lending a hot yet fresh flavour. The karai beef ramen with chillies and coriander was the perfect antidote to a cold night, and we also loved the prawn gyoza (£3.90) – deep-fried prawn dumplings served with a tangy dip. For quality, quantity and price, Fujiyama can't be faulted.

Open: Mon-Thurs 5pm-11pm, Fri 5pm-midnight, Sat noon-midnight, Sun noon-11pm; reservations advisable; licensed, no BYO

Map 17 E3
Tube/rail: Brixton (300m)

Separate smoke-free dining available

starter £3.50
main £5.15-£8.95
wine £8.20-£11.95

DC JCB MC V; SW

BRIXTON

Map 17 E2
Tube/rail: Brixton, then bus 159 (bus stop: 15m)
Smoking throughout

The Gallery
Portuguese

☎ 8671 8311
256a Brixton Hill SW2

Behind the takeaway disguise (go through the door by the counter) is a Portuguese restaurant in the style of a sunny Atlantic-coast villa. With bona-fide Portuguese ownership and colourful wall paintings of Madeira seas, you wonder if the food can match the ambience. To a large extent it does, but be adventurous when choosing your meal as gastronomic satisfaction favours the brave here. More ordinary sounding dishes such as lamb cutlets (£9) are more ordinary tasting, but platters that hint at the exotic, such as the Portuguese grilled sausages (£2.50) or the old Goa chicken curry (£9), will not disappoint. As a finale, the sweet memory of the Molotov dessert (an egg- and syrup-based pudding; £3) will linger long after you step back from Portugal to Brixton Hill.

starter £3.50-£8.50
main £8.50-£13
dessert £3
wine £7.50-£55
DC MC V; SW

Open: Mon-Sat 7pm-10.30pm, Sun noon-10pm; reservations advisable; licensed, no BYO

Map 17 3
Tube/rail: Brixton (300m)
Wheelchair access
Entertainment: DJ Sat evening
Smoking throughout

Satay Bar
Indonesian

☎ 7326 5001
447-450 Coldharbour Lane SW9

Favoured by a young, trendy crowd, the Satay Bar is bustling and congenial, even on week nights. Decorated with constantly changing artwork, it's alive with funky music and the animated shouts of the waiters. There's an extensive cocktail list (£3.95 each, £12 per jug) and a good range of international bottled beers. The choice of dishes is extensive, good value and unpronounceable! The chicken satay (£5.50) is slightly hotter than most, with a delicious rich sauce, while the duck with peach in a mild rice wine sauce (bebek hijau; £5.95) offers an interesting combination of flavours. The hot and spicy prawns (sambai udang; £6.75) are tender and tasty, and to soak up the plethora of sauces there's boiled coconut rice (£1.65) or noodles (£4.75), which are a meal in themselves (hence the price). And if you can cope with another taste sensation, green pancakes (£2.95) make a great way to finish.

starter £3.25-£6.15
main £4.50-£8.25
dessert £2.95
set menu £13.95
wine £8-£13
AE MC V; SW

Open: Mon-Fri noon-3pm, Mon-Thurs 6pm-11pm, Fri 6pm-1am, Sat 1pm-1am, Sun 1pm-10pm; reservations advisable; licensed, no BYO

CAMBERWELL

Sun & Doves
Mediterranean

☎ 7733 1525
61 Coldharbour Lane SE5

Though predominantly a pub where drinkers fill up two-thirds of the interior, the Sun & Doves offers Mediterranean snacks and meals which are a step beyond normal pub fare. In the restaurant area, paintings by local artists fill the walls. The staff are friendly, and happy to make recommendations – the house red, a Merlot (£9.95), proved to be exactly what we were told: very good. Skewered grills (one: £4.95, two: £7.25, three: £9.25), served with pleasantly fluffy couscous and delicious roast vegetables, are a speciality. The swordfish and king prawn skewers were both succulent and flavoursome, but the lamb and chicken alternatives were disappointing – even the accompanying dips couldn't deflect attention from the dried-out and tasteless meat. But we loved the crunchy, garlicky bruschetta (£3.75) and chocolate torte (£4.25), which was firm and light, with a hint of almond and rum.

Open: Mon-Fri 11am-11pm, Sat noon-11pm, Sun noon-10.30pm; reservations advisable at weekends; licensed, no BYO

Rail: Loughborough Junction (550m)
Entertainment: bands occasionally
Nonsmoking tables available
Garden tables

starter £1.50-£5.25
main £4.95-£10.95
dessert £4.25
wine £9.95-£28.75
AE DC MC V; SW

CLAPHAM

blackpepper
Modern Mediterranean

☎ 7978 4863
133 Lavender Hill SW11

Erstwhile Pepe Nero, now refurbished blackpepper, is a family affair. Husband, wife and siblings have pooled talents to create a cosy interior in bold colours, where you get great Italian food with a modern twist. Grilled scallops (£7) with bacon and red-pepper vinaigrette were stunning; the fish melted away on the tongue almost too quickly. A hearty octopus salad (£6.50) came in the form of one tentacle, diced and buried in a mass of foliage. Scotch sirloin steak (£11.50) was a good cut and grilled precisely to spec. Not everything impressed though. Aubergine and ricotta cannelloni (£6.60) was smooth but bland. So too the side of peas with pancetta (£1.60): the ham's flavour failed to permeate. Of the desserts, crêpe Sophia (£3.50), a pancake filled with chantilly cream laced with a head-spinning splash of amaretto, stood out. Family pride shines through in the friendly, chatty service.

Open: Mon-Fri noon-2pm, 7pm-11pm, Sat 7pm-11pm, Sun 11am-4pm; reservations advisable; licensed, no BYO

Map 16 A2
Rail: Clapham Junction (700m)
Smoking throughout
Pavement tables

starter £3.50-£7
main £6.40-£12.75
dessert £3.50
wine £10-£60
AE DC MC V; SW

CLAPHAM

Map 16 D2
Tube: Clapham South (250m)

Smoking throughout

Bombay Bicycle Club
Indian

☎ 8673 6217
95 Nightingale Lane SW12

Forget flock wallpaper and screechy background music, this is an Indian restaurant with a difference. Huge vases of lilies and roses, attentive Polish waitresses and Nepalese chefs are part of a successful package that the management proudly proclaims to be '100% non-authentic' Indian. Everything is freshly cooked, and regular favourites such as the spicy chicken dhansak (£8.75) are supplemented with daily specials. The fish samosas (£5) are exceedingly good, the filling generous and the pastry crisp and not the least greasy, and we were most impressed with the pasanda khybari (£8), lamb in a sweet creamy sauce, which went down very nicely with the flaky pilau rice (£4.50). The chicken murgh mangalore (£8.55) is much spicier and provides the perfect excuse to indulge in a syrupy mango and papaya sorbet (£3) for dessert.

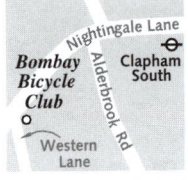

starter £4.50-£9.50
main £6.50-£12
dessert £3-£3.15
wine £11-£36.50

AE DC MC V; SW

Open: Mon-Sat 7pm-11pm; reservations advisable; licensed, no BYO

Rail: Clapham Junction (600m)
Nonsmoking tables available
Pavement tables

Cantuccio
Italian

☎ 7924 5588
143 St John's Hill SW11

Cantuccio serves up authentic Italian fare at affordable prices. The ambience and style of this unpretentious restaurant is just what you'd encounter in small-town *Italia*, and the service is friendly, solicitous and efficient. We enjoyed the pappardelle (£6.95), pasta with a tomato sauce enlivened by pale strips of rabbit, and the thick cut of pork loin (£9.75), which comes with crunchy carrots and delicious mushy-inside baked chestnuts. Though the marinara pizza (£5.50) base is pleasantly light and crisp, we thought it too salty and left most of it on our plate. Our waiter was genuinely apologetic, and immediately offered a replacement (and he didn't know we were writing this review). Desserts were excellent: home-made chocolate mousse (£3.75) was smooth and rich with a cake-like texture and we couldn't get enough of the panna cotta (£3.75) – a dense portion of cooked cream firmed up by gelatin – imported from Italy.

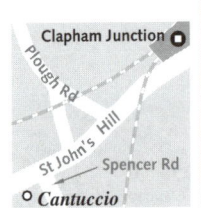

starter £3.50-£6.95
main £5.50-£10.95
dessert £2.95-£3.75
wine £9.50-£30

MC V; SW

Open: Tues-Fri 6.30pm-11pm, Sat noon-11.30pm, Sun noon-10pm; reservations advisable; licensed, no BYO

CLAPHAM

Carmen
Spanish

☎ 7622 6848
6 Clapham Common South Side SW4

The ochre-washed walls and blue-toned Hispanic tiles add credence to the authenticity of the cuisine of this small tapas bar. Coax the taste buds into a Mediterranean mood with spicy gazpacho (£3.95), shiny fat olives (£1.95) and chilli-tinged patatas bravas (spicy potatoes in tomato; £3.30). Vegetarians are spoiled for choice, with a range of almost 20 tapas and salad dishes to choose from. Try champiñones a la crema (£3.95), mushrooms and spinach smothered in a herby béchamel. Fish fiends do almost as well, with tantalising anchovies, mussels, prawns, whitebait and cod. The calamares a la romana (deep-fried battered squid rings; £4.95) are reassuringly tender, with subtle citrus undertones. The croquetas de pollo (£4.60), chicken in a tangy tomato sauce, also satisfies many a hungry customer. With friendly service, huge jugs of sangria, and tapas as tempting as you'll find this side of Seville, Carmen serves up a taste of sunny *España*.

Open: Mon-Thurs 6pm-midnight, Fri-Sun noon-midnight; reservations advisable Sun-Thurs, not accepted Fri & Sat; licensed, no BYO

Map 16 A5
Tube: Clapham Common (50m)
Smoking throughout

main £2.80-£7.35
dessert £2.95-£3.95
wine £9.85-£14.90
cash or cheque only

The Drawing Room
Modern International

☎ 7350 2564
103 Lavender Hill SW11

Full of character, The Drawing Room, a former antique shop, and the adjacent Sofa Bar, are a treasure trove of weird and wonderful curios: tapestries, clocks, candelabras, chandeliers and sumptuous silks. The food is equally striking, with more than a few creative combinations on offer. For the sweet toothed, the crispy filo parcel starter oozes warm goat's cheese (£5.95) with just a hint of mango and sits indulgently on a bed of white chocolate sauce. Otherwise the smoked haddock and potato tortilla (£5.95) fills the room with a pleasant aroma and then bursts with flavour. Main courses include a juicy chicken breast (£10.95) braised in white-wine sauce, with just the right amount of smoked bacon, or oven-baked spinach gnocchi (£9.75) in a zesty tomato and basil sauce. We finished off with a creamy banoffee pie (£4.50) and then started eyeing up the nearest sofa.

Open: Tue-Fri 6pm-midnight, Sat & Sun 11am-midnight; reservations advisable; licensed, no BYO

Map 16 A2
Rail: Clapham Junction
Smoking throughout
Pavement tables

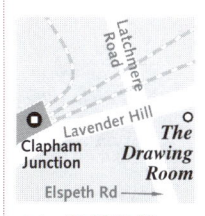

starter £4.95-£5.95
main £9.75-£13.50
dessert £4-£5
set menu Tues-Thurs & Sun £12.95
wine £9.95-£17.50
MC V

CLAPHAM

Map 16 A5
Tube: Clapham Common (100m)
Nonsmoking tables available

Eco
Italian

☎ 7978 1108
162 Clapham High St SW4
www.ecorestaurants.com

Clapham is very Eco, or Eco is very Clapham: youthful, sleek (the Anand Zenz-designed interior is innovative and spare, almost uncomfortable), attitude-laden – service is brisk, almost to the point of being brusque – and bustling with the upwardly mobile. It's hard to reconcile this self-conscious vibe with the wood-fired oven churning out pizzas to make your mama in Milan envious. Starters are almost incidental; baked lemongrass prawns (£5.20), though plentiful and well-prepared, a mere distraction. Pizza bases are beautifully crisp throughout and imaginative toppings include a range of very Mediterranean vegetables – sweet roasted repper and aubergine (£6.90), complemented by fresh coriander, present marvellous contrasting flavours, while the parma (£7.90) is strewn with generous slices of beautifully cured Italian ham. There's pasta and salad too, but really – why bother? *Also at 4 Market Row, Electric Lane, Brixton, SW9* ☎ *7738 3021 and 66 Baker St, W1U* ☎ *7486 6888.*

starter £1.40-£6.50
main £5.20-£10.50
dessert £3.70-£4.70
wine £10.25-£12.95
AE DC MC V; SW

Open: Mon-Thurs noon-4pm, 6.30pm-11pm, Fri noon-4pm, 6.30pm-11.30pm, Sat noon-5pm, 6pm-11.30pm, Sun noon-5pm, 6pm-11pm; reservations advisable; licensed, no BYO

Rail: Clapham Junction (250m)
Smoking throughout

Fish in a Tie
French & Italian

☎ 7924 1913
105 Falcon Rd SW11

It'll surely come as no great revelation that fish make a strong showing here. They scale the walls via glittery pictures and ambient lampshades, reside on the tables as candlesticks and feature heavily on the menu (though there is also a decent choice of meat dishes). Prices are modest and portions are large, yet they make a half-decent stab at culinary quality. The asparagus starter (£3.25) is crisp and fresh. The huge platter of seafood linguine allo scoglio (£7.75) has a tomato sauce that almost masks a pleasant hint of chilli, but the accompanying impressive-looking half-lobster was disappointingly chewy. The trout (£5.95) is a treat, albeit served with overly-sweet carrots and an unusual crème fraîche-based hollandaise sauce, and the house wine surprisingly smooth considering it's just £2.10 for a generous glass. It can get noisy at night, but Fish in a Tie isn't a bad choice for a cheap and cheerful date.

starter £2.95-£3.50
main £4.95-£7.75
dessert £2.25
set menu £5
wine £8.25-£17.85
MC V; SW

Open: Mon-Sat noon-3pm, 6pm-midnight, Sun noon-11pm; reservations advisable; licensed, no BYO

Fish in a Tie (Carl Drury)

Moxon's
Fish

☎ **7627 2468**
14 Clapham Park Rd SW4

You know you're in a fish restaurant as soon as you walk into Moxon's. The walls are adorned with tasteful fish compositions and even the toilets provide a slice of water life, depicting fish and their vital statistics and the best time to eat them! A chilled-out atmosphere presides and the waiters are friendly and honest, suggesting the best, as opposed to the most expensive, wine on the list for the dishes ordered. And Moxon's knows its fish: the menu changes according to the fish season. Already won over by the complimentary prawns, we weren't at all surprised to find that the salmon with asparagus (£11.95) was delightfully tender and melt-in-your-mouth fresh, as was the equally flavoursome tuna in black-bean salsa (£12.95). The imaginatively presented roast peach with cherries (£4.50) and strawberries in champagne gratin with ice cream (£4.50) both tasted as good as they looked.

Open: Mon-Sat 6.30pm-11pm; reservations advisable (essential weekends); licensed, no BYO

Map 16 A5
Tube: Clapham Common (250m)

Smoking throughout

SOUTH

Clapham Common — Clapham High St — Clapham Park Rd
Moxon's

starter £3.50-£6.95
main £9.50-£14.50
dessert £4.50
set menu £12.50
wine £13.70-£150
MC V; SW

CLAPHAM 167

CLAPHAM

Map 16 B5
Tube: Clapham Common (25m)
Nonsmoking tables available
Pavement tables

The Pepper Tree ☎ 7622 1758
Thai
19 Clapham Common South Side SW4

This popular Thai restaurant operates on the 'stack 'em high, sell 'em fast, sell 'em cheap' principle, which it achieves without compromising on quality – the food tastes truly authentic and the service is friendly. The meat on the grilled chicken satay (£2.95) is properly seared, and the tord man fishcakes (£2.95) are smooth and subtle. The green chicken curry (£3.75) raises a sweat without being too firey, and the pad Thai noodles (£4.50) balance the fish and peanut flavours perfectly. The mix of crunchy, hot, sour and fresh is also just right in the green papaya salad (£3.75). Among the few desserts are the surprisingly light Thai beancakes (£2.65) and exotically flavoured ice creams (£1.95) such as stem ginger. Décor includes discrete designer touches and long, communal tables and benches. You'll have to queue to be seated on weekend evenings, but use the time to sup a beer.

starter £2.25-£2.95
main £3.50-£4.95
dessert £1.95-£2.65
wine £8.50-£11.95

MC V; SW

Open: Mon noon-3pm, 6pm-10.30pm, Tues-Sat noon-3pm, 6pm-11pm, Sun noon-10.30pm; reservations not accepted; licensed & BYO (corkage wine £2/bottle, beer 50p/bottle)

Map 16 B5
Tube: Clapham Common (250m) or Clapham North
Wheelchair access
Entertainment: DJ Fri-Sun evenings
Smoking throughout

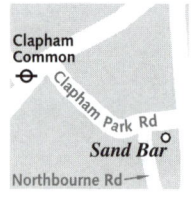

Sand Bar & Restaurant ☎ 7622 3022
New European
156 Clapham Park Rd SW4
www.sandbarrestaurant.co.uk

Sand attracts a young, trendy crowd who come because of the late licence, good food and (at the weekends) DJ. Soft leather sofas and an open fire create a relaxed, laid-back atmosphere in the early evening, but it livens up considerably as the party-goers arrive later on. Dark Moroccan screens allow diners to escape from the crush of the bar and enjoy dishes from the tempting menu. The subtle taste of the scallops (£6.75) is set off by coriander and chilli, while crab risotto (£5) is creamy and rich, almost too filling for a starter. Hard though it is to decide from the large selection of mains, the roasted sea bass (£14.50) with saffron mash and fennel has an interesting combination of flavours and is an excellent choice. Sand is the perfect place to come if you're looking for fantastic food and a lively, late evening out.

starter £3.75-£7
main £9.75-£14.50
dessert £3.50-£5
wine £11-£28

MC V; SW

Open: Mon-Sat 5pm-2am, Sun 5pm-1am; reservations advisable; licensed, no BYO

CLAPHAM

SO.UK
North African

☎ 7622 4004
165 Clapham High St SW4

SO.UK has a truly Moroccan feel. The design is simple with large silver trays acting as tables, pierced Moorish lanterns and low seating stacked high with cushions. By the addition of a full stop the management have bought the Arabic word 'souk' into the dot.com era, reflecting the trendy Clapham clientele. But don't expect to find your traditional tajine here – the tapas-style menu, which includes Asian dishes, has a light slant on North African cuisine. Very affordable options include delicious houmous and babaganoush dips with flatbread (£1.95), crispy tiger prawns with a sweet Thai sauce (£3.50) and flavoursome smoky salmon and tuna sushi with a rich sauce.
On weekend nights SO.UK is more of a bar than a restaurant and you'll find it difficult to get served a drink, let alone find a table.

Open: Mon-Thurs 4pm-midnight, Fri-Sat 11am-midnight, Sun 11am-11.30pm; reservations not accepted; licensed, no BYO

Map 16 A5
Tube: Clapham Common (100m)
Wheelchair access
Entertainment: DJ Tues-Sat evening
Smoking throughout
Pavement tables

main £1.95-£3.50
dessert £4.50
wine £13.50-£36
AE DC MC V; SW

DULWICH

Belair House
Classical French

☎ 8299 9788
Gallery Rd SE21
www.belairhouse.co.uk

Elegant but unstuffy, Belair House serves beautifully presented food in a restored Georgian mansion surrounded by Dulwich Park's green lawns. Top-quality, seasonal ingredients feature on the inspired Euro-friendly menu. The complimentary appetiser – a small cup of smooth, spicy gazpacho – was an appreciated gesture and put us in the mood for starters such as the stilton parfait and poached pear salad, and lobster and truffle cocktail. The roast fillet of salmon and tender duck breast drizzled with cinnamon cherry sauce maintained the high standards and came with garnishes such as perfectly cooked spinach or asparagus. The palette of sorbets – intensely flavoured scoops of blackcurrant, coconut, passion fruit and mango ices atop an orange-infused crisp biscuit – made for a sensational finale, with extra applause reserved for the wide range of coffees. Service was friendly throughout. This might be treat territory, but it's an affordable indulgence.

Open: Tues-Sat noon-2.30pm, 7pm-10.30pm, Sun noon-3pm; reservations advisable; licensed, no BYO

Rail: West Dulwich (400m)
Wheelchair access
Smoking throughout
Terrace tables

set lunch £17.95 or £21.95
set dinner £29.95
Sund lunch £25.95
wine £16-£165
AE DC JCB MC V; SW

GREENWICH

Rail/DLR: Greenwich (125m)
Wheelchair access
Smoking throughout

Inside
Modern European

☎/fax 8265 5060
19 Greenwich South St SE10
www.inside.org.uk

Appearing somewhat spartan from the outside, Inside – with its eminently tasteful aubergine-dark and cool-white walls – proves a polished, tranquil place to settle for a few hours. Feeding up youngish, smartish SE10ers, this friendly neighbourhood restaurant is a place to root for. It's striving to fill Greenwich's gastronomic gap and, with starters such as an angelically dainty spring salad of grilled asparagus, broad beans and new potatoes with goat's cheese quenelle (£5.95) and tangy mussels tagliatelle (£4.95), it's succeeding. Corn-fed chicken with spinach, tomato and sage risotto (£13.95) is deeply satisfying, but for us the flaky buttery pastry of a truffled oyster mushroom, aubergine and baby spinach tart (£4.95) was too much of a good thing. Rampaging chocoholics will be quietened for months by a thickly rich chocolate tart (£4.95) while less ferocious creatures may prefer an airier choice: try raspberry crème brûlée (£4.95).

starter £3.50-£5.95
main £9.50-£14.95
dessert £4.95-£5.95
set lunch £11
wine £9.50-£60

MC V; SW

Open: Tues-Fri noon-2.30pm, Tues-Sat 6.30pm-11pm, Sat & Sun 11am-3pm; reservations advisable; licensed, no BYO

KENNINGTON

Tube: Kennington (1000m)
Smoking throughout
Courtyard tables

Kennington Lane Restaurant & Bar
Modern European

☎ 7793 8313
205-209 Kennington Lane
SE11

Symbolic of Kennington's up-and-coming status, this restaurant is a handsome trendsetter. Its French master of ceremonies chirpily ushers you into the bustling arena of diners, where the rest of the continental crew are on hand. Noise levels, amplified by the wooden floor, are a result of people having a good time. The cuisine also speaks volumes, with a 'pick me!' range of dishes. For a cheesy start try feta salad with toasted pine nuts (£5.00) or for a moreish and filling bread-based approach, go for the Italian panzanella (£4.50). If you're out to catch a bird you'll find no better than the tender and voluptuously ample portion of duck breast with creamy mashed potatoes (£10.50). Fish fanciers, on the other hand, can sample the magnificent tuna steak (£10.95). If wine beckons, then trust Sancerre (half-bottle; £12) to wash away those gastronomic sins.

starter £4.25-£6.50
main £9.50-£12.95
dessert £5-£5.25
wine £10.50-£43

AE DC JCB MC V; SW

Open: Mon-Fri noon-3pm, 6pm-10.30pm, Sat 6pm-10.30pm, Sun noon-4pm, 6pm-10.30pm; reservations advisable; licensed, no BYO

KENNINGTON

The Lobster Pot
French/Seafood

☎ 7582 5556
3 Kennington Lane SE11

Tube: Kennington (500m)

Smoking throughout

Why did French owner/chef Hervé choose a bleak junction in south London for his nautically themed restaurant? Perhaps the grim surroundings account for the effort he has put into creating such a charming interior. The wood-panelled room is decked out to look like the cabin of a small boat, complete with fishing nets hanging from the ceilings and portholes that open on to fish-filled aquaria. Seafood dominates the menu and prices are correspondingly high. We tried the marinated salmon (£7.50), grilled garlic prawns (£8.50) and bouillabaisse (£16.50) – all well prepared with strong, clear flavours. But don't expect any exciting twists – the accent is firmly on the hearty and traditional. Desserts – including a crêpe filled with crème brûlée (£5.30) – are exquisite. The slow but attentive service encourages lingering, so save The Lobster Pot for an evening when you can do just that.

Open: Tues-Sat noon-2.30pm, 7pm-11pm; reservations essential; licensed, no BYO

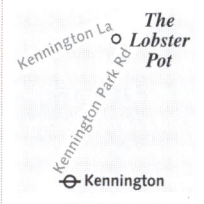

starter £6.50-£11.50
main £14.50-£22.50
dessert £5.30-£7.30
set menu £10, £13.50, £19.50 or £39.50
wine £10.50-£47.50

AE DC JCB MC V; SW

NEW CROSS

Thailand
Thai/Lao

☎ 8691 4040
15 Lewisham Way SE14

Tube/rail: New Cross (450m)

The design is an eccentric, endearing collision of country-house tapestry and DIY Thai. Service is stressed – perhaps because staff work in a space that, at best, would make a fair-sized sitting room – but friendly. There is a vast menu, and the Lao dishes are particularly outstanding. Try the chilled yet fierce taste of the hot and sour papaya salad with fish sauce, lime, garlic and chilli (£6.95) or delicious tangy bamboo shoots in Lao herbs and spices (£6.95). Duck breast (£6.95) with lime juice and pounded, toasted rice wrapped in lettuce leaves is almost too authentic for timid palates; for those playing it safe there are many milder options on offer, such as sweet, pungent Thai red vegetable curry with coconut (£4.95). Traditional Lao sticky rice (£2.95) served in woven pots is a solid accompaniment. There's real scope to be adventurous here, an unusual proposition in New Cross.

Open: Mon-Fri noon-2.30pm, 6pm-11pm, Sat & Sun 6pm-11.30pm; reservations essential Fri & Sat evenings; licensed, no BYO

starter £3.95-£6.95
main £4.95-£8.95
dessert £2.95-£3.95
set lunch £3.95
wine £9.99-£18

MC V; SW

SOUTH BANK

Tube: Westminster (250m)
Entertainment: pianist Mon-Sat evening, jazz band Sun lunch
Nonsmoking tables available

The County Hall Restaurant ☎ 7902 8000
Modern British **London Marriott Hotel County Hall, Westminster Bridge Rd SE1**

Housed in, you guessed it, the County Hall, this imaginatively named restaurant concedes nothing to the building's past. Large pieces of colourful art adorn wood-panelled walls, a pianist plays in the corner and diners sit at tables covered with pristine white tablecloths admiring views over the Thames. Chef Gregg Brown serves up an interesting selection of dishes where presentation is all and taste is pretty good too. The beautifully arranged terrine of vegetables (£9) is crunchy, fresh and delicately flavoured; the rump of lamb (£18) is wonderfully rare and served with a heavenly thyme jus that does justice to both the meat and the finely grilled vegetables. To finish, the County Hall tiramisù (£5.95) is thick, creamy and has just the right number of coffee beans to give it a lift. Served up by friendly international staff in a relaxed yet refined establishment, dining here is an enjoyable experience.

starter £7.75-£14.50
main £13.50-£24.50
dessert £5.95
pre-theatre menu £20.50 or £23
wine £16-£55

AE DC JCB MC V; SW

Open: Mon-Fri 6.30am-10.30am, Sat & Sun 7am-11am, Mon-Sat noon-2.30pm, 5pm-11pm, Sun 12.30pm-3pm, 5pm-10.30pm; reservations advisable; licensed & BYO (corkage £5/bottle)

Tube/rail: Waterloo (250m)
Wheelchair access
Nonsmoking tables available

fish! ☎ 7234 3333
Fish **3b Belvedere Rd SE1**
www.fishdiner.co.uk

Behind the über-in County Hall buildings on the Thames, glass-walled fish! restaurant serves up its trademark nonfussy fishy fare. The quietish area by the bar is perfect for politician watching with a double espresso and a tart (at £3.85 the lemon tart was a little thin but the pastry is buttery and the filling tangy). For those who can stand the heat, a counter runs the length of the kitchen allowing you to watch the low-fat, high-taste brill get a grilling (£12.50) and organic salmon (£9.90) get smothered in rich hollandaise sauce. Both come with a rather meagre portion of salty vegetables so order the ravishingly crunchy chips (£1.90) as well. *Also at 41a Queenstown Rd, Battersea, SW8, Cathedral St, London Bridge, SE1, Hanover House, Westferry Circus, E14, 92-94 Waterford Rd, Fulham, SW6, 296-298 Upper Richmond Rd, Putney, SW15. Reservations can be made online or by calling the central number above.*

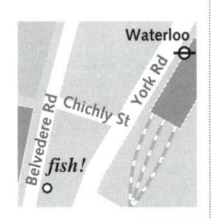

starter £1-£6.50
main £7.80-£14.50
dessert £3.95
wine £9.90-£15

AE DC JCB MC V; SW

Open: Mon-Sat 11.30am-11pm, Sun noon-10.30pm; reservations advisable; licensed, no BYO

SOUTH BANK

Little Saigon
Vietnamese/Chinese

☎ **7928 5415**
139 Westminster Bridge Rd SE1

Tube: Lambeth North (200m)

Smoking throughout

In many ways this is an unremarkable, inexpensive oriental restaurant. There's the usual Asian décor, background music and people popping in to collect takeaways. The starters we tested were also unexceptional – the butterfly king prawns (£3.20) were fine but the barbecued spare ribs (£3.30) were on the dry side. However, if you choose carefully there are a few gems on the main menu. We couldn't get enough of the fabulous Saigon duck (£6.50) – flaky meat cooked in a rich, thick sauce laced with star anise spice. The Vietnamese special noodles (£4) were also good, with the thick noodles mixed with diced meats and topped off with a generous selection of vegetables (broccoli, courgettes, carrots and so on). Desserts (£3) were pretty much a non-event: only a couple of choices were available ('Sorry, no lychees') and sorbets were offered in a wide range of one flavour (lemon).

Open: daily 5.30pm-11.30pm, Mon-Fri noon-3pm; reservations not accepted; licensed, no BYO

starter £3.20-£9
main £6.20-£15
dessert £3
set menu £18
wine £8-£20

AE DC MC V; SW

fish! (Carl Drury)

SOUTH BANK

Meson Don Felipe
Spanish

☎ 7928 3237
53 The Cut SE1

Map 15 B1
Tube: Southwark (200m), tube/rail: Waterloo
Entertainment: flamenco guitar Mon-Sat evening
Smoking throughout

Felipe of this *meson* is actually a Philip – a Brit, and don of the diminutive converted bank for a decade-and-a-half. Don't be misled by this detail, though: service, fare and nightly flamenco guitar are Hispanic to the heart. Join the pre- and post-theatre masses that pack the place to sample the extensive selection of riojas, cavas and sherries – accompanied by appropriate bites, naturally. The essential benchmarks of tapas are surpassed: fluffy-fried potato chunks are doused but not overpowered by chilli-tinged tomato sauce (patatas bravas; £2.95), calamari (£4.25) is delightfully succulent, and the flavour of the champiñones con chorizo (mushrooms stuffed with spicy Spanish sausage; £3.95) is balanced and terribly moreish. If you can't bag one of the few tables, perch on a high stool at the central bar and rack up the bottles and dishes.

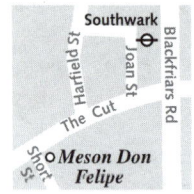

main £1.95-£4.95
wine £9.95-£65
MC V; SW

Open: Mon-Sat noon-11pm; reservations advisable; fully licensed, no BYO

Oxo Tower Restaurant
Modern European

☎ 7803 3888
Oxo Tower Wharf, Barge House St SE1
www.harveynichols.com

Map 15 A1
Tube: Southwark (250), tube/rail: Waterloo
Wheelchair access
Smoking throughout
Balcony tables

Escaping demolition thanks to a tenacious grassroots campaign fought by local residents, this former bouillon-cube warehouse underwent a top-floor makeover in 1995 courtesy of architects Lifschutz Davidson and fine-living torch-bearers Harvey Nichols. Your eye is drawn outward along the avian sweep of the louvred ceiling through the full-length plate-glass wall to a fabulous panorama that encompasses the Thames and St Paul's. This intoxicating aperitif leads in to a menu of classy Anglo-French hybrids and worldly seafood concoctions. Lunch (£27.50), recommended, includes dessert, heavy on fruit-fusion creations such as banana and pear chocolate strudel. Fresh-off-the-hook smooth roasted salmon on a lurid pea purée and yieldingly textured risotto alla Milanese were winners, not so much the gooey crépinette of oxtail or the expansive, vegetable-deficient roast rump of lamb. Service is considerate.

starter £5-£19
main £11-£26
dessert £6.50-£8
set lunch £27.50
wine £12.50-£1275
AE DC MC V; SW

Open: Mon-Fri noon-3pm, 6.30pm-11.30pm, Sat 6.30pm-11.30pm, Sun noon-3pm, 6.30pm-10.30pm; reservations essential; licensed, no BYO

SOUTH BANK

R Cooke
Traditional English

☎ **7298 5931**
84 The Cut SE1

Map 15 B1
Tube: Southwark (300m)

Smoking throughout

Pie, mash and jellied eels isn't everyone's idea of a good meal but this traditional Cockney concoction must be experienced once, if not again and again. And where better to cut your teeth than at R Cooke where it all comes with a dose of healthy banter. The menu is basic, each item a different combination of pie, mash and eels. We went for the pie and mash (£1.60) with a portion of rubbery but very tasty eels (£1.80). The minced-beef pie (traditionally made from leftovers) with a puff-pastry lid comes swimming in liquor – a very green, very watery parsley sauce – and with plain mash. You can take-away but we recommend sitting on the hard canteen-esque benches at the Formica-topped tables. Join the regulars – a mix of housewives, suits, labourers and young kids – as they queue down the road; it's all part of the experience.

Open: Tues-Sat 10am-2.30pm; reservations not accepted; unlicensed

main £1.60-£3.80
cash only

Oxo Tower Restaurant (Carl Drury)

SOUTH BANK

Map 15 B1
Tube/rail: Waterloo (500m)
Smoking throughout

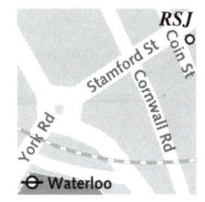

RSJ
Modern English

☎ 7928 4554
13a Coin St SE1

The money RSJ saved on its classroom décor has clearly gone into the wine list, a lavish work of love. Our food got off to a shaky start, however: having called in advance to confirm there would be vegetarian choices, we were faced with a veggie-free menu and an irritable waiter who scratched his head for a while before proposing chorizo risotto. The *maître d'* swept to our rescue with a custom-built couscous with vegetables, the only dud of the evening. Both the salty chorizo risotto (£5) and fragrant pan-roasted scallops with black pudding (£8.25) were superb. Roast haddock with bubble and squeak (£13.95) was a juicy wedge of perfectly seasoned firm, fall-apart fish; oven-roasted sea bass (£15.95) on a tomato salad was meltingly savoury. Desserts – and dessert wines by the glass – are no mere afterthought either: skip coffee and try the dreamily light coffee crème brûlée (£5.25) instead.

starter £6.50-£8.25
main £13.95-£17.95
dessert £4.75-£5.25
set menu £15.95 or £16.95
wine £12.50-£50
DC MC V; SW

Open: Mon-Fri noon-2pm, 5.30pm-11pm, Sat 5.30pm-11pm; reservations advisable; licensed, no BYO

Map 15 A2
Tube/rail: Blackfriars (500m)
Wheelchair access

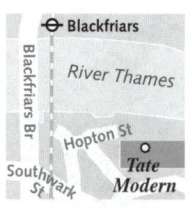

Tate Modern
Modern British

☎ 7401 5020
**Seventh Floor,
Tate Modern, Sumner St SE1**
www.tate.org.uk

Once you're done staring at all that art, come stare at London. The sheer size of Tate Modern's slick restaurant (on floor seven – don't get confused with the level-two restaurant: the menu's the same, the views aren't) makes it feel a bit like a school cafeteria, but what it lacks in interior atmosphere it makes up for with majestic views of the Thames, St Paul's and the BA London Eye. And the food's not bad either: our antipasti (£6.25) came in the kind of unfortunate stack favoured by chefs of pretension but tasted great. The same couldn't be said of the tough steak (£10.50) but, happily, the mixed-leaf salad (£2.25) was so fresh, tasty and cheap it brought us back from this way of thinking. And by the time the luscious apple crumble (£3.50) was gobbled up we'd forgotten the food and were back to looking out the windows.

starter £3.50-£8.50
main £5.80-£10.50
dessert £3.25-£4.75
wine £12.20-£48
AE DC JCB MC V; SW

Open: Sun-Thu 10am-6pm, Fri & Sat 10am-9.30pm; reservations not accepted; licensed, no BYO

SOUTHWARK

Fina Estampa
Peruvian

☎/fax **7403 1342**
150 Tooley St SE1

London's only Peruvian eatery, with its family ambience and smiley service, combines an unusual dining experience with high standards. The menu is not extensive (if you don't like seafood or nuts, go elsewhere) but the chef does have an innate ability to make simple-sounding staple dishes look like genuine gastro creations. The ocopa (£6.95), mixing potatoes and prawns in a rich, creamy paste, had a smooth nutty flavour which was intriguing yet subtle, while carapulco (£10.95), a meaty stew of potatoes, chicken and yucca, came with a rich flavoursome sauce, best complemented by a heavy Chilean Merlot (£14.95). Mains are large and desserts (all £3.50) feel superfluous. Ask for details of occasional Peruvian desserts such as alfajores, Peruvian-filled short pastry with ice cream. Fina Estampa is both unusual and tasty, although the rather hearty nature of dishes makes it more of a winter treat.

Open: Mon-Fri noon-3pm, 6.30pm-10.30pm, Sat 6.30pm-10.30pm; reservations advisable; licensed, no BYO

Map 15 B4
Tube/rail: London Bridge (500m)
Entertainment: Latin music Mon evening

Smoking throughout

starter £4.50-£9.50
main £7.95-£14.95
dessert £3.50
wine £12.50-£24.50

AE DC MC V; SW

Laughing Gravy
International

☎/fax **7721 7055**
154 Blackfriars Rd SE1

Laughing Gravy's cosy atmosphere immediately compensates for its bleak location. The décor of the restaurant, situated behind a bar of chattering pre-dinner drinkers, is reminiscent of a family dining room with piano, sideboard and child's drawing tacked to the wall. The ambitious and varying menu, however, is nothing like home-cooking. Tender scallops come with stewed-tasting bacon and red pepper coulis (£6.75), and slimy octopus is served on deliciously dressed peperoncino parsley (£15.95). Less inventive but more confident mains include rich haddock fishcakes (£8.95) and tuna steak with aubergine mash (£12.95). The expansive dessert menu makes simple dishes interesting. Wattlesead ice cream (£4.75) has an earthy taste, and sticky toffee and banana pudding (£4.75) swims in caramel. Prices reflect substantial portions and quality ingredients, but the service may leave you feeling slightly cheated. But when the overall experience is this pleasant, imperfections are easily forgiven.

Open: Mon-Fri 11am-11pm, Sat 6.30pm-midnight; reservations advisable; licensed, no BYO

Map 15 B1
Tube: Southwark (450m)

Smoking throughout
Pavement tables

starter £4.50-£6.75
main £8.95-£13.25
dessert £4.75
set menu £5.95-£27.95
wine £9.95-£26.75

AE DC JCB MC V; SW

SOUTH BANK

Tas
Turkish

☎ 7403 7200
72 Borough High St SE1

Map 15 B3
Tube/rail: London Bridge (450m)
Wheelchair access
Entertainment: Turkish guitar evenings
Nonsmoking tables available

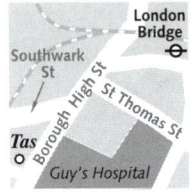

starter £2.75-£3.45
main £4.45-£14.45
dessert £2.25-£3.25
set menu £6.45-£17.95
wine £8.90-£23.50
AE JCB MC V; SW

Tas has a rather Ikea-showroom-like interior, personable (albeit slightly erratic) service and food presented to maximise its bright summery colours. However, while it makes for a perfectly satisfactory dining experience, with a little effort this could be an outstanding one. Both the pirasali kofte (lamb kebab; £6.95), arriving without its advertised leek accompaniment, and the mercan baligi, a rather listless fish dish hugely overpriced at £14.45, were dryer than a Clive Anderson delivery and felt as though they'd been thrown together hurriedly to precipitate shooing us out. A redeeming feature, thankfully, was desert: kayisi tatlisi (£2.25) added a spark of flair to the preparation of sundried apricots that the mains could only dream of. Prices are moderate and the vegetarian choice notable, but Tas fails to impress. And, by setting its sights firmly on the mediocre, its long-term staying power seems doubtful. *Also at 33 The Cut, Waterloo, SE1* ☎ *7928 1444/2111.*

Open: Mon-Sat 11.30am-11.30pm, Sun noon-10.30pm; reservations advisable; licensed, no BYO

STOCKWELL

Café Portugal
Portuguse/Spanish

☎ 7587 1962
5a-6a Victoria House,
South Lambeth Rd SW8

Map 17 A1
Tube: Vauxhall (575m) or Stockwell
Entertainment: occasional *fado*
Smoking throughout
Pavement tables

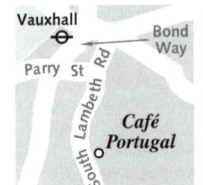

starter 95p-£4.95
main £6.50-£12.50
dessert £2.50
wine £8.50-£28

(£10 min) AE MC V; SW

After a change of ownership, this is now 'Little Portugal's' classiest option. There's a great Portuguese wine list and the menu is a roll call of national classics, with a nod towards Spain. Ingredients are high quality but seasoning can be disappointing: plump Spanish-style octopus (£4) was bland despite the paprika, and king prawns in chilli sauce (95p each) lacked the expected fiery citrus punch. No such problem with the main courses. Porco a Alentejana (£8) was an accomplished dish of potatoes, pork, clams and, oddly, gherkins; Arroz de marisco (£10.50), an enormous rice stew, revealed oceans of seafood. Puddings include pudim flan (crème caramel) and orange roll. Delicious, and a steal at £2.50 each. In contrast to the elegant dining room, the adjoining tapas bar retains its earthy charm, with Portuguese football on TV and a collection of framed shirts – including that of Eusebio, who ate here recently.

Open: daily 8am-11pm; reservations advisable Fri-Sun; licensed & BYO (corkage £5/bottle, no corkage with tapas)

STOCKWELL

Estrela Bar
Portuguese/Spanish/Italian

☎ **7793 1051**
111-115 South Lambeth Rd SW8

A great spot for an off-the-cuff meal when you fancy a dose of genuine Portuguese sunshine, Estrela's sizeable bar leads up to a narrow restaurant with starry ceiling and chandeliers. The menu embraces everything from fish, meat and pasta to tapas, sandwiches and omelettes. Don't expect haute cuisine – some dishes are pretty basic. The ham and cheese salad (£4) looked processed and the bacalhau frito con miho de tomatada (salt cod in tomato sauce; £9) was chewy. That aside, clams Estrela style (£5) were absolute stars in a delicious sauce. Caldo verde (£2) – traditional cabbage soup – also hit the spot. Despite a faintly artificial flavour, pork Alentejana (£9) was good, and puds were homely indulgences. There's crème caramel two ways – we loved the 'heavy based' version (£2) – and a naughty tiramisù-like doce de casa (£2). The wine list provides a great introduction to the Portuguese grape.

Open: Mon-Sat 8am-midnight, Sun 10am-11pm; reservations advisable Fri-Sun; licensed, no BYO

Map 17 A1
Tube: Vauxhall (600m) or Stockwell

Nonsmoking tables available

Pavement tables

starter £1-£5
main £4.50-£10.50
dessert £1-£3
wine £7.50-£15.50
AE DC MC V; SW

O Cantinho
Portuguese

☎ **7924 0218**
137 Stockwell Rd SW9

Less well known than some of its 'Little Portugal' rivals, O Cantinho is nevertheless a useful no-frills pit stop. It's tiled, not with beautiful azulezos from the homeland but in faux marble, and service, like the place itself, is friendly but not showy. The tapas bar offers sanctuary to Portuguese regulars wanting to see the match back home, and the restaurant dishes up mammoth portions of uncomplicated, authentic fare to local families. A bowl of fleshy octopus salad (£4.50) was brim full. Grilled sea bream (£7.80) was unexceptional and the 'special' with pork and mushrooms (£8) wasn't very, with chewy meat and a slightly medicinal taste. Better by far was the squid (£7.80), smothered in a rich garlicky sauce. Rice pudding and crème caramel (both £2) weren't fabulous, but at these prices who cares? The wine list provides those bottles you loved on holiday but can't find in the supermarket.

Open: daily 10am-midnight; reservations advisable; licensed & BYO (corkage £5/bottle)

Map 17 C2
Tube: Brixton (550m) or Stockwell

Smoking throughout

starter £2-£6.50
main £6-£9
dessert £2
wine £7-£20
(£10 min) V; SW

TOOTING

Tube: Tooting Broadway (500m)

Smoking throughout

Kastoori
Indian/African Vegetarian

☎ 8767 7027
188 Upper Tooting Rd SW17

Gujarati cuisine is sadly under-represented in the pantheon of British Indian restaurants; shame – rich, tomato-based dishes offer a delightful, slightly sweeter twist on familiar south Indian vegetarian equivalents. For nearly 15 years the Thanki family have been proudly treating Tooting to the joys of their own unique masala blends. Samosas (£1.95) and puris (£2.75) are lent sparkle by hot, coriander-laced green chutney and minted yoghurt. Deep-fried vegetable kofta balls (£4.50) lie in a dense, chunky vegetable sauce – spicier and less creamy than expected, and none the worse for it. Kastoori dal (£2.50) is smooth, cumin-laden and tomato-red; soak up the flavour with a unique bhatura (£1.20), fried chapati-like bread with fenugreek and sesame. Ugandan influences are also betrayed – chilli banana (£4.75) won't be on the menu in Ahmedabad but it's on the hit-list for our next visit. Restrained décor and thoughtful service complete the experience. A gem.

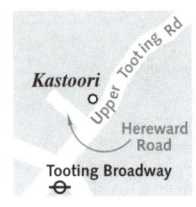

starter £1.95-£2.75
main £3.95-£5.95
dessert £2.25-£3.25
Thalis £8.25 & £15.75; Sun special menu £7.95
wine £7.75-£24.95
MC V

Open: Wed-Sun 12.30pm-2.30pm, daily 6pm-10.30pm; reservations advisable; licensed, no BYO

WANDSWORTH

Map 16 E1
Rail: Wandsworth Common (300m)

Smoking throughout

Chez Bruce
Modern French

☎ 8672 0114
2 Bellevue Rd SW17

For proof that fine dining in London needn't cost the earth nor involve an inquisition by the style police, head south of the Thames to Chez Bruce. The interior of this restaurant is a curious but relaxed mix of fake Spanish farmhouse with modern art and closely packed tables. The set menus change regularly to take advantage of the season's best produce. Foie gras and chicken liver parfait with toasted brioche is a heavenly starter. The hunk of roast turbot on a broad bean and pea risotto is worth the additional charge (£5), while the whole Tuscan pigeon yields just enough slightly gamey meat to complement the accompanying lentils, artichokes and balsamic sauce. And desserts are colourful: Sauternes crème caramel comes surrounded by sliced strawberries and kiwi fruit. With friendly service to boot, you could hardly wish for more.

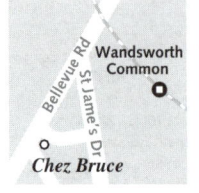

set lunch £21.50
set dinner £27.50
wine £16-£200
AE DC JCB MC V; SW

Open: Mon-Fri noon-2pm, Sat 12.30pm-2.30pm, Mon-Thurs 7pm-10.30pm, Fri & Sat 6.30pm-10.30pm, Sun 12.30pm-3pm; reservations essential; licensed, no BYO

WIMBLEDON

light house
Italian Fusion

☎ **8944 6338**
75-77 Ridgway SW19

Tube/rail: Wimbledon (1200m)

Wheelchair access

Nonsmoking tables available

Courtyard tables

The name describes the interior perfectly, for this spacious, uncluttered restaurant has pale walls, big windows and a high ceiling. There's evidence of care and quality throughout, ranging from the willing service to the herb-infused bread and the well-chosen wines. Beautifully tender braised octopus (£7.70) comes with a nicely balanced, non-stodgy risotto. The roast sea bass (£14.50) is excellent – crisp outside, moist inside, and enhanced with a satay-style sauce. The cheaper set lunch (£12.50) betrays no short cuts, and looks just as good on the plate. Among the starters is a piquant chorizo sausage, well complemented by rocket though the capers and olives perhaps overdid the salty aspect. The chicken main manages the crisp-yet-juicy trick, and comes with sweet potato, sliced courgette and a complex, slightly sharp kumquat chutney. In comparison, desserts were on the disappointing side – the polenta and pistachio cake (£4.75) was rather dry and nondescript.

Open: Mon-Sat noon-2.30pm, 6.30pm-10.30pm, Sun 12.30pm-3pm, 6.30pm-9pm; reservations advisable; licensed, no BYO

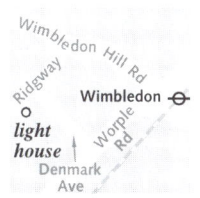

starter £4.50-£7.70
main £9.70-£16
dessert £4.75
set lunch Mon-Sat £12.50
wine £11.50-£70

AE JCB MC V; SW

(Simon Bracken)

Sunday Best

Sunday, a day of rest, recovery and roasts. And what better way to combine all three than by visiting one of these pubs. They all serve up a decent traditional Sunday lunch and lots of lazy Sunday atmosphere – and they're all deservedly popular so arrive early.

The Albion
10 Thornhill Rd, Islington, N1 ☎ 7607 7450
A pretty little pub in the backwaters of Islington, The Albion is worth any detour. Service is quick and the food (£7.25; served noon-5pm and 6pm-9pm) remarkably good considering the speed at which it appears. There's a lovely beer garden out the back in which to sit and read the papers. (map 9 D1)

Crocker's Folly
24 Aberdeen Place, Marylebone, NW8 ☎ 7286 6608
Perfect after a walk along Regent's Canal, you can munch for £6.95 (served noon-8pm) in the dining room before retiring to the dim comfort of the big sofas or the lighter sports bar to watch the footie. Ask who Crocker was – and what his folly was - and you'll understand the ornate ceilings and marble mirrors. (map 4 A1)

The Flask
77 Highgate West Hill, Highgate, N6, ☎ 8348 7346, www.theflaskhighgate.co.uk
A long-standing favourite with those exploring Highgate Cemetery or Hampstead Heath, the Flask's roast (£6.95; served noon-4pm, 7pm-9.30pm) can be hit-and-miss but its ambience is not. There are lots of nooks and crannies to tuck yourself away in and a large garden for those sunny moments.

The Frog and Forget-Me-Not
The Pavement, Clapham, SW4 ☎ 7622 5230
Unusually for trendy Clapham, this is a down-to-earth local pub where you can collapse on shabby armchairs and enjoy a good feed for £6.95 (served 1pm-4pm). Crayons are provided for budding artists to draw on the tablecloths. (map 16 A5)

The Phene Arms
9 Phene St, Chelsea, SW3 ☎ 7352 3294
On a quiet Chelsea side street, this small pub has been attracting a loyal following of all ages for over 150 years. The dining room is tiny but atmospheric, and there's plenty of space to spill out into when the sun shines. And the food (£6.95 or £7.95; served noon-6pm) – as the Egon Ronay certificates testify – is good. (map 19 D5)

The Royal Inn on the Park
111 Lauriston Rd, Hackney, E9 ☎ 8985 3321 www.theroyalinn.co.uk
Situated on the edge of Victoria Park, this pub has everything covered: roasts (£7.50) or other dishes, indoors or outdoors, kids-free and DJ upstairs or child-friendly and piped music downstairs. A beautiful pub that gets that Sunday vibe just right. Food served noon-4pm. (map 12 A3)

The Settle Inn
186 Battersea Bridge Rd, SW11 ☎ 7228 0395 www.thesettleinn.co.uk
The *Evening Standard*'s Pub of the Year 2001, this pub is all pine, pine and more pine – with a little bit of atmosphere and a lot of good food thrown in. There are games on hand for rainy days and a beer garden for when the sun shines. Lunch costs £9 (served noon-9.30pm); reservations are advisable. (map 19 6E)

Imogen Franks

Acton
Bayswater
Chelsea
Chiswick
Ealing
WEST
Fulham
Hammersmith
Holland Park
Kensal Rise
Kensington
Kensington Olympia
Kew
Kilburn
Knightsbridge
Ladbroke Grove
Lancaster Gate
Mortlake
Notting Hill
Putney
Queens Park
Richmond
Shepherd's Bush
South Kensington
Teddington
Westbourne Park

FAVOURITE

- **British**
  The Glasshouse
  (p209)

- **Chinese**
  Mandarin Kitchen
  (187)

- **French**
  La Trompette
  (p195)

- **Gastropub**
  The Salusbury Pub
  and Dining Room
  (p227)

- **Indian**
  Chutney Mary
  (p198)

- **Italian**
  Assaggi (p220)

- **Modern European**
  Bibendum (p230)

- **South-East Asian**
  Churchill Arms
  (p221)

- **Vegetarian**
  Blah Blah Blah!
  (p228)

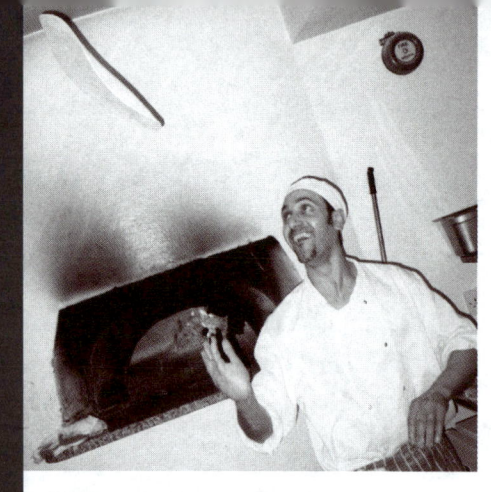

West London

In the early 18th century, the influx of foreign migrants to London led to the expansion of the working-class areas to the east and the south while the more affluent high-tailed it to the north and, to an even greater extent, the west. Places such as Chelsea, South Kensington and Knightsbridge became synonymous with 'posh' – as they are to this very day. The foreigners did eventually make it to these 'villages', though nowadays they are expatriate businesspeople living in corporate flats and mobs of tourists cruising past the snazzy shops and parading like lemmings into Harrods. When the accent you hear is British, it's likely to be from the upper end of the scale, and the dozens of expensive and/or established restaurants here feed this well-heeled crowd everything from classic French and silver-service Polish to modern Chinese and newfangled tapas. Neighbourhoods farther afield, such as Fulham and Hammersmith, are less homogenous and have a mix of residents from working class to upper management; much of the action is generated by and for locals, and the choice and quality of restaurants vary greatly. To the north, workaday Shepherd's Bush has some decent ethnic and vegetarian options while the dining scene in Notting Hill has undergone a transformation ever since *that* film put it on the world map and drove property prices through the roof. Traditionally home to a multicultural mix that was reflected in its restaurants (African, Caribbean, Thai), we're now seeing a lot of both fusion and confusion being served up with plenty of attitude on the side. This area is particularly strong in Italian restaurants, serving both classic and 21st-century *cucina italiana*. Queensway in Bayswater to the east has Greek and Middle Eastern restaurants and is also something of a mini Chinatown; aficionados of Chinese food generally acknowledge that it is better here than it is in Soho.

ACTON

Rasputin
Russian

☎ 8993 5802
265 High St W3

Tube: Acton Town (500m)

Smoking throughout

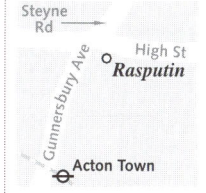

With its warm décor, subdued lighting and monochrome prints of the eponymous rascal, Rasputin has a very inviting ambience, added to which is the friendly welcome from the chatty owner. The inventive menu ranges from the standard to the original. The mushroom sauté in rich sour cream and cheese sauce (£3.95) and the blinis (Russian pancakes) with sour cream (£3.50) are both delicious, satisfying starters, while the salmon fillet sautéed in dill sauce (£10.95) is beautifully tender and the stuffed quail with apricot and plums (£9.95) an exquisite melee of flavours. We couldn't resist the Charlotte russe (£3.50), with its wonderfully light apricot mousse, and crêpes with plum preserve (£3.50) – both garnished with cream and strawberry slices. The Russian tea (£2.50) – served with a helping of the owner's favourite organic honey – or a shot of vodka (£2.25-£2.75) ends the meal on a warm high.

Open: daily noon-3pm, 6pm-11.30pm; reservations accepted; licensed, no BYO

starter £3.95-£24.95
main £9.50-£14.95
dessert £2.95-£3.50
wine £8.50-£35.50

MC V; SW

BAYSWATER

Alwaha
Lebanese

☎ 7229 0806
75 Westbourne Grove W2

Map 20 B4
Tube: Bayswater (500m) or Queensway

Smoking throughout

Pavement tables

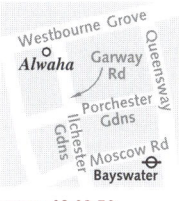

Patience is a prerequisite for the waiters at this leafy, split-level oasis (alwaha) – ordering takes time as the menu is a saga of Lebanese treats (53 starters, fish, grills and daily specials). Herbivores should keep to meze – there's nothing for them in the list of lamb and chicken mains – but that's no hardship. Olives and crudités were fabulous, as was the house white (£9). Smooth nutty houmous (£3) came with seedy flatbread. Falafel (£3.50) and pizza-like kallaj bil jiben with halloumi and mint (£4.25) were a cut above, and Armenian sausages (sojuk sadah; £4.50) had a paprika kick. But don't overlook the mains; many are recipes borrowed from the chef's mother. We tried the Tuesday special, sheihkal mahshi (£9), a homely stew of aubergine stuffed with lamb, and finished off with delightful honey-soaked pastries (£3) from the cabinet and some strong, sweet Lebanese coffee (£1.75), infused with cardamom.

Open: daily noon-midnight; reservations advisable; licensed, no BYO

starter £3-£6.50
main £8.50-£18
dessert £3
set menu £20
wine £9-£35

AE DC MC V

WEST

ACTON & BAYSWATER 185

BAYSWATER

Map 20 C5
Tube: Bayswater (100m) or Queensway
Smoking throughout

Hung To
Chinese

☎ 7727 5753
51 Queensway W2

Frills are sparse but taste is plenty in this David among Goliaths on the Queensway Chinese restaurant beat. With classroom ceilings and stockpiled soft drinks, clearly no décor expense is dared, but the hard-working dumbwaiter soon proves where the priorities lie. The food does all the talking here. The menu is not for the calorie conscious but with aromas this good, who cares? From the impressive and cheap selection, the chicken and duck congee (£4) is tasty, although the fried king prawns (£7.10) were disappointingly bland for the price. If we have to be picky (and we do!), go for the succulent and tangy char siu pork (£4.90) or the chicken in black-bean sauce (£4.90); both are well matched by the special fried rice (£3.90). Forget the spartan surroundings – cuisine triumphs over *feng shui*, as the reassuringly sizable Chinese clientele would agree.

starter £2-£2.50
main £5-£7.50
set menu £10.50 or £12.50

cash or cheque only

Open: daily 11am-11pm; reservations not accepted; BYO (corkage wine £2/bottle, beer 50p/bottle)

Map 20 B4
Tube: Bayswater (400m) or Notting Hill Gate
Smoking throughout

Inaho
Japanese

☎ 7221 8495
4 Hereford Rd W2

You could easily miss this ultra-compact restaurant, but once inside you'll be glad you didn't. The décor resembles that of an Alpine cabin but the abundant Japanese prints give it away. The impressive menu runs through the expected standards, with some outstanding starters – the sunomono (marinated seafood; £4.50) includes generous pieces of deliciously fresh fish and seaweed, and the agedashidofu (tofu with ginger sauce and daikon; £3.80) is fried to the perfect texture. The main courses are satisfying and equally tasty – try the soba noodles with prawn tempura in piping-hot soup (£6) – and a selection of good sushi is also on offer, dosed with perfect amounts of wasabi. Desserts are limited, but the yokan (adzuki bean jelly; £3.25) is splendid. The only reservation we had was the ridiculously overstretched and somewhat abrasive service, but perhaps this was a temporary blip; in any event the delicious, excellent-value food should offer sufficient compensation.

starter £2.50-£4.50
main £5-£9.50
dessert £1.50-£3
set lunch £8-£10
set dinner £20-£22
wine £8-£57

MC V

Open: Mon-Fri 12.30pm-2.30pm, 7pm-11pm, Sat 7pm-11pm; reservations advisable; licensed, no BYO

BAYSWATER

L'Accento
Italian

☎/fax 7243 2201
16 Garway Rd W2

L'Accento attracts a well-heeled, well-groomed crowd. Lively but not loud, simply furnished with white walls and well-spaced tables that allow for discreet conversation, it's equally suitable as a venue for a business lunch, a romantic tête à tête or dinner with your parents. The menu is limited but all the options are enticing. The pumpkin ravioli (£6) with sage and melted butter was succulent though the portion was disappointingly small. After such a memorable combination of sweetness and delicacy, the main courses – lamb shank (£12) in a red wine and shallot sauce and fillet of beef (£14) with a rucola and dolce latte sauce – seemed a little heavy, but you couldn't fault the preparation. A third course of chocolate cake with crème pâtissière (£4) was pure greed but well worth the extra effort. L'Accento sets very high culinary standards for itself, and the service is correspondingly slick.

Open: Mon-Sat 12.30pm-2.30pm, 6.30pm-11.15pm, Sun 6.30pm-10.30pm; reservations advisable (essential weekends); licensed & BYO (corkage £5-£10/bottle)

Map 20 B4
Tube: Bayswater (300m) or Queensway

Smoking throughout

Patio tables

starter £6-£7.50
main £12-£14
dessert £4
set menu £12.50
wine £10.50-£44

AE MC V; SW

Mandarin Kitchen
Chinese Seafood

☎ 7727 9012
14-16 Queensway W2

You'll have plenty of time to admire the white stucco cave-like dining room while you wait for a table here, but once you're in you'll find that the sleek down-lighting keeps the focus on the food. Everything slapped in front of you by the brusque staff has been prepared to emphasise colour, subtle flavour and careful texturing. Each airy mouthful of fried crispy seaweed (£4.90) begins bitter, passes through sweet and finishes savoury. It's hard to fault anything across the long and varied menu, from a delicately flavoured fish and 'thousand years egg' soup (£7.90 for two), with nuggets of grey egg and heaps of fresh coriander, to braised bean curd with pork strips and Chinese mushrooms (£5.90) in a scrumptious sauce. Don't ignore the seafood though: whole sea bass with garlic and black-bean sauce (around £20 depending on the season) is exquisitely simple, the flesh tenderly steamed to perfumed, fall-apart perfection.

Open: daily noon-11.30pm; reservations advisable; licensed, no BYO

Map 20 C5
Tube: Queensway (50m) or Bayswater

Smoking throughout

starter £4.90-£10.90
main £5.90-£23.50
dessert £4-£7.90
wine £10.50-£550

AE DC MC V; SW

WEST

BAYSWATER

Map 20 B4
Tube: Bayswater (600m) or Queensway

Entertainment: traditional Austrian music each evening
Nonsmoking tables available

starter £3.50-£5
main £8.50-£13.50
dessert £3.50-£4.50
wine £11.50-£19.50
AE DC MC V; SW

Tiroler Hut
Austrian

☎ 7727 3981
27 Westbourne Grove W2
www.tirolerhut.co.uk

The Tiroler Hut is easily the most fun Austrian restaurant outside of the homeland. It's a warren of low-ceilinged rooms, entered through a narrow door and down a steep staircase. Try to get a table close to the assortment of cow bells. Most of the starters are purely functional, although the champignons Tiroler art (£5.50) are nicely garlicky mushrooms and the goulash soup (£3.50) is redolent with paprika. Most mains are – as expected – pork, and there's really no reason not to opt for the huge and tender wiener schnitzel (£9.60) – this is pretty much an Austrian theme park, after all. Entertainment is provided by the delightful owner, Joseph Friedman, who works the cow bells and other instruments in a boisterous show that encourages audience participation and inspires even more boisterous behaviour in the lager-fuelled diners. Come with a crowd and expect to make friends.

Open: Tues-Sun 6.30pm-12.30am; reservations advisable (essential Thurs-Sat); licensed, no BYO

Tiroler Hut (Carl Drury)

CHELSEA

Bluebird
Modern British

☎ 7559 1111
350 King's Rd SW3
www.conran.com

Bluebird is a wonderful venue for a long, relaxed lunch. A high translucent glass ceiling makes the most of London's fleeting sunlight, and on weekends piano music echoes dreamily about the huge dining hall. Scattered greenery reinforces the open-air sensation and images of the land-speed record-setting car, Bluebird, adorn the walls. The theme is appropriate given the building's history as an automobile showroom; look out for car-shaped ashtrays. The food is unforgettably fresh and served in elegant fashion. A massive bowl of invitingly pink langoustines (£13.50), eighty legs in all, kept us busy for hours – and that was the small portion! Chunky tuna steak with crushed potatoes and olives (£15.25) came flame-grilled to perfection, and a bottle of Sancerre (£25) proved the meal's ideal accompaniment. Cherry pavlova (£6) was a drop-dead gorgeous finger-licking finisher.

Open: Mon-Fri noon-3pm, 6pm-11pm, Sat 11am-3.30pm, 6pm-11pm, Sun 11am-3.30pm, 6pm-10pm; reservations advisable (essential evenings and weekends); licensed, no BYO

Map 19 D4
Tube: Sloane Square, then bus 11/19/22/211/319 (bus stop: 25m)
Wheelchair access
Entertainment: piano at weekends
Smoking throughout

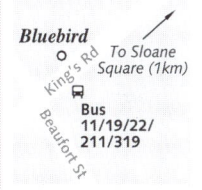

starter £6.50-£12.75
main £9.50-£30
dessert £4.50-£6.50
set lunch £12.50-£21.50
wine £12.75-£70

AE MC V; SW

Buona Sera at the Jam
Italian

☎ 7352 8827
289a King's Rd SW3

Buona Sera at the Jam has carved out a niche for itself with its imaginative décor and inexpensive Italian food. Inside, the wooden booths are literally stacked on top of each other, with the desirable 'upstairs' seating reached by ladders between the ground-level tables. Every booth has adjustable mood lighting and a radio playing golden oldies. The food doesn't quite match up to the inspired interior, but this is fun rather than formal dining. Start with an Italian staple such as hearty minestrone soup (£3.50) or the inevitable antipasti (£4.60). At least half the pasta options are vegetarian and there are crowd pleasers such as lasagna bologna (£6.80) for meat-eaters, plus a long list of *secondi platti* (second courses). Dessert is the best course, with some classic ice-cream bombes and other creations (all £3.50). Turn down the lights, turn up the radio and enjoy booth culture.

Open: Tues-Sun noon-3pm, 6pm-11pm; reservations accepted; licensed, no BYO

Map 19 D4
Tube: Sloane Square, then bus 11/19/22/211/319 (bus stop: 50m)
Smoking throughout

starter £2.50-£4.60
main £6.80-£10.90
dessert £3.50
wine £9.50-£36

AE MC V; SW

CHELSEA

Map 19 E3
Tube: Fulham Broadway (900m)

Smoking throughout
Pavement tables

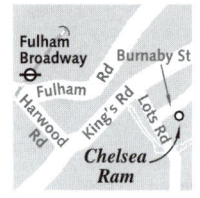

starter £3.45-£7.95
main £4.95-£11.95
dessert £3.95-£4.45
wine £9.95-£24.95

AE JCB MC V; SW

The Chelsea Ram
Modern Global

☎/fax 7351 4008
32 Burnaby St SW10
www.chelsearam.com

A popular choice for Sunday lunch, the menu at the cheerful Chelsea Ram strikes a good balance between ambitious cuisine and traditional fare. Broccoli and stilton soup (£3.45) is flavourful and vegetable crostini (£6.95), presented as a starter but suitable for a main, is a feast of roasted vegetables. The pause between courses (as we struggle to wrest the attention of the staff from the demands of customers at the bar) allows us to replenish appetites for a butternut risotto (£8.95), lifted from creamy obscurity by the generous inclusion of herbs, and farfalle with sundried tomatoes and deliciously pungent goat's cheese (£6.95). Perhaps the huge portions are designed to discourage customers from ordering puddings as they make a disappointing finish; the brownie (£3.95) is bland and the crème brûlée (£3.95) more reminiscent of custard. While not top in the gastropub league and unremarkably decorated, the Ram serves good value, tasty food.

Open: daily noon-3pm, 7pm-10pm; reservations advisable; licensed, no BYO

Map 19 D3
Tube: South Kensington, then bus 14 (bus stop: 20m)

Smoking throughout
Pavement & terrace tables

starter £4.50-£5.50
main £9.50-£10.50
dessert £4
wine £14.50-£79

AE JCB MC V; SW

Chives
Modern European

☎ 7351 4747
204 Fulham Rd SW10

This latest offering from the Red Pepper Group is already the most highly regarded of its restaurants. Its secret? An innovative chef, charming management and understated elegance in two dining rooms. The menu is short – only three choices per course at lunch – so not good for picky palates. A neatly stacked spring vegetable starter (£5.50) is everything you'd expect of a salad, though tortellini of soft pork confit (£4.50), gorgeous in a rich wild mushroom sauce, is more revolutionary. Taste-buds rejoice over the perfectly cooked leg of lamb (£10.50) with pommes cocotte and garlic. The rump of veal (£9.50) is succulent though its mozzarella base and pea and bean fricassée do little to lift flavour or texture. Banishing all thoughts of mediocrity is a brave, exquisite raspberry soufflé (£4) – the perfect finish. One word of advice – if you like a little atmosphere with your meal, book an evening sitting.

Open: Sat 12.30pm-2.30pm, Sun noon-3.30pm, Mon-Sat 7pm-10.30pm, Sun 6.30pm-10pm; reservations advisable Fri & Sat; licensed, no BYO

CHELSEA

Gordon Ramsay
French/Mediterranean

☎ **7352 4441**
68 Royal Hospital Rd SW3

Gordon Ramsay's rough-diamond reputation proceeds him but, as far as his cooking is concerned, we can confirm that the accolades are richly deserved. Whatever the kitchen dramas, all in the intimate, elegant beige dining room is well mannered. Service is flamboyantly Gallic, yet convivial rather than poncy. Gourmands will want to go for the £75 seven-course dinner, which includes Ramsay's signature dishes of lobster pasta and salad of scallops and new potatoes – but you certainly won't be short-changed by the briefer £30 lunch option, which also comes with all the haute cuisine trimmings. A sublime foie gras terrine is marbled with swirling layers of duck meat, and the gamey venison ideally matched with wild mushrooms and celeriac. Fans of *fromage* are well-advised to graze from the trolley of at least 15 premium French cheeses and get their sugar fix from the marvellous petits fours.

Open: Mon-Fri noon-2.30pm, 6.45pm-11pm; reservations essential (one month in advance); licensed, no BYO

Map 19 D6
Tube: Sloane Square (950m)
Wheelchair access
Smoking throughout

set lunch £30,
à la carte menu £60
prestige menu £75
wine £15-£1000

AE DC MC V; SW

Made in Italy
Italian

☎ **7352 1880**
249 King's Rd SW3

This intimate restaurant is always packed and rightly so – the pizzas here must be the best in London. Italian staff rush around, creating an authentically chaotic atmosphere, while the open kitchen allows you to watch your pizza being created and cooked in the wood-burning oven, which gives a distinct smoky taste and a delicious crispy base. Served on long, raised wooden platters, your orders will arrive as one giant pizza, so there is no chance of being possessive over a particular favourite. All the classics are here from margherita (£6) to capricciosa (£7.80), as well as some more innovative combinations including saltimbocca (£7.80), a folded pizza stuffed with mozzarella, basil, parma ham and parmesan. Don't bother with the desserts, a very disappointing selection of rather tired cakes that have seen better days. Keep to the pizzas and you'll have a very enjoyable, reasonably priced meal.

Open: Mon-Fri 6.30pm-11pm, Sat-Sun 1pm-4pm, Sat 6.30pm-11.30pm, Sun 6.30pm-10.30pm; reservations essential; licensed, no BYO

Map 19 D4
Tube: Sloane Square, then bus 11/19/22/211/319 (bus stop: 25m)
Smoking throughout
Terrace tables

starter £6.50-£9
main £5.50-£14
dessert £3.50
set menu £19.50
wine £11-£23

MC V; S

CHELSEA

Phat Phuc Noodle Bar
Vietnamese

☎ 0976 276808
The Courtyard, Sundance Market, 151 Sydney St SW3

Map 19 C5
Tube: South Kensington (750m) or Sloane Square
Wheelchair access
Smoking throughout
Courtyard tables

Phat Phuc (meaning happy Buddha) is a wonderful concept – a Vietnamese-style street stall in the tranquil surroundings of a courtyard. Seating is outdoors, either on a bench or at the counter. Simply place your order and sit back and enjoy a live cookery demonstration. Only two dishes are prepared each day: steaming bowls of meat or vegetarian pho, a clear Vietnamese broth filled with delicate spices, noodles, fresh coriander and spring onions. The vegetable pho (£4.95) is packed with thin rice stick noodles, tasty tofu, three types of oriental mushroom and green vegetables, while the beef pho (£4.95) is simpler fare with fat, slippery noodles. Visit the neighbouring farmers market if you want some drinks to take along.

main £4.95
cash or cheque only

Open: daily 11.30am-5pm (later in summer); reservations not accepted; unlicensed

---

The Thai Bar & Restaurant
Thai

☎/fax 7584 4788
93 Pelham St SW3

Map 19 B5
Tube: South Kensington (400m)
Smoking throughout

From the traditional Thai *wai* greeting to the smiley service, this upscale eatery is keen to please. The interior – contemporary designer chic upstairs, casual bar area and traditional Thai downstairs – makes for a very stylish setting. Where it falls down, however, is the menu. Like so many Thai restaurants, it offers a rather generic selection of foreigner-friendly dishes, namely green curry (£7.25) and pad thai (£7.25). They're well prepared and presentation is excellent, but our tom kha gai soup lacked consistency and coconut flavour. However, the mad sa man (£7.95), a Muslim beef curry, packed a satay peanut punch and the pla nung (£8.95), steamed fish with ginger, offered hunks of fleshy meat to complement a side order of crunchy garlic broccoli (£5.50). Definitely best suited to those seeking Thai food 'lite' in a cool ambience and preferring to keep the lining of their mouths intact for dessert.

starter £4.95-£8.95
main £6.95-£8.95
dessert £3.95-£5.50
set lunch £8.95
set dinner £21.95-£25.95
wine £10.95-£45
AE DC JCB MC V; SW

Open: Mon-Sun 11.30am-3.30pm, 6.30pm-11.30pm; reservations advisable Fri & Sat; licensed, no BYO

Phat Phuc Noodle Bar (Carl Drury)

CHISWICK

The Chiswick Restaurant
Modern British

☎ 8994 6887
131 Chiswick High Rd W4

This family-run restaurant prides itself on the top quality of its ingredients. Local suppliers provide free-range, farm-assured, non-GM food for use in each dish. The menu reflects this: the breast of widgeon with red cabbage and garlic (£9.75) is rich in the flavour so often lacking in factory-farmed duck. A disappointing, tasteless starter of warm leek vinaigrette (£5) is soon forgotten thanks to the delicious mains – a tasty vegetarian option is violet artichoke, oyster mushroom and linguine with truffles (£9.50). Leave room for the heavenly sweet chocolate fondant (£4.50), served with contrasting sharp lemon sorbet. The extensive wine list offers some excellent quality wines – reflecting the smart Chiswick clientele who come here in droves. On Sundays families enjoy the welcoming, relaxed atmosphere, and in summer the French windows are thrown open, giving the restaurant a bistro feel.

Open: Mon-Fri 12.30pm-2.45pm, Sun noon-3pm, Mon-Sat 7pm-11pm; reservations advisable; licensed, no BYO

Tube: Turnham Green (300m)

Nonsmoking tables available

Pavement tables

starter £4.50-£9
main £8.50-£14.25
dessert £4-£4.50
set lunch Mon-Thurs £9.50 or £12.95, set dinner £12.95 or £15.50
wine £11.50-£59
AE DC MC V; SW

WEST

CHISWICK

CHISWICK

Rail: Chiswick (800m),
tube/rail: Gunnersbury

Wheelchair access

Smoking throughout

Pavement tables

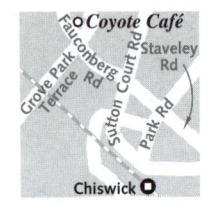

Coyote Café
South-West American

☎ 8742 8545
2 Fauconberg Rd W4

Most South-West American food in London should cause a protest to the highest levels at the American embassy: gooey cheese over tasteless piles of meat, beans and cardboard tortillas. Coyote Café, by contrast, is a small local that draws fans from far beyond its patch. Granted, there are some concessions to the expectations of the masses but you can request a real margarita instead of the fake frozen variety and the nachos (£5.95) are layered with fiery jalapeño peppers. The star of the mains is the blackened rib-eye steak (£11.95), which radiates spice and has a fine chipotle sauce infused with the smoky taste of peppers. Chicken fajitas (£8.95) are sizzling and fresh, and the meat has a nice tangy lime marinade. Service can get harried, but on temperate nights you can sit outside and mingle with the Chiswick swells while supping a nice cold beer.

starter £4.50-£6.95
main £7.95-£13
dessert £4.25
wine £10.95-£20

AE MC V; SW

Open: Mon-Thurs 5pm-11pm, Fri-Sat 11am-11pm, Sun 11am-10.30pm; reservations essential; licensed, no BYO

Rail: Kew Bridge (750m),
tube: Gunnersbury

Wheelchair access

Nonsmoking tables available

Grano
Modern Italian

☎ 8995 0120
162 Thames Rd W4

One of London's best Italian restaurants is hidden away in residential Chiswick. Affluent locals love it for its exceptional menu and impeccable service, and rightly so. Presentation is the key here, with the dishes sculpted into mini constructions and beautifully crafted artworks, such as the tender slices of beef carpaccio perched precariously on a tower of baby aubergine and crunchy lettuce. This starter is matched by the rich and substantial pumpkin tagliatelle with sausage and chestnut, an interesting combination of textures. Other dishes are equally delicious and include succulent veal stuffed with smoked cheese on a bed of fresh spinach and roasted peppers, and subtly flavoured monkfish served with bitter olives and red cabbage. Grano is a real find.

starter £4-£6
main £7.50-£14
dessert £4
wine £12.50-£40

MC V; SW

Open: Tues-Fri & Sun noon-3pm, Tues-Sat 7pm-10.30pm; reservations advisable; licensed, no BYO

CHISWICK

La Trompette
French

☎ 8747 1836
5-7 Devonshire Rd W4

Tube: Turnham Green (400m)

Smoking with neighbour's permission

Pavement tables

With West End quality at west London prices, it's no surprise that La Trompette boasts a capacity crowd of cheerful professionals each sitting. An elegant tan and brown Deco-esque interior and professional service are careful not to detract from the main focus – the food. Standards are set high with fine starters: neatly presented tuna steak with guacamole is rare and tender, and the goat's cheese and tomato tart a delicate rendering of the type. For mains, haddock on a bed of seafood risotto is well balanced and retains the freshness of the ocean; while the chicken and asparagus has a decent bite to contrast with silky mashed morel. There are interesting concoctions to finish, including melt-in-the-mouth blueberry and almond pud with lemon-curd ice cream and crisp apple tart with gooey caramel ice-cream. Combine all this with a discerning wine list, and you'll understand the recommendation to book in advance. Flawless.

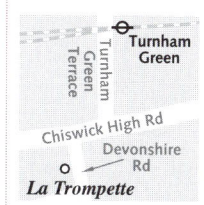

Open: Mon-Sat noon-2.30pm, 6.30pm-10.30pm, Sun 12.30pm-3pm; reservations essential; licensed, no BYO

set lunch £19.50
set dinner £25
wine £11.50-£130

AE JCB MC V; SW

Pug
International

☎ 8987 9988
68 Chiswick High Rd W4

Tube: Stamford Brook (300m)

Wheelchair access

Smoking throughout

Courtyard tables

Named after Hogarth's favourite pet, Pug is a stylish new restaurant catering for the families and young professionals of Chiswick. The interior design screams 1960s chic: black and chrome furniture, retro lights and dark wooden tables. In summer the large courtyard is much more appealing. Dishes on offer are interesting and varied, and the tempting set menu changes daily. Char-grilled baby squid (£4.95) to start is incredibly fresh, a rare treat in London, and served with a tangy red pepper and chilli salsa. Substantial mains include a precarious pile of aubergine, red pepper, tomato and halloumi tourte (£9.25), somewhat lacking in pastry but the only light dish available, and pan-fried cured salmon on sweet potato mash (£10.25) topped with crispy deep-fried basil. Put any dieting ideas on hold when you look at the dessert menu, the banoffee cheesecake with mocha sauce (£4.50) is deliciously rich and extremely calorific!

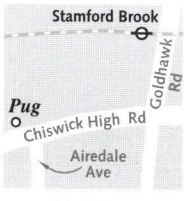

Open: Mon-Sun noon-3pm, Mon-Sat 6.30pm-10.30pm, Sun 6.30pm-10pm; reservations advisable; licensed, no BYO

starter £4.25-£5.25
main £9.25-£13.50
dessert £4.25-£4.75
set menu £14.50
wine £11.95-£45

AE MC V; SW

CHISWICK

Tube: Turnham Green (300m)
Separate smoke-free dining available
Pavement tables

Springbok Café
Modern South African

☎ 8742 3149
42 Devonshire Rd W4
www.springbokcafecuisine.com

On our first taste of Springbok cuisine (complimentary spinach bread) we congratulated ourselves on our ringside seat – there was obviously some superior cooking going on in the open kitchen. Our South African waiter proudly described unfamiliar dishes (many ingredients are flown fresh from home). Sweet pumpkin was sharpened with parmesan (£4.50) and seared calamari creatively partnered with dandelion leaves (£6.50). We lingered on unbelievably fresh kobeljou (£13.25), similar to sea bass, with klakvelds (purple potatoes), and were rewarded for risking the vinegar pudding (£5.00) with a sweet sponge that had a slightly tart aftertaste. Chocolate mielie meal pudding (£5.00), with a spongy texture and liquid chocolate centre, was delicious. The intimate décor, open kitchen and small tables created an atmosphere that encouraged chefs and customers to feed off each other's enjoyment. Definitely worth a visit.

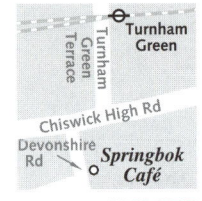

starter £4.50-£6.50
main £11.50-£16.50
dessert £3.75-£5
wine £12-£40
DC JCB MC V; SW

Open: Mon-Sat 6.30pm-11pm; reservations advisable; licensed & BYO (corkage £15/bottle, no corkage if South African wine)

EALING

Tube: Ealing Common (50m)

Sushi-Hiro
Japanese

☎ 8896 3175
1 Station Parade, Uxbridge Rd W5

Sushi aficionados will find a trip out to Sushi-Hiro well worth their while – this small, quietly confident restaurant is the real McCoy. A long counter lines one wall, behind which industrious chefs toil ceaselessly to keep customers supplied. The wide range on offer may be somewhat daunting, but don't be afraid to dive in and try something new. Of the nigiri-sushi, the crab (£1.80) is especially good, while the futomaki-sushi (£8.50 per roll) is deliciously succulent. Be prepared to wait a while as your selections are prepared; whatever you choose, the freshness of the ingredients and the vitality of their flavours are sure to impress. The friendly, helpful service and the thoughtful, understated decoration add to the pleasure of dining here, but remember to bring enough dough with you – payment is strictly cash only and the nearest ATM is quite a jog away.

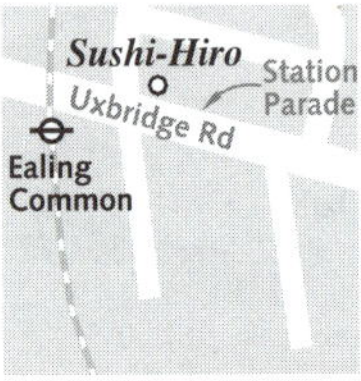

main 60p-£8.50
set menu £5-£14
plum wine £4
cash only

Open: Tues-Sun 11am-2pm, 4.30pm-9.30pm; reservations accepted; licensed, no BYO

A Tipple by the Thames

Two of the great things about London's riverside pubs are their lovely views and historic backgrounds. Here are eight of the best:

The Bell and Crown 72 Strand on the Green, Chiswick W4 ☎ 8994 4164
One of several ancient watering holes in the vicinity and once the dropping point for smugglers' wares, this is a pub for all seasons with a fireplace, conservatory, terrace and towpath patio. On busy days, people perch on the river wall.

The Dove 19 Upper Mall, Hammersmith W6 ☎ 8748 5405
With its beams, settles, fireplace and river terraces, The Dove is perhaps the most appealing of Hammersmith's bankside hostelries. Legend has it 'Rule Britannia' was written here. Past drinkers include Ernest Hemmingway and Graham Greene. (map 21 B1)

The Ship Inn Jews Row, Wandsworth SW18 ☎ 8870 9667
Difficult to find, but worth it when you do, this 19th-century riverside inn has an attractive public bar, conservatory, restaurant and garden with its own bar and cracking summer barbecues. It's a great party venue.

Anchor Bankside 34 Park St, Southwark SE1 ☎ 7407 1577
A tavern has stood here for 1000 years, though this incarnation dates from 1670 and is a warren of little rooms, cubby holes and creaking floorboards. Pepys watched the Great Fire here and Samuel Johnson wrote his dictionary upstairs. There's a restaurant, terrace and courtyard. (map 15 A3)

Prospect of Whitby 57 Wapping Wall, Wapping E1 ☎ 7481 1095
This is London's oldest riverside pub (est. 1520) and was formally the hangout of smugglers and pirates – a gibbet on the balcony marks the spot where the unlucky ones met their death. Tourists love the original flagstone floor, pewter bar, wooden beams and good restaurant. (map 14 A3)

The Mayflower 117 Rotherhithe St, Rotherhithe SE16, ☎ 7237 4088
Complete with settles, snugs, a fireplace, jetty and restaurant, this charismatic pub is a big hit with American tourists. The Pilgrim Fathers set sail from this area, and their ship's captain is buried nearby. (map 14 2B)

The Grapes 76 Narrow St, Limehouse, Docklands E14 ☎ 7987 4396
Dating from 1583, The Grapes can tell tales of drownings and press gangs. A listed (and listing) building, with an open fire and wonky walls, The Grapes has rickety stairs leading to a pleasant fish restaurant and deck.

The Trafalgar Tavern Park Row, Greenwich SE10 ☎ 8858 2437
Built in 1837, the stately Trafalgar Tavern is a huge Regency affair, with three bars, guest ales and classy food. Past regulars include Charles Dickens (The Trafalgar is mentioned in *Our Mutual Friend*) and William Thackeray.

Susan Grimshaw

FULHAM

Chutney Mary
Regional Indian Gourmet

☎ 7351 3113
535 King's Rd SW10
www.chutneymary.com

Map 19 E2
Tube: Fulham Broadway (650m)
Entertainment: live jazz Sun lunch
Separate smoke-free dining available

starter £3-£7.50
main £9.25-£16.75
dessert £4.50-£6.50
set lunch and pre-theatre menu £11 or £14
Sunday brunch £15
wine £11.50-£80

AE DC MC V; SW

Don't have so much as one pint of lager before you visit Chutney Mary. Go in fresh and enjoy a G&T, for this place is class. It's even nicely decorated. The food is a mix of traditional Indian, Anglo-Indian and a regularly changing selection of regional specialities. To start, try one of the top-notch staples including samosas (£4.50) or 'flavour of the month' baked crab with mustard and red chilli (£8.50). We thoroughly enjoyed the lobster with mango, tamarind and coconut (£19) and spicy lamb shanks (£13), while the Goan green curry (£11.50) was good value. The best pudding on the menu was a lovely spiced bread-and-butter pudding (£6), not too sweet. We swapped a lot of spoons, so we reckon the tasting menu (£32) is the best way of sampling all the unusual flavours and combinations.

Open: Mon-Fri 12.30pm-2.30pm, Sat & Sun 12.30pm-3pm, Mon-Sat 6.30pm-11.30pm, Sun 6.30pm-10.30pm; reservations essential; licensed, no BYO

Montana
Contemporary American

☎ 7385 9500
125-129 Dawes Rd SW6
www.montanafood.co.uk

Map 19 E1
Tube: Fulham Broadway (650m)
Entertainment: jazz Tues-Sat evening
Nonsmoking tables available

starter £5-£8
main £11-£22
dessert £4-£5
wine £12-£65

AE MC V; SW

From a distance Montana shines. The white table settings and large wine glasses sparkle against the rich ochre walls, enticing you inside. But you can't just wander in, as the equally sparkling cuisine ensures that booking is essential. The ever-changing menu draws from America: the rich flavours of the South West predominate but other regions get their due as well. Smoked salmon fishcakes (£7) are a rich alternative to the norm, while the New England seafood chowder (£6) would do any Bostonian proud. The Cajun-spiced northern albacore tuna (£14) is a hearty grilled fish, nicely teamed with coriander cream and a delicate red bean burrito. Everything comes with a selection of wholegrain breads that surprise with chillies and other flavourings. Service is smooth and professional, and the wine list has several good choices under £15. On most nights there's some combination of live jazz – piano and/or vocalists.

Open: daily 6pm-11pm, Sat noon-4pm, Sun 11.30am-4pm; reservations advisable (essential weekends); licensed, no BYO

FULHAM

The Salisbury Tavern
Modern British

☎ 7381 4005
1 Sherbrooke Rd SW6

Map 19 E1

Tube: Fulham Broadway (700m)

Wheelchair access

Smoking throughout

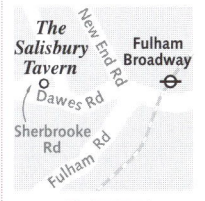

In the heart of hooray heaven, nicely spoken, crisply ironed folk – safely surrounded by similar types – tuck into esoteric delicacies. The chef is Charlie Rushton, formerly of Mirabelle, the place a glass-roofed, softly lit room adjoining a cheery pub. Suitably Elysian are a variety of classic, inviting openers, such as marinated artichoke, green bean and calamata olive salad (£5.75), with a jumble of textures in each bite. Seared fillet of seabass with tagiatelle of vegetables in a coriander, sesame and soy sauce (£11.75) typifies the delicate, inventive combinations on offer, complemented by crisp vegetables (£2) or a creamy, sloppy mustard mash (£2). Traditional peach and bread-and-butter pudding with clotted cream (£4.50) is a delicious though sturdy finish, and there are lighter delights too. The verdict: fine food served in bland central.

starter £3.95-£7.50
main £7.75-£18
dessert £4.50
wine £11-£80

AE MC V; SW

Open: daily noon-11pm; reservations advisable; licensed, no BYO

(Simon Bracken)

HAMMERSMITH

Map 21 A1
Tube: Ravenscourt Park (600m)

Smoking throughout
Patio tables

The Anglesea Arms
Modern British/European

☎ 8749 1291
35 Wingate Rd W6

The Anglesea Arms is an all-too-rare independent pub serving fine ale, decent wine and fresh, often innovative, food. There are only a handful of tables in the bar area so it feels spacious despite the traditional dark wooden interior. On a balmy evening there was plenty of supping and chatting going on outside, while inside there wasn't a free seat – but it was only an ale's wait to get a table in the dining area. Starters included an unusual but lovely marinated feta salad (£4.95) and a sweet onion and Emmental tart (£3.95). A classic main of calf's liver, pancetta and rosemary (£8.95) was nicely done, as was the wild mushroom risotto (£7.50) with parmesan and rocket. Home-made puddings included a ricotta cheesecake and an amply rich chocolate mousse/cake/sorbet combination (both £3.95). With proper coffee and decent service, it's well worth the trip out west.

starter £4-£6
main £7-£10
dessert £3.50-£4.50
wine £10-£25

DC MC V; SW

Open: Mon-Sat 12.30pm-2.45pm, 7.30pm-10.45pm, Sun 1pm-3.30pm, 7.30pm-10.15pm; reservations not accepted; licensed, no BYO

Map 21 B2
Tube: Hammersmith (300m)

Smoking throughout
Courtyard tables

The Gate
Modern British Vegetarian

☎ 8748 6932
51 Queen Caroline St W6
www.gateveg.co.uk

This vegetarian haven has a menu so delicious it should convert even the most confirmed meat-lover. The premises are rented from the neighbouring church, lending the décor a village-hall atmosphere despite the eclectic pop art that adorns the bright yellow walls. The small menu changes monthly, and all the dishes are interesting, varied and beautifully presented. The butternut gnocchi (£4.90) and goat's cheese and pear salad (£4.90) are rich and flavoursome. Mains such as rocket panzerotti (£8.90) – fresh rocket pasta filled with grilled aubergine and oven-dried tomatoes topped with shaved parmesan and a tangy sage and lemon butter – are equally sumptuous. Innovative desserts include nectarines in filo (£4.75) and blackberry and kirsch brûlée (£4.25).

starter £3.50-£5.75
main £9.50-£10.50
dessert £3.75-£5.50
wine £9.75-£26.50

AE DC MC V; SW

Open: Mon-Fri noon-3pm, Mon-Sat 6pm-11pm; reservations advisable (essential at weekends); licensed, no BYO

WEST

200 LONELY PLANET OUT TO EAT

The Gate (Carl Drury)

Paulo's
Brazilian

☎ **7385 9264**
30 Greyhound Rd W6

Map 21 B3
Tube: Hammersmith (700m)
Smoking throughout
Garden tables

This small restaurant serves up an impressive Brazilian buffet. The emphasis is on home cooking, and the home-style ambience extends to the personal welcome each guest receives. Though there are starters, the range of the eat-all-you-can buffet (the only option for the main course) makes them all but unnecessary unless you fancy something unusual, such as the asparagus-like palm hearts salad (£3.85). Paulo will explain the buffet dishes and suggest the best combinations. Hot and cold options include salads, plantain fritters, chicken, slightly watery refried beans and shrimp-dominated fish dishes. We particularly enjoyed the creamy pork dish (porco com molho branco) which incorporates béchemel sauce and (on occasion) fluffy pumpkin. If you have room for more, you could try quindim (£2.95), a Brazilian dessert reminiscent of crème caramel but with a coconut-biscuit base.

Open: Tues-Fri noon-2.30pm, Tues-Sat 7.30pm-10.30pm, Sun 1pm-3.30pm; reservations advisable; licensed, no BYO

Hammersmith
Hammersmith Flyover
Fulham Palace Rd
Charing Cross Hospital
Paulo's ○ Greyhound Rd

starter 95p-£3.85
main £10.50 (lunch & Tues evening £8.50)
dessert £2.95
wine £10.85-£13.60
JCB MC V; SW

WEST

HAMMERSMITH 201

HOLLAND PARK

Map 20 D1
Tube: Holland Park (525m)
Smoking throughout
Patio tables

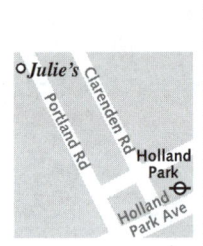

Julie's
British

☎ 7229 8331
135 Portland Rd W11
www.juliesrestaurant.com

Got wedding-proposal jitters? Take a test run in Julie's. This elegant and charismatic restaurant has put tremendous energy into its décor. Julie's maze of downstairs rooms features mirrors, soft white plaster-walls and pillars, and a comfortable, intimate sitting area. Soothing contemporary music plays as couples toast one other in corners. The compact menu, featuring stylised British delicacies, holds some exotics – though the partridge breast in port sauce (£15.95) was overly chewy. Indeed, overall we found the food lacklustre. But for the Roquefort cheese, the angel-hair noodle starter salad would have been oily and bland, and the filo pastry main (£12.95) wasn't saved by dollops of goat's cheese and wads of spinach. Our best dish was dessert – warm banana coconut crêpes soaked in a pool of chocolate sauce (£6.95). But food is really an afterthought at Julie's – go to indulge in romance, and to experience a London tradition.

starter £3.95-£7.95
main £12.95-£16.50
dessert £6.95
set dinner £28 or £35
wine £14.95-£42

AE MC V; SW

Open: Mon-Fri 12.30pm-2.45pm, Sun 12.30pm-3pm, Mon-Sat 7.30pm-11.15pm, Sun 7.30pm-10.15pm; reservations advisable; licensed, no BYO

Map 20 D1
Tube: Holland Park (150m)
Nonsmoking tables available
Pavement tables

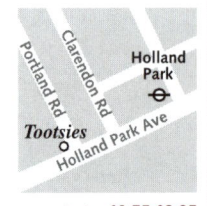

Tootsies
American

☎ 7229 8567
120 Holland Park Ave W11

Tootsies is ever popular, serving American-style fodder to the local neighbourhood. Although the clientele is mixed, Sunday is a family day with waitresses handing out crayons to children. Free-range eggs are used, and vegetarians will be delighted to find meat-free sausages and burgers on offer. If you can't decide how to start, then try it all – the selection plate of appetisers (£8.95) is to share, and includes crispy, deep-fried onion rings with sweet chilli dipping sauce, potato skins with sour cream and chicken satay sticks with a spicy peanut dipping sauce. The signature dish, the hamburger (£7.75), comes with fries and a choice of toppings. Mesquite barbecue sauce gives the meat a sweet, smoky flavour. The warm chicken salad (£6.95) is packed with spinach leaves and bacon, and it eventually got the better of us – thankfully, the helpful staff are only too happy to pack leftovers into a doggy bag.

starter £2.75-£8.95
main £5.50-£9.75
dessert £3.75
wine £9.95-£16.50

AE JCB MC V; SW

Open: Sun-Thurs 9am-11pm, Fri & Sat 9am-11.30pm, Sun 9am-11pm; reservations not accepted; licensed, no BYO

HOLLAND PARK

Wiz
International

☎ **7229 1500**
123a Clarendon Rd W11
www.wizandwoz.com

Owned by Antony Worrall Thomson, the TV-celebrity chef, this tavern-like restaurant offers a splendid array of tapas grouped by geographic category, as well as our favourite, the 'Spice Trail'. Three dishes each should do; if you simply can't choose, the well-informed staff can reel off suggestions. Seared tuna (£6.75), a perennial first choice, arrives as thimble-sized slivers of pink tuna deliciously seasoned with soy, ginger and lemon grass. The chilli salt squid (£6.75) is a spicy delight, the North African lamb with sweet tomato tajine (£6.95) is tender and zesty, and the Greek salad (£4.95) is just right. For dessert, the chocolate tart (£4.50), topped with ice cream and floating in marbled chocolate sauce, rates among the all-time most blissful (and beautiful) puddings. Wooden tables, wicker chairs, comfy benches and brick walls provide a cosy welcome in winter, but alfresco summer dining really brings Wiz into its own.

Open: Tues-Fri noon-3pm, Sat & Sun noon-4pm, Mon-Thurs 6.30pm-11pm, Fri & Sat 6.30pm-midnight; reservations advisable; licensed, no BYO

Map 20 C1
Tube: Holland Park (700m) or Ladbroke Grove

Smoking throughout
Roof-terrace tables

main £3.95-£8.45
dessert £4
wine £10.95-£95
AE JCB MC V; SW

KENSAL RISE

Astons
International/Fish

☎ **8969 2184**
2 Regent St NW10

This funky gastropub has an incredible pull that makes you want to stay all day. It's casual and the food is fab. With a menu that changes daily and a chef adept at conjuring up new dishes, you'll be gorging on a mish-mash of global fish dishes. The goodies picked from our lucky dip (two-courses £15.50) were chunky tiger prawns in a pool of chilli oil and vegetarian spicy parsnip and coconut soup (with a Thai twist). The fine starters were backed up by tender seared salmon with juicy stuffed peppers and, mighty as the name suggests, grilled swordfish with mash. We sighed over the hot sticky-toffee pudding (£4.50) for a second, before wolfing it down. Late-afternoon diners left the waitress overstretched, not a problem if you've come – as you should – to chill.

Open: Mon-Sun noon-4pm, 6pm-10.30pm; reservations essential; licensed, no BYO

Map 20 A1
Tube: Kensal Green (300m)
Entertainment: jazz Sun

Smoking throughout
Pavement tables

starter £3.50-£6
main £7.50-£13.50
dessert £4.50
set menu £15.50
wine £9.50-£38
MC V; SW

WEST

HOLLAND PARK & KENSAL RISE

KENSAL RISE

Map 20 A1
Tube: Kensal Green (300m)
Wheelchair access
Smoking throughout
Garden tables

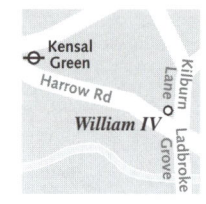

William IV
Modern British

☎ 8969 5944
786 Harrow Rd NW10
www.william-iv.co.uk

Attracting young families and old trendies alike, the restaurant at William IV has a lively feel as the staff engage the punters in friendly banter and the highs and lows of conversations fill the room. The small space is open and well-lit; colourful mosaics line the fireplace and a local artist's paintings on the wall give it an added warmth. The daily menu is interesting but not cutting edge. Rough chunks of mozzarella with juicy vine tomatoes (£4.50) is perhaps not the most original of starters but this winning combination is served to a tasty perfection. The explosion of rosemary in the rich chump of lamb (£10.90) is refreshingly good, the pommes dauphinoise are creamy and herb rich, and the recommended Gamay Anjou Richou (£15) proves an excellent companion. With good food and happy service, relaxed and welcoming William IV is hugely popular and deservedly so.

starter £3.75-£5
main £7-£12.90
dessert £4-£5
set lunch Mon-Thurs £7.50
Sun lunch £12 or £15
wine £10.50-£26

AE DC JCB MC V; SW

Open: Mon-Wed noon-3pm, 6pm-10.30pm, Thurs & Fri noon-3pm, 6pm-11pm, Sat noon-4pm, 7pm-11pm, Sun noon-4pm, 7pm-10pm; reservations essential at weekends; licensed, no BYO

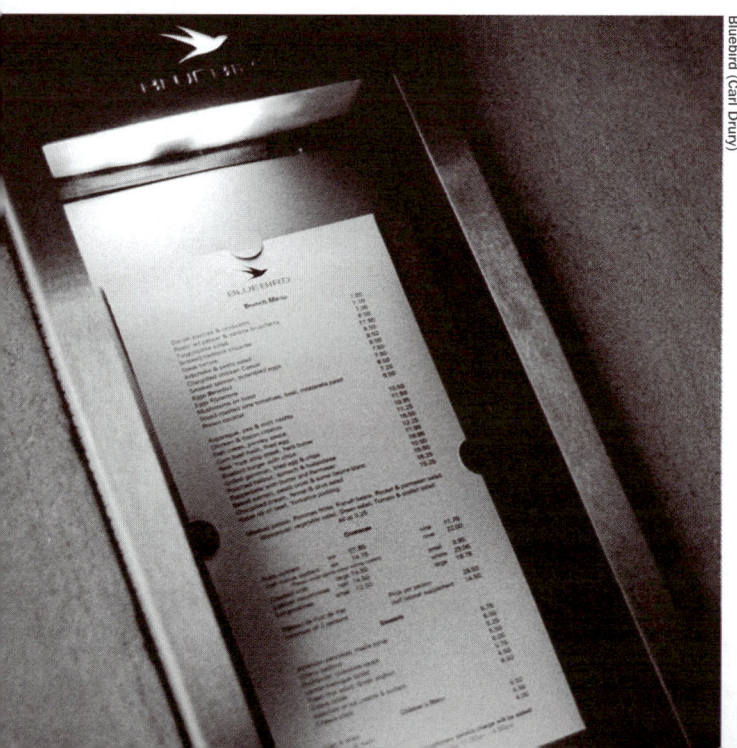

Bluebird (Carl Drury)

KENSINGTON

L'Anis
Mediterranean

☎ 7795 6533
1 Kensington High St W8

L'Anis, conforming to current trends, resides in a converted bank. The dining room has a courtroom air with its wood panelling and ornate stonework. The menu offers six to eight items per course and classy ingredients are lavishly presented. Waiters were in no hurry and forgot our side order, but all was forgiven when we tasted the food. An amusette of pumpkin soup transformed the stringy vegetable beyond recognition and the winter celeriac soup was luxuriously buttery with morels lurking at the bottom like blackened loofahs. Braised beef skirt was not as tender as expected, but no less rich, with snail and garlic mash arriving separately in a copper pan. A rack of pork, black pudding, foie gras and truffle and pear mash was flavour-packed, and creamy lemon tart was studded with perfectly round citrus crisps. We washed the lot down with a storming bottle of 1997 Rioja (£19).

Open: Mon-Fri & Sun noon-2.45pm, Mon-Sat 6pm-10.45pm; reservations essential; licenced & BYO (pre-arrangede only, corkage £10/bottle)

Map 20 E5
Tube: High Street Kensington (400m)

Smoking throughout

set lunch £13.50-£21.50
set dinner £14.50-£25.50
wine £13.50-£3,000

AE MC V; SW

Maggie Jones's
British

☎ 7937 6462
6 Old Court Place, Kensington Church St W8

This place *is* a grandmother's kitchen – there's Victorian memorabilia everywhere – but the clientele is definitely up to date; we dined alongside media types, tourists and even a toff, his girlfriend and their transsexual sidekick. The set dinner (£20.95) menu has a choice of seven dishes per course, but the starter to try is Maggie's tart, a creamed fish pie made from a traditional recipe with boiled eggs and plenty of fish, cased in perfect pastry. The roast guinea fowl (£12.50) is a classic favourite, and diners who like to experiment will love the rabbit and mustard casserole (£14.75). There's a good choice of puddings (£4), and with over 55 wine varieties to choose from you'll be sure to find one to your liking. The lunch menus have lighter portions and less variety, but you can still expect to eat well.

Open: Mon-Sun 12.30pm-2.30pm, Mon-Sat 6.30pm-11pm, Sun 6.30pm-10.30pm; reservations advisable (essential for dinner); licensed, no BYO

Map 20 E4
Tube: High Street Kensington (350m)

Smoking throughout

starter £4.85-£6.80
main £8.75-£14.75
dessert £4
set lunch Mon-Fri £13.75
Sun lunch £14.95
set dinner £20.95
wine £23-£47

AE DC MC V; SW

KENSINGTON

Map 19 A2
Tube: Gloucester Road
(600m)

Smoking throughout

Pasha
Morroccan/Maghreb

☎ 7589 7969
1 Gloucester Rd SW7
www.pasha-restaurant.co.uk

Step through Pasha's ornate metal doors and you'll be instantly whisked away to medieval Marrakesh, complete with flickering lanterns, mosaic fountains, Islamic arches and waiters in robes. Theming a restaurant like this can be touch and go but Pasha pulls it off with real panache. The meze (£7) – a tasty selection of vegetarian dips served with conical Lebanese bread – is almost obligatory. The main menu is dominated, unsurprisingly, by couscous and tajines, backed up by an interesting array of meats and fish. Topping the bill is the couscous royale (£14.50) with tender lamb, chicken and merguez sausage. Mashed potato with black olives and red onions (£2.75) is delicious on the side, but save some space for crème brûlée with Turkish delight (£4.50). The best tables are tucked away in private alcoves downstairs.

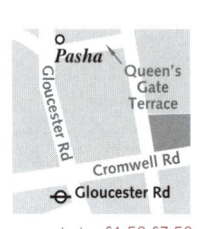

starter £1.50-£7.50
main £9.90-£16.50
dessert £3.50-£4.50
wine £13.50-£50

AE DC JCB MC V; SW

Open: daily noon-3pm, Mon-Sat 7pm-11.30pm; reservations advisable; licensed, no BYO

Map 20 E4
Tube: High Street Kensington
(200m)

Smoking throughout

Terrace tables

The Terrace
Modern British

☎ 7937 3224
33c Holland St W8

A small, elegant, understated neighbourhood restaurant, The Terrace is loveliest in summer when it spills out into the salubrious Kensington street. Starters include tender, delicate scallops with buttery leek (£10), and goat's cheese sensuously melting over a roasted salad (£7.50). Firm monkfish wrapped in salty parma ham is imaginatively paired with succulent beetroot (£18.50) and an extravagant option couples duck breast with the fine, syrupy flavours of parsnip purée, caramelised shallots, girolle mushrooms and maderia jus (£19.50). The requisite simple sides include silky mashed potato and crisp French beans. Wines are varied and reasonably priced, and some fine wines are held in limited quantities. Service is as immaculate as the clientele's hairstyles. Feather-light comfort puddings include renditions of rice and bread-and-butter puddings that leave you ready to float away skywards – there's no chance: you're hauled down to earth by the bill.

starter £5.50-£11
main £11.50-£20
dessert £5.50-£5.75
wine £11.50-£80

AE DC MC V; SW

Open: Mon-Sat noon-2.30pm, 7pm-10.30pm, Sun 12.30pm-3pm; reservations advisable (essential at weekends); licensed, no BYO

KENSINGTON

Wódka
Polish/Eastern European

☎ 7937 6513
12 St Alban's Grove W8

You'll find several healthy-sounding fish options on Wódka's menu, but this friendly local remains a temple to a cuisine largely unreconstructed by dietary science. The Kraców-chic ambience is unmistakable, too: Polish vodka and cocktails rule the drinks list and staff chat in what sounds like authentic Polish. The staff are equally helpful in English, though the robust flavours of cheese and leek dumplings (£5.75) tossed with chunks of fatty bacon and wild mushrooms need no explanation – nor, perhaps, quite so much oil. The kasza salad is tossed with eye-watering doses of fresh mint and shallots (£2.50), but the fishcakes alone make a visit to Wódka essential: two plump pucks of juicy shredded fish seasoned with dill and served in a deliciously salty leek and cream sauce (£10.50). Try the unctuous white chocolate cheesecake (£4.50), then book yourself in for that cholesterol test while you still can.

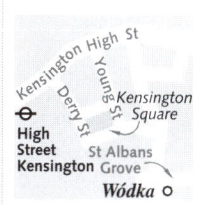

Open: Mon-Fri 12.30pm-2.30pm, Mon-Sun 7pm-11.15pm; reservations advisable; licensed & BYO (corkage £6/bottle)

Map 20 E5
Tube: High Street Kensington (450m)

Smoking throughout

starter £4.90-£7.90
main £11.50-£13.50
dessert £4.50-£4.90
set lunch £10.50 or £13.50
wine £10.50-£33

AE DC MC V; SW

KENSINGTON OLYMPIA

Cotto
Modern European

☎ 7602 9333
44 Blythe Rd W14

Swanky and contemporary Cotto offers a minimalist approach to dining. Perched boldly on a corner, its stark-white walls and black chairs are enlivened by blazing modern art, bringing a flush of colour to its pale face. In this calm setting, Samson-esque waiters sidle round the mixed clientele wielding nibble-worthy walnut rolls. And it's best to say yes as the supreme flavours come in dainty portions. Among the exceptionally stylish gastronomic pleasures is the cuttlefish and braised beef combination (£7.00), created to perk up the senses. The velvety velouté of wild mushrooms (£4.95) slips down a treat and if you follow it with pan-fried brill, purple flowering broccoli and anchovy relish (£13.50), you'll be entranced. The sautéed scallops, Jerusalem artichokes and sage (£14.50) looked a tad scant but were a lip-licking triumph. And flower lovers will appreciate the prettily carved carrots too.

Open: Mon-Fri noon-2.30pm, 7pm-10.30pm, Sat 7pm-10.30pm; reservations advisable; licensed & BYO (corkage £12.50/bottle)

Map 21 A3
Tube: Kensington (Olympia) (300m)

Smoking throughout

Pavement tables

starter £4.95-£8.50
main £11.95-£15
dessert £5.50-£6
set lunch £12.50 or £15.50
wine £12-£45

MC V; SW

KENSINGTON OLYMPIA

Map 21 A3

Tube: Kensington (Olympia) (650m)

Smoking throughout

Popeseye
British

☎ 7610 4578
108 Blythe Rd W14

There's no difficulty in deciding what to order in Popeseye – the choice is steak or steak. There aren't any distracting starters. Simply plump for a rump (known as 'popeseye' in Scotland), sirloin or fillet, and select a size between 6oz and 20oz. As they only do one thing, you can be sure that they do it well. The meat is of the highest quality (Aberdeen Angus, hung for at least two weeks) and is served with thick-cut chips and a platter of mustards and sauces. We tried the sirloin and the fillet – both were supremely tender and char-grilled exactly to our requirements – and finished with a lovely moist and crumbly sticky toffee pudding (£3.95) and a selection of three cheeses (£3.95). This small, softly-lit restaurant also offers a fine selection of malt Scotch whiskies (well, the owner is Scottish). *Also at 277 Upper Richmond Rd, Putney, SW15* ☎ *8788 7733.*

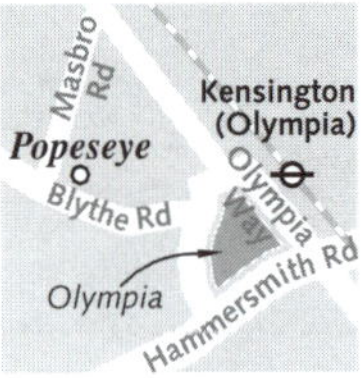

main £9.45-£29.95
dessert £3.95
wine £11.50-£75

cash or cheque only

Open: Mon-Sat 7pm-10.30pm; reservations advisable; licensed & BYO (corkage £8/bottle)

Tube: Kensington (Olympia) (200m)

Smoking throughout

Yas
Persian

☎ 7603 9148
7 Hammersmith Rd W14
www.yasrestaurant.com

Yas, Iranian for jasmine, proudly trumpets it reputation as London's first Persian restaurant. Justly so. This no-nonsense eatery is split across two floors (the lower is more intimate), and boasts a vegetarian-friendly menu and pleasant ambience. The Persian bread, baked in a large mosaic oven by the door, wafted enticing smells across the room as we perused the menu. Unfortunately, the staff wafted across the room pretty sharpish too, hurrying us to decide and then whisking away starters before we were ready for mains. That said, the food is good quality, albeit a little uninspired. Khoresh-e gheime bademjan (£8), stewed lamb with aubergine, is alive with flavours of the Mediterranean while yoghurt-based starters, such as mast-o khiar (£3.50) with its crunchy cucumber pieces, complement the warm bread perfectly. Yas is about good-value hearty fare and no frills – not a special-occasion venue but a reliable standby for a flavour of something different.

starter £3.50
main £6-£25
dessert £3
wine £9-£16

AE DC JCB MC V; SW

Open: daily noon-5am; reservations advisable; licensed, no BYO

KEW

The Glasshouse
Modern British

☎ 8940 6777
14 Station Parade TW9

From the exterior, The Glasshouse looks a rather unassuming, low-key eatery. And long may it remain so for it's actually a little gem. Service is immaculate, quality excellent and the ambience pleasantly smart without being overbearing. It adopts a strict set-menu format with a short but interesting selection that changes daily. Our warm duck salad starter was superb – a delicately constructed tower of tender meat and crunchy lardons, worthy of a place in the Tate Modern, which succeeded in matching its aesthetic promise with rich flavours. The lamb was also tender and fresh; only the plaice, served in a squid ink sauce, looked more interesting than it tasted. Presentation is excellent with the chef really bringing out the colours and textures of the food without dishes becoming *nouvelle cuisine* gastro-porn. A real treasure. Just keep it between us.

Open: Mon-Thurs noon-2.30pm, 7pm-10.30pm, Fri & Sat noon-2.30pm, 6.30pm-10.30pm, Sun 12.30pm-3pm; reservations advisable; licensed & BYO (corkage £15/bottle)

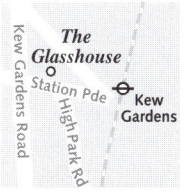

Tube/rail: Kew Gardens (50m)

Smoking throughout

set lunch Mon-Sat £15-£19.50, Sun £15-£23.50
set dinner £15-£25
wine £13.50-£85

AE MC V; SW

KILBURN

Vijay
South Indian

☎ 7328 1087
49 Willesden Lane NW6

The English are fiercely loyal to their local Indian restaurants and in the case of Vijay, this loyalty is well deserved. Well off the main drag, Vijay manages to pull in punters from across London with a huge menu of north Indian favourites and south Indian specialities that will evoke a sigh of nostalgia from anyone who has spent time in the subcontinent. Add friendly staff and reasonable prices and it's easy to see the attraction. South Indian standards such as masala dosa (an outsized lentil pancake stuffed with spiced potato; £4.95) or idly sambar (steamed rice cakes with a fiery dipping sauce; £4.30) should put you in the right mood. Mains run the gamut from hot concoctions of bhindi (okra) and saag (spinach) to unusual 'non-veg' creations such as chicken mehti (£4.60), a spicy curry flavoured with braised onion and fenugreek leaves. Friendly, well-organised and excellent value, Vijay comes highly recommended.

Open: daily noon-2.45pm, Sun-Thurs 6pm-10.45pm, Fri & Sat 6pm-11.45pm; reservations accepted; licensed, no BYO

Rail: Brondesbury (800m), tube: Kilburn

Nonsmoking tables available

starter £1.10-£4.95
main £2.95-£5.95
dessert £1.70-£2
wine £8.10-£12.75

MC V; SW

KNIGHTSBRIDGE

Map 18 B1
Tube: Knightsbridge (500m)
Entertainment: live Russian music every night
Smoking throughout

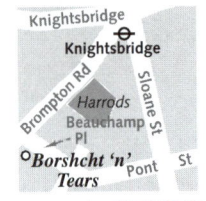

Borshcht 'n' Tears
Russian

☎ 7584 9911
46 Beauchamp Place SW3

The best thing about Borshcht 'n' Tears is that it's refreshingly unpretentious. Decked in red wallpaper, the long split-level dining room is cosy and engaging, and there's live music every night. The menu and paper placemats, reproduced virtually unchanged since the 1970s, poke fun at communists, capitalists and famous Russians. We started with borshcht (beetroot soup; £3.15), which was disappointingly watery. But the accompanying piroshki (£2.95), small pasties filled with minced meat, were just right – juicy with a soft shell. Beef stroganoff (£10.55) consisted of thin slivers of tender beef in a creamy sauce doused liberally and to great effect with tarragon. The accompanying rice and vegetables were less memorable. Rated on gastronomic merits alone this place is expensive, but on a wintry night, eating heavy Slavonic fare to the strains of a polka – accompanied by generous shots of vodka – can prove thoroughly enjoyable.

starter £2.50-£5.50
main £6-£12
dessert £3.40
wine £10-£15

AE MC V; SW

Open: daily 6pm-1am; reservations essential; licensed, no BYO

Map 18 A2
Tube: Knightsbridge (25m)
Wheelchair access
Dress code: no jeans or trainers
Separate smoke-free dining available

Foliage
Modern European

☎ 7235 2000
**Mandarin Oriental Hyde Park,
66 Knightsbridge SW1X**

Gazing out over Hyde Park, Foliage is a firm favourite of diplomats and executives. Although understated, the small dining room is full of stylish touches, from real ivy leaves on the place mats to a magnificently stocked, walk-through wine cellar and, of course, the famous view. If the wallet stretches to the £42.50 set menu, you can feast on such delights as poached lobster with crab vinaigrette, sliced venison with foie gras cannelloni and hot Cuban chocolate fondant. The more modest £24 set lunch offers a choice of three starters and mains; we opted for salty herring salad followed by tender roast chicken with a brochette of ceps and herb tagliatelle. The best was saved till last – death by chocolate courtesy of the bitter chocolate tart. It's worth sticking to the smart side of 'smart casual' for your visit.

set lunch £24
set dinner £42.50
gourmet set dinner £55
wine £19.50-£1750

AE DC JCB MC V; SW

Open: Mon-Fri noon-2.30pm, Mon-Sat 7pm-10.30pm; reservations advised; licensed, no BYO

KNIGHTSBRIDGE

Isola
Italian

☎ **7838 1044**
145 Knightsbridge SW1X
www.gruppo.co.uk

Map 18 A2
Tube: Knightsbridge (100m)
Smoking throughout

Over-hyped, over-priced, but so what? The décor's knockout, as are the cocktails – but then Oliver 'Atlantic Bar' Peyton does own the joint. The exhaustive wine list mentions probably every single Italian producer, with plenty by the glass or as part of a sampler. Isola is at the vanguard of the 1970s sci-fi retro look, with kitsch red leather seating and 'Space-Age' lights. The menu is brief, but offers beautifully presented platefuls. A starter of tuna carpaccio (£9) was upturned with a ball of translucent fish encasing a mass of rocket. Buffalo mozzarella and roasted peppers (£8) came with a lovely balsamic reduction. Wild mushroom risotto (£14.50) tasted meaty, but rack of lamb (£17.50), while rare, was chewy. Chocolate tartelette (£7.50) oozed fabulous goo, although the accompanying coffee ice cream was more like a sorbet and strega zabaglione (£6.50) just stayed the right side of sickly with sharp red fruits. Service was engaging, if erratic.

Open: Mon-Sat noon-3pm, 6pm-11pm, Sun 6pm-9.30pm; reservations advisable; licensed & BYO (corkage varies)

starter £6-£12
main £7-£20
dessert £5.50-£8
set lunch Mon-Fri £17.50 & £19.50, Sat & Sun brunch £17.50 (children under 10 eat free)
wine £13.50-£570

AE DC MC V; SW

Isola (Carl Drury)

KNIGHTSBRIDGE

Map 18 A3
Tube: Hyde Park Corner (550m)
Wheelchair access
Dress code: jacket
Nonsmoking tables available

Hyde Park
Knightsbridge
Hyde Park Corner
La Tante Claire
Wilton Pl

starter £22-£30
main £27-£40
dessert £11-£12.50
set lunch £28
wine £16-£1100
AE DC MC V; SW

La Tante Claire
French

☎ 7823 2003
The Berkeley, Wilton Place SW1X
www.savoy-group.co.uk

Scrawny French waiters struggle to manoeuvre large carts between tables occupied by bankers, oil barons and wealthy Japanese tourists at stuffy La Tante Claire. Poor Auntie, her golden age is gone; nowadays most folk want a less intimidating ambience and livelier inventions than those conjured up by chef Pierre Koffmann. But there are some flashes of brilliance, chief among which are the magical between-course offerings, especially green-apple Calvados sorbet. Generously portioned confit of duck (£29) and lofty pistachio soufflé (£12) were also sublime, but too many dishes failed to stimulate (starters were downright bland) – unlike the presentation of the bill, a reverie-wrenching anvil-clang to the head. Service is laughably cloying, with so many waiters on hand there's even a 'fromagelier' and a 'liqueurier'. For value, try the set lunch.

Open: Mon-Fri 12.30pm-2pm, 7pm-11pm, Sat 7pm-11pm; reservations essential; licensed, no BYO

Map 18 B2
Tube: Knightsbridge (250m)
Smoking throughout

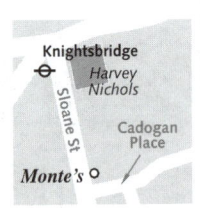

Knightsbridge
Harvey Nichols
Sloane St
Cadogan Place
Monte's

starter £7-£10.50
main £17-£25
dessert £6
set lunch £19.50 or £23
wine £17.50-£2,550
AE DC JCB MC V; SW

Monte's
Modern European

☎ 7245 0896
164 Sloane St SW1X
www.montes.co.uk

The light, modern design and relaxed service of Monte's first-floor restaurant sets the tone for a stylish lunch, which is the only meal you'll be having unless you're a member. Linger over the preliminaries (bread served with a pool of grassy olive oil or an aperitif from the superb wine list) as you name-check the crowd and savour a menu designed by Jamie Oliver and head chef Ben O'Donoghue. Traces of clubby cuisine remain but a tender sheath of seasoned squid (£8.50) is more typical of the kitchen's Mediterranean outlook. The exquisite flavours of roasted sweet garlic, leeks and wild marjoram made the mascarpone risotto (£7.50) the highlight. Guinea fowl breast (£16.50) is huge and juicy but rare venison dumplings (£17.50) will be too heavy for some. 'Puds', however, are delicate and uniformly superb. Try the monte bianco (£6), foaming chestnut praline strewn with shavings of bitter chocolate.

Open: Mon-Sat 12.15pm-3pm; reservations advisable; licensed, no BYO

WEST

KNIGHTSBRIDGE

Mr Chow
Beijing Chinese

☎ 7589 7347
151 Knightsbridge SW1X
www.mrchow.com

Map 18 A2
Tube: Knightsbridge (50m)

Smoking throughout

A visit to Mr Chow is like a step back in time to the 1970s – the long, narrow dining room has brown banquettes and once 'mod' touches. But the gardenias are fragrant and new, and the ingratiating waiters younger than the décor. The media-savvy Mr Chow – whose address book you just know reads like a 1975 issue of *Hello* – limits his menu to a single page, but the waiters strongly encourage you to sit back and let them do the ordering. It's not a bad idea, if your sense of adventure – and wallet – can handle it. The green prawns (£12.50) are spicy and succulent, and Mr Chow's trademark Peking duck (£28 per person) is a showy dish served from a special cart that just wouldn't work with a post-'70s name like, say, Beijing duck. Mr Chow is a fun throwback, especially if someone else is paying.

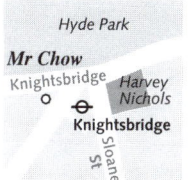

starter £6.50-£14.50
main £14.50-£18.50
dessert £6
wine £13.50-£385
AE DC JCB MC V; SW

Open: daily 12.30pm-3pm, 7pm-midnight ; reservations advisable; licensed, no BYO

O Fado
Portuguese

☎/fax 7589 3002
49-50 Beauchamp Place SW3

Map 18 B1
Tube: Knightsbridge (450m) or South Kensington

Dress code: jacket & collared shirt

Entertainment: *fado* Tues-Sun evening

Smoking throughout

An extensive menu and well-prepared food will keep regulars loyal but to newcomers O Fado feels rather austere. A typical Portuguese restaurant is synonymous with a relaxed atmosphere and hearty fare. By pitching solely at business people, O Fado sacrifices national charm for a formal dining experience. Nevertheless, quality is good and service impeccable. The huge wild boar steak (£11.95), not so much a rack of meat as a veritable stampede, is gamey in a richly tasty way. Seafood is a speciality but the cured cod with potatoes and olives (£9.90) was dryer than an Algarve summer. The dessert selection was also disappointing and the Portuguese icon pastéis de nata (custard cream tart) was conspicuous by its absence; ask for the chef's secret supply. And remember to budget for a £1.10 cover charge per person *and* a 12.5% service charge. Better still, charge it to expenses.

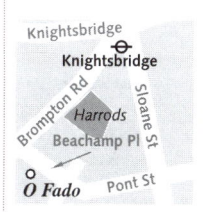

starter £3.50-£6.90
main £7.20-£14.95
wine £11.50-£82
AE JCB MC V; SW

Open: daily noon-3pm, 6.30pm-1am; reservations advisable; licensed, no BYO

WEST

KNIGHTSBRIDGE

KNIGHTSBRIDGE

Pan-Asian Canteen
Modern Asian

☎ 7589 6627
153 Knightsbridge SW1X

Map 18 A2
Tube: Knightsbridge (150m)
Nonsmoking tables available

Occupying a floor above The Paxton's Head pub, just three large tables and a bar fill the quietly lit pine-wood interior of Pan-Asian Canteen. It's restful and relaxing; convivial bench-style seating encourages conversation between groups and the staff are very genial. The menu covers anything from Japanese to Malay dishes, served on elegant concave, rectangular china saras. Starters were delicate and moreish, with a chicken yakitori (£3.95) beautifully skewered together with spring onions. Crisp won ton wraps (£3.45) were stuffed with a juicy mix of seafood while red snapper fillet and sambal (£7.55) came coated in a thick red curry. A small mountain of five spice scallops (£6.75) packed a punch, each tiny mouthful overflowing with zippy flavours. Mango and cardamom brûlée (£3.55), while pleasantly scented, was the wrong consistency, but pandan pancake with coconut ice cream (£3.55) made a great finish.

starter £3.15-£6.25
main £5.95-£7.55
dessert £3.35-£3.55
wine £10.85-£22

AE MC V; SW

Open: daily noon-10.30pm; reservations advisable; licensed, no BYO

Scalini
Italian

☎ 7225 2301
1-3 Walton St SW3

Map 18 B1
Tube: Knightsbridge (750m)
Dress code: collared shirt
Smoking throughout

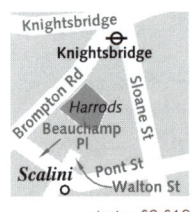

A bastion of authentic Italian cooking, Scalini is busy, bright and full of well-heeled, long-experienced ladies (and gentlemen) who lunch. Although the calamari antipasti (£11) was slightly overcooked, it arrived in the most delicious rich tomato and garlic sauce. Avocado caldo (warm avocado; £12), though tasty, lost its more delicate flavour to the crab and cheese sauce. The menu offers a good choice of traditional pasta dishes but we chose veal escalopes (£12.50), stuffed with ham and mozzarella in a tomato and mushroom sauce, beautifully executed but extremely heavy. The beef fillet (£18) was perfectly judged and presented in an artistically inspired mix of two contrasting pepper sauces. Last up was a colourful trolley of desserts (£4) that failed to live up to appearances. A dry tart and frozen cheesecake confirmed our opinion that Scalini is above average but not quite exceptional.

starter £6-£18
main £8-£23.50
dessert £4
wine £14-£185

AE MC V; SW

Open: daily noon-3pm, 7pm-midnight; reservations advisable; licensed, no BYO

KNIGHTSBRIDGE

Vong
French/Thai

☎ 7235 1010
**The Berkeley,
Wilton Place SW1X**
www.jean-georges.com

Map 18 A3

Tube: Hyde Park Corner (300m) or Knightsbridge

Nonsmoking tables available

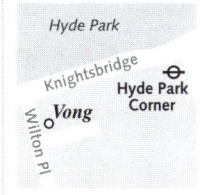

Stylish, contemporary and restrained, this spacious outpost of chef Jean-Georges Vongerichten's restaurant empire serves up a lively synthesis of French and Thai gourmet. Portions are generous, presentation is gorgeous and service is meticulous. Tuna spring rolls (£9.20), garnished with a soy-bean blend and tiny bundles of fish eggs, make a savoury starter, as does the zinging chicken and coconut milk soup (£7.50). Request the vegetarian menu to round out the appealing list of mains; the macadamia nut and vegetable stir-fry (£13.50), served over paddles of silky white rice-noodles, is varied and delicious. For dessert, the terrine of gingered apple (£7) blends superbly with a layer of icy green-apple sorbet. With mirrored pillars, a semi-open kitchen and muted but still striking colours, Vong blends trend with comfort and, above all, delightful cuisine.

starter £5.25-£13 (lunch only)
main £12-£30 (lunch only)
dessert £7-£9
set lunch £21
set dinner £32-£50
pre- & post theatre £22.50
wine £20-£131

AE DC JCB MC V; SW

Open: Mon-Fri noon-2.30pm, 6pm-11.30pm, Sat 11.30am-2pm, 6pm-11.30pm, Sun 11.30am-2pm, 6pm-10.30pm; reservations essential; licensed, no BYO

Zafferano
Italian

☎ 7235 5800
15-16 Lowndes St SW1X

Map 18 B3

Tube: Knightsbridge (300m)

Smoking throughout

Diamonds, perma-tans and glamour. Zafferano attracts people who like to dress up. But for all that, this smart two-roomed restaurant is understated. The menu, too, offers comparatively straightforward dishes, albeit expertly cooked using top-notch ingredients. At only an extra fiver for four courses (£39.50), the full Italian dining experience is hard to refuse, particularly as the staples – pasta and polenta – are sheer perfection. Another forte, perhaps unsurprisingly, is ice cream. The wine in a 'cooked wine' version had lost none of its heady fruity body and counterbalanced crumbly polenta cake perfectly. Beef carpaccio was thickish but tender, and had a garlicky kick. Delicious slivers of cured pork were spotted with syrupy balsamic vinegar. Walnut pasta tasted wonderfully fresh, but lobster linguine wasn't worth the £5 supplement. The *pièce de résistance* was rabbit with Parma ham, which arrived with fluffy polenta that was a breed apart from the supermarket stuff.

set lunch £18.50-£21.50
set dinner £29.50-£39.50
wine £12.30-£900

AE DC MC V; SW

Open: daily noon-2.30pm, 7pm-10.45pm; reservations essential; licensed & BYO (corkage £20-£30/bottle)

LADBROKE GROVE

Map 20 A1
Tube: Ladbroke Grove (450m)

Smoking throughout
Pavement tables

starter £4.25-£9.95
main £9.95-£15.95
dessert £4-£5.50
set lunch Mon-Fri £11.95
wine £10.95-£34.95
AE JCB MC V; SW

Brasserie du Marché aux Puces
French

☎ 8968 5828
349 Portobello Rd W10

Brasserie du Marché aux Puces is a very pleasant surprise in overrun (and often overpriced) Notting Hill. Part of the appeal is its location on a quieter stretch of Portobello Rd, a few blocks away from the antique and curio market. On a sunny day you can grab a table outside, order a decent bottle of wine (starting from £10) and tuck into solid fare at reasonable prices. Our Sunday lunch menu offered roast pork with country potatoes and green beans, roast cod fillet with ratatouille, and a generous charcuterie plate that included salami, duck pâté, smoked ham and chorizo with a rocket salad – all for under £12. The restaurant graciously welcomes children, but in true French style the kids are expected to behave and order from the adult menu.

Open: Mon-Sat 10am-11pm, Sun 11am-10pm; reservations advisable; licensed, no BYO

Map 20 B1
Tube: Ladbroke Grove (600m)

Smoking throughout
Pavement tables

starter 20p-£2
main £2.70-£6
dessert 60p-£1
cash only

Yum Yum
Caribbean

☎/fax 8968 1477
312 Ladbroke Grove W10

Holes in the wall have a certain habit of churning out the heartiest, most flavourful food – and humble Yum Yum is no exception. On offer in this teeny Caribbean diner is a range of dirt-cheap dishes – chicken roasted or fried, fish, lamb, burgers and more. The brown fish stew (£3.50) is exactly that, with a rich, musky flavour. The large bean feast (£4.50) is chunky and delicious, and whatever your main, yam (£1) is a worthwhile complement to sponge up the sauce. But nobody really comes to sit down – after all, there are only two tables in front of the counter. Locals swing by for the takeout (the sweetish slab of banana cake, tellingly, comes pre-wrapped to go). If you're in the neighbourhood and feeling famished but broke, Yum Yum is worth a stop.

Open: Mon-Thurs 10am-10pm, Fri & Sat 10am-11pm; reservations not accepted; unlicensed

LANCASTER GATE

Bistro Daniel
French

☎ **7723 8395**
**26 Sussex Place,
Lancaster Gate W2**

The bistro below Amandier is possibly the darkest dining room in London. It's very Provence, with bare candlelit tables, pottery crickets stuffed with lavender and framed images of French life. The simple menu – the posh stuff goes upstairs – is served from a shared kitchen over which husband and wife preside. Service was knowledgeable and food was good, barring a starter of smoked salmon (£6) somewhat overpowered by goat's cheese. Deep-fried Camembert (£4.95) was unusually mild and came with a mustard dressing – but could have been enlivened with redcurrant jelly. A seabream main was perched atop good, chunky ratatouille and a delicious knuckle of lamb came with caramel carrots. A side order of gratin dauphinois (£1.95) was superb and haricots verts (£1.95) had the requisite crunch. Then followed a velvety duo of white and dark chocolate mousse (£3.95) and a rich, but not noticeably gingery, pear and ginger bread-and-butter pudding (£3.95).

Open: Mon-Fri noon-2.30pm, 7pm-10.30pm, Sat 7pm-10.30pm; reservations accepted (advisable for groups); licensed, no BYO

Tube: Lancaster Gate (200m) or Paddington
Separate smoke-free dining available
Pavement tables

starter £3.95-£5.80
main £7.80-£12.95
dessert £3.95-£4.50
set lunch £9.95 or £12.95
wine £9.95-£72

AE DC MC V; SW

(Simon Bracken)

MORTLAKE

Rail: Barnes Bridge (200m)
Separate smoke-free dining available
Courtyard tables

starter £3.80-£6.50
main £8.75-£13.50
dessert £4.50
set lunch Mon-Fri £9.95
set dinner Mon-Thurs £13.50
wine £10.50-£38
AE DC MC V; SW

The Depôt
Modern British

☎ 8878 9462
**Tideway Yard,
Mortlake High St SW14**

This restaurant serves up palatable, well-presented food and offers a commanding view of the Thames. The menu is not long but it's varied, encompassing European, Middle-Eastern and Asian influences on its modern British cuisine. Several dishes feature chillies. The cream chilli dressing goes wonderfully with the superb and succulent queen scallops (£6.50) starter, as does the sweet chilli dressing on the tender, pan-fried Thai marinated salmon (£9.75). However, the tomato-heavy chilli sauce that came with the roast duck breast (£10.50) was surprisingly spicy and tasted burnt. The sticky toffee pudding (£4.50) is (as promised) sticky, and (as expected) calorie-laden, though our favourite dessert is the lemon grass and lime brûlée (£4.50), with its subtle yet distinctive flavours. Notable features of this converted warehouse include rustic-style natural wood tables, starched linen napkins, high ceilings and picture windows. On Saturday lunchtime the place is full of well-to-do families.

Open: Mon-Sat noon-3pm, 6pm-11pm, Sun noon-10pm; reservations advisable (essential at weekends); licensed, no BYO

Rail: Mortlake (150m)
Smoking throughout
Pavement tables

starter £3.95-£5.50
main £9.75-£13.95
dessert £4
wine £9.75-£24
MC V; SW

Fish Tank
*Modern European
Fish & Seafood*

☎ 8878 3535
45 Sheen Lane SW14

Eat fish and be like fish at this tank-like restaurant where, if you notice the chap dangling his bait, you'll catch the drift. It's a local place that serves its patch but it's a snappy little number, offering strikingly prepared, freshly caught fish in generous proportions. The man at the helm meandered from guest to guest a trifle leisurely but patience paid off. The circular parcels of crab and grapefruit (£4.50) are a jaw-stretching feast of tangy crab and the moist orange roughy (£12.50) falls apart with awesome ease. The wafting scents of the top-tasting Thai fish curry (£9.75) give the nostrils a good massage, and you'll start feeling the satisfaction of eating food that's good for you. Only thing is, don't bank on having the dessert of your choice.

Open: Mon-Sat 7pm-midnight; reservations advisable; licensed, no BYO

MORTLAKE

Redmond's
Modern British

☎ 8878 1922
170 Upper Richmond Rd West SW14

Everything about Redmond's conveys quality – the ambience, the furnishings, the vibrant modern art on the walls, and most importantly of all, the food. The service is leisurely and friendly. Dishes are arranged like art on the plates, with drizzles of sauces or oils round the sides. Unusual ingredients are often combined to great effect, and the results transcend menu descriptions. The tartare of smoked haddock is enlivened by tangy sushi ginger and softened with parsley crème fraîche; chicken breast is served on a moist and creamy bed of butternut squash polenta, which offsets the sharper taste of the accompanying lentils. Seared black bream is hot from the pan, but came with a perhaps slightly dry mix of couscous and ratatouille. Desserts, such as rhubarb and brûlee tart with blood orange sorbet, are also superb and the wine, though slightly pricey, will not disappoint.

Open: Mon-Fri noon-2pm, Mon-Sat 7pm-10.30pm, Sun noon-2.30pm; reservations advisable; licensed, no BYO

Rail: Mortlake (500m)

Smoking throughout

set lunch Mon-Fri £10 or £21, Sun £16.50 or £19.50
set dinner Mon-Sat £23 or £27
wine £13.50-£75
MC V; SW

NOTTING HILL

192
Modern British

☎ 7229 0482
192 Kensington Park Rd W11

Red velvet seating, fresh flowers, inspired cooking and a youthful, animated crowd combine to make 192 one of Notting Hill's buzziest restaurants. Not only is the food, drawn from an ever-changing menu of intriguing modern dishes, consistently excellent, it also doubles as deftly sculpted art. Adventurers among us relished the bacon-draped figs stuffed with gorgonzola, tallegio and goat's cheese (£7). Another fun dish is the pan-fried sardines – the largest sardines we've ever seen, and full-flavoured to boot. Juices from the roast chicken breast with sundried tomatoes (£12.50) can be delectably soaked up by an accompanying slice of olive polenta, while the irresistible chocolate tart (£4.25) proves a rich, silken wedge attended by a cone of hazelnut ice cream and a dollop of cherries. The rush on the staff means that service could be a smidgen more attentive – a small price to pay for this restaurant's verve.

Open: Mon-Fri 12.30pm-3pm, 6.30pm-11pm, Sat 12.30pm-3.30pm, 6.30pm-11.30pm, Sun 12.30pm-3.30pm, 6.30pm-11pm; reservations essential; licensed, no BYO

Map 20 B2
Tube: Ladbroke Grove (400m)

Smoking throughout

Pavement tables

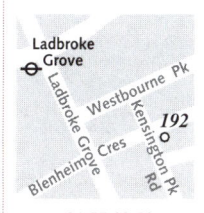

starter £4.75-£8.50
main £8.50-£15.50
dessert £4-£5
wine £10.50-£40
AE DC JCB MC V; SW

NOTTING HILL

Map 20 C3
Tube: Notting Hill Gate (450m)

Smoking throughout

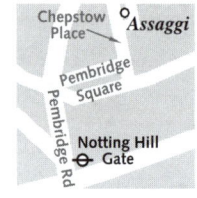

starter £7.95-£10.95
main £9.95-£18.75
dessert £5.75
wine £11.95-£170

AE DC JCB MC V; SW

Assaggi
Italian

☎ 7792 5501
39 Chepstow Place W2

Any restaurant requiring one month's advance booking certainly ought to serve heavenly food – and award-winning Assaggi comfortably clears the bar. The menu includes, for starters, an excellent scallop and squid salad (£10.95), as well as grilled vegetables (£7.95) tinged with just enough olive oil. Mains offer a choice of pasta or meat and fish dishes. The gnocchi (£9.95) is lovely and subtle and the calf's liver (£15.95) is perfectly done and beautifully presented. For dessert, a wedge of chocolate sponge cake (£5.75) with a dollop of ice cream offers exquisite indulgence. With just 11 tables, Assaggi feels homey and relaxed: décor features wooden floors and Rothko-esque paintings, and service is helpful and attentive. Also worth a look is the (unaffiliated) pub downstairs where there's no need to make month-ahead reservations.

Open: Mon-Fri 12.30pm-2.30pm, 7.30pm-11pm, Sat 1pm-2.30pm, 7.30pm-11pm; reservations essential; licensed, no BYO

Map 20 C3
Tube: Notting Hill Gate (400m)

Smoking throughout

starter £5.95-£11.95
main £12.75-£18.50
dessert £5.50
wine £13-£99.50

AE DC MC V; SW

Beach Blanket Babylon
Mediterranean/Thai

☎ 7229 2907
45 Ledbury Rd W11

This stylish but terribly self-conscious eatery has been pulling in the in-crowd for close to a decade with its unique blend of gothic sophistication and theatrical camp. The vault-like restaurant is reached via a fantasy staircase behind the bar and features several extravagant rooms with roaring fireplaces, flickering candles and plenty of ivy. Although there are a few Asian choices, modern European dishes dominate the menu, including an inspired combination of pan-fried pigeon breast (£7.55) with poached pear and rocket, and a splendid roast rack of lamb (£17.95) with a mélange of beans flavoured with tarragon and tomato. Side dishes such as velvety mash with cream (£3.50) are extra. For dessert, cleanse your palate with the French-style strawberry sorbet (£5.50). The staff here can come over as a little cooler-than-thou and it's certainly an expensive night out, but the excellent food makes it worth the splurge.

Open: Mon-Fri noon-3pm, Sat & Sun noon-4pm, daily 7pm-11pm; reservations accepted (advisable at weekends); licensed, no BYO

NOTTING HILL

Churchill Arms
Thai

☎ 7727 4242
119 Kensington Church St W8

Pub grub doesn't get much better than this for the price. In true Thai fashion, the menu gets down to basics by dispensing with starters. There's the usual mix 'n' match offerings of chilli and soya stir-fries, and red, green or jungle curries – all of which can be ordered with pork, beef, chicken or prawns. While this means there's an impressive-sounding 100-odd permutations on offer, the reality is that dishes tend to blur into that generic sameness of meals cooked from the same pot. Portions are large and Churchill's popularity guarantees freshness, but the downside is the occasional lack of attention to detail. It can all be a bit alarming when your table 'slot' is strictly for one and a half hours (just one hour for couples) – but where else in London are you able to eat restaurant-standard food while enjoying a pint in an indoor beer 'garden'?

Open: Mon-Sat noon-2.30pm, 6pm-9.30pm, Sun noon-2.30pm; reservations advisable (essential for dinner); licensed, no BYO

Map 20 D3
Tube: Notting Hill Gate (400m)
Wheelchair access
Smoking throughout

main £5.25-£5.50
dessert £1.75-£1.95
wine £9.95-£15.50

AE DC MC V; SW

(Simon Bracken)

NOTTING HILL

Map 20 D2
Tube: Notting Hill Gate (300m)

Smoking throughout
Terrace tables

starter £3.95-£6
main £9.50-£13
dessert £3.50-£6
wine £10.75-£26.50
MC V; SW

The Ladbroke Arms
Modern British

☎/fax 7727 6648
54 Ladbroke Rd W11

You might have to fight your way through a front bar packed with regulars to get to the old-fashioned dining room, but it's worth the struggle. Some of these locals may lament the transformation from neighbourhood nosh joint to gastropub – you won't. The menu seems a little ho-hum, but the food is star-quality and it's backed up by an eclectic list of affordable wines. Grilled sardines (£6) had the gutsy smokey flavour of classy pub grub, but extremely tender salt-baked salmon (£6), which was served cold, is more typical of the kitchen's contemporary flair. Chopped squid added complexity to the rich reduction pooled around scorched fillets of pan-fried seabass (£13) and moist pan-fried chicken breast (£12) blended beautifully with capers and anchovies. Simple desserts included a powerfully rich chocolate brownie on home-made ice cream (£5.50) which arrived – of course – on an expanse of elegant white china.

Open: Mon-Fri noon-2.30pm, 7pm-9.45pm, Sat & Sun 12.30pm-3pm, 7pm-9.45pm; reservations advisable; licensed, no BYO

(Simon Bracken)

NOTTING HILL

Mandola
Sudanese

☎ 7229 4734
139-141 Westbourne Grove W11

Map 20 B3

Tube: Notting Hill Gate (400m) or Queensway

Smoking throughout

When most people think of Sudan they don't necessarily think of food. You won't be taken on a gastronomic tour at Mandola, but you can expect simple and authentic food served in a cosy atmosphere. Lighting is provided by ruby red candles on the mahogany tables casually arranged in two connecting rooms – it's a bit like being at a large dinner party. Gold paper moons hang in the window and terracotta urns are dotted about. With a BYO policy and a wine shop next door, Mandola is great for big parties. The mixed salad bar (£7.95 for two) is not to be missed: a selection of falafel, baked aubergine, sesame dip, spiced yoghurt, feta and tomato salad, and mixed vegetables, accompanied by oven-baked pita. A word of caution: treat the house 'chilli' with the respect it deserves!

Open: daily noon-5pm, 6pm-11pm; reservations advisable; BYO (corkage £2/bottle)

starter £2.90-£5.50
main £6.50-£10.50
set menu £20
MC V; S

Notting Hill Brasserie
Modern British

☎ 7229 4481
92 Kensington Park Rd W11
www.firmdale.com

Map 20 C2

Tube: Notting Hill Gate (650m)

Smoking throughout

Refined and understated, the Notting Hill Brasserie, owned by Firmdale Hotels, is the latest venture of chef Nial McKenna, an Ireland native specialising in British cuisine. This restaurant's inspiration lies in the décor – unusual wall decorations suggest an intriguing African theme, and the chequered frosted glass on the windows is a classy touch. Flavours of the dishes, an arty spectrum of British cuisine, are similarly subtle – often, alas, a bit too subtle. The papardelle with portobello mushrooms and truffle oil (£6) was a smooth but unremarkable starter, while the feta and olive salad (£5.50), shaped into an elegant column, resonated of, well, feta. For a main, the salmon fishcakes with champagne gratin (£13) were gently textured but needed a good rolling in the sauce to extract any flavour. Service is attentive and helps to make this restaurant an agreeable, if not exceptional, choice for a tête à tête.

Open: Mon-Fri noon-2.30pm, Sat & Sun noon-3pm, daily 6.45pm-10.30pm; reservations advisable (essential at weekends); licensed, no BYO

starter £4.50-£8
main £12-£17
dessert £5.50
set lunch £14.50-£19.50
wine £11.50-£140
AE JCB MC V; SW

NOTTING HILL 223

Map 20 C3
Tube: Notting Hill Gate (400m)

Smoking throughout

Zucca
Contemporary Italian

☎ 7727 0060
188 Westbourne Grove W11

A cocktail in the basement bar is a good place to start: you can survey the hip crowd, listen to mobile phone jingles and admire the hip severity of concrete floors and wooden tables. The lively pulse, in the evening at least, in no way detracts from Zucca's focus on creative comfort food though. The menu is deservedly popular with local vegetarians and full of thoughtful touches. Mr Vine's leaves with goat's cheese (£5.75) combines tangy saltiness with pine nuts and quails eggs, and chicken liver parfait (£7) is a generous hunk of gamey pâté served with eye-watering pickled cabbage. Several designer pizzas are listed, but our helpful waitress steered us towards the delicately flavoured wood-roasted monkfish (£13.50) and a wonderfully creamy roast butternut squash and mascarpone risotto (£8.50). Don't ignore the excellent wine list: a glass of Vin Santo tasted like it had been made with our sublime almond tart (£4.75) in mind.

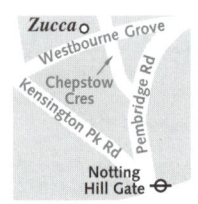

starter £4.50-£7.50
main £7.75-£13.50
dessert £3.75-£5.50
set lunch £12.50 or £14.50
wine £10.75-£76
JCB MC V; SW

Open: Mon-Sat 12.30pm-3pm, 7pm-11pm, Sun 11.30am-3.30pm, 7pm-10.30pm; reservations essential for dinner; licensed, no BYO

Zucca (Carl Drury)

PUTNEY

Ma Goa
Goan

☎ 8780 1767
242-244 Upper Richmond Rd SW15
www.magoa.co.uk

For an Indian that's not quite an Indian, head to the comfortable environment of Ma Goa. Its speciality is the Portuguese-influenced cuisine of Goa. The food (served in glazed terracotta bowls) is infused with fresh herbs and pungent tastes, and the welcome is friendly. Ma Goa's pork sausages (£4) are delicious and spicy, and have a distinct cinnamon flavour. Konkan gallina aur baigan (£8.50) is chunks of chicken breast and aubergine, which initially tastes fairly bland but gradually builds in intensity. The slow cooking method of chini raan xhacutti (£9.50) allows the large cut of lamb shank to thoroughly invest the accompanying tomato-based sauce with lip-smacking juices. Add an extra layer of taste to your main course by opting for the basmati rice cooked in rich vegetable stock (£2.50). If you don't have room for one of the home-made desserts, finish up with a smooth, sweet lassi (£1.95).

Open: Tues-Sat 6.30pm-11pm, Sun 6pm-10pm; reservations advisable; licensed, no BYO

Rail: Putney (250m), tube: East Putney

Entertainment: jazz occasionally on Sunday

Smoking throughout

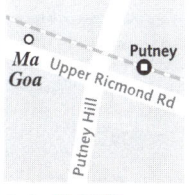

starter £3-£4.50
main £6.50-£9.50
dessert £3.50-£4.50
wine £11.45-£19.65

AE DC JCB MC V; SW

Ma Goa (Carl Drury)

PUTNEY

Tube: Putney Bridge (400m)
Wheelchair access
Smoking throughout

Putney Bridge Restaurant
French

☎ 8780 1811
2 Lower Richmond Rd SW15
www.putneybridgerestaurant.com

The glassy, ship-like Putney Bridge has a curvy leather bar below deck and a classy restaurant above. Linen-clad tables face the river and service is as polished as all that glass. This is premier stuff with stunning amusettes, pre-desserts and nibbles. The displayed crockery is by Picasso, and there's similar artistry in the presentation of the food. The eight or so choices per course are fancier than the menu suggests. A starter of roast squid, marinated seafood and red pepper purée was an over-complex hotch-potch of titbits and highly coloured sauces. Pumpkin and Parmesan crème brûlée was better judged. Several mains were to share – Donald Russell '28-day aged' Scotch rib of beef was worth the wait, although the crushed potatoes weren't great. To finish, caramelised orange with Muscat jelly and a bergamot biscuit was sublime and we didn't know roasted pineapple could taste so good.

à la carte menu £34-£42.50
set lunch Mon-Sat £19.50
Sun lunch £24.50
set dinner £24.50
menu gourmand £69.50
wine £14.50-£2000
AE DC MC V; SW

Open: Tues-Sat noon-2.30pm, Sun 12.30pm-3.30pm, Tues-Thurs 7pm-10.30pm, Fri & Sat 7pm-11pm; reservations advisable; licensed, no BYO

Putney Bridge Restaurant (Carl Drury)

QUEENS PARK

The Salusbury Pub and Dining Room
Modern Italian

☎/fax 7328 3286
50 Salusbury Rd NW6

Diners pass through the vibrant pub to the establishment's calmer other half. Fronted by elegant glass panels, there are higgledy-piggledy paintings covering the deep red walls, a tangle of bamboo on a dark wood counter and big globes of light hanging above the jumble of tables. You could linger here for hours, trying out Venetian chef Enrico Salter's buttery chickpea soup with rosemary (£4) or tender, smoky pan-fried squid with chilli and rocket (£6.50). There are several risottos on offer, such as Swiss chard and pumpkin (£9), in which the disintegrating pumpkin (£9) is an ideal foil to the bite of the rice. A divine cartoccio of seabass fillets with mushrooms and radicchio (£13) allows an intense concentration of flavour. Delicious. But desserts are not for the fainthearted: amaretto, ricotta and almond pudding (£3.95) is nutty and rich, and syroppino proves a savage shot of grappa (£3.95) – perhaps an acquired taste.

Open: Tues-Sun 12.30pm-3.30pm, Mon-Sat 7pm-10.30pm, Sun 7pm-10pm; reservations advisable; licensed, no BYO

Tube/rail: Queens Park (200m)

Smoking throughout

Pavement tables

starter £4-£11
main £9.50-£15
dessert £3.95
wine £9.75-£40

MC V; SW

RICHMOND

Canyon
Contemporary South-West American

☎ 8948 2944
The Tow Path, Riverside (near Richmond Bridge) TW10
www.canyonfood.co.uk

Canyon's modern, airy environment is perfect for sampling its attractively presented American cuisine. Seating overlooks the Thames-lapped garden (landscaped to evoke Arizona) and the riverside promenade provides the only access, so expect some walking or telephone ahead to be met by their electric buggy. From the regularly changing menu, we started with roast vegetables (£5) – a flavoursome combination of courgette, aubergine, sweet potato and bell pepper, accompanied by a tangy tomato sauce. We loved the pheasant (£12), cooked to perfection and resting on a bed of creamy mashed potato, and the fish and chips (£9), enlivened by a chunky tartare sauce. All portions were large, including the dessert of moist chocolate bourbon tart (£5). Service, though slow, was friendly. Weekend brunches are a speciality, with a wide choice from fruit salad to breakfast tortillas.

Open: Mon-Fri noon-3.30pm, 6pm-10.45pm, Sat 11am-4pm, 6pm-10.45pm, Sun 11am-4pm, 6pm-10.30pm; reservations advisable; licensed, no BYO

Tube/rail: Richmond (900m)
Wheelchair access
Nonsmoking areas available
Terrace & courtyard tables

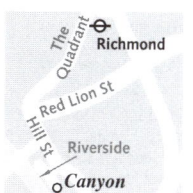

starter £5-£8
main £11-£16
dessert £5
set lunch Mon-Fri £12.95
wine £12-£60

AE JCB MC V; SW

SHEPHERD'S BUSH

Map 21 A2
Tube: Goldhawk Road (100m)

Smoking throughout

starter £3.95-£4.95
main £7.95-£8.95
dessert £4.50

cash or cheque only

Blah Blah Blah!
Vegetarian

☎ 8746 1337
78 Goldhawk Rd W12

Now is a good time to be vegetarian in London. Gourmet cuisine is the primary *raison d'être* of the current meat-free restaurant movement. In common with other such places, this 10-year-old veteran at the vanguard of the scene boasts cheerful staff, a lack of front-of-house pretension, and ambition in the kitchen, where global influences and fresh ingredients provide regular inspiration (the menu changes every six weeks or so). It seems churlish to select only one or two dishes for praise when all are highly desirable, but the boconccini (deep-fried risotto rice fritters filled with mozzarella and dolcelatte, anointed with creamy pesto sauce; £4.50) won our fickle affections, only to have them stolen by the mushroom and gruyere potato cake (£8.95) – wars have been declared over more trifling affairs than the accompanying porcini and Madeira sauce. We tutted impatiently between courses – deliberately relaxed service to heighten anticipation? If so, it worked. Gorgeous.

Open: Mon-Sat 12.30pm-2.30pm, 7pm-11pm; reservations advisable (essential Thurs-Sat); BYO (corkage £1.25/person)

Map 21 A2
Tube: Goldhawk Road (100m)

Wheelchair access
Nonsmoking tables available

starter £3-£6
main £8-£14.75
dessert £3.50-£4.50
set lunch & pre-theatre menu £10
wine £10-£55

MC V; SW

Bush Bar & Grill
French/British

☎ 8746 2111
45a Goldhawk Rd W12

Set back from the road, this dimly lit cocktail bar and restaurant must be doing something right – it's packed with sharply dressed thirty-somethings on a Tuesday night. The food is a major part of the appeal. The fish soup (£4.75) is fabulous: rich, thick and with a strong crustacean flavour. The sizeable bowl of mussels (£5) comes with an understated soup of white wine and garlic. Our entrecôte steak (£14.75) was tender and juicy, though 'medium rare' looked decidedly 'medium' to us and we thought it terribly oversalted. The calves liver (£9) had the desired melt-in-the-mouth quality but was also too salty for our taste. Things were back on form for the desserts: the lychee sorbet (£3.50) is very refreshing, while the chocolate brownies (£4.50) are nutty and moist. If you ask them to lay off the salt, you can have a great meal here.

Open: Mon-Sat noon-3.30pm, 6.30pm-11.30pm, Sun noon-4pm, 7pm-11pm; reservations advisable; licensed, no BYO

Organic Street Preachers

Foot and mouth, mad cow disease and the GM (genetically modified) food controversy have done much to drive the organic point home. Out is the hippy image and in are restaurants that use organic ingredients, such as **The Crown Organic Pub** (page 140), **The Duke of Cambridge** (page 116) and **SauCe** (page 102), organic markets (see Farmers Markets, page 146), and sleek designer shops where the healthy ethos reigns. So if you fancy eating in rather than out and are after some clean-living fare, why not visit one of these:

As Nature Intended 201 Chiswick High Road, Chiswick W4 ☎ 8742 8838
Light, spacious designer organic supermarket with around 4,000 products ranging from quality meats and lush fruit to household goods and natural remedies. There's an excellent choice of wines, preserves and baby food.

Bumblebee 30-33 Brecknock Rd, Kentish Town N7 ☎ 7607 1936
Bumblebee has provided organic, vegetarian and wholefood produce since 1980. With around 1,200 organic lines, specialities include delicious organic cheeses, olive oils and wines. Lunchtime vegetarian takeaway is available and there's a local delivery service.

Fresh & Wild 49 Parkway, Camden NW1 ☎ 7428 7575
This hip, good-looking supermarket sells fruit, veg, breads, wines, meat, fish and Epicurean groceries that look far too tempting to be healthy. There's also an impressive deli and juice bar, and branches in Clapham, Old Street, Soho, Stoke Newington and Westbourne Grove.

Kelly's Organic Foods 46 Northcote Rd, Clapham SW11 ☎ 7207 3967
Kelly's is spacious – and popular, not least because of the mouth-watering deli counter. Appropriately for a store in 'Nappy Valley', in among the tables of greens, wheat-free breads and dairy-free produce you can find every kind of organic baby food imaginable.

Old Spitalfields Organic Market 65 Brushfield St, City E1 ☎ 01279 444663
Purporting to be London's largest organic market, Spitalfields is hard to beat for good-value organic fruit and veg sold by registered producers. You'll also find a range of organic meats, dairy products, wines and wholefoods. Check out the hemp stall.

Planet Organic 42 Westbourne Grove, Bayswater W2 ☎ 7221 7171
Planet Organic is healthy supermarket shopping, with a great range of good quality organic fruit, veg, meat, fish, cheeses, wines and beers, all clearly labelled. Health supplements, beauty products, magazines, plants and flowers are also available, as well as mail order, a delivery service and another branch in Fitzrovia.

Ye Olde English Organic Greengrocer Junction Rd, Archway N19 ☎ 7263 8565
This store is a cut above with 200-plus lines, including superior fresh produce, an impressive collection of olive oils and mounds of oozing ripe cheeses. Try their exclusive organic breads and delicious deli fare.

Susan Grimshaw

SOUTH KENSINGTON

Map 19 B5
Tube: South Kensington (450m)

Smoking throughout

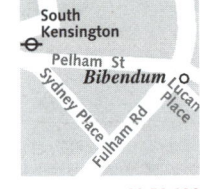

Bibendum
Modern European

☎ **7581 5817**
81 Fulham Rd SW3
www.conran.com

Approaching Bibendum it's easy to picture the glint in Terence Conran's eye when he took a gamble and decided to transform a decrepit Michelin garage into a gleaming phoenix of architectural and gastronomic eclecticism. Constructed in 1909, the building is an inspired jumble of Art Nouveau styles; sunlight falling through aquamarine stained-glass windows bathes diners in an oceanic glow. Bibendum's rich, trans-European menu is as marvellously varied as the surroundings. Ballotine of fresh foie gras (£19.50) was nothing to honk about, but the strapping escargots de Bourgogne (£17.50) slid willingly from their shells, a sensuous delight. Main dishes were consistently fine; stalwart roast rabbit (£18.50) wrapped in dainty cones of bacon and juicy, humongous grilled Bresse pigeon (£21) left little room for the divine pithiviers au chocolat (chocolate pastry cake; £8.50). Ask the engaging staff for assistance in deciphering the hefty wine list, 900-bottles strong.

starter £6.50-£32
main £15.50-£27
dessert £6.50-£8.50
set lunch Mon-Fri £24.50 or £28
wine £17.50-£1100
AE DC MC V; SW

Open: Mon-Fri noon-2.30pm, 7pm-11.30pm, Sat noon-3pm, 7pm-11.30pm, Sun noon-3pm, 7pm-10.30pm; reservations essential; licensed, no BYO

Bibendum (Carl Drury)

SOUTH KENSINGTON

Cambio de Tercio
Modern Spanish

☎ 7244 8970
163 Old Brompton Rd SW5

Cambio de tercio is a bull-fighting term – hence the matador-red chairs and memorabilia on the deep orange walls of this vibrant restaurant. Gourmet fare remains true to Spain and service stays friendly, despite the crowds. Do as Spaniards do and opt for the later of the two evening sittings. Likewise with starters: share them as tapas. The jamón de Jabugo (£14), from an acorn-fed rare pig breed, should be sampled. Cod-mousse-stuffed pimentos (£7.50), another Spanish classic, are excellent and smothered in a creamy red sauce. A main of melt-in-the-mouth oxtail (£13.90) contrasts wonderfully with crispy potato rounds. Simple fish dishes of cod in olive oil and hake with clams (both £13.50) are subtle. Leche frita (fried milk; £4.90) is a Spanish-style nursery pud, offset by apricot sorbet and peppermint tea sauce. A plate of Spanish cheeses (£7) comes with a first-rate membrillo (quince marmalade).

Open: daily noon-2.30pm, Mon-Sat 7pm-11.30pm, Sun 7pm-11pm; reservations advisable (essential for dinner); licensed, no BYO

Map 19 C2
Tube: Gloucester Road (500m)
Smoking throughout
Pavement tables

starter £6-£14
main £12.50-£14.90
dessert £4.90
menu degustation £30
wine £13.50-£390
AE JCB MC V; SW

Daquise
Polish/Continental

☎ 7589 6117
20 Thurloe St SW7

Entering Daquise is a bit like stepping into an old-fashioned, sepia-toned picture. The décor is in varying shades of brown, cream and yellow, and the only sound you can hear above the soft buzz of conversation is the creaking of the dumb waiter. It's all very Polish but awfully English at the same time – serious, but pleasantly eccentric. The service is of the no-nonsense variety and the food is solid, cold-climate fare (potato pancakes, hunters stew, meatballs) that's best appreciated after a winter's day walk across Hyde Park. The blinis (Russian pancakes) with smoked salmon (£3.50) were satisfyingly fat and full of buckwheat flavour, but they left plenty of room for the chunky, mildly spicy pork sausage (£6) served with a mountain of just-caramelised fried onion and mashed potato. There's also a an alluring range of pâtisseries such as cheesecake, apple strudel and home-made Polish doughnuts with rose jam.

Open: daily 11am-11pm; reservations advisable; licensed & BYO (corkage £5/bottle)

Map 19 B4
Tube: South Kensington (50m)
Nonsmoking tables available

starter £2.50-£3.50
main £5.50-£12.50
dessert £1.20-£4
set lunch Mon-Fri £7.50
wine £8.50-£12.50
MC V; SW

SOUTH KENSINGTON

Map 19 B5
Tube: South Kensington (500m)

Smoking throughout

El Rincón
Modern Spanish

☎ 7584 6655
2a Pond Place SW3

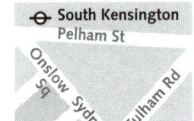

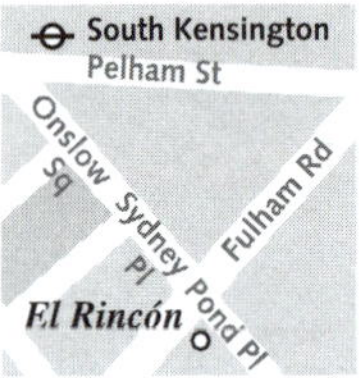

With minimalist décor and careful use of light and space, those at the helm of El Rincón have successfully transformed a fusty dance club into an attractive restaurant. We chose to browse the small menu in the comfort of the bar. Once at the table we found the selection of tapas (£7.50) a perfect launch pad into the world of *nouveau Éspagnol*. The platter included the full compliment of starters. Pears with blue cheese were exceptional, as were the sardines. After skipping through the tapas, the rich flavours of the mains demanded more attention. Tender salmon (£13.95) was enhanced by orange roasted chicory, while roasted cod (£13.25) was ancillary to the delicious saffron mash. With a subtle cinnamon taste, créme Catalan (crème brûlée; £4.50) was an appropriately sweet end to the meal. Service was efficient and cheerful, and we left confident that sometimes it is worth paying a little more.

South Kensington
Pelham St
El Rincón

starter £4.50-£7.50
main £11.50-£14.25
dessert £4.50-£5.50
wine £11.50-£52

AE DC MC V; SW

Open: Mon 6pm-11pm, Tues-Sat noon-3pm, 6pm-11pm; reservations accepted; licensed & BYO (corkage £10/bottle)

Map 19 B3
Tube: Gloucester Road (500m)

Smoking throughout

Pavement tables

Lundum's
Danish

☎ 7373 7774
119 Old Brompton Rd SW7

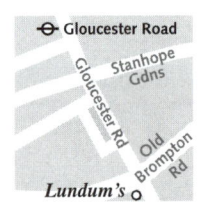

This snug, family-run restaurant serves up fabulous Danish fare in a comfortably serene setting. Lunch offerings include a smorgasbord of open sandwiches featuring smoked eel, salt beef and other traditional Danish treats. Dinner blends Danish and French cuisine – doubtless a tribute to the talented chef, Franck Dietrich, who is himself of both nations. The seafood at Lundum's is superb – for dinner, the oven-baked monkfish (£15.25), bathed with a red wine and shallot sauce, is restrained and wonderful. Another worthy delicacy is the salted salmon starter with salmon caviar and horseradish cream (£6.75). Mr Dietrich's mastery extends well beyond fish – the roast duck in Medoc sauce (£14.75) comes pink and divine, rich but pure. As for beverages, the nine-page wine list provides helpful suggestions on matching wines with dishes. Service is capable and efficient, and the sprinkling of tweed jackets suggests that plenty of Danes have discovered Lundum's delights.

Gloucester Road
Stanhope Gdns
Lundum's

starter £3-£8
main £6-£16
dessert £3.50-£8
set lunch £12.50 or £15.50
set dinner £21.50
wine £12.50-£160

AE DC JCB MC V; SW

Open: Mon-Sat noon-4pm, 6pm-10pm, Sun noon-1.30pm; reservations advisable (essential for dinner and Sunday); licensed, no BYO

SOUTH KENSINGTON

Ognisko
Polish

☎ 7589 4635
55 Exhibition Rd SW7

Spinning past the V&A, the cab driver informed me that 'there ain't no restaurants on Prince's Gate, love'. Granted, Ognisko is more of a club for Polish gentry – the ancestors of whom hang immortalised on the walls – than a restaurant. Nevertheless, the golden chandeliers, cornices and marble pillars unite with salmon walls and a soundtrack of Chopin to invite diners unconditionally to be their guest. We tried the Ukrainian beetroot soup (£4.30) laced with delicate creamy spirals and topped with parsley – delicious. All the Polish favourites are represented, including the ubiquitous dumplings, game and meat platters. The shashlik (£10.80) was a tangy skewer of lamb with smoky, roasted peppers and onions on a bed of rocket, with mange touts, haricot verts, courgettes and leeks a veritable emerald treat on the side. Put your glad rags on because pure indulgence is fabulous once in a while.

Open: daily noon-3pm, 6.30pm-11pm; reservations advisable; licensed, no BYO

Map 19 A4
Tube: South Kensington (500m)

Nonsmoking tables available

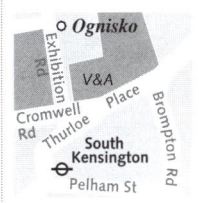

Terrace tables

starter £3-£11.20
main £7.20-£13.90
dessert £2.50-£3.90
set lunch £8
wine £9.80-£27

AE DC MC V; SW

Texas Lone Star Saloon
Tex-Mex

☎ 7370 5625
154 Gloucester Rd SW7

Bring all the family, a hearty appetite and a sense of fun to the bustling, lively Western-style Lone Star, London's oldest and most popular tex-mex saloon where everything comes in Texan-sized portions. Try the bowls of nachos piled mountain high (£3.95), a monster slab of spare ribs (£9.50) or the whopping 12oz steaks (£12.50) – a must for meat-lovers. Even the frozen fruit margaritas come by the jugful (£21) and the beers by the bucket (£14.40). The spicy three-bean Mexican soup (£3.45) set the taste buds tingling, but didn't score highly on presentation. The succulent beef and chicken fajitas (£8.95), served with the usual colourful lashings of sour cream, guacamole and salsa, more than compensated. The giant stuffed moose on the wall eagerly eyed our meal throughout, but the leftovers came home with us in true American style – in a doggy bag. *Also at 50-54 Turnham Green Terrace, W4* ☎ *8747 0001.*

Open: daily noon-11.30pm; reservations accepted; licensed no BYO

Map 19 B3
Tube: Gloucester Road (150m)
Entertainment: live music Wed, Thurs & Sun evening

Separate smoke-free dining available

starter £2.60-£5.25
main £5.75-£14.50
dessert £2.50-£4.95
wine £8.95-£15.45

AE MC V; SW

TEDDINGTON

Rail: Teddington (900m)
Wheelchair access
Entertainment: live band Thurs evening
Nonsmoking tables available
Terrace tables

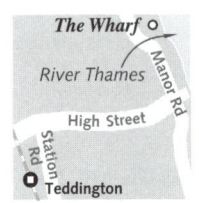

The Wharf
Modern European

☎ 8977 6333
22 Manor Rd TW11
www.walk-on-water.co.uk

starter £4.50-£7
main £8.50-£13.50
dessert £5.50
set menu £22.50
wine £11-£110
AE MC V; SW

'Location, location, location' say estate agents. The same formula applies to eating out and The Wharf provides it in spades – customers can enjoy the view over Teddington lock, where boats and pedestrians meander to and fro. Upstairs, the oriental room (open Monday to Saturday evenings) has a good reputation. Downstairs the brasserie, packed with families for Sunday lunch, serves competent European fare. The rocket salad (£4.50) was fresh if unremarkable and the potato gnocchi (£11) too gooey and heavy. The braised lamb shank (£10.50) was better – the sauce tangy and the meat falling nicely off the bone. Desserts (£5.50) were a mixed bag. The chocolate and raspberry tart didn't work too well, and the 'amaretto' ice cream tasted only of apricot. The Wharf is best enjoyed in summer when the roof is rolled back. Consider getting there via an enjoyable appetite-building riverside walk from Kingston or Twickenham.

Open: Mon-Sat noon-11pm, Sun noon-5pm, 6pm-11pm; reservations accepted (except Sat evenings); licensed, no BYO

WESTBOURNE PARK

Bali Sugar
Fusion

☎ 7221 4477
33a All Saints Rd W11

The name Bali Sugar doesn't do this exquisite little restaurant justice. Images of some typical Asian joint serving up piles of so-so nasi goreng are far from reality as chef Claudio Aprile melds Asian and Latin cooking in a way that could almost put some life back into the overused moniker 'fusion'. The char-grilled squid starter (£7.90) with black-bean salsa and Thai dressing is a mélange of fresh flavours and spices which perfectly captures the ethos of the place. The grilled chorizo salad (£8.50) shows the potential of a dish that is so often just a pile of mixed greens. Mains include crispy salmon (£15.90) that comes perched on a beautiful arrangement of sweet potato tempura and cucumber kimchi. While the wine list reflects the eclectic menu, the décor is spare but elegant – the perfect backdrop to the food and your companions.

Open: Sat & Sun 11.30am-3.30pm, daily 6.30pm-11pm; reservations essential; licensed, no BYO

Map 20 B2
Tube: Ladbroke Grove (350m) or Westbourne Park
No smoking (one level), smoking throughout (one level)
Garden tables

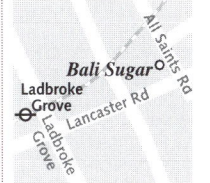

starter £4.50-£11.50
main £13.10-£18
dessert £5.50
weekend brunch £12.50
wine £11.50-£250
AE DC JCB MC V; SW

The Cow
Modern British

☎ 7221 5400
89 Westbourne Park Rd W2

It seems the owner, Tom Conran, has inherited his father Terence's style. This little pub looks unassuming from the outside, and its pretty unassuming inside: it simply provides great atmosphere and great food at prices that don't offend. The downstairs bistro and bar does an excellent lunch; upstairs is a posher nosherie, but the fare coming out of chef James Rix's kitchen is well worth the couple of pounds extra. We ate downstairs on our most recent visit and had the rare bavette steak (£9.50), as sickeningly blue as it was excellent, and the perfectly prepared French onion tart (£7.75). The only sweet option was crème brûlée (£4.50), which took some breaking into – effort well spent. If you're eating upstairs, be prepared to be subjected to odious fumes from smokers indulging in the cigar selection, and to the sort of folk who smoke cigars. But it's a small price to pay.

Open: Mon-Fri 12.30pm-3pm, Sat & Sun 12.30pm-4pm, Mon-Sat 7pm-11pm, Sun 7.30pm-10.30pm; reservations advisable; licensed, no BYO

Map 20 A3
Tube: Royal Oak (450m) or Westbourne Park
Nonsmoking tables available
Pavement tables

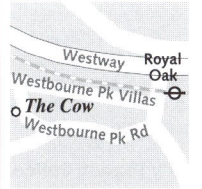

starter £4.50-£8.50
main £12-£16
dessert £5.25
wine £12-£25
AE MC V; SW

Lonely Planet Products

City Products

City Guides offer an in-depth view to over 50 cities around the globe. Featuring the top restaurants, bars and clubs as well as information on accommodation and transport, these guides are suited to long-term and business travellers and anyone who wants to know everything about a city. They come with reliable, easy-to-use maps, cultural and historical facts and a run-down on attractions, old and new.

For the discerning short-term visitor, **Condensed** guides highlight the best a destination has to offer in a full-colour pocket-sized format designed for quick access. From top sights and walking tours to opinionated reviews of where to eat, stay, shop and have fun.

CitySync lets travellers use their Palm™ or Visor™ hand-held computers to guide them through a city's highlights with quick tips on transport, history, cultural life, major sights and shopping and entertainment options. It can also quickly search and sort hundreds of reviews of hotels, restaurants and attractions and pinpoint the place on scrollable street maps. CitySync can be downloaded from www.citysync.com.

City Maps

Lonely Planet's **City Maps** feature downtown and metropolitan maps as well as transit routes and walking tours. The maps come complete with an index of streets, a listing of sights and plastic coated for extra durability.

Food Guides

For people who live to eat, drink and travel, **World Food** guides explore the culinary culture of each country. Entertaining and adventurous, each guide is packed with detail on staples and specialities, regional cuisine and local markets, as well as sumptuous recipes, comprehensive culinary dictionaries and lavish photos good enough to eat.

Lonely Planet Online

Lonely Planet's award-winning Web site, has insider information on hundreds of destinations from Amsterdam to Zimbabwe complete with interactive maps and relevant links. The site also offers the latest travel news, recent reports from travellers on the road, guidebook upgrades, a travel links site, an online book-buying option and a lively traveller's bulletin board. It can be viewed at www.lonelyplanet.com or AOL keyword: lp.

Lonely Planet Offices

Australia
90 Maribyrnong St, Locked Bag 1,
Footscray VIC 3011
☎ 03 9689 4666
fax 03 9689 6833
email: out2eat@lonelyplanet.com.au
talk2us@lonelyplanet.com.au

USA
150 Linden St, Oakland,
CA 94607
☎ 510 893 8555
TOLL FREE: 800 275 8555
fax 510 893 8572
email: info@lonelyplanet.com

UK
10a Spring Place, London NW5 3BH
☎ 020 7428 4800
fax 020 7428 4828
email: go@lonelyplanet.co.uk

France
1 rue du Dahomey, 75011 Paris
☎ 01 55 25 33 00
fax 01 55 25 33 01
email: bip@lonelyplanet.fr

Web
www.lonelyplanet.com or AOL keyword: lp

Lonely Planet Images
lpi@lonelyplanet.com.au

Thanks

Thanks to all the restaurants who kindly allowed us to take photographs for this edition:

Asia de Cuba, Bah Humbug, Bam-Bou, Belgo, Bengal Clipper, Bibendum, Bluebird, The Café in the Crypt, China City, The Conservatory at the Lanesborough, The Crown, fish!, Fish in a Tie, The Gate, Gay Hussar, Isola, Le Pont de la Tour, Lemongrass, Ma Goa, Mezzo, Mô tea-room, Oxo Tower Restaurant, Patogh, The Pepper Tree, Phat Phuc Noodle Bar, PJ's Restaurant, Putney Bridge Restaurant, Quilon, Ransome's Dock, The Real Greek, The Rock and Sole Plaice, satsuma, Tiroler Hut, Vic Naylor, Villandry, Yo! Sushi, Zamoyski and Zucca.

INDEX

RESTAURANT NAME	PAGE NUMBER	Wheelchair access	Child friendly	Outdoor	Private room	Business	Romantic
1 Blossom Street, City ☎ 7247 6532	25	●			●	●	
192, Notting Hill ☎ 7229 0482	219		●	●			●
291, Bethnal Green ☎ 7613 5675	127	●	●	●	●		●
Abeno, Bloomsbury ☎ 7405 3211	19		●				
Abu Ali, Edgware Road ☎ 7724 6338	39			●			
The Admiralty, Aldwych ☎ 7724 6338	15	●	●		●	●	
Afghan Kitchen, Islington ☎ 7359 8019	113		●				
a.k.a bar & restaurant, Bloomsbury ☎ 7836 0110	136	●			●		
Al Dar, Edgware Road ☎ 7402 2541	39		●	●			
Alastair Little, Soho ☎ 7734 5183	73		●		●	●	
The Albion, Islington ☎ 7607 7450	182	●	●	●			
Alwaha, Bayswater ☎ 7229 0806	185		●			●	●
Anchor Bankside, Southwark ☎ 7407 1577	197		●	●	●		●
Andrew Edmunds, Soho ☎ 7437 5708	73						
The Anglesea Arms, Hammersmith ☎ 8749 1291	200		●	●			
Antipasto & Pasta, Battersea ☎ 7223 9765	149		●	●	●		
Aperitivo, Soho ☎ 7287 2057	74		●		●		
The Apprentice, Bermondsey ☎ 7234 0254	153	●	●			●	
Arancia, Bermondsey ☎ 7394 1751	154				●		●
The Ard-Ri Dining Room, Marylebone ☎ 7696 8994	51				●	●	●
Arkansas Café, Spitalfields ☎ 7377 6999	144		●	●	●		
Aroma II, Chinatown ☎/fax 7437 0377	22		●		●		
Artigiano, Belsize Park ☎ 7794 4288	98			●		●	●
Asia de Cuba, Covent Garden ☎ 7300 5500	32	●				●	●
Asmara, Brixton ☎ 7737 4144	159		●				●
Assaggi, Notting Hill ☎ 7792 5501	220		●			●	●
Astons, Kensal Rise ☎ 8969 2184	203		●	●			

INDEX

RESTAURANT NAME	PAGE NUMBER	Wheelchair access	Child friendly	Outdoor	Private room	Business	Romantic
Aurora, Soho ☎ 7494 0514	75		●	●	●		●
The Avenue, Mayfair ☎ 7321 2111	55	●	●			●	
Bah Humbug, Brixton ☎ 7738 3184	160	●	●	●			
Bali Sugar, Westbourne Park ☎ 7221 4477	235			●	●		●
Bam-Bou, Fitzrovia ☎ 7323 9130	43			●	●	●	●
Bank Aldwych, Aldwych ☎ 7379 9797	15	●	●			●	
Bank Westminster, Westminster ☎ 7379 9797	92		●	●		●	●
Bar and Dining House, Islington ☎ 7704 8789	114		●				
Baradero, Docklands ☎ 7321 2111	134	●	●	●	●	●	●
Beach Blanket Babylon, Notting Hill ☎ 7229 2907	220			●	●		●
Belair House, Dulwich ☎ 8299 9788	169	●	●	●	●	●	●
The Bell and Crown, Chiswick ☎ 8994 4164	197	●		●			
Bengal Clipper, Bermondsey ☎ 7357 9001	154		●			●	
Benihana, Piccadilly ☎ 7494 2525	65		●		●		
Bibendum, South Kensington ☎ 7581 5817	230		●			●	●
Bistro Daniel, Lancaster Gate ☎ 7723 8395	217			●	●	●	●
blackpepper, Clapham ☎ 7978 4863	163		●	●			●
Blah Blah Blah!, Shepherd's Bush ☎ 8746 1337	228		●				
Bleeding Heart Bistro, Clerkenwell ☎ 7242 8238	130		●	●	●	●	●
Bluebird, Chelsea ☎ 7559 1111	189	●	●	●	●	●	●
Blues Bistro & Bar, Soho ☎ 7494 1966	75	●	●		●		
Boardwalk, Soho ☎ 7287 2051	136						
Bombay Bicycle Club, Clapham ☎ 8673 6217	164		●		●		●
Borshcht 'n' Tears, Knightsbridge ☎ 7584 9911	210		●		●		●
Brasserie du Marché, Ladbroke Grove ☎ 8968 5828	216		●	●	●		●
The Bridge Brasserie & Bar, City ☎ 7236 0000	25	●	●	●		●	
Brixtonian Havana Club, Brixton ☎ 7924 9262	161			●			

INDEX 239

INDEX

RESTAURANT NAME	PAGE NUMBER	Wheelchair access	Child friendly	Outdoor	Private room	Business	Romantic
Brown's Hotel, Mayfair ☎ 7493 6020	50	●	●				
Buchan's, Battersea ☎ 7228 0888	150		●	●		●	●
Buona Sera at the Jam, Chelsea ☎ 7352 8827	189						
Bush Bar & Grill, Shepherd's Bush ☎ 8746 2111	228	●	●		●		
Butlers Wharf Chop House, Bermondsey ☎ 7403 3403	155	●	●	●		●	●
Café Bintang, Camden ☎ 7428 9603	98						
Café des Amis, Covent Garden ☎ 7379 3444	32		●	●	●	●	
Café Emm, Soho ☎ 7437 0723	76		●				
Café Espana, Soho ☎ 7494 1271	76		●			●	
The Café in the Crypt, Trafalgar Square ☎ 7839 4342	90		●		●		
Café Japan, Golders Green ☎ 8455 6854	108						
Café Naz, Brick Lane ☎ 7247 0234	128				●		
Café Portugal, Stockwell ☎ 7587 1962	178		●	●		●	●
Cafe Sol, Clapham ☎ 7498 8558	136	●	●	●			
Cafe Spice Namaste, City ☎ 7488 9242	26		●		●	●	
Calabash, Covent Garden ☎ 7836 1976	33		●		●		●
Cambio de Tercio, South Kensington ☎ 7244 8970	231			●	●	●	●
Cantina Italia, Islington ☎ 7226 9791	114		●				
Cantina del Ponte, Bermondsey ☎ 7403 5403	156		●	●			
Cantuccio, Clapham ☎ 7924 5588	164						
Canyon, Richmond ☎ 8948 2944	227	●	●	●		●	
Cargo, Shoreditch ☎ 7739 3440	136	●	●	●			
Carmen, Clapham ☎ 7622 6848	165		●				
Carnevale, Hoxton ☎ 7250 3452	141		●				
Centrale, Soho ☎ 7437 5513	77		●				
Che, St James's ☎ 7747 9380	70	●			●	●	
The Chelsea Ram, Chelsea ☎ 7351 4008	190	●		●	●		

240 LONELY PLANET OUT TO EAT

INDEX

RESTAURANT NAME	PAGE NUMBER	Wheelchair access	Child friendly	Outdoor	Private room	Business	Romantic
Chez Bruce, Wandsworth ☎ 8672 0114	180		●		●	●	●
cheznico, Mayfair ☎ 7409 1290	55	●	●		●	●	●
China City, Chinatown ☎ 7734 3388	22				●	●	
China House, Piccadilly ☎ 7499 6996	66		●			●	
The Chiswick Restaurant, Chiswick ☎ 8994 6887	193		●	●		●	●
Chives, Fulham ☎ 7351 4747	198		●	●	●	●	
Christopher's, Covent Garden ☎ 7240 4222	33		●		●	●	●
Churchill Arms, Notting Hill ☎ 7727 4242	221	●					
Chutney Mary, Fulham ☎ 7351 3113	198		●		●	●	
Cigala, Holborn ☎ 7405 1717	47		●	●			●
Cinnamon Club, Westminster ☎ 7222 2555	93	●	●		●	●	●
Circus Restaurant & Bar, Soho ☎ 7534 4000	77		●		●	●	
City Rhodes, City ☎ 7583 1313	26	●	●		●	●	
Claridge's Hotel, Mayfair ☎ 7629 8860	50	●	●				
The Connaught, Mayfair ☎ 7499 7070	56		●		●	●	
The Conservatory, Belgravia ☎ 7259 5599	17	●	●			●	●
Coopers, Holborn ☎ 7831 6211	48					●	
Cotto, Kensington Olympia ☎ 7602 9333	207		●	●		●	●
Country Life, Soho ☎ 7434 2922	78				●	●	
The County Hall Restaurant, South Bank ☎ 7902 8000	172		●		●	●	
Court Restaurant, Bloomsbury ☎ 7323 8990	19	●	●		●	●	
The Cow, Westbourne Park ☎ 7221 5400	235		●	●		●	●
Coyote Café, Chiswick ☎ 8742 8545	194	●	●	●			
The Criterion, Piccadilly ☎ 7930 0488	66	●	●			●	●
Crocker's Folly, Marylebone ☎ 7286 6608	182	●	●	●			
The Crown, Islington ☎ 8742 8545	115		●	●			●
The Crown & Goose, Camden ☎ 8742 8545	99		●	●	●		●

INDEX

RESTAURANT NAME	PAGE NUMBER	Wheelchair access	Child friendly	Outdoor	Private room	Business	Romantic
The Crown Organic Pub, Hackney ☎ 8742 8545	140	●	●	●	●		●
Cuba Libra, Islington ☎ 7354 9998	136		●				
Cucina, Hampstead ☎ 7435 7814	109		●			●	
Daquise, South Kensington ☎ 7589 6117	231		●		●		
Delfina Studio Café, Bermondsey ☎ 7357 0244	156	●	●		●	●	
The Depôt, Mortlake ☎ 8878 9462	218		●	●			
Detroit, Covent Garden ☎ 7240 2662	34				●		●
The Dining Room, Barnsbury ☎ 7609 3009	97		●	●			
Dish Dash, Fitzrovia ☎ 7037 7474	44		●				
Diwana Bhel Poori House, Euston ☎ 7387 5556	42		●		●		
Don Pepe, Edgware Road ☎ 7262 3834/7723 9749	40		●			●	●
The Don Restaurant and Bistro, City ☎ 7626 2606	27					●	
The Dove, Hammersmith ☎ 8748 5405	197			●		●	
The Drawing Room, Clapham ☎ 7350 2564	165		●	●	●		●
The Duke of Cambridge, Islington ☎ 7359 9450	116		●	●	●		●
The Eagle, Clerkenwell ☎ 7837 1353	130		●	●			
Eco, Clapham ☎ 7978 1108	166		●				
El Parador, Camden ☎ 7387 2789	99		●	●	●		●
El Rincón, South Kensington ☎ 7584 6655	232					●	●
The Engineer, Primrose Hill ☎ 7722 0950	119	●	●	●			●
Estrela Bar, Stockwell ☎ 7793 1051	179		●	●	●		●
Fairuz, Marylebone ☎ 7486 8108	52		●			●	●
Fiction, Crouch End ☎ 8340 3403	103		●	●	●	●	●
Fina Estampa, Southwark ☎/fax 7403 1342	177		●		●	●	
First Edition, Docklands ☎ 7513 0300	135		●	●		●	
fish!, South Bank ☎ 7234 3333	172	●	●			●	●
Fish in a Tie, Clapham ☎ 7513 0300	166				●		●

242 LONELY PLANET OUT TO EAT

INDEX

RESTAURANT NAME	PAGE NUMBER	Wheelchair access	Child friendly	Outdoor	Private room	Business	Romantic
Fish Tank, Mortlake ☎ 8878 3535	218			●		●	●
The Flask, Highgate ☎ 8348 7346	182		●	●	●		
Foliage, Knightsbridge ☎ 7235 2000	210	●				●	
Fortnum & Mason, Piccadilly ☎ 7734 8040	50	●	●				
Frederick's, Islington ☎ 7359 2888	116		●	●	●	●	●
French House Dining Room, Soho ☎ 7437 2477	78		●			●	●
The Frog and Forget-Me-Not, Clapham ☎ 7622 5230	182	●	●	●			
Fujiyama, Brixton ☎ 7737 2369	161		●		●		
Fung Shing, Chinatown ☎ 7437 1539	23				●	●	
Futures Café-Bar, City ☎ 74638 6341	27	●	●	●			
Galiano's, Highbury ☎ 7359 9042	112		●				●
The Gallery, Brixton ☎ 7671 8311	162		●				●
Garbo's, Marylebone ☎/fax 7262 6582	52		●		●		●
The Gate, Hammersmith ☎/fax 7262 6582	200			●		●	●
Gaudi, Clerkenwell ☎ 7608 3220	131		●		●		
Gay Hussar, Soho ☎ 7437 0973	79		●		●	●	●
Giotto, Bloomsbury ☎/fax 7323 0891	20		●			●	
Giovanni's, Covent Garden ☎ 7240 2877	34		●			●	●
The Glasshouse, Kew ☎ 8940 6777	209		●				
Gordon Ramsay, Chelsea ☎ 7352 4441	191	●	●			●	●
The Goring Dining Room, Victoria ☎ 7396 9000	91	●	●		●		
Grano, Chiswick ☎ 8995 0120	194	●	●		●	●	●
The Grapes, Docklands ☎ 7987 4396	197			●	●		●
Great Eastern Dining Room, Shoreditch ☎ 7613 4545	141		●		●	●	
High Holborn, Holborn ☎ 7404 3338	48	●				●	●
Home, Shoreditch ☎ 7684 8618	142	●			●	●	●
Honest Cabbage, Bermondsey ☎ 7234 0080	157	●	●				

INDEX 243

INDEX

RESTAURANT NAME	PAGE NUMBER	Wheelchair access	Child friendly	Outdoor	Private room	Business	Romantic
The House, Hampstead ☎ 7435 8037	109	●	●	●			
Hujo's, Soho ☎ 7734 5144	80		●				●
Hunan, Pimlico ☎ 7730 5712	68						●
Hung To, Bayswater ☎ 7727 5753	186		●				
hush, Mayfair ☎ 7659 1500	56	●		●	●	●	●
Idaho, Highgate ☎ 8341 6633	112	●	●	●	●	●	
Ikkyu, Japanese ☎ 7636 9280	44				●		
Inaho, Bayswater ☎ 7221 8495	186						
Incognico, Leicester Square ☎ 7836 8866	49		●			●	
Inside, Greenwich ☎/fax 8265 5060	170	●				●	●
Isola, Knightsbridge ☎ 7838 1044	211		●			●	●
The Ivy, Covent Garden ☎ 7836 4751	35		●		●	●	●
Jack's Place, Battersea ☎ 7228 8519	151		●				
Jashan, Turnpike Lane ☎ 8340 9880	124		●			●	
Jason's Wharf, Maida Vale ☎ 7286 6752	118	●	●	●	●	●	●
Jen, Chinatown ☎ 7287 8193	24				●		
Jenny Lo's Tea House, Victoria ☎ 7259 0399	92			●	●		
Jerusalem, Soho ☎ 7255 1120	137						
Julie's, Holland Park ☎ 7229 8331	202		●	●	●		●
Kam-Pai!, Islington ☎ 7833 1380	117		●				
Kastoori, Tooting ☎ 8767 7027	180						
Kennington Lane, Kennington ☎ 7793 8313	170		●	●			
Kettners, Soho ☎ 7734 6112	80		●		●		
La Bota, Crouch End ☎ 8340 3082	103						
La Brocca, West Hampstead ☎ 7433 1989	124		●	●			●
La Porchetta, Finsbury Park ☎ 7281 2892	105		●		●		
La Porte des Indes, Marble Arch ☎ 7224 0055	51		●		●	●	●

INDEX

RESTAURANT NAME	PAGE NUMBER	Wheelchair access	Child friendly	Outdoor	Private room	Business	Romantic
La Poule au Pot, Pimlico ☎ 7730 7763	69		●	●	●		●
La Tante Claire, Knightsbridge ☎ 7823 2003	212	●	●		●	●	
La Trompette, Chiswick ☎ 8747 1836	195			●		●	●
Lal Qila, Bloomsbury ☎ 7387 4570	20		●				
L'Accento, Bayswater ☎/fax 7243 2201	187			●	●	●	●
The Ladbroke Arms, Notting Hill ☎ 7727 6648	222			●			●
Lalibela, Tufnell Park ☎ 7284 0600	123		●		●		
L'Anis, Kensington ☎ 7795 6533	205					●	●
L'Artiste Muscle, Mayfair ☎ 7493 6150	57		●		●		●
Laughing Buddha, Blackheath ☎/fax 8852 4161	158		●		●		●
Laughing Gravy, Southwark ☎/fax 7721 7055	177		●		●	●	●
Laurent, Golders Green ☎ 7794 3603	108		●				
L'Autre, Mayfair ☎ 7499 4680	57			●			●
L'Aventure, St John's Wood ☎ 7624 6232	122			●			●
Le Bistro Savoir Faire, Bloomsbury ☎ 7436 0707	21		●		●		
Le Café du Marche, Farringdon ☎ 7608 1609	138		●		●	●	
Le Gavroche, Mayfair ☎ 7499 1826	58		●		●	●	●
Le Mercury, Islington ☎ 7354 4088	117		●		●		●
Le Mignon, Camden ☎ 7387 0600	100			●			●
Le Pont de la Tour, Bermondsey ☎ 7403 8403	157		●	●	●	●	●
Le Taj, Brick Lane ☎ 7247 4210	128		●				
Lemongrass, Camden ☎/fax 7284 1116	101						●
Les Trois Garçons, Shoreditch ☎ 7613 1924	142				●		
L'Escargot, Soho ☎ 7437 6828	81		●		●	●	●
Levant, Marylebone ☎ 7224 1111	53				●		●
light house, Wimbledon ☎ 8944 6338	181	●	●	●		●	●
Little Georgia, Haggerston ☎ 7249 9070	140		●	●			●

INDEX

RESTAURANT NAME	PAGE NUMBER	Wheelchair access	Child friendly	Outdoor	Private room	Business	Romantic
Little Saigon, South Bank ☎ 7928 5415	173						
The Lobster Pot, Kennington ☎ 7582 5556	171		●		●		●
L'Oranger, Mayfair ☎ 7839 3774	58		●	●	●	●	●
Lundum's, South Kensington ☎ 7373 7774	232		●	●		●	●
Ma Goa, Putney ☎ 8780 1767	225		●		●		●
Made in Italy, Chelsea ☎ 7352 1880	191			●			●
Maggie Jones's, Kensington ☎ 7937 6462	205		●				●
Maison Novelli, Clerkenwell ☎ 7251 6606	131			●	●	●	●
Malabar Junction, Bloomsbury ☎ 7580 5230	21		●			●	●
Mandalay, Edgware Road ☎/fax 7258 3696	40		●				
Mandarin Kitchen, Bayswater ☎ 7727 9012	187		●			●	
Mandola, Notting Hill ☎ 7229 4734	223	●	●				●
Mango Room, Camden ☎ 7482 5065	101		●				●
Manna, Primrose Hill ☎ 7722 8028	120		●	●		●	●
MPW The Oak Room, Piccadilly ☎ 7437 0202	67	●				●	●
The Mayflower, Rotherhithe ☎ 7237 4088	197			●	●		
Mesclun, Stoke Newington ☎ 7249 5029	122	●	●			●	●
Meson Don Filippe, South Bank ☎ 7928 3237	174		●				
Metrogusto, Battersea ☎ 7720 0204	151		●				
Mezzo, Soho ☎ 7314 4000	82	●			●	●	●
Mildreds, Soho ☎/fax 7494 1634	82		●	●			
Mirabelle, Mayfair ☎ 7499 4636	59			●	●	●	●
Mr Chow, Knightsbridge ☎ 7589 7347	213		●		●	●	●
Mô tea-room, Mayfair ☎ 7734 3999	59		●	●			
Momo Restaurant Familial, Mayfair ☎ 7434 4040	60			●	●		●
Mon Plaisir, Covent Garden ☎ 7836 7243	35				●	●	●
Monitor, Islington ☎ 7607 7710	118		●	●		●	●

INDEX

RESTAURANT NAME	PAGE NUMBER	Wheelchair access	Child friendly	Outdoor	Private room	Business	Romantic
Montana, Fulham ☎ 7385 9500	198		●				●
Monte's, Knightsbridge ☎ 7245 0896	212	●	●		●	●	●
Moro, Clerkenwell ☎ 7833 8336	132	●		●	●		●
Moxon's, Clapham ☎ 7627 2468	167		●			●	
Mulberry, Belgravia ☎ 7201 1905	17		●			●	
Nam Dae Moon, Soho ☎ 7836 7235	83						
Navarro's, Fitzrovia ☎ 7637 7713	45		●	●	●	●	●
New Tayyab's, Whitechapel ☎ 7247 9543	145		●				
New World, Chinatown ☎ 7734 0396	24		●		●		
Nobu, Mayfair ☎ 7447 4747	61	●			●	●	●
Nottting Hill Brasserie, Notting Hill ☎ 7229 4481	223		●		●	●	●
O Cantinho, Stockwell ☎ 7924 0218	179		●				
O Fado, Knightsbridge ☎/fax 7589 3002	213				●	●	
Odette's, Primrose Hill ☎ 7586 5486	120		●	●	●		●
Ognisko, South Kensington ☎ 7589 4635	233	●	●	●	●	●	●
The Old Europeans, East Finchley ☎ 8833 3964	104		●				
Opium, Soho ☎ 7287 9608	83						●
Orangery, Kensington ☎ 7376 0239	50	●	●				
O's Thai Café, Crouch End ☎ 8348 6898	104		●				
Oscar, Fitzrovia ☎ 7907 4005	45	●	●	●	●	●	●
Oshobasho Café, Highgate ☎ 8444 1505	113	●	●	●			
Oxo Tower Restaurant, South Bank ☎ 7803 3888	174	●	●	●	●	●	●
Ozer, Oxford Circus ☎ 7323 0505	64	●	●	●		●	●
Pan-Asian Canteen, Knightsbridge ☎ 7589 6627	214		●				
Parco's, Aldgate ☎ 7488 2817	127		●			●	
Paris London Café, Archway ☎/fax 7561 0330	97		●				●
Pasha, Kensington ☎ 7589 7969	206				●	●	●

INDEX

RESTAURANT NAME	PAGE NUMBER	Wheelchair access	Child friendly	Outdoor	Private room	Business	Romantic
Patogh, Edgware Road ☎ 7262 4015	41						
Paulo's, Hammersmith ☎ 7385 9264	201		●	●			●
The Pepper Tree, Clapham ☎ 7622 1758	167		●	●			
Perc%nto, City ☎ 7778 0010	28	●		●	●	●	
Pescador, Camden ☎/fax 7482 7008	102		●				●
Phat Phuc Noodle Bar, Chelsea ☎ 0976 276808	192	●	●	●			
The Phene Arms, Chelsea ☎ 7352 3294	182			●	●		
Pied à Terre, Fitzrovia ☎ 7636 1178	46		●		●	●	
PJ's Restaurant, Hampstead ☎ 7435 3608	110	●			●	●	
The Place Below, City ☎ 7329 0789	28		●	●			
Popeseye, Kensington Olympia ☎ 7610 4578	208						
The Porterhouse, Covent Garden ☎ 7379 7917	36	●			●		
The Portrait Restaurant, Trafalgar Square ☎ 7312 2490	90	●			●	●	●
Posh Nosh, Tufnell Park ☎ 7916 1047	123		●				
Prospect of Whitby, Wapping ☎ 7481 1095	197			●	●		
Pug, Chiswick ☎ 8987 9988	195	●	●	●		●	●
Putney Bridge Restaurant, Putney ☎ 8780 1811	226	●				●	●
Quality Chop House, Clerkenwell ☎ 7837 5093	132		●			●	
Quilon, St James's ☎ 7821 1899	71		●			●	
Quo Vadis, Soho ☎ 7437 9585	84	●	●		●	●	
R Cooke, Southwark ☎ 7298 5931	175		●				
Ramen Seto, Soho ☎ 7434 0309	84		●				
Randall & Aubin, Soho ☎ 7287 4447	85		●				
Rani, Finchley ☎ 8349 4386	105					●	●
Ransome's Dock, Battersea ☎ 7223 1611	152	●	●	●		●	●
Rasa Samudra, Fitzrovia ☎ 7637 0222	46				●	●	
Rasputin, Acton ☎ 8993 5802	185				●		●

INDEX

RESTAURANT NAME	PAGE NUMBER	Wheelchair access	Child friendly	Outdoor	Private room	Business	Romantic
Ravi Shankar, Euston ☎ 7388 6458	42	●	●				
The Real Greek, Shoreditch ☎ 7739 8212	143				●		●
Red Cube Bar & Grill, Leicester Square ☎ 7287 0101	137	●			●		
Redmond's, Mortlake ☎ 8878 1922	219		●			●	●
RIBA Café, Marylebone ☎ 7631 0467	53	●	●	●	●	●	
Richard Corrigan at Lindsay House, Soho ☎ 7439 0450	85				●		
The Ritz, Piccadilly ☎ 7493 8181	50	●	●				
RK Stanleys, Oxford Circus ☎ 7462 0099	64	●	●				●
The Rock & Sole Plaice, Covent Garden ☎ 7836 3785	36		●	●			
Roussillon, Pimlico ☎ 7730 5550	69				●	●	●
The Royal Inn on the Park, Hackney ☎ 8985 3321	182	●	●	●			
RSJ, South Bank ☎ 7928 4554	176				●	●	
Rules, Covent Garden ☎ 7836 5314	37		●		●	●	●
St John, Clerkenwell ☎ 7251 0848	133		●		●	●	
The Salisbury Tavern, Fulham ☎ 7381 4005	199	●	●				●
The Salusbury Dining Room, Queens Park ☎ 7328 3286	227		●				●
Sand Bar & Restaurant, Clapham ☎ 7622 3022	168	●					
Sarastro, Covent Garden ☎ 7836 0101	38	●	●		●		●
Sardo, Fitzrovia ☎ 7387 2521	47		●	●	●		●
Satay Bar, Brixton ☎ 7326 5001	162	●					
satsuma, Soho ☎ 7437 8338	86	●					
SauCe, Camden ☎ 7482 0777	102		●				
The Savoy (Thames Foyer), Aldwych ☎ 7836 4343	50		●				
The Savoy Grill, Aldwych ☎ 7836 4343	16				●	●	
Scalini, Knightsbridge ☎ 7225 2301	214					●	●
The Settle Inn, Battersea ☎ 7228 0395	182		●	●	●		
Seven, Leicester Square ☎ 7909 1177	49	●	●	●	●	●	●

INDEX 249

INDEX

RESTAURANT NAME	PAGE NUMBER	Wheelchair access	Child friendly	Outdoor	Private room	Business	Romantic
Shampan, Brick Lane ☎ 7375 0475	129		●				
The Ship Inn, Wandsworth ☎ 8870 9667	197			●	●		
Singapura, City ☎ 7329 1133	29	●	●		●	●	
Six-13, Marylebone ☎ 7629 6133	54	●	●		●	●	●
'Smiths' of Smithfield, Farringdon ☎ 7236 6666	138	●	●			●	●
Sotheby's Café, Mayfair ☎ 7293 5000	61					●	
SO.UK, Clapham ☎ 7622 4004	169	●		●			
The Springbok Café, Chiswick ☎ 8742 3149	196						●
The Square, Mayfair ☎ 7495 7100	62	●	●		●	●	
Stepping Stone, Battersea ☎ 7622 0555	152					●	●
Stream Bubble & Shell, Clerkenwell ☎ 7796 0070	133					●	●
Sugar Club, Soho ☎ 7437 7776	87		●		●	●	
Sugar Reef, Soho ☎ 7851 0800	87	●			●	●	
Sun & Doves, Camberwell ☎ 7733 1525	163		●				
Sushi-Hiro, Ealing ☎ 8896 3175	196		●			●	
Sweetings, City ☎ 7248 3062	29				●		
Tabaq, Balham ☎ 8673 7820	149						
Tabla, Docklands ☎ 7345 0345	135		●	●	●		
Tamarind, Mayfair ☎ 7629 3561	62		●			●	
Tas, Southwark ☎ 7403 7200	178	●					
Tate Modern, South Bank ☎ 7401 5020	176	●	●			●	●
Tatsuso, City ☎ 7638 5863	30				●	●	
The Terrace, Kensington ☎ 7937 3224	206		●				●
Texas Embassy Cantina, Westminster ☎ 7925 0077	93	●	●	●	●		
Texas Lone Star Saloon, South Kensington ☎ 7370 5625	233		●				
The Thai Bar & Restaurant, Chelsea ☎/fax 7584 4788	192		●		●		
Thailand, New Cross ☎ 8691 4040	171		●				●

INDEX

RESTAURANT NAME	PAGE NUMBER	Wheelchair access	Child friendly	Outdoor	Private room	Business	Romantic
Thyme, Blackheath ☎ 8293 9183	159			●			●
Tiroler Hut, Bayswater ☎ 7727 3981	188		●				
Titanic, Soho ☎ 7437 1912	88	●					
Toff's, Muswell Hill ☎ 7437 1912	119		●				
Tootsies, Holland Park ☎ 7229 8567	202		●	●		●	
The Toucan, Soho ☎ 7437 4123	88						
The Trafalgar Tavern, Greenwich ☎ 8858 2437	197	●	●	●	●		●
Troika, Primrose Hill ☎ 7483 3765	121		●	●		●	
Truc Vert, Mayfair ☎ 7491 9988	63		●				
Tsunami Brasserie, City ☎ 7481 0972	30	●	●	●	●	●	
Vasco & Piero's, Soho ☎ 7437 8774	89		●		●	●	
Vertigo 42, City ☎ 7877 7842	31	●				●	●
Vic Naylor, Farringdon ☎ 7608 2181	139		●				
Viet Hoa Café, Shoreditch ☎/fax 7729 8293	144		●				
Vijay, Kilburn ☎ 7328 1087	209						
Villandry, Marylebone ☎ 7631 3131	54		●			●	●
Vong, Knightsbridge ☎ 7235 1010	215		●			●	
Waldorf Meridien, Aldwych ☎ 7836 2400	50		●				
Wapping Food, Wapping ☎ 7680 2080	145		●			●	●
The Well, Camberwell ☎ 7251 9363	134			●			
The Wharf, Teddington ☎ 8977 6333	234	●	●	●		●	●
William IV, Kensal Rise ☎ 8969 5944	204	●	●	●	●	●	
Wiltons, St James's ☎ 7629 9955	71				●	●	●
Wiz, Holland Park ☎ 7229 1500	203		●	●	●		●
Wódka, Kensington ☎ 7937 6513	207		●		●	●	●
Woodlands, Piccadilly ☎ 7839 7258	67						
World Food Cafe, Covent Garden ☎ 7379 0298	38		●				

INDEX

RESTAURANT NAME	PAGE NUMBER	Wheelchair access	Child friendly	Outdoor	Private room	Business	Romantic
Yas, Kensington Olympia ☎ 7603 9148	208		●				
Yoshino, Piccadilly ☎ 7287 6622	68		●			●	●
Yum Yum, Ladbroke Grove ☎/fax 8968 1477	216		●	●			
Zafferano, Knightsbridge ☎ 7235 5800	215					●	●
Zamoyski, Hampstead ☎ 7794 4792	111		●		●		●
Zilli Fish, Soho ☎ 7734 8649	89		●				
Zinc Bar & Grill, Mayfair ☎ 7255 8899	63	●	●	●	●	●	
Zucca, Notting Hill ☎ 7727 0060	224		●			●	●

INDEX

By Cuisine

Afghan

Afghan Kitchen 113
Islington

African

Calabash 33
Covent Garden
Kastoori 180
Tooting

American

(see also Tex-Mex)
Arkansas Café 144
Spitalfields
Canyon 227
Richmond
Christopher's American
Grill 33
Covent Garden
Coyote Café 194
Chiswick
Idaho 112
Highgate
Montana 198
Fulham
Sugar Reef 87
Soho
Tootsies 202
Holland Park

Asian

Asia de Cuba 32
Covent Garden
Pan-Asian Canteen 214
Knightsbridge
Sugar Club 87
Soho

Australian

Monitor 118
Islington

Austrian

Tiroler Hut 188
Bayswater

Bangladeshi

Café Naz 128
Brick Lane
Shampan 129
Brick Lane

Brazilian

Paulo's 201
Hammersmith

British

(see also Modern British)
The Albion 182
Islington
Bleeding Heart Bistro 130
Clerkenwell
Brown's Hotel 50
Mayfair
Bush Bar & Grill 228
Shepherd's Bush
Butlers Wharf
Chop House 155
Bermondsey
The Café in the Crypt 90
Trafalgar Square
Claridge's Hotel 50
Mayfair
The Connaught 56
Mayfair
Crocker's Folly 182
Marylebone
The Dove 197
Hammersmith
The Flask 182
Highgate
Fortnum & Mason 50
Piccadilly
The Frog and
Forget-Me-Not 182
Clapham
The Goring Dining Room 91
Victoria
The Grapes 197
Docklands
Jack's Place 151
Battersea
Julie's 202
Holland Park
Maggie Jones's 205
Kensington
The Mayflower 197
Rotherhithe
Orangery 50
Kensington
The Phene Arms 182
Chelsea
Popeseye 208
Kensington Olympia
Prospect of Whitby 197
Wapping
Quality Chop House 132
Clerkenwell
R Cooke 175
South Bank
The Ritz 50
Piccadilly
RK Stanleys 64
Oxford Circus
The Rock & Sole
Plaice 36
Covent Garden

The Royal Inn
on the Park 182
Hackney
Rules 37
Convent Garden
The Savoy (Thames Foyer) 50
Aldwych
The Savoy Grill 16
Aldwych
The Settle Inn 182
Battersea
The Ship Inn 197
Wandsworth
St John 133
Clerkenwell
Toff's 119
Muswell Hill
The Trafalgar Tavern 197
Greenwich
Vic Naylor 139
Farringdon
Waldorf Meridien 50
Aldwych
Wiltons 71
St James's

Burmese

Mandalay 40
Edgware Road

Caribbean

Brixtonian Havana
Club 161
Brixton
Mango Room 101
Camden
Posh Nosh 123
Tufnell Park
Yum Yum 216
Ladbroke Grove

Chinese

Aroma II 22
Chinatown
China City 22
Chinatown
China House 66
Piccadilly
Fung Shing 23
Chinatown
Hunan 68
Pimlico
Hung To 186
Bayswater
Jen 24
Chinatown
Jenny Lo's Tea House 92
Victoria
Laughing Buddha 158
Blackheath

INDEX

By Cuisine

Little Saigon 173
South Bank

Mandarin Kitchen 187
Bayswater

Mr Chow 213
Knightsbridge

New World 24
Chinatown

Cuban

Asia de Cuba 32
Covent Garden

Cuba Libra 136
Islington

Danish

Lundum's 232
South Kensington

Eastern European

Troika 121
Primrose Hill

Wódka 207
Kensington

Zamoyski 111
Hampstead

Eritrean

Asmara 159
Brixton

Ethiopian

Lalibela 123
Tufnell Park

European

(see also Modern European)

Café Espana 76
Soho

Daquise 231
South Kensington

The Dining Room 97
Barnsbury

Fish & Seafood

Astons 203
Kensal Rise

fish! 172
South Bank

Fish Tank 218
Mortlake

The Grapes 197
Docklands

Jason's Wharf 118
Maida Vale

The Lobster Pot 171
Kennington

Mandarin Kitchen 187
Bayswater

Moxon's 167
Clapham

The Rock & Sole Plaice 36
Covent Garden

Stream Bubble & Shell 133
Clerkenwell

Sweetings 29
City

Toff's 119
Muswell Hill

Vertigo 42 31
City

Zilli Fish 89
Soho

French

(see also Modern French)

The Admiralty 15
Aldwych

Bam-Bou 43
Fitzrovia

Belair House 169
Dulwich

Bistro Daniel 217
Lancaster Gate

Bleeding Heart Bistro 130
Clerkenwell

Brasserie du Marché aux Puces 216
Ladbroke Grove

Bush Bar & Grill 228
Shepherd's Bush

cheznico 55
Mayfair

The Connaught 56
Mayfair

Fish in a Tie 166
Clapham

Gordon Ramsay 191
Chelsea

Incognico 49
Leicester Square

La Poule au Pot 69
Pimlico

La Tante Claire 212
Knightsbridge

La Trompette 195
Chiswick

L'Artiste Muscle 57
Mayfair

L'Aventure 122
St John's Wood

Le Bistro Savoir Faire 21
Bloomsbury

Le Café du Marché 138
Farringdon

Le Gavroche 58
Mayfair

Le Mercury 117
Islington

Les Trois Garçons 142
Shoreditch

L'Escargot 81
Soho

The Lobster Pot 171
Kennington

L'Oranger 58
Mayfair

Marco Pierre White The Oak Room 67
Piccadilly

Mirabelle 59
Mayfair

Mon Plaisir 35
Covent Garden

Opium 83
Soho

Paris London Café 97
Archway

Putney Bridge Restaurant 226
Putney

The Savoy Grill 16
Aldwych

Truc Vert 63
Mayfair

Vong 215
Knightsbridge

Georgian

Little Georgia 140
Haggerston

Greek

The Real Greek 143
Shoreditch

Hungarian

Gay Hussar 79
Soho

The Old Europeans 104
East Finchley

Indian

Bengal Clipper 154
Bermondsey

Bombay Bicycle Club 164
Clapham

Cafe Spice Namaste 26
City

Chutney Mary 198
Fulham

Cinnamon Club 93
Westminster

254 LONELY PLANET OUT TO EAT

Diwana Bhel Poori House Euston	42	**The Chelsea Ram** Chelsea	198	**Cantina Italia** Islington	114
Jashan Turnpike Lane	124	**The Conservatory at the Lanesborough** Belgravia	17	**Cantina del Ponte** Bermondsey	156
Kastoori Tooting	180	**Delfina Studio Café** Bermondsey	156	**Cantuccio** Clapham	164
La Porte des Indes Marble Arch	51	**Detroit** Covent Garden	34	**Centrale** Soho	77
Lal Qila Bloomsbury	20	**The Drawing Room** Clapham	165	**Eco** Clapham	166
Le Taj Brick Lane	128	**Home** Shoreditch	142	**Estrela Bar** Stockwell	179
Ma Goa Putney	225	**First Edition Restaurant and Wine Bar** Docklands	135	**Fish in a Tie** Clapham	166
Malabar Junction Bloomsbury	21	**Futures Café-Bar** City	27	**Galiano's** Highbury	112
Quilon St James's	71	**Kettners** Soho	80	**Giotto** Bloomsbury	20
Rani Finchley	105	**Laughing Gravy** Southwark	177	**Giovanni's** Covent Garden	34
Rasa Samudra Fitzrovia	46	**Mulberry** Belgravia	17	**Isola** Knightsbridge	211
Ravi Shankar Euston	42	**Pug** Chiswick	195	**La Brocca** West Hampstead	124
Shampan Brick Lane	129	**Randall & Aubin** Soho	85	**La Porchetta** Finsbury Park	105
Tabla Docklands	135	**Tsunami Brasserie & Waterside Terrace** City	30	**L'Accento** Bayswater	187
Tamarind Mayfair	62	**Wiz** Holland Park	203	**light house** Wimbledon	181
Vijay Kilburn	209	**World Food Cafe** Covent Garden	38	**Made in Italy** Chelsea	191
Woodlands Piccadilly	67	**Iranian**		**Perc%nto** City	28
Indonesian		*(see Persian)*		**Sardo** Fitzrovia	47
Satay Bar Brixton	162	**Irish**		**Scalini** Knightsbridge	214
International		**The Ard-Ri Dining Room** Marylebone	51	**Vasco & Piero's Pavilion Restaurant** Soho	89
a.k.a. bar & restaurant Bloomsbury	136	**The Porterhouse Stout & Oyster Bar** Covent Garden	36	**Zafferano** Knightsbridge	215
Astons Kensal Rise	203	**The Toucan** Soho	88	**Zilli Fish** Soho	89
Bali Sugar Westbourne Park	235	**Italian**		**Japanese**	
The Bell and Crown Chiswick	197	*(see also Modern Italian)*		**Abeno** Bloomsbury	19
Blues Bistro & Bar Soho	75	**Antipasto & Pasta** Battersea	149	**Benihana** Piccadilly	65
Boardwalk Soho	136	**Aperitivo** Soho	74	**Café Japan** Golders Green	108
The Bridge Brasserie & Bar City	25	**Arancia** Bermondsey	154	**Fujiyama** Brixton	161
Café Emm Soho	76	**Assaggi** Notting Hill	220	**Ikkyu** Fitzrovia	44
Cargo Shoreditch	136	**Buona Sera at the Jam** Chelsea	189	**Inaho** Bayswater	186
				Kam-Pai! Islington	117

INDEX

By Cuisine

Nobu 61
Mayfair

Ramen Seto 84
Soho

satsuma 86
Soho

Sushi-Hiro 196
Ealing

Tatsuso 30
City

Yoshino 68
Piccadilly

Korean

Nam Dae Moon 83
Soho

Kosher

Six-13 54
Marylebone

Lao

Thailand 171
New Cross

Lebanese

Abu Ali 39
Edgware Road

Al Dar 39
Edgware Road

Alwaha 185
Bayswater

Fairuz 52
Marylebone

Le Mignon 100
Camden

Levant 53
Marylebone

Mauritian

Jason's Wharf 118
Maida Vale

Mediterranean

Beach Blanket Babylon 220
Notting Hill

blackpepper 163
Clapham

The Eagle 130
Clerkenwell

Fairuz 52
Marylebone

Gordon Ramsay 191
Chelsea

Hujo's 80
Soho

Kam-Pai! 117
Islington

L'Anis 205
Kensington

Sarastro 38
Covent Garden

Sun & Doves 163
Camberwell

Titanic 88
Soho

The Well 134
Clerkenwell

Mexican

L'Autre 57
Mayfair

Modern British

192 219
Notting Hill

Alastair Little 73
Soho

Anchor Bankside 197
Southwark

The Anglesea Arms 200
Hammersmith

The Apprentice 153
Bermondsey

Bah Humbug 160
Brixton

Bank Aldwych 15
Aldwych

Bank Westminster & Zander Bar 92
Westminster

Bluebird 189
Chelsea

Che 70
St James's

The Chiswick Restaurant 193
Chiswick

City Rhodes 26
City

The Cow 235
Westbourne Park

Court Restaurant 19
Bloomsbury

The Crown 114
Modern British

The Crown Organic Pub 140
Hackney

The County Hall Restaurant 172
South Bank

The Depôt 218
Mortlake

The Duke of Cambridge 116
Islington

The Engineer 119
Primrose Hill

Frederick's 116
Islington

French House Dining Room 78
Soho

The Gate 200
Hammersmith

The Glasshouse 209
Kew

Honest Cabbage 157
Bermondsey

Jerusalem 137
Soho

The Ladbroke Arms 222
Notting Hill

Mesclun 122
Stoke Newington

Notting Hill Brasserie 223
Notting Hill

Oscar 45
Fitzrovia

The Place Below 28
City

The Portrait Restaurant 90
Trafalgar Square

Red Cube Bar & Grill 137
Leicester Square

Redmond's 219
Mortlake

RIBA Cafe 53
Marylebone

Richard Corrigan at Lindsay House 85
Soho

RSJ 176
South Bank

The Salisbury Tavern 199
Fulham

SauCe 102
Camden

Seven 49
Leicester Square

'Smiths' of Smithfield 138
Farringdon

Sotheby's Café 61
Mayfair

Stepping Stone 152
Battersea

Tate Modern 176
South Bank

The Terrace 206
Kensington

Wapping Food 145
Wapping

William IV 204
Kensal Rise

256 LONELY PLANET OUT TO EAT

Modern European

1 Blossom Street City	25
291 Bethnal Green	127
Andrew Edmunds Soho	73
The Anglesea Arms Hammersmith	200
The Ard-Ri Dining Room Marylebone	51
Aurora Soho	75
The Avenue Mayfair	55
Bank Westminster & Zander Bar Westminster	92
Bar and Dining House Islington	114
Bibendum South Kensington	230
Chives Chelsea	190
Circus Restaurant & Bar Soho	77
Coopers Holborn	48
Cotto Kensington Olympia	207
The Crown & Goose Camden	99
Cucina Hampstead	109
The Don Restaurant and Bistro City	27
Fish Tank Mortlake	218
Foliage Knightsbridge	210
The House Hampstead	109
Inside Greenwich	170
The Ivy Covent Garden	35
Kennington Lane Restaurant & Bar Kennington	170
Le Pont de la Tour Bermondsey	157
Mesclun Stoke Newington	122
Mezzo Soho	82
Monte's Knightsbridge	212
Odette's Primrose Hill	120
Oxo Tower Restaurant South Bank	174
PJ's Restaurant Hampstead	110
Quo Vadis Soho	84
Ransome's Dock Battersea	152
Sand Bar & Restaurant Clapham	168
The Ship Inn Wandsworth	197
Thyme Blackheath	159
Titanic Soho	88
Truc Vert Mayfair	63
Villandry Marylebone	54
The Wharf Teddington	234
Zinc Bar & Grill Mayfair	63

Modern French

Bank Aldwych Aldwych	15
Café des Amis Covent Garden	32
Chez Bruce Wandsworth	180
The Criterion Piccadilly	66
High Holborn Holborn	48
hush Mayfair	56
Maison Novelli Clerkenwell	131
Pied à Terre Fitzrovia	46
Roussillon Pimlico	69
The Square Mayfair	62

Modern Italian

Artigiano Belsize Park	98
blackpepper Clapham	163
Grano Chiswick	194
Great Eastern Dining Room Shoreditch	141
Metrogusto Battersea	151

Parco's Aldgate	127
The Salusbury Pub and Dining Room Queens Park	227
Zucca Notting Hill	224

Modern Spanish

Cambio de Tercio South Kensington	231
El Rincón South Kensington	232
Gaudi Clerkenwell	131

Moroccan

Mô tea-room Mayfair	59
Pasha Kensington	206

North African

Laurent Golders Green	108
Momo Restaurant Familial Mayfair	60
Moro Clerkenwell	132
SO.UK Clapham	169

Organic

The Crown Organic Pub Hackney	140
The Duke of Cambridge Islington	116
SauCe Camden	102

Ottoman

Ozer Oxford Circus	64

Pakistani

New Tayyab's Whitechapel	145
Tabaq Balham	149

Persian

Dish Dash Fitzrovia	44
Patogh Edgware Road	41
Yas Kensington Olympia	208

INDEX

By Cuisine

Peruvian

Fina Estampa Southwark	177

Polish

Daquise South Kensington	231
L'Autre Mayfair	57
Ognisko South Kensington	233
Wódka Kensington	207

Portuguese

Café Portugal Stockwell	178
Estrela Bar Stockwell	179
The Gallery Brixton	162
O Cantinho Stockwell	179
O Fado Knightsbridge	213
Pescador Camden	102

Russian

Borshcht 'n' Tears Knightsbridge	210
Rasputin Acton	185
Troika Primrose Hill	121

Scottish

Buchan's Battersea	150

Seafood

(see Fish & Seafood)

South African

Springbok Café Chiswick	196

South-East Asian

Café Bintang Camden	98
Lemongrass Camden	101
Singapura City	29

Spanish

(see also Modern Spanish)

Baradero Docklands	134
Café Espana Soho	76
Café Portugal Stockwell	178
Carmen Clapham	165
Cigala Holborn	47
Don Pepe Edgware Road	40
El Parador Camden	99
Estrela Bar Stockwell	179
La Bota Crouch End	103
Meson Don Felipe South Bank	174
Moro Clerkenwell	132
Navarro's Fitzrovia	45

Sudanese

Mandola Notting Hill	223

Swedish

Garbo's Marylebone	52

Tex-Mex

Cafe Sol Clapham	136
Texas Embassy Cantina Westminster	93
Texas Lone Star Saloon South Kensington	233

Thai

Beach Blanket Babylon Notting Hill	220
Churchill Arms Notting Hill	221
O's Thai Café Crouch End	104
The Pepper Tree Clapham	168
The Porterhouse Stout & Oyster Bar Covent Garden	36
The Thai Bar & Restaurant Chelsea	192
Thailand New Cross	171
Vong Knightsbridge	215

Turkish

Tas Southwark	178

Vegan

Country Life Soho	78

Vegetarian

Blah Blah Blah! Shepherd's Bush	228
Carnevale Hoxton	141
Diwana Bhel Poori House Euston	42
Fiction Crouch End	103
Futures Café-Bar City	27
The Gate Hammersmith	200
Kastoori Tooting	180
Manna Primrose Hill	120
Mildreds Soho	82
Oshobasho Café Highgate	113
The Place Below City	28
Rani Finchley	105
Woodlands Piccadilly	67
World Food Cafe Covent Garden	38

Vietnamese

Bam-Bou Fitzrovia	43
Little Saigon South Bank	173
Opium Soho	83
Phat Phuc Noodle Bar Chelsea	192
Viet Hoa Café Shoreditch	144

INDEX

By Neighbourhood

Acton

Rasputin 185
Russian

Aldgate

Parco's 127
Modern Italian

Aldwych

The Admiralty 15
French Regional

Bank Aldwych 15
Modern British, Liberated French

The Savoy (Thames Foyer) 54
British

The Savoy Grill 16
British/French

Waldorf Meridien 50
British

Archway

Paris London Café 97
French

Balham

Tabaq 149
Pakistani

Barnsbury

The Dining Room 97
Country European

Battersea

Antipasto & Pasta 149
Traditional Italian

Buchan's 150
Modern Scottish

Jack's Place 151
British

Metrogusto 151
Progressive Italian

Ransome's Dock 152
Modern European

The Settle Inn 182
British

Stepping Stone 152
Modern British

Bayswater

Alwaha 185
Lebanese

Hung To 186
Chinese

Inaho 186
Japanese

L'Accento 187
Italian

Mandarin Kitchen 187
Chinese Seafood

Tiroler Hut 188
Austrian

Belgravia

The Conservatory at the Lanesborough 17
International

Mulberry 17
International

Belsize Park

Artigiano 98
Modern Italian

Bermondsey

The Apprentice 153
Modern British

Arancia 154
Italian

Bengal Clipper 154
Indian

Butlers Wharf Chop House 155
Traditional British

Cantina del Ponte 156
Italian

Delfina Studio Café 156
Global

Honest Cabbage 157
Modern British

Le Pont de la Tour 157
Modern European

Bethnal Green

291 127
Modern European

Blackheath

Laughing Buddha 158
Chinese

Thyme 159
Modern European

Bloomsbury

Abeno 19
Japanese

a.k.a bar & restaurant 136
Global

Court Restaurant 19
Modern British

Giotto 20
Italian

Lal Qila 20
Indian

Le Bistro Savoir Faire 21
French

Malabar Junction 21
South Indian

Brick Lane

Café Naz 128
Contemporary Bangladeshi

Le Taj 128
Indian

Shampan 129
Bangladeshi/Indian

Brixton

Asmara 159
Eritrean

Bah Humbug 160
Modern British

Brixtonian Havana Club 161
West Indian

Fujiyama 161
Japanese

The Gallery 162
Portuguese

Satay Bar 162
Indonesian

Camberwell

Sun & Doves 163
Mediterranean

Camden

Café Bintang 98
South-East Asian

The Crown & Goose 99
Modern European

El Parador 99
Spanish

Le Mignon 100
Lebanese

Lemongrass 101
South-East Asian

Mango Room 101
Traditional & Modern Caribbean

Pescador 102
Portuguese

SauCe 102
Modern British

Chelsea

Bluebird 189
Modern British

Buona Sera at the Jam 189
Italian

The Chelsea Ram 190
Modern Global

INDEX BY NEIGHBOURHOOD 259

INDEX

By Neighbourhood

Chives 190
Modern European

Gordon Ramsay 191
French/Mediterranean

Made in Italy 191
Italian

Phat Phuc Noodle Bar 192
Vietnamese

The Phene Arms 182
British

The Thai Bar & Restaurant 192
Thai

Chinatown

Aroma II 22
Chinese

China City 22
Chinese

Fung Shing 22
Chinese

Jen 24
Hong Kong

New World 24
Chinese

Chiswick

The Chiswick Restaurant 193
Modern British

Coyote Café 194
South-West American

Grano 194
Modern Italian

La Trompette 195
French

Pug 195
International

Springbok Café 196
Modern South African

The Bell and Crown 197
International

City

1 Blossom Street 25
Modern European

The Bridge Brasserie & Bar 25
International

Cafe Spice Namaste 26
Indian

City Rhodes 26
Modern British

The Don Restaurant and Bistro 27
Modern European

Futures Café-Bar 27
International Vegetarian

Perc%nto 28
Italian

The Place Below 28
Modern British Vegetarian

Singapura 29
South-East Asian

Sweetings 29
Seafood

Tatsuso 30
Japanese

Tsunami Brasserie & Waterside Terrace 30
International

Vertigo 42 31
Seafood

Clapham

blackpepper 163
Modern Mediterranean

Bombay Bicycle Club 164
Indian

Cafe Sol 136
Tex-Mex

Cantuccio 164
Italian

Carmen 165
Spanish

The Drawing Room 165
Modern International

Eco 166
Italian

Fish in a Tie 166
French & Italian

Moxon's 167
Fish

The Pepper Tree 168
Thai

Sand Bar & Restaurant 168
New European

SO.UK 169
North African

The Frog and Forget-Me-Not 182
British

Clerkenwell

Bleeding Heart Bistro 130
British

The Eagle 130
Mediterranean

Gaudi 131
Modern Spanish

Maison Novelli 131
Modern French

Moro 132
Spanish/North African

The Quality Chop House 132
British

St John 133
British

Stream Bubble & Shell 133
Seafood

The Well 134
Mediterranean

Covent Garden

Asia de Cuba 32
Asian/Cuban

Café des Amis 32
Modern French

Calabash 33
African

Christopher's American Grill 33
American

Detroit 34
International

Giovanni's 34
Italian

The Ivy 35
Modern European

Mon Plaisir 35
French

The Porterhouse Stout & Oyster Bar 36
Irish/Thai

The Rock & Sole Plaice 36
British/Fish

Rules 37
British

Sarastro 38
Mediterranean

World Food Cafe 38
Global Vegetarian

Crouch End

Fiction 103
Vegetarian

La Bota 103
Spanish

O's Thai Café 104
Thai

Docklands

Baradero 134
Spanish

First Edition Restaurant and Wine Bar 135
International

The Grapes 197
British/Fish

Tabla 135
Indian

Dulwich

Belair House 169
Classical French

260 LONELY PLANET OUT TO EAT

Ealing

Sushi-Hiro 196
Japanese

East Finchley

The Old Europeans 104
Hungarian

Edgware Road

Abu Ali 39
Lebanese

Al Dar 39
Lebanese

Don Pepe 40
Spanish

Mandalay 40
Burmese

Patogh 41
Iranian

Euston

Diwana Bhel Poori House 42
Indian Vegetarian

Ravi Shankar 42
Indian

Farringdon

Le Café du Marché 138
French

'Smiths' of Smithfield 138
Modern British

Vic Naylor 139
Eccentric British

Finchley

Rani 105
Indian Vegetarian

Finsbury Park

La Porchetta 105
Italian

Fitzrovia

Bam-Bou 43
French-Vietnamese

Dish Dash 44
Anglo-Persian

Ikkyu 44
Japanese

Navarro's 45
Spanish

Oscar 45
Modern British

Pied à Terre 46
Contemporary French

Rasa Samudra 46
South Indian

Sardo 47
Italian

Fulham

Chutney Mary 198
Indian

Montana 198
Contemporary American

The Salisbury Tavern 199
Modern British

Golders Green

Café Japan 108
Japanese

Laurent 108
North African

Greenwich

Inside 170
Modern European

The Trafalgar Tavern 197
British

Hackney

The Crown Organic Pub 140
Modern British

The Royal Inn on the Park 182
British

Haggerston

Little Georgia 140
Georgian

Hammersmith

The Anglesea Arms 200
Modern British/European

The Dove 197
British

The Gate 200
Modern British Vegetarian

Paulo's 201
Brazilian

Hampstead

Cucina 109
Modern European

The House 109
Modern European

PJ's Restaurant 110
Modern European

Zamoyski 111
Eastern European

Highbury

Galiano's 112
Italian

Highgate

The Flask 182
British

Idaho 112
Contemporary South-West American

Oshobasho Café 113
Vegetarian

Holborn

Cigala 47
Spanish

Coopers 48
Modern European

High Holborn 48
Modern French

Holland Park

Julie's 202
British

Tootsies 202
American

Wiz 203
International

Hoxton

Carnevale 141
Vegetarian

Islington

Afghan Kitchen 113
Afghan

The Albion 182
British

Bar and Dining House 114
Modern European

Cantina Italia 114
Italian

The Crown 115
Modern British

Cuba Libra 136
Cuban

The Duke of Cambridge 116
Modern British

Frederick's 116
Modern British

Kam-Pai! 117
Japanese/Mediterranean

Le Mercury 117
French

Monitor 118
Australian

Kennington

Kennington Lane Restaurant & Bar 170
Modern European

INDEX

By Neighbourhood

The Lobster Pot 171
French/Seafood

Kensal Rise

Astons 203
International/Fish

William IV 204
Modern British

Kensington

L'Anis 205
Mediterranean

Maggie Jones's 205
British

Pasha 206
Morroccan/Maghreb

The Terrace 206
Modern British

Wódka 206
Polish/Eastern European

Orangery 50
British

Kensington Olympia

Cotto 207
Modern European

Popeseye 208
British

Yas 208
Persian

Kew

The Glasshouse 209
Modern British

Kilburn

Vijay 209
South Indian

Knightsbridge

Borshtch 'n' Tears 210
Russian

Foliage 210
Modern European

Isola 211
Italian

La Tante Claire 212
French

Monte's 212
Modern European

Mr Chow 213
Beijing Chinese

O Fado 213
Portuguese

Pan-Asian Canteen 214
Modern Asian

Scalini 214
Italian

Vong 215
French/Thai

Zafferano 215
Italian

Ladbroke Grove

Brasserie du Marché aux
Puces 216
French

Yum Yum 216
Caribbean

Lancaster Gate

Bistro Daniel 217
French

Leicester Square

Incognico 49
French

Red Cube Bar & Grill 137
Modern British

Seven 49
Modern British

Maida Vale

Jason's Wharf 118
Mauritian Fish & Seafood

Marble Arch

La Porte des Indes 51
Indian

Marylebone

The Ard-Ri Dining
Room 51
Modern European/Irish

Crocker's Folly 182
British

Fairuz 52
Lebanese/Mediterranean

Garbo's 52
Swedish

Levant 53
Lebanese

RIBA Cafe 53
Modern British

Six-13 54
Kosher

Villandry 54
Modern European

Mayfair

The Avenue 55
Modern European

Brown's Hotel 50
British

cheznico 55
Classical French

Claridge's Hotel 50
British

The Connaught 56
Classic French/
Traditional British

hush 56
Modern French

L'Artiste Muscle 57
French

L'Autre 57
Polish/Mexican

L'Oranger 58
French Provençal

Le Gavroche 58
French

Mirabelle 59
French

Mô tea-room 59
Moroccan

Momo Restaurant
Familial 60
North African

Nobu 61
Japanese

Sotheby's Café 61
Modern British

The Square 62
Modern French

Tamarind 62
Modern North Indian

Truc Vert 63
French/Modern European

Zinc Bar & Grill 63
Modern European

Mortlake

The Depôt 218
Modern British

Fish Tank 218
Modern European Fish &
Seafood

Redmond's 219
Modern British

Muswell Hill

Toff's 119
British/Fish

New Cross

Thailand 171
Thai/Lao

Notting Hill

192 219
Modern British

Assaggi 220
Italian

INDEX

Beach Blanket Babylon 220
Mediterranean/Thai
Churchill Arms 221
Thai
The Ladbroke Arms 222
Modern British
Mandola 223
Sudanese
Notting Hill Brasserie 223
Modern British
Zucca 224
Contemporary Italian

Oxford Circus

Ozer 64
Modern Ottoman
RK Stanleys 64
British

Piccadilly

Benihana 74
Japanese
China House 66
Chinese
The Criterion 67
Modern French
Fortnum & Mason 50
British
MPW The Oak Room 67
French
The Ritz 50
British
Woodlands 67
South Indian Vegetarian
Yoshino 68
Japanese

Pimlico

Hunan 68
Chinese
La Poule au Pot 69
French
Roussillon 69
Modern French

Primrose Hill

The Engineer 119
Modern British
Manna 120
Vegetarian
Odette's 120
Modern European
Troika 121
Russian/Eastern European

Putney

Ma Goa 225
Goan

Putney Bridge
Restaurant 226
French

Queens Park

The Salusbury Pub and
Dining Room 227
Modern Italian

Richmond

Canyon 227
Contemporary South-West
American

Rotherhithe

The Mayflower 197
British

St James's

Che 70
Modern British
Quilon 71
South Indian
Wiltons 71
Traditional English

St John's Wood

L'Aventure 122
Traditional French

Shepherd's Bush

Blah Blah Blah! 228
Vegetarian
Bush Bar & Grill 228
French/British

Shoreditch

Cargo 136
Global
Great Eastern Dining
Room 141
Modern Italian
Home 142
International
Les Trois Garçons 142
French
The Real Greek 143
Greek
Viet Hoa Café 144
Vietnamese

Soho

Alastair Little 73
Modern British
Andrew Edmunds 73
Modern European
Aperitivo 74
Italian

Aurora 75
Modern European
Blues Bistro & Bar 75
International
Boardwalk 136
Global
Café Emm 76
International
Café Espana 76
Spanish/Continental
Centrale 77
Italian
Circus Restaurant & Bar 77
Modern European
Country Life 78
Vegan
French House Dining
Room 78
Modern British
Gay Hussar 79
Hungarian
Hujo's 80
Mediterranean
Jerusalem 137
Modern British
Kettners 80
International
L'Escargot 80
French
Mezzo 82
Modern European
Mildreds 82
Wholefood Vegetarian
Nam Dae Moon 83
Korean
Opium 83
Vietnamese/French
Quo Vadis 84
Modern European
Ramen Seto 84
Japanese
Randall & Aubin 85
International
Richard Corrigan at Lindsay
House 85
Modern British
satsuma 86
Japanese
Sugar Club 87
Asian Fusion
Sugar Reef 87
Pan American
Titanic 88
Modern European
The Toucan 88
Irish
Vasco & Piero's Pavilion
Restaurant 89
Italian
Zilli Fish 89
Italian seafood

INDEX BY NEIGHBOURHOOD 263

INDEX

By Neighbourhood

South Bank

The County Hall Restaurant Modern British	172
fish! Fish	172
Little Saigon Vietnamese/Chinese	173
Meson Don Felipe Spanish	174
Oxo Tower Restaurant Modern European	174
R Cooke Traditional English	175
RSJ Modern English	176
Tate Modern Modern British	176

South Kensington

Bibendum Modern European	230
Cambio de Tercio Modern Spanish	231
Daquise Polish/Continental	231
El Rincón Modern Spanish	232
Lundum's Danish	232
Ognisko Polish	233
Texas Lone Star Saloon Tex-Mex	233

Southwark

Anchor Bankside Modern British	197
Fina Estampa Peruvian	177
Laughing Gravy International	177
Tas Turkish	178

Spitalfields

Arkansas Café American Barbecue	144

Stockwell

Café Portugal Portuguese/Spanish	178
Estrela Bar Portuguese/Spanish/Italian	179
O Cantinho Portuguese	179

Stoke Newington

Mesclun Modern British/European	122

Teddington

The Wharf Modern European	234

Tooting

Kastoori Indian/African Vegetarian	180

Trafalgar Square

The Café in the Crypt British	90
The Portrait Restaurant Modern British	90

Tufnell Park

Lalibela Ethiopian	123
Posh Nosh Caribbean	123

Turnpike Lane

Jashan Indian	124

Victoria

The Goring Dining Room Traditional British	91
Jenny Lo's Tea House Chinese	92

Wandsworth

Chez Bruce Modern French	180
The Ship Inn Modern European	197

Wapping

Prospect of Whitby British	197
Wapping Food Modern British	145

West Hampstead

La Brocca Italian	124

Westbourne Park

Bali Sugar Fusion	235
The Cow Modern British	235

Westminster

Bank Westminster & Zander Bar Modern English/European	92
Cinnamon Club Indian	93
Texas Embassy Cantina Tex-Mex	93

Whitechapel

New Tayyab's Pakistani	145

Wimbledon

light house Italian Fusion	181

LONDON MAPS

Outer London
Inner London
Soho
Holborn & Covent Garden
Fitzrovia & Bloombury
Marylebone
Mayfair
City
Victoria
Hampstead
Islington
Camden & Primrose Hill
Shoreditch & Spitalfields
Bethnal Green & Haggerston
Clerkenwell & Farringdon
Wapping
South Bank to Bermondsey
Clapham
Brixton & Stockwell
Knightsbridge
South Kensington & Chelsea
Notting Hill & Kensington
Hammersmith

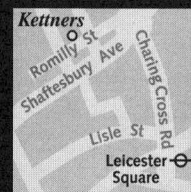

Outer London

To the North
HENDON
A406
HIGHGATE
GOLDERS GREEN
Hampstead Heath
M1
North Circular Rd
A41
Map 8 - North: Hampstead p277
HAMPSTEAD
Inner London pp268-9
WEMBLEY
A406
WILLESDEN
KILBURN
A5
HARLESDEN
To Oxford
A40
EALING
A40(M)
BAYSWATER
Paddington
ACTON
SHEPHERD'S BUSH
NOTTING HILL
Hyde Park
Map 21 - West: Hammersmith p294
Map 19 - West: South Kensington & Chelsea pp290-1
KENSINGTON
A406
To Bristol
Gunnersbury Park
M4
HAMMERSMITH
A4
EARL'S COURT
CHELSEA
A4
To Heathrow Airport
CHISWICK
Kew Gardens
KEW
Old Deer Park
BARNES
FULHAM
River Thames
BATTERSEA
A205
PUTNEY
WANDSWORTH
A316
To M3 & Southampton
RICHMOND
Richmond Park
A308
UPPER TOOTING
TWICKENHAM
A24
WIMBLEDON

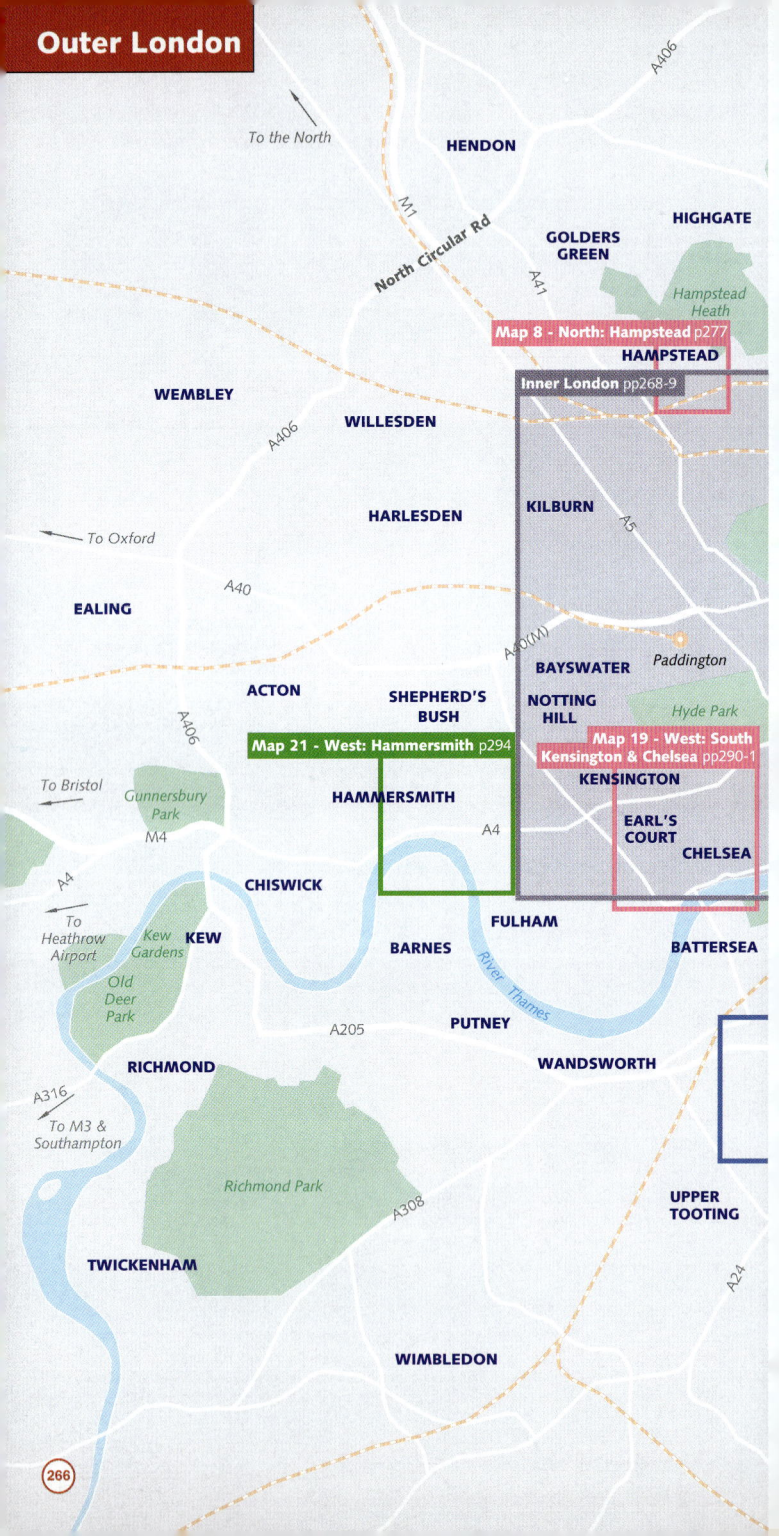

(266)

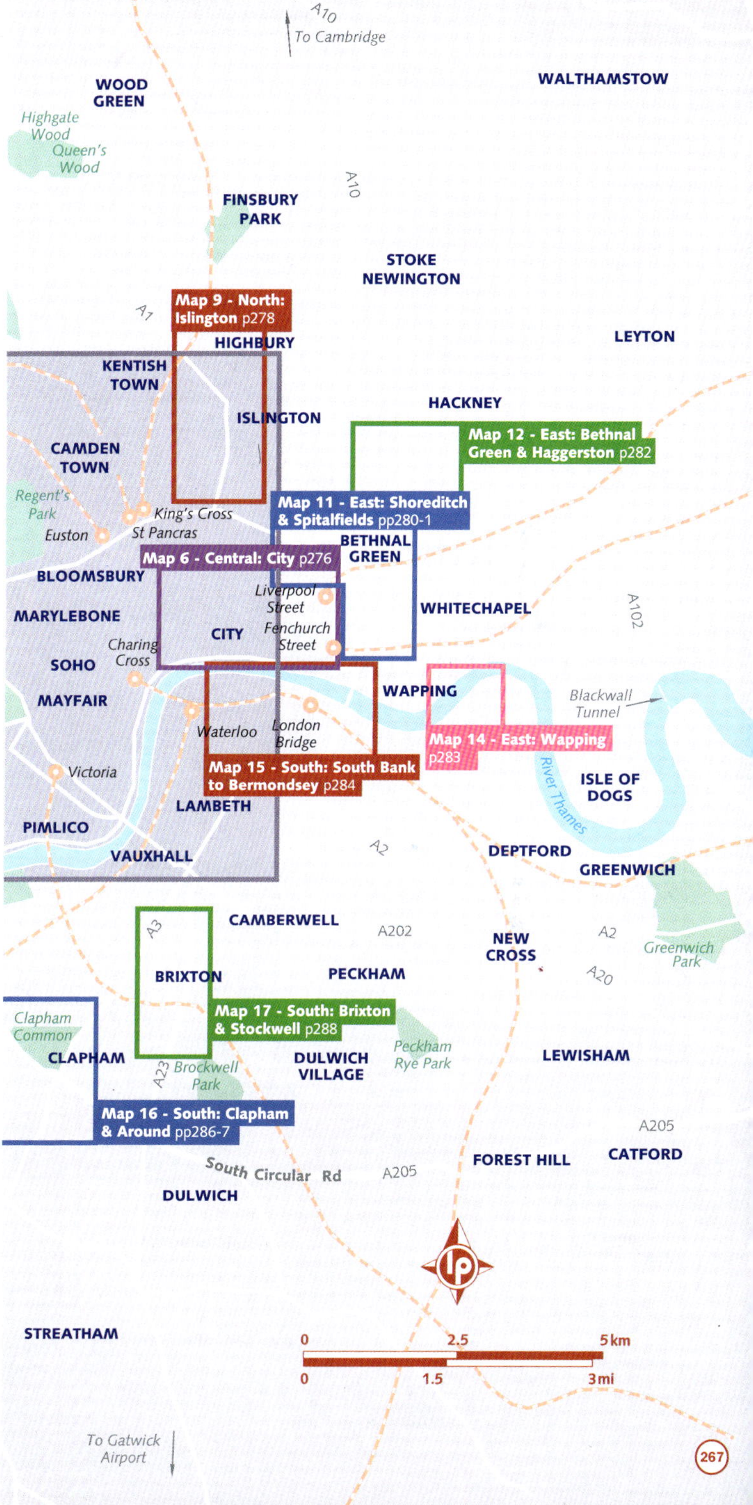

A10
To Cambridge
WOOD GREEN
WALTHAMSTOW
Highgate Wood
Queen's Wood
A10
FINSBURY PARK
STOKE NEWINGTON
A1
Map 9 - North: Islington p278
HIGHBURY
LEYTON
KENTISH TOWN
HACKNEY
ISLINGTON
Map 12 - East: Bethnal Green & Haggerston p282
CAMDEN TOWN
Regent's Park
King's Cross
St Pancras
Euston
Map 11 - East: Shoreditch & Spitalfields pp280-1
BETHNAL GREEN
Map 6 - Central: City p276
BLOOMSBURY
Liverpool Street
MARYLEBONE
WHITECHAPEL
A102
CITY
Fenchurch Street
Charing Cross
SOHO
MAYFAIR
WAPPING
Blackwall Tunnel
Waterloo
London Bridge
Map 14 - East: Wapping p283
Victoria
Map 15 - South: South Bank to Bermondsey p284
River Thames
ISLE OF DOGS
LAMBETH
PIMLICO
A2
VAUXHALL
DEPTFORD
GREENWICH
CAMBERWELL
A3
A202
NEW CROSS
A2
Greenwich Park
A20
BRIXTON
PECKHAM
Map 17 - South: Brixton & Stockwell p288
Clapham Common
Peckham Rye Park
CLAPHAM
A23
Brockwell Park
DULWICH VILLAGE
LEWISHAM
Map 16 - South: Clapham & Around pp286-7
A205
South Circular Rd
A205
FOREST HILL
CATFORD
DULWICH
STREATHAM
0
2.5
5km
0
1.5
3mi
To Gatwick Airport

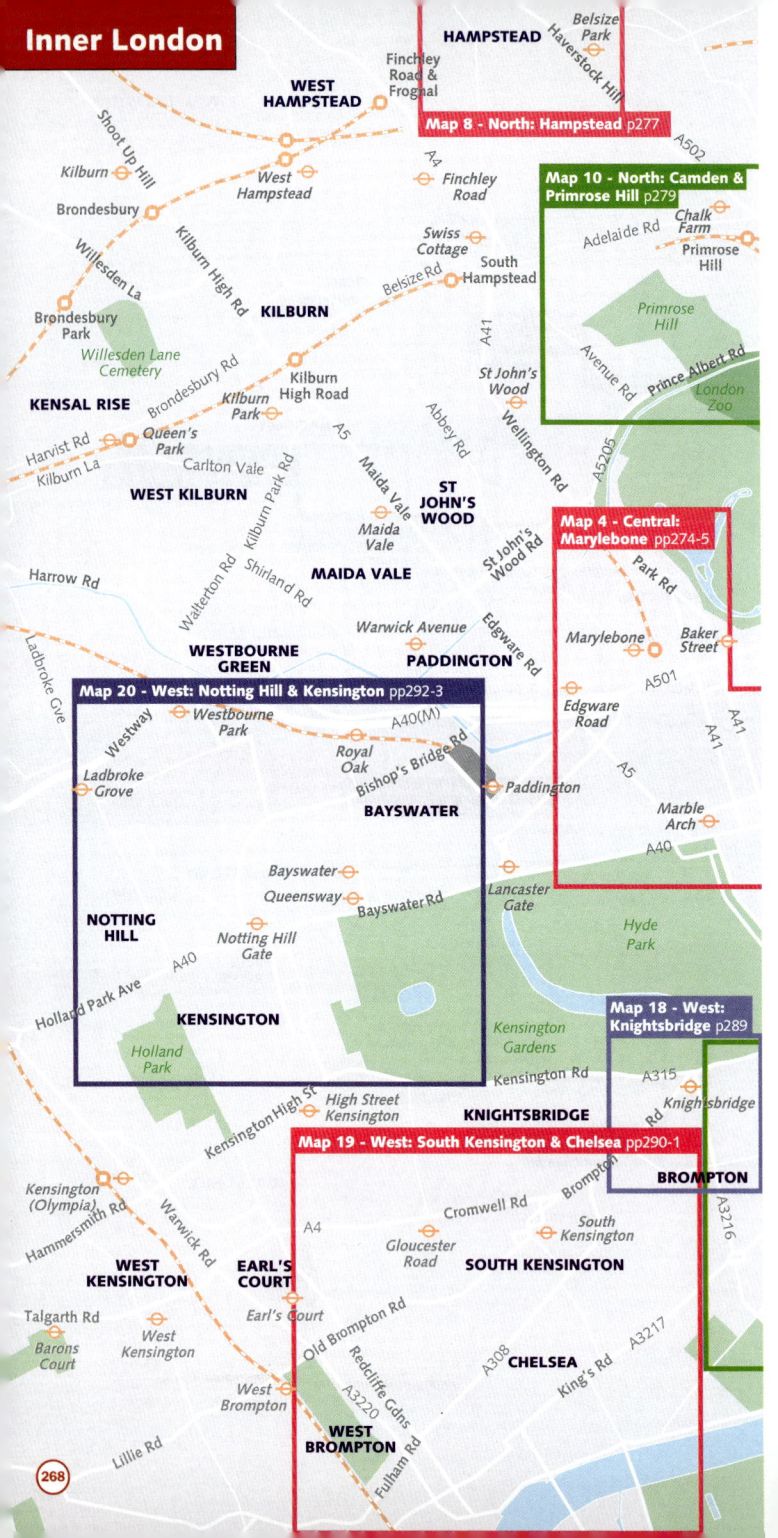

Inner London

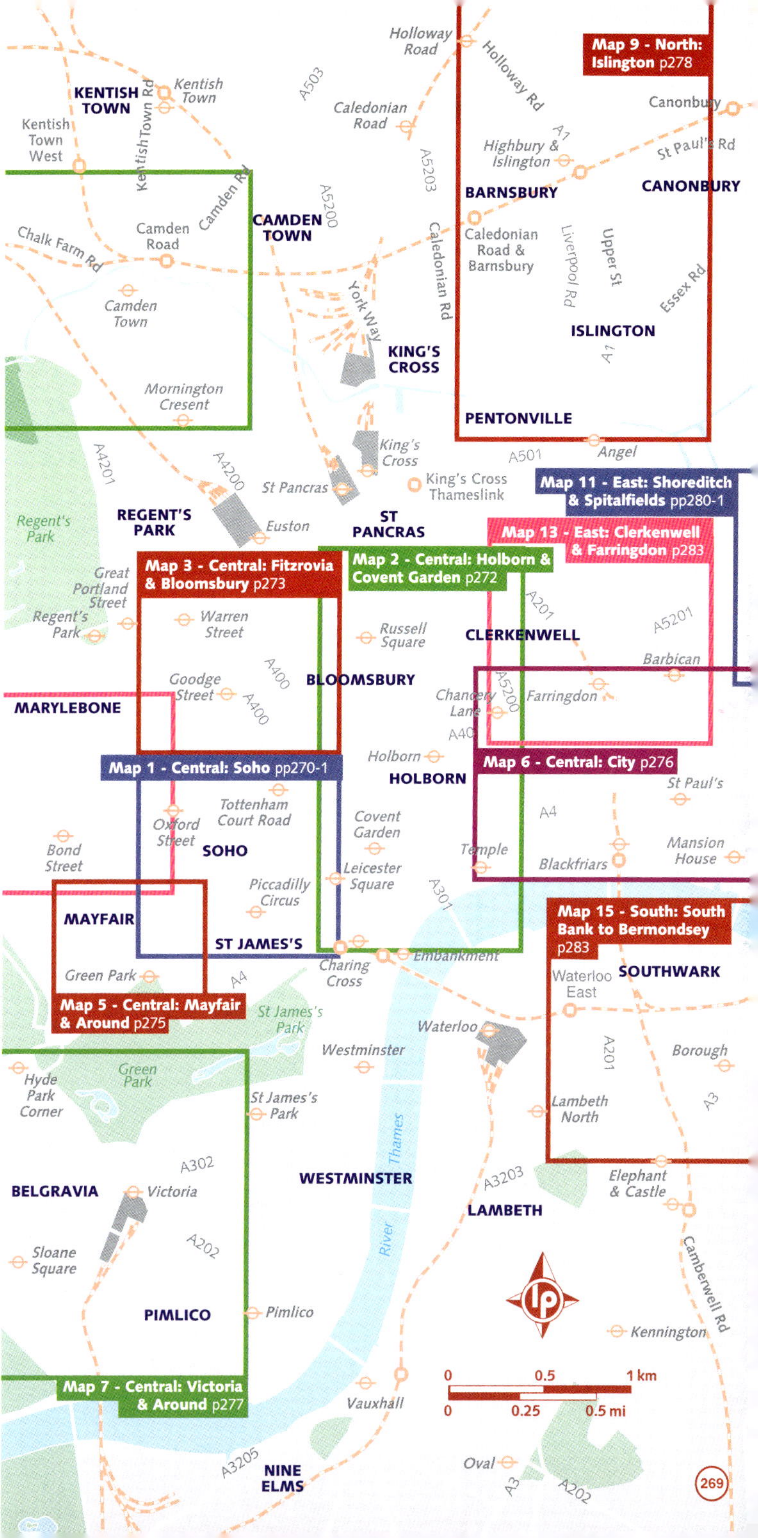

Map 9 - North: Islington p278
Map 11 - East: Shoreditch & Spitalfields pp280-1
Map 13 - East: Clerkenwell & Farringdon p283
Map 3 - Central: Fitzrovia & Bloomsbury p273
Map 2 - Central: Holborn & Covent Garden p272
Map 1 - Central: Soho pp270-1
Map 6 - Central: City p276
Map 15 - South: South Bank to Bermondsey p283
Map 5 - Central: Mayfair & Around p275
Map 7 - Central: Victoria & Around p277
KENTISH TOWN
CAMDEN TOWN
KING'S CROSS
BARNSBURY
CANONBURY
ISLINGTON
PENTONVILLE
REGENT'S PARK
ST PANCRAS
CLERKENWELL
BLOOMSBURY
MARYLEBONE
HOLBORN
SOHO
MAYFAIR
ST JAMES'S
SOUTHWARK
BELGRAVIA
WESTMINSTER
LAMBETH
PIMLICO
NINE ELMS
Holloway Road
Kentish Town
Kentish Town West
Caledonian Road
Canonbury
Highbury & Islington
Camden Road
Caledonian Road & Barnsbury
Camden Town
Mornington Cresent
King's Cross
St Pancras
King's Cross Thameslink
Angel
Euston
Great Portland Street
Regent's Park
Warren Street
Russell Square
Barbican
Goodge Street
Chancery Lane
Farringdon
Holborn
St Paul's
Tottenham Court Road
Oxford Street
Bond Street
Covent Garden
Temple
Blackfriars
Mansion House
Leicester Square
Piccadilly Circus
Charing Cross
Embankment
Green Park
Waterloo East
Waterloo
Westminster
Borough
Hyde Park Corner
St James's Park
Lambeth North
Elephant & Castle
Victoria
Sloane Square
Pimlico
Kennington
Vauxhall
Oval
Regent's Park
Green Park
St James's Park
River Thames
Holloway Rd
Kentish Town Rd
Camden Rd
Chalk Farm Rd
York Way
Caledonian Rd
Liverpool Rd
Upper St
Essex Rd
St Paul's Rd
Camberwell Rd
A503
A5203
A5200
A1
A4201
A4200
A501
A201
A5201
A400
A40
A4
A301
A302
A202
A3203
A3
A3205
0 0.5 1 km
0 0.25 0.5 mi

Map 1 - Central: Soho

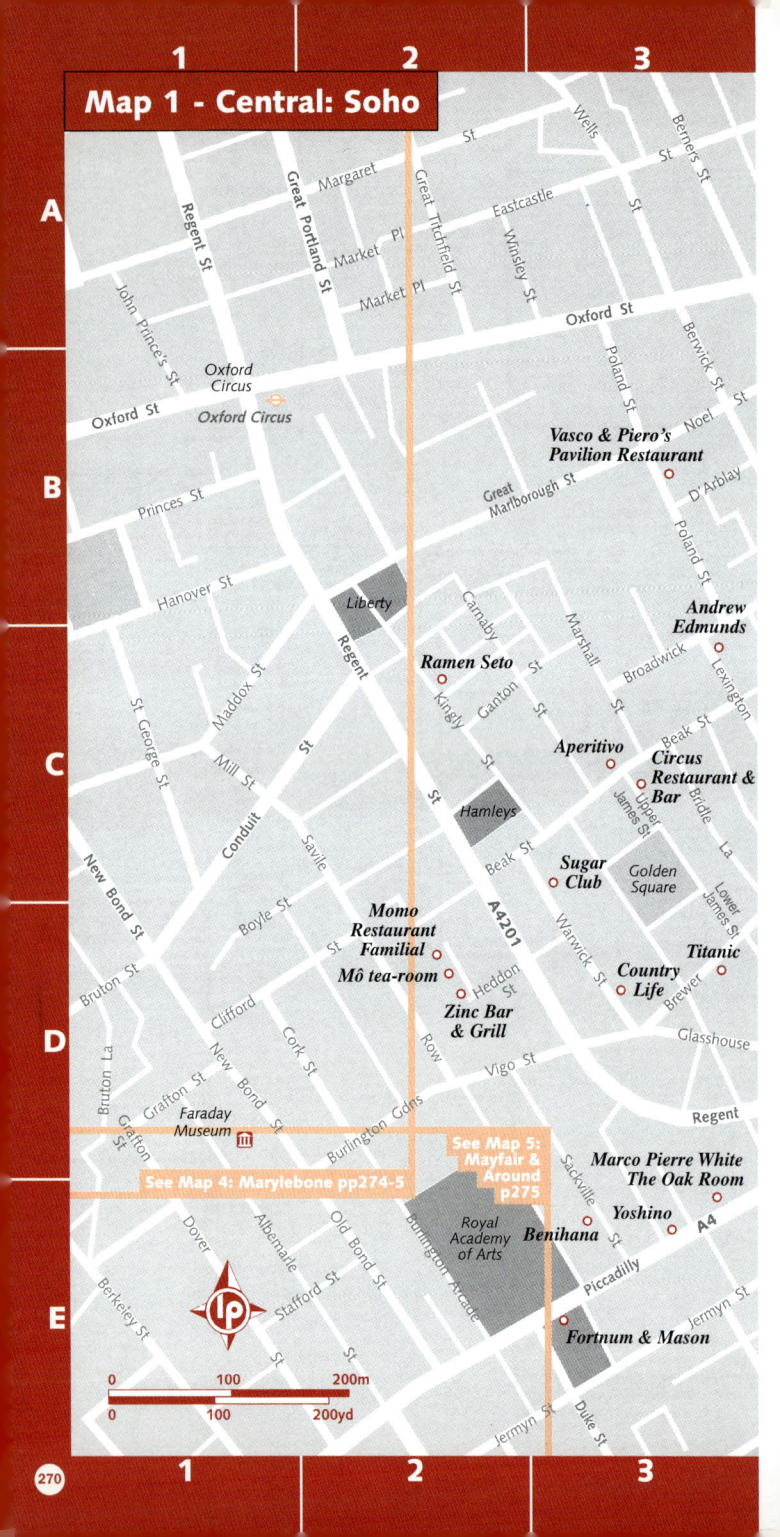

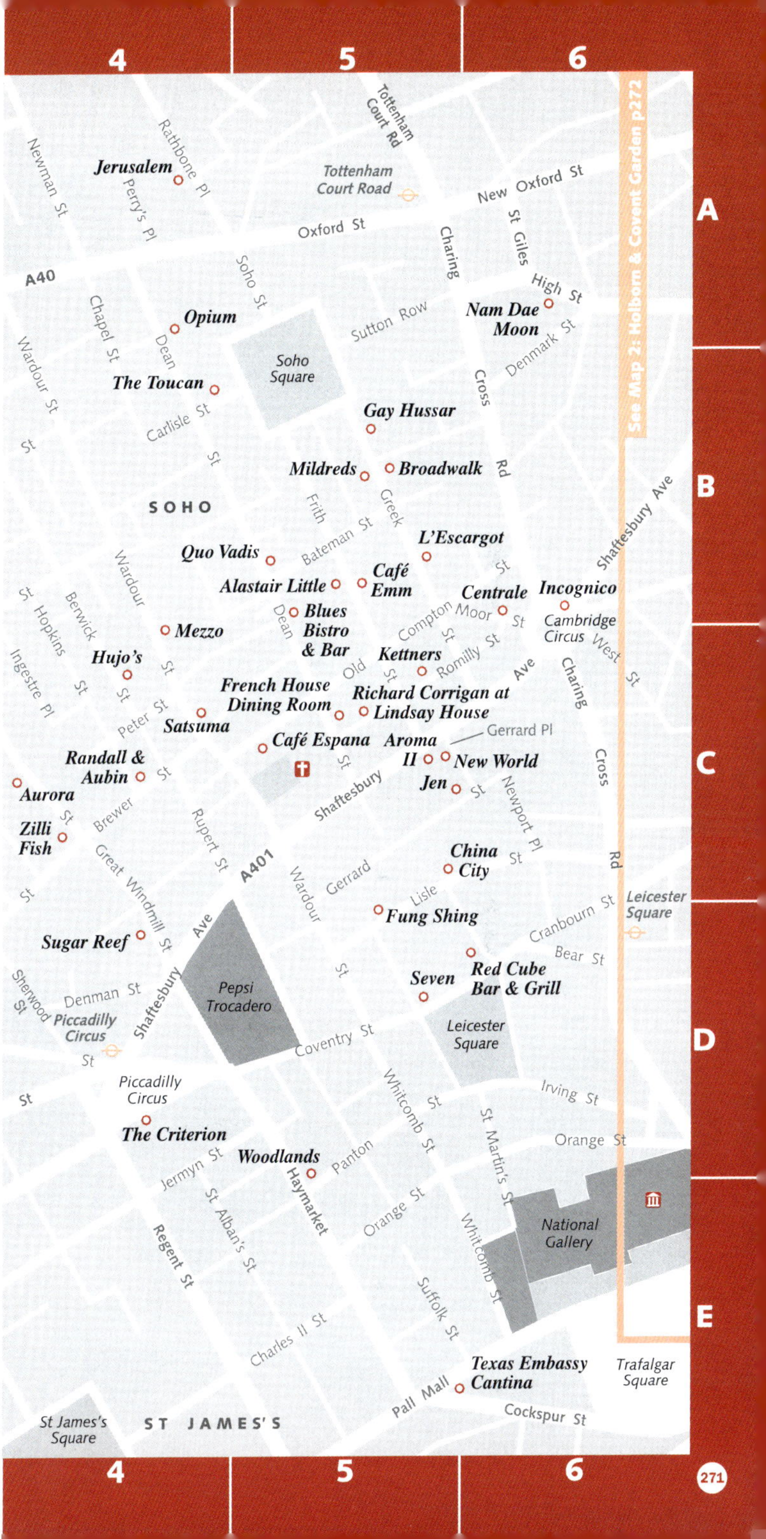

See Map 2: Holborn & Covent Garden p272

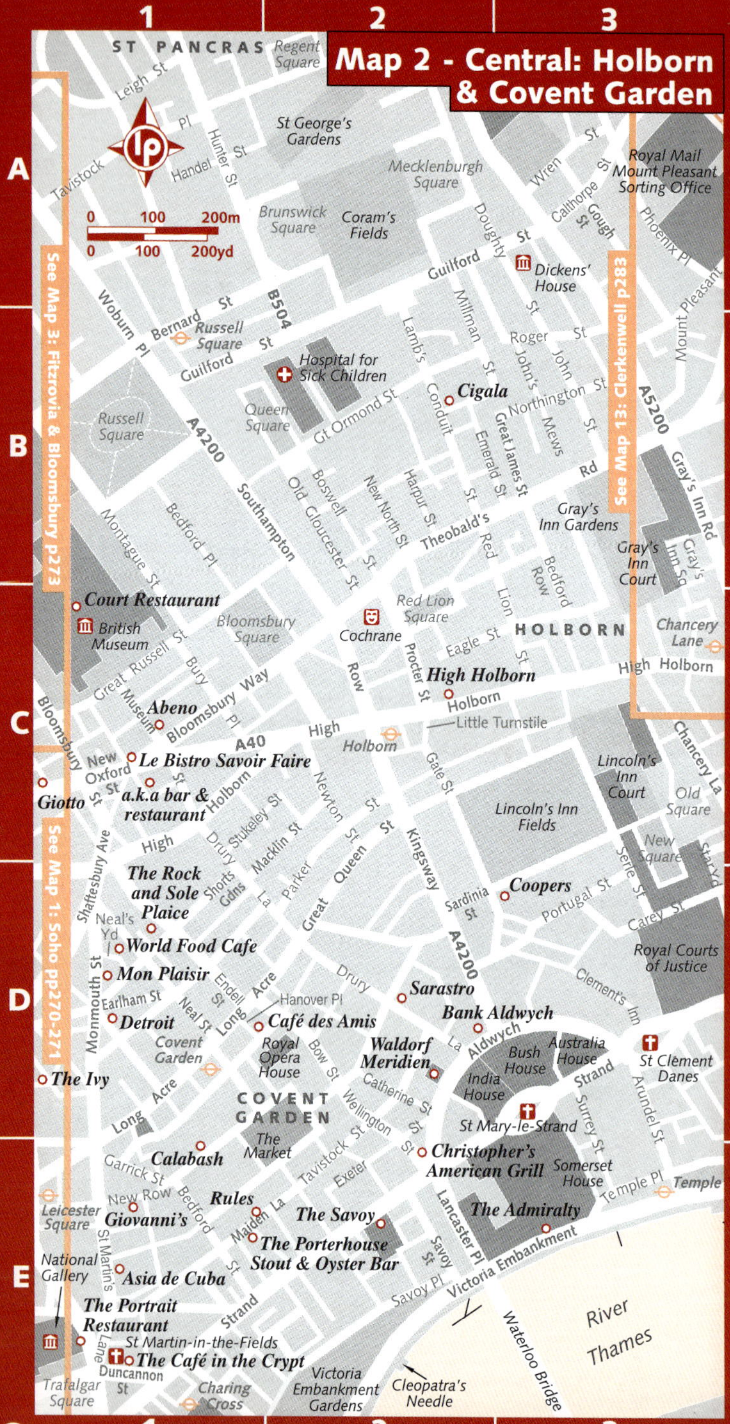
Map 2 - Central: Holborn & Covent Garden
1
2
3
A
B
C
D
E
0
100
200m
0
100
200yd
See Map 3: Fitzrovia & Bloomsbury p273
See Map 13: Clerkenwell p283
See Map 1: Soho pp270-271
ST PANCRAS
Regent Square
St George's Gardens
Mecklenburgh Square
Brunswick Square
Coram's Fields
Royal Mail Mount Pleasant Sorting Office
Dickens' House
Hospital for Sick Children
Cigala
Russell Square
Queen Square
Gray's Inn Gardens
Gray's Inn Court
Court Restaurant
British Museum
Bloomsbury Square
Red Lion Square
Cochrane
HOLBORN
Chancery Lane
High Holborn
Little Turnstile
Holborn
Abeno
Le Bistro Savoir Faire
a.k.a bar & restaurant
Giotto
Lincoln's Inn Court
Old Square
Lincoln's Inn Fields
New Square
The Rock and Sole Plaice
Coopers
World Food Cafe
Mon Plaisir
Detroit
Royal Courts of Justice
Sarastro
Bank Aldwych
Café des Amis
Hanover Pl
Royal Opera House
Waldorf Meridien
Bush House
Australia House
India House
St Clement Danes
Covent Garden
The Ivy
COVENT GARDEN
The Market
St Mary-le-Strand
Calabash
Christopher's American Grill
Somerset House
Temple
Rules
Leicester Square
Giovanni's
The Savoy
The Admiralty
The Porterhouse Stout & Oyster Bar
National Gallery
Asia de Cuba
The Portrait Restaurant
St Martin-in-the-Fields
The Café in the Crypt
River Thames
Victoria Embankment Gardens
Cleopatra's Needle
Trafalgar Square
Charing Cross
Waterloo Bridge
Victoria Embankment
Tavistock
Leigh St
Handel St
Hunter St
Woburn Pl
Bernard St
Guilford St
B504
A4200
A40
A5200
Southampton Row
Bedford Pl
Montague St
Great Russell St
Museum St
Bloomsbury Way
Bloomsbury Pl
New Oxford St
Shaftesbury Ave
Neal's Yd
Monmouth St
Earlham St
Neal St
Endell St
Long Acre
Garrick St
New Row
Bedford St
Maiden La
St Martin's La
Duncannon St
Strand
Savoy Pl
Savoy St
Lancaster Pl
Exeter St
Tavistock St
Wellington St
Catherine St
Bow St
Drury La
Great Queen St
Kingsway
Sardinia St
Portugal St
Serle St
Carey St
Clement's Inn
Surrey St
Arundel St
Temple Pl
Aldwych
Gt Ormond St
Boswell St
Old Gloucester St
New North St
Harpur St
Lamb's Conduit St
Theobald's Rd
Red Lion St
Eagle St
Procter St
Gate St
Newton St
Parker St
Macklin St
Stukeley St
Shorts Gdns
Mecklenburgh
Doughty St
Millman St
Great James St
Emerald St
John's Mews
John St
Northington St
Roger St
Guilford St
Wren St
Calthorpe St
Gough St
Phoenix Pl
Mount Pleasant
Gray's Inn Rd
Gray's Inn Sq
Bedford Row
Chancery La
Star Yd
High Holborn

Map 3 - Central: Fitzrovia & Bloomsbury

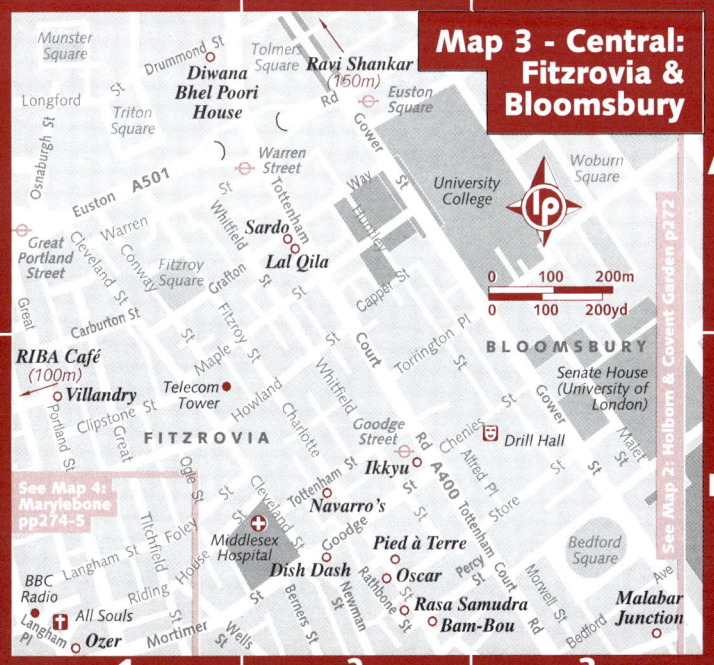

- Munster Square
- Drummond St
- Tolmers Square
- Ravi Shankar (160m)
- Longford St
- Diwana Bhel Poori House
- Triton Square
- Euston Rd
- Euston Square
- Osnaburgh St
- Euston A501
- Warren Street
- Gower St
- Woburn Square
- University College
- Great Portland Street
- Cleveland St
- Warren St
- Conway St
- Whitfield St
- Tottenham Court Rd
- Sardo
- Huntley St
- Fitzroy Square
- Grafton Way
- Lal Qila
- Carburton St
- Capper St
- **BLOOMSBURY**
- RIBA Café (100m)
- Maple St
- Fitzroy St
- Torrington Pl
- Senate House (University of London)
- Villandry
- Clipstone St
- Telecom Tower
- Howland St
- Whitfield St
- Charlotte St
- Gower St
- Great Portland St
- Goodge Street
- Chenies St
- Drill Hall
- Malet St
- See Map 4: Marylebone pp274-5
- **FITZROVIA**
- Ogle St
- Cleveland St
- Tottenham Ct Rd
- Ikkyu
- A400 Tottenham Court Rd
- Alfred Pl
- Store St
- Titchfield St
- Foley St
- Goodge St
- Navarro's
- Bedford Square
- Middlesex Hospital
- Pied à Terre
- Rathbone Pl
- Newman St
- Percy St
- BBC Radio
- Langham St
- Riding House St
- Berners St
- Dish Dash
- Oscar
- Rasa Samudra
- Morwell St
- Bedford Ave
- Malabar Junction
- All Souls
- Langham Pl
- Ozer
- Mortimer St
- Wells St
- Bam-Bou

See Map 2: Holborn & Covent Garden p272

0 100 200m
0 100 200yd

273

Map 4 - Central: Marylebone

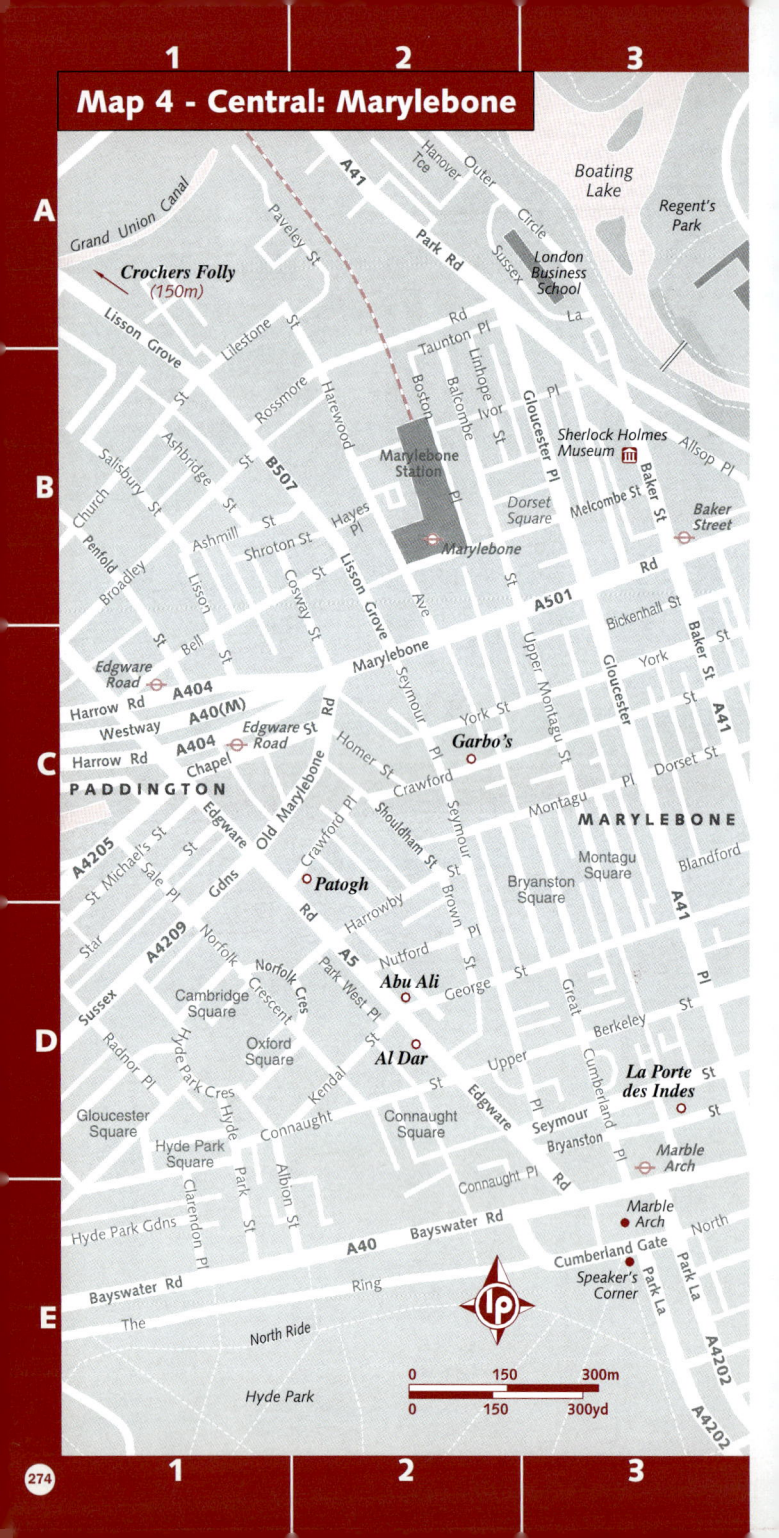

Map 5 - Central: Mayfair & Around

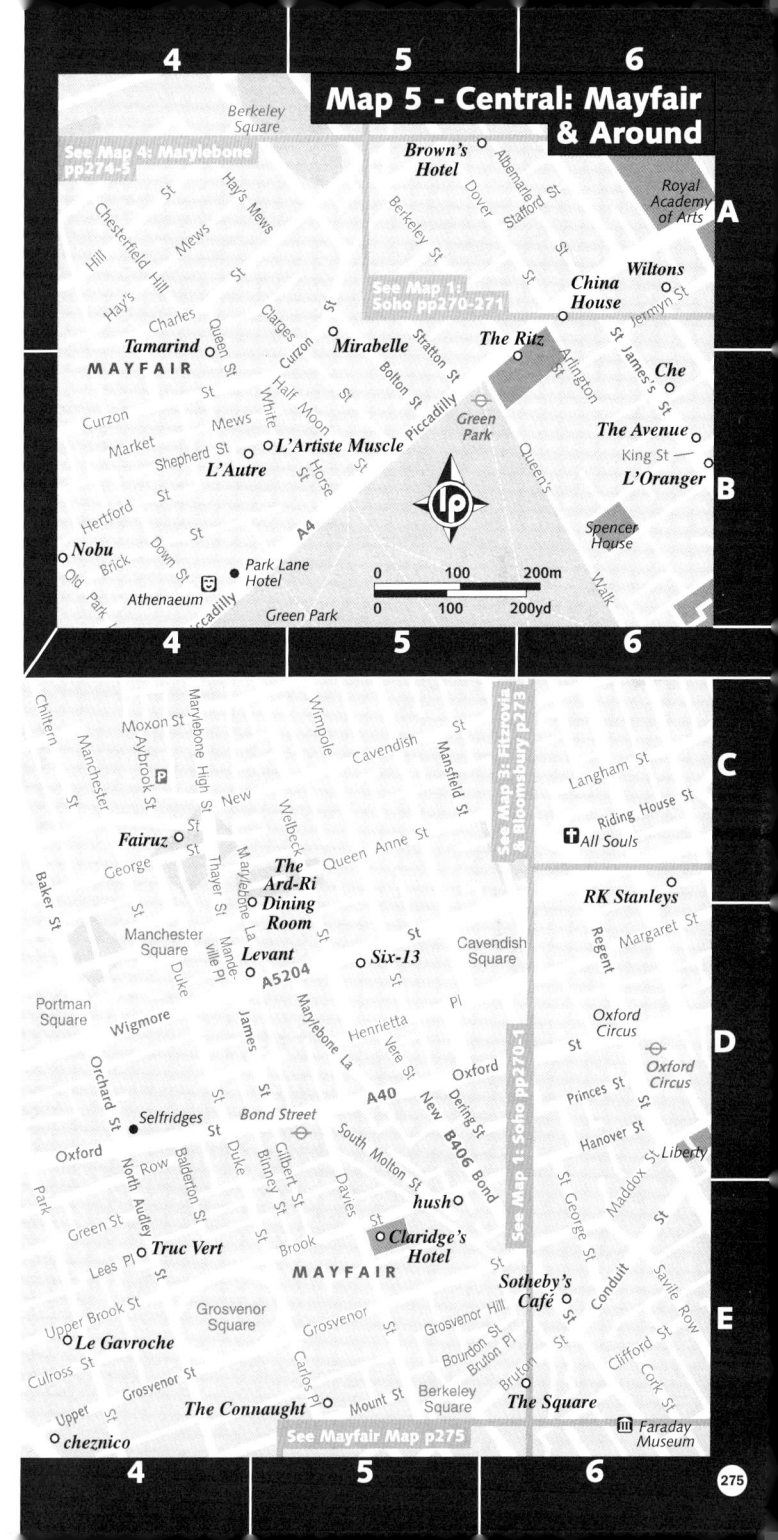

Map 6 - Central: City

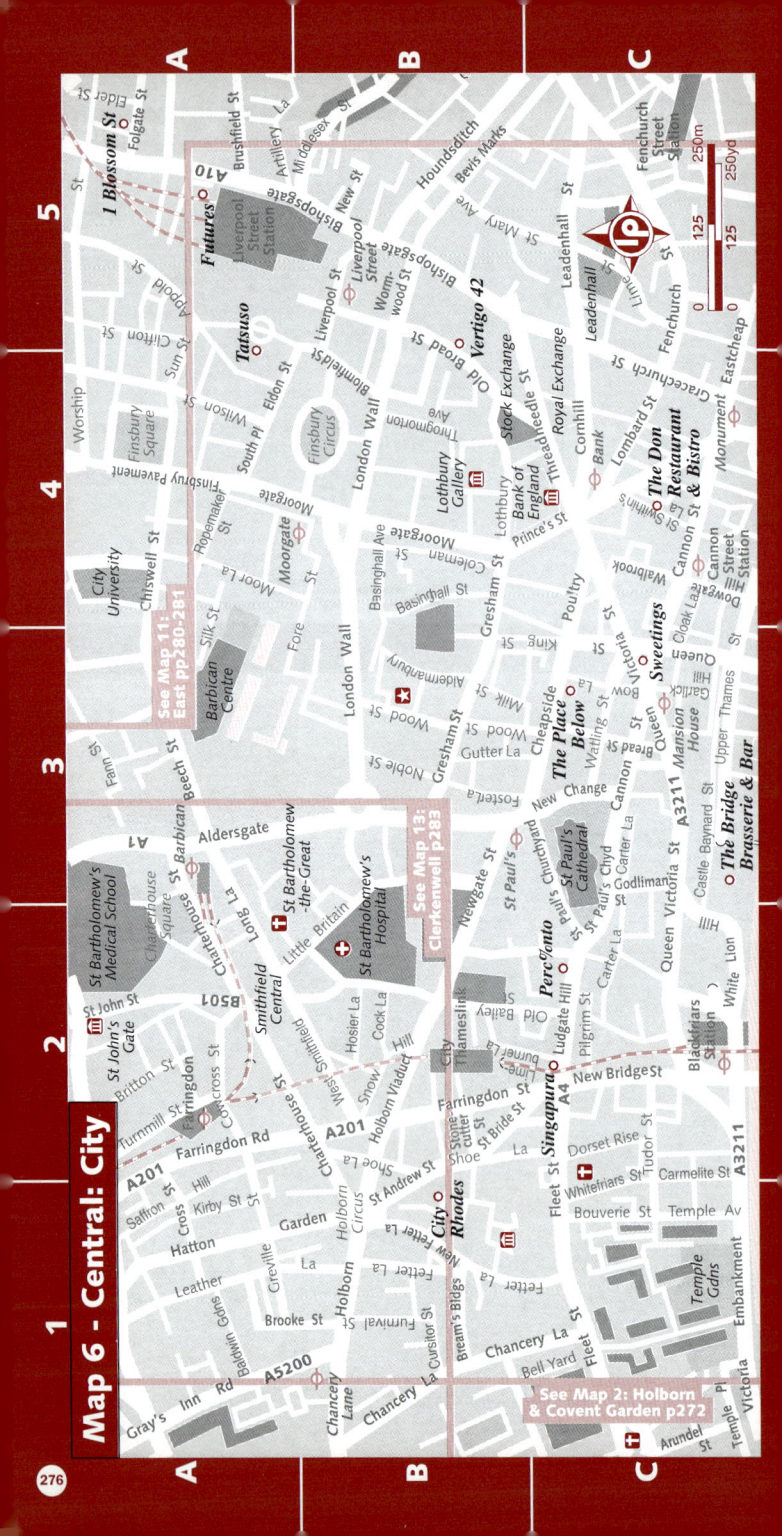

Map 7 - Central: Victoria & Around

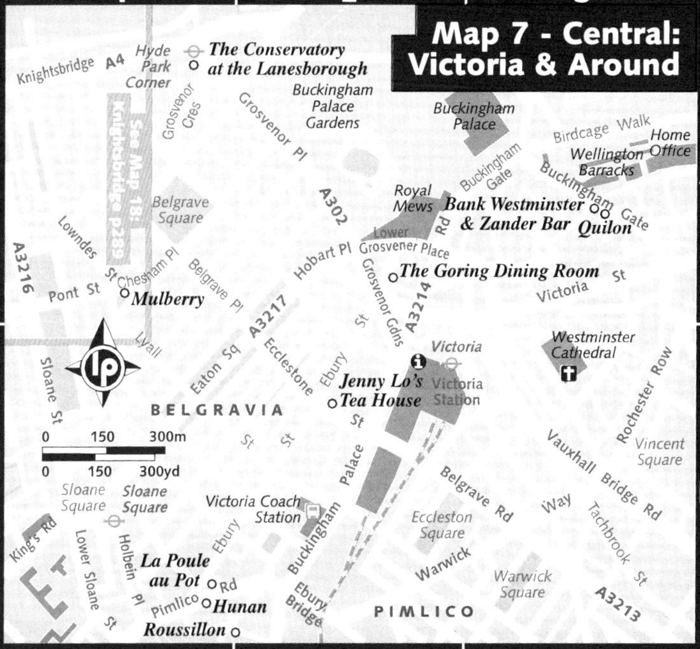

Map 8 - North: Hampstead

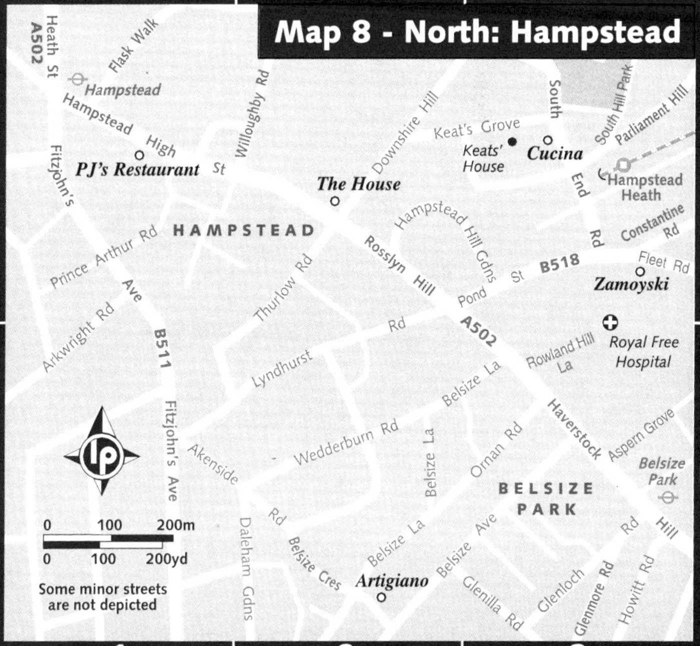

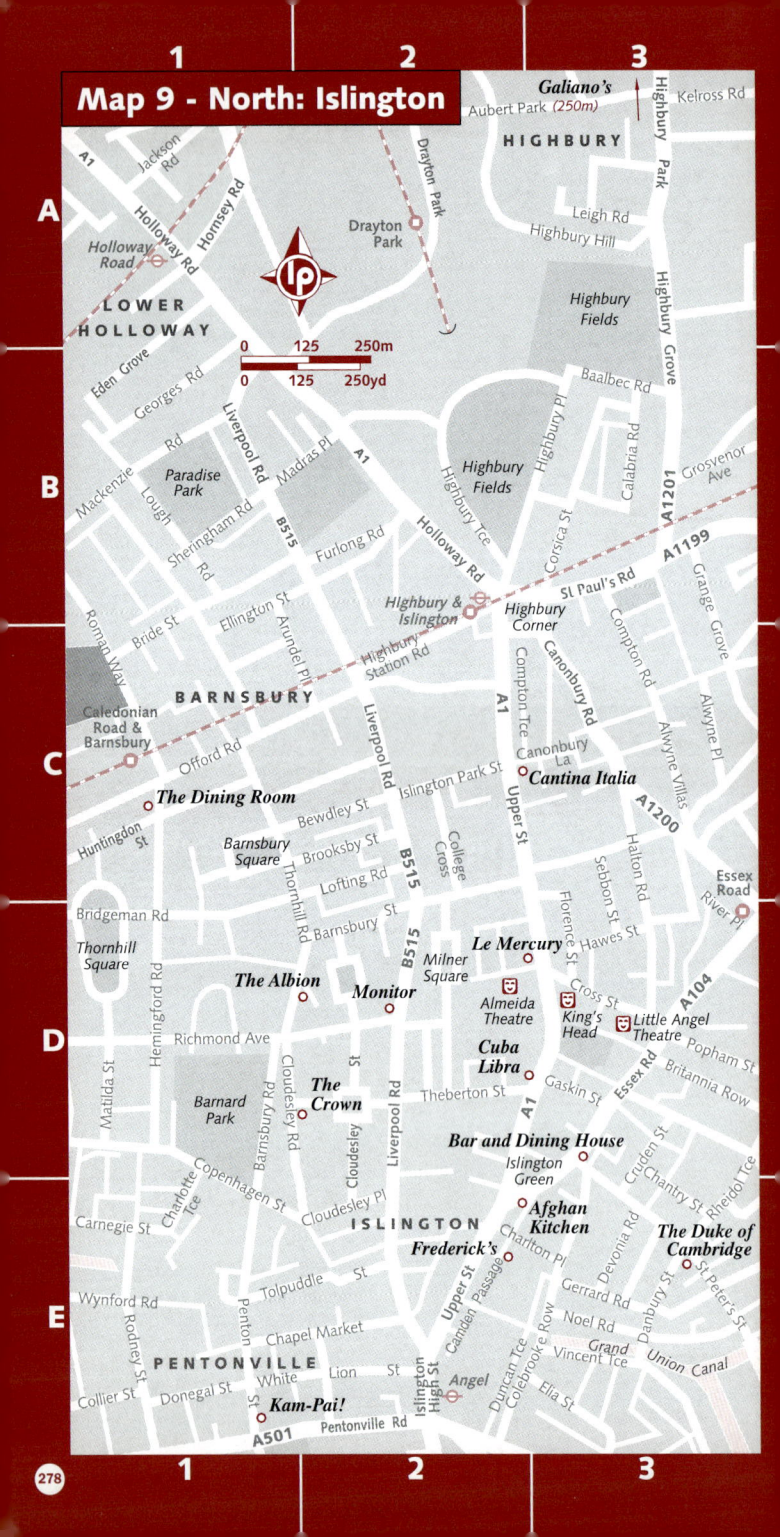

Map 9 - North: Islington

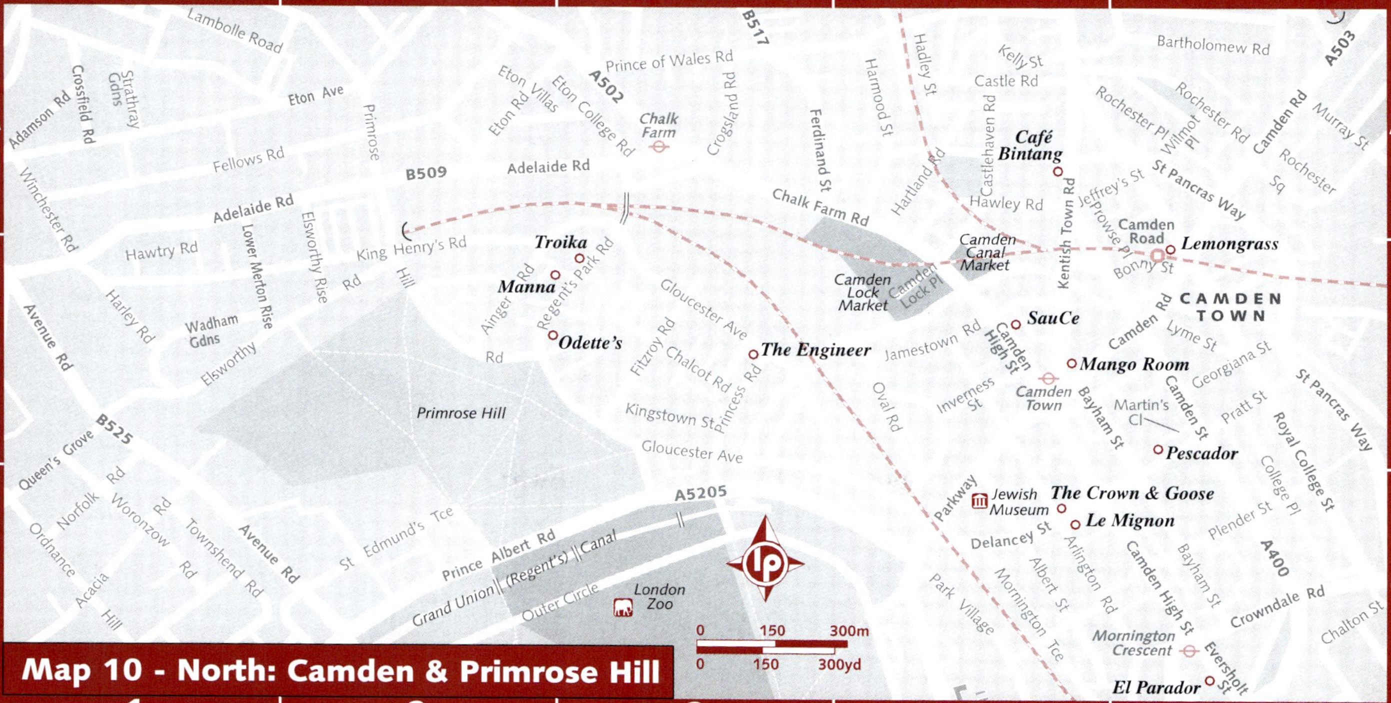

Map 10 - North: Camden & Primrose Hill

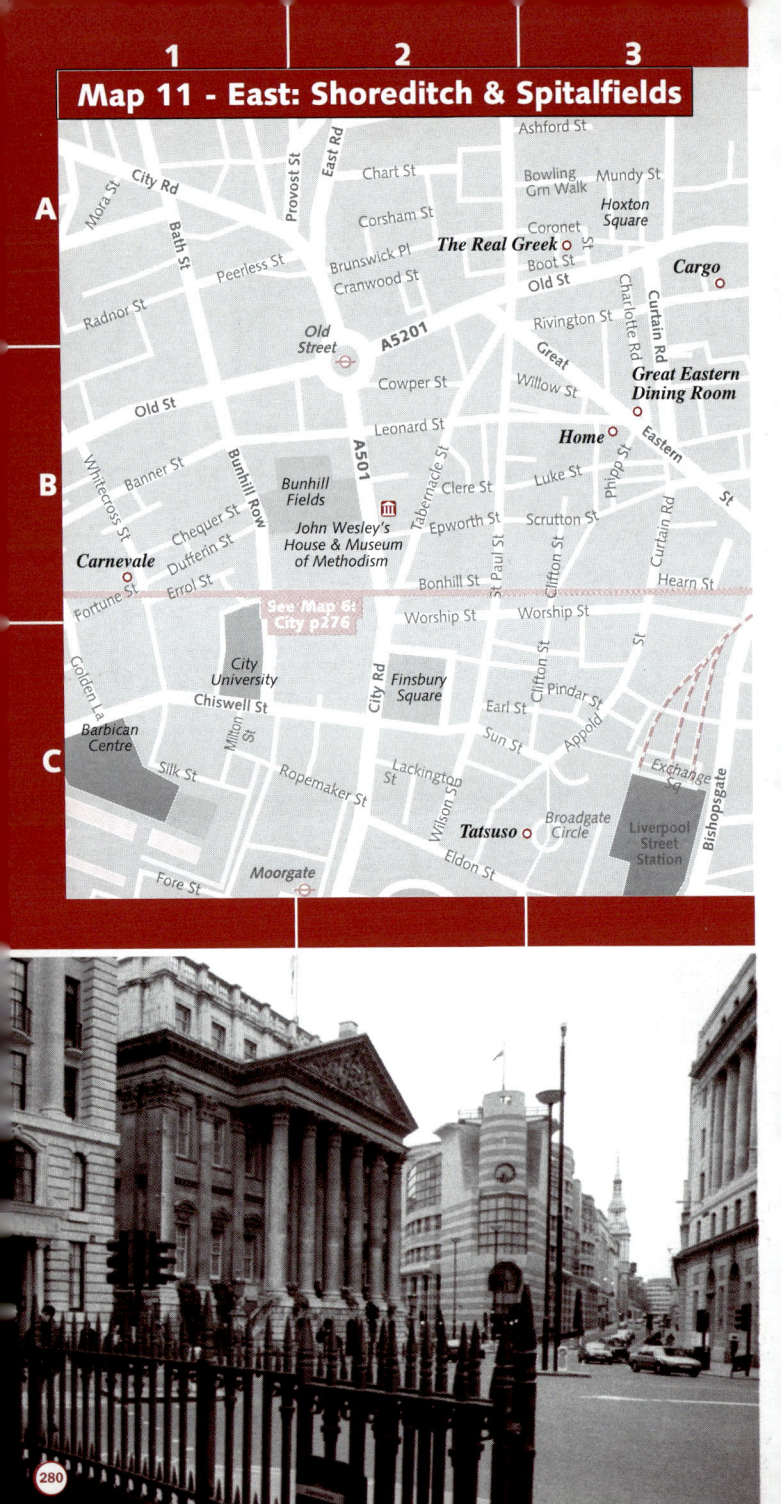

Map 11 - East: Shoreditch & Spitalfields

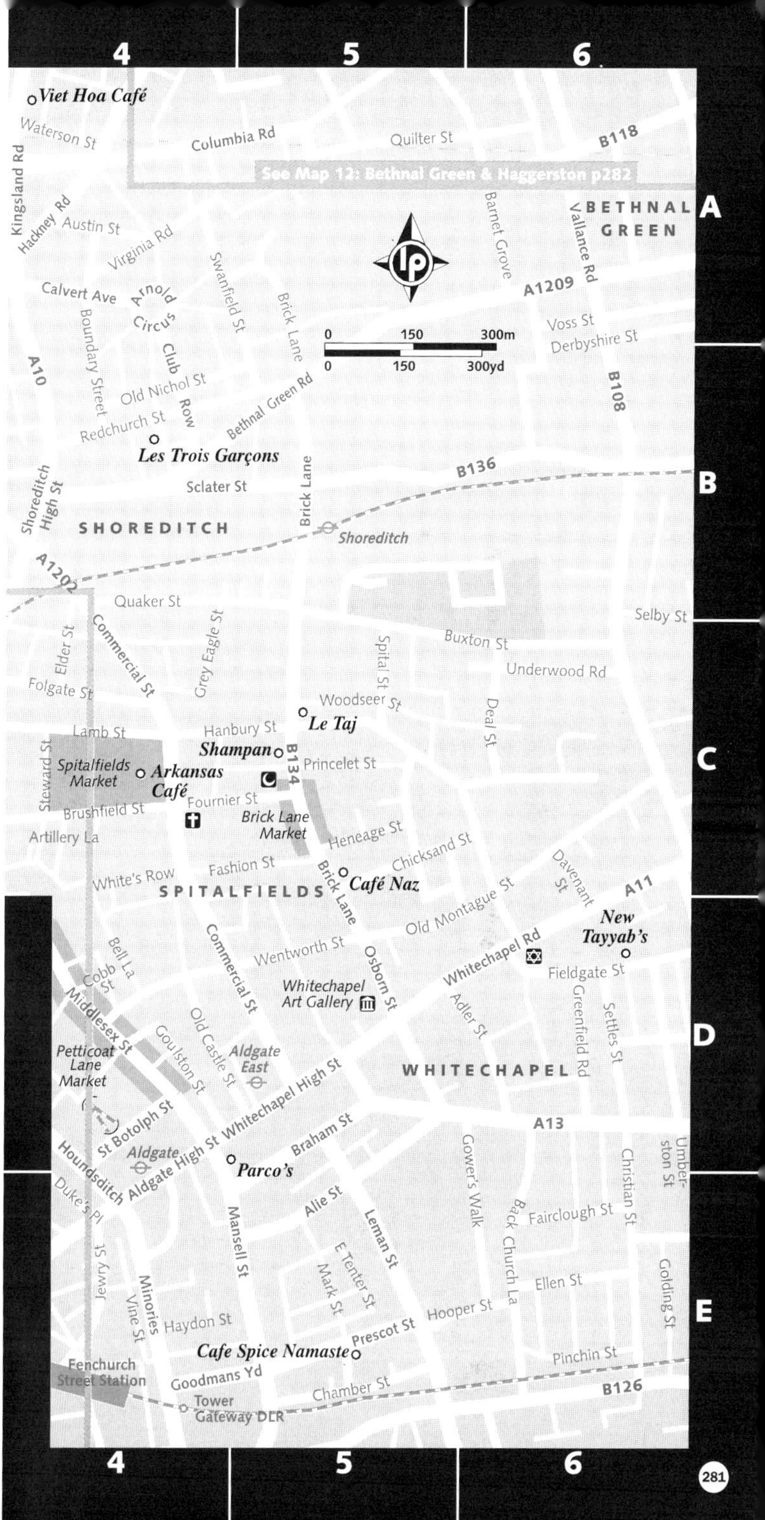
4
5
6
Viet Hoa Café
Waterson St
Columbia Rd
Quilter St
B118
See Map 12: Bethnal Green & Haggerston p282
Kingsland Rd
Hackney Rd
Austin St
Virginia Rd
Swanfield St
Barnet Grove
Vallance Rd
BETHNAL GREEN
A
Calvert Ave
Arnold Circus
Brick Lane
A1209
Boundary Street
Club Row
0
150
300m
0
150
300yd
Voss St
Derbyshire St
A10
Old Nichol St
Bethnal Green Rd
B108
Redchurch St
Les Trois Garçons
B136
Sclater St
B
Shoreditch High St
SHOREDITCH
Shoreditch
A1202
Quaker St
Selby St
Elder St
Commercial St
Grey Eagle St
Spital St
Buxton St
Underwood Rd
Folgate St
Woodseer St
Le Taj
Deal St
Lamb St
Hanbury St
Shampan
B134
Princelet St
C
Steward St
Spitalfields Market
Arkansas Café
Fournier St
Brushfield St
Brick Lane Market
Artillery La
Heneage St
Chicksand St
Davenant St
Fashion St
White's Row
Café Naz
SPITALFIELDS
A11
Old Montague St
New Tayyab's
Bell La
Wentworth St
Osborn St
Whitechapel Rd
Cobb St
Fieldgate St
Whitechapel Art Gallery
Middlesex St
Commercial St
Adler St
Greenfield Rd
Settles St
Old Castle St
Goulston St
Aldgate East
D
Petticoat Lane Market
WHITECHAPEL
Whitechapel High St
St Botolph St
A13
Braham St
Gower's Walk
Aldgate
Aldgate High St
Parco's
Christian St
Umberston St
Houndsditch
Duke's Pl
Alie St
Mansell St
Leman St
Back Church La
Fairclough St
Jewry St
E Tenter St
Mark St
Ellen St
Golding St
Minories
Vine St
Haydon St
Hooper St
E
Prescot St
Cafe Spice Namaste
Pinchin St
Fenchurch Street Station
Goodmans Yd
Tower Gateway DLR
Chamber St
B126
4
5
6

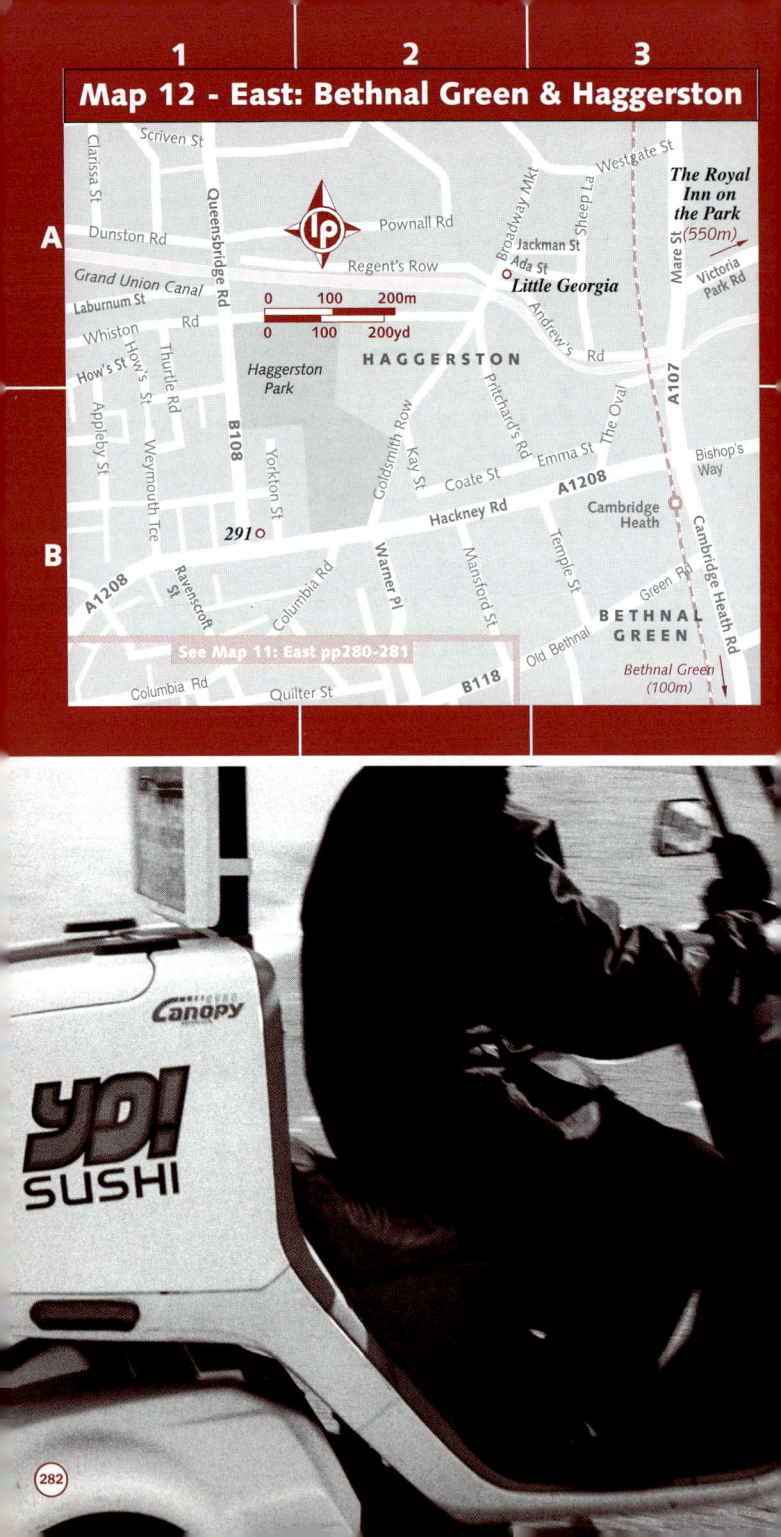

Map 12 - East: Bethnal Green & Haggerston

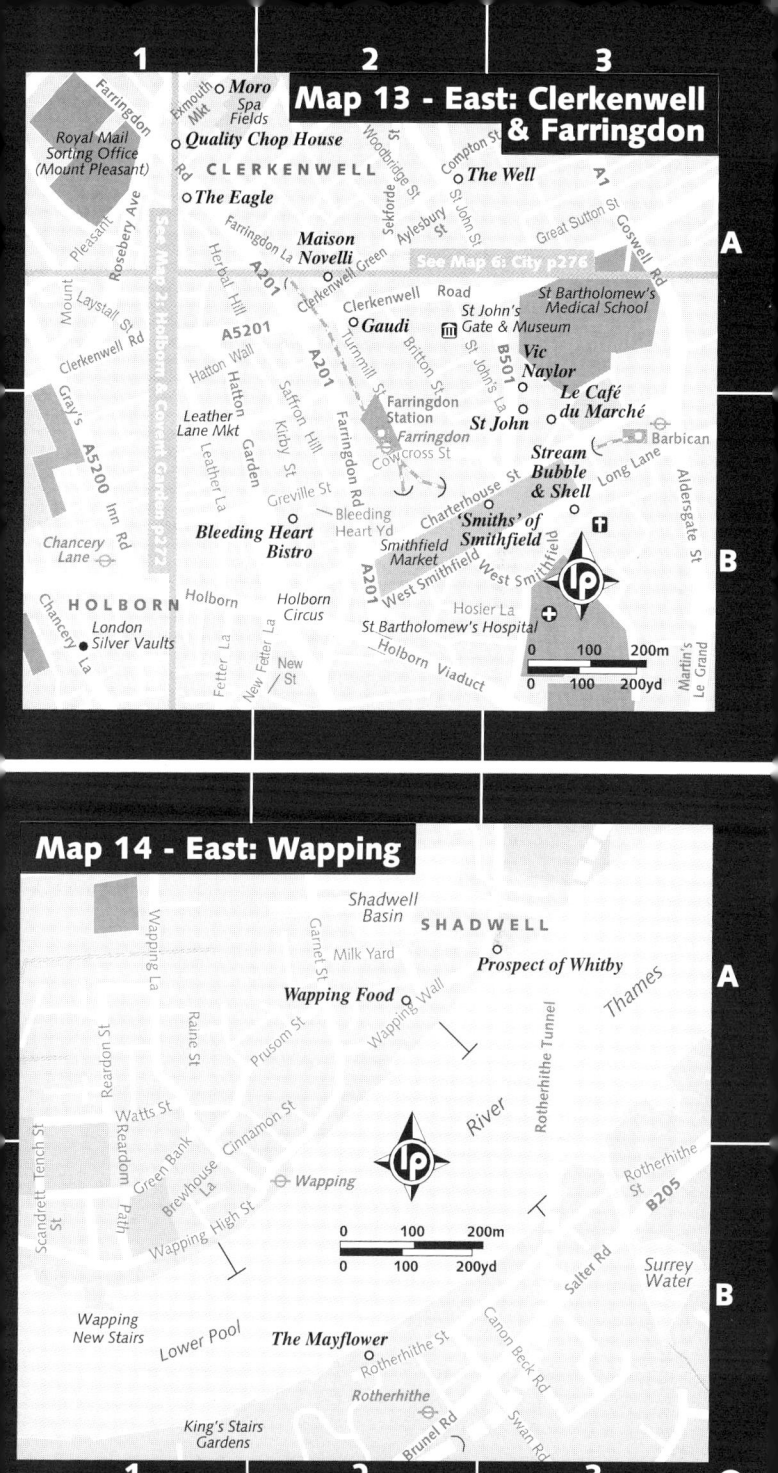

Map 13 - East: Clerkenwell & Farringdon

- Moro
- Quality Chop House
- The Eagle
- The Well
- Maison Novelli
- Gaudi
- St Bartholomew's Medical School
- St John's Gate & Museum
- Vic Naylor
- Le Café du Marché
- St John
- Stream Bubble & Shell
- Bleeding Heart Bistro
- Smiths' of Smithfield

Map 14 - East: Wapping

- Prospect of Whitby
- Wapping Food
- The Mayflower

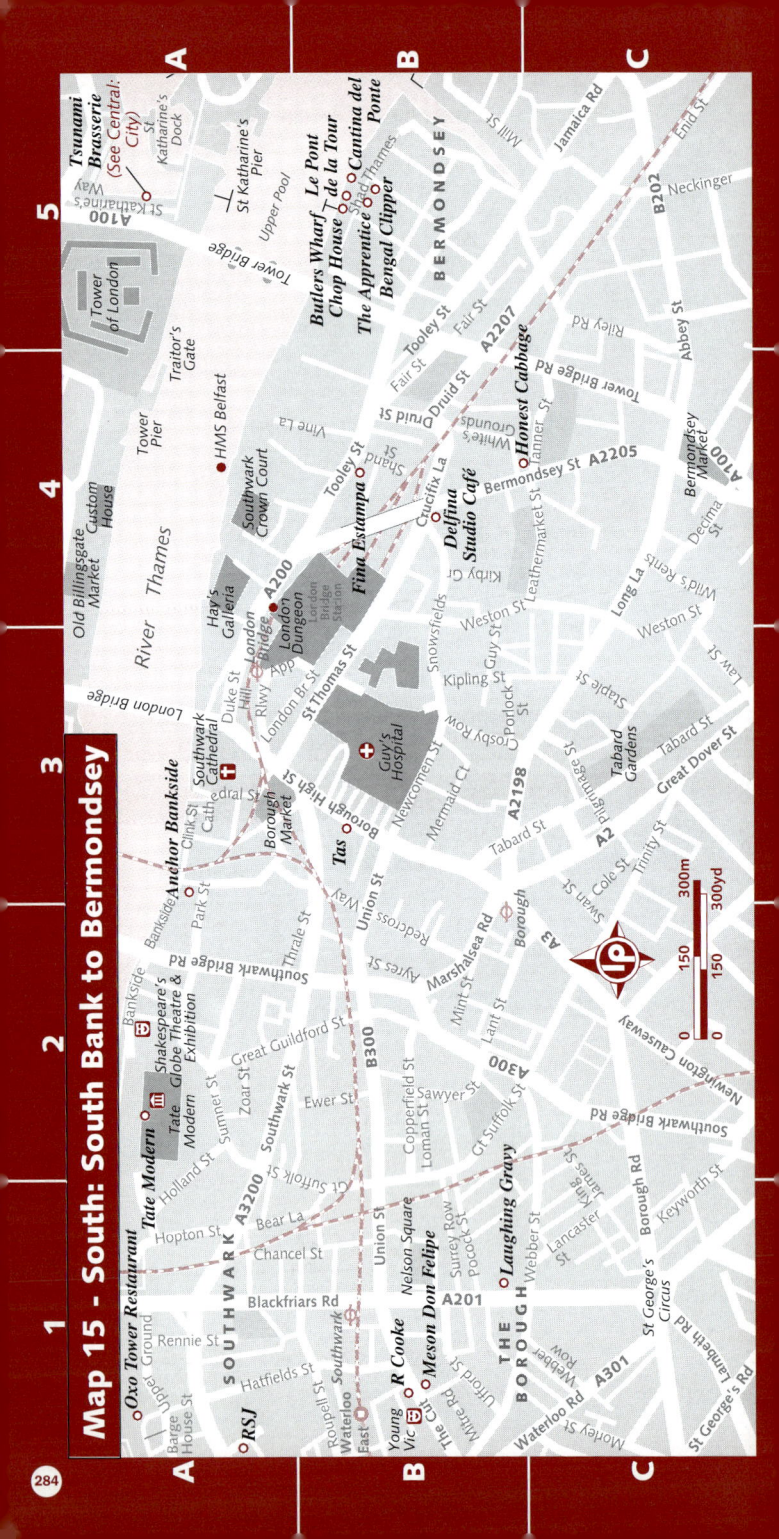

Map 15 - South: South Bank to Bermondsey

Restaurants/Places labeled:

- Oxo Tower Restaurant
- RSJ
- Tate Modern
- Shakespeare's Globe Theatre & Exhibition
- Anchor Bankside
- Southwark Cathedral
- Tas
- Young Vic
- R Cooke
- Meson Don Felipe
- Laughing Gravy
- Fina Estampa
- Delfina Studio Café
- Honest Cabbage
- Butlers Wharf Chop House
- Le Pont de la Tour
- The Apprentice
- Bengal Clipper
- Cantina del Ponte
- Tsunami Brasserie (See Central: City)

Landmarks:

- Tower of London
- Traitor's Gate
- Tower Pier
- HMS Belfast
- St Katharine's Dock
- St Katharine's Pier
- Upper Pool
- Tower Bridge
- Southwark Crown Court
- Hay's Galleria
- London Bridge
- London Bridge Station
- London Dungeon
- St Thomas St
- Guy's Hospital
- Borough Market
- Custom House
- Old Billingsgate Market
- River Thames

Streets and areas:

- SOUTHWARK
- BERMONDSEY
- THE BOROUGH
- Bermondsey Market
- A100 St Katharine's Way
- A3200
- A2207 Tooley St
- A2205 Bermondsey St
- Tower Bridge Rd
- A2198 Tabard St
- A3 Great Dover St
- A198
- A300 Borough
- A301 Waterloo Rd
- A201 Blackfriars Rd
- B300 Southwark Bridge Rd
- Jamaica Rd
- Neckinger
- B202
- Mill St
- End St
- Abbey St
- Riley Rd
- Druid St
- Fair St
- Vine La
- Shand St
- Tanner St
- Leathermarket St
- White's Grounds
- Crucifix La
- Kirby Gr
- Weston St
- Snowsfields
- Kipling St
- Guy St
- Crosby Row
- Porlock St
- Mermaid Ct
- Newcomen St
- Borough High St
- Redcross Way
- Union St
- Ayres St
- Marshalsea Rd
- Mint St
- Lant St
- Swan St
- Cole St
- Trinity St
- Pilgrimage St
- Tabard Gardens
- Staple St
- Long La
- Wild's Rents
- Decima St
- Morley St
- St George's Rd
- Lancaster St
- Webber St
- Keyworth St
- Borough Rd
- St George's Circus
- Newington Causeway
- Southwark Bridge Rd
- Pocock St
- Gt Suffolk St
- Sawyer St
- Loman St
- Copperfield St
- Nelson Square
- Union St
- Bear La
- Chancel St
- Hopton St
- Holland St
- Sumner St
- Zoar St
- Ewer St
- Great Guildford St
- Southwark St
- Park St
- Clink St
- Cathedral St
- Duke St Hill
- London Br St
- Rwly App
- Thrale St
- Bankside
- Hatfields St
- Roupell St
- Waterloo East
- The Cut
- Mitre Rd
- Ufford St
- Surrey Row
- Rennie St
- Upper Ground
- Barge House St
- London Bridge

300m / 300yd
150 / 150
0 / 0

284

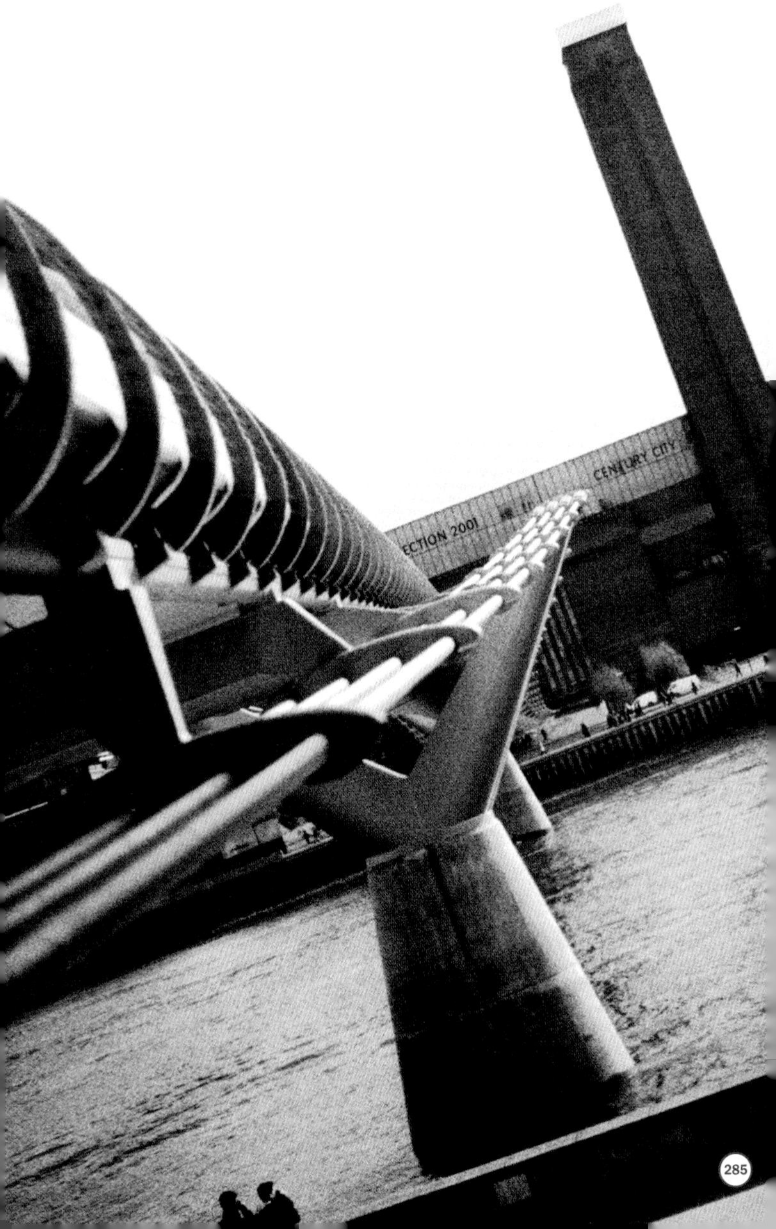
CENTURY CITY
ECTION 2001

Map 16 - South: Clapham & Around

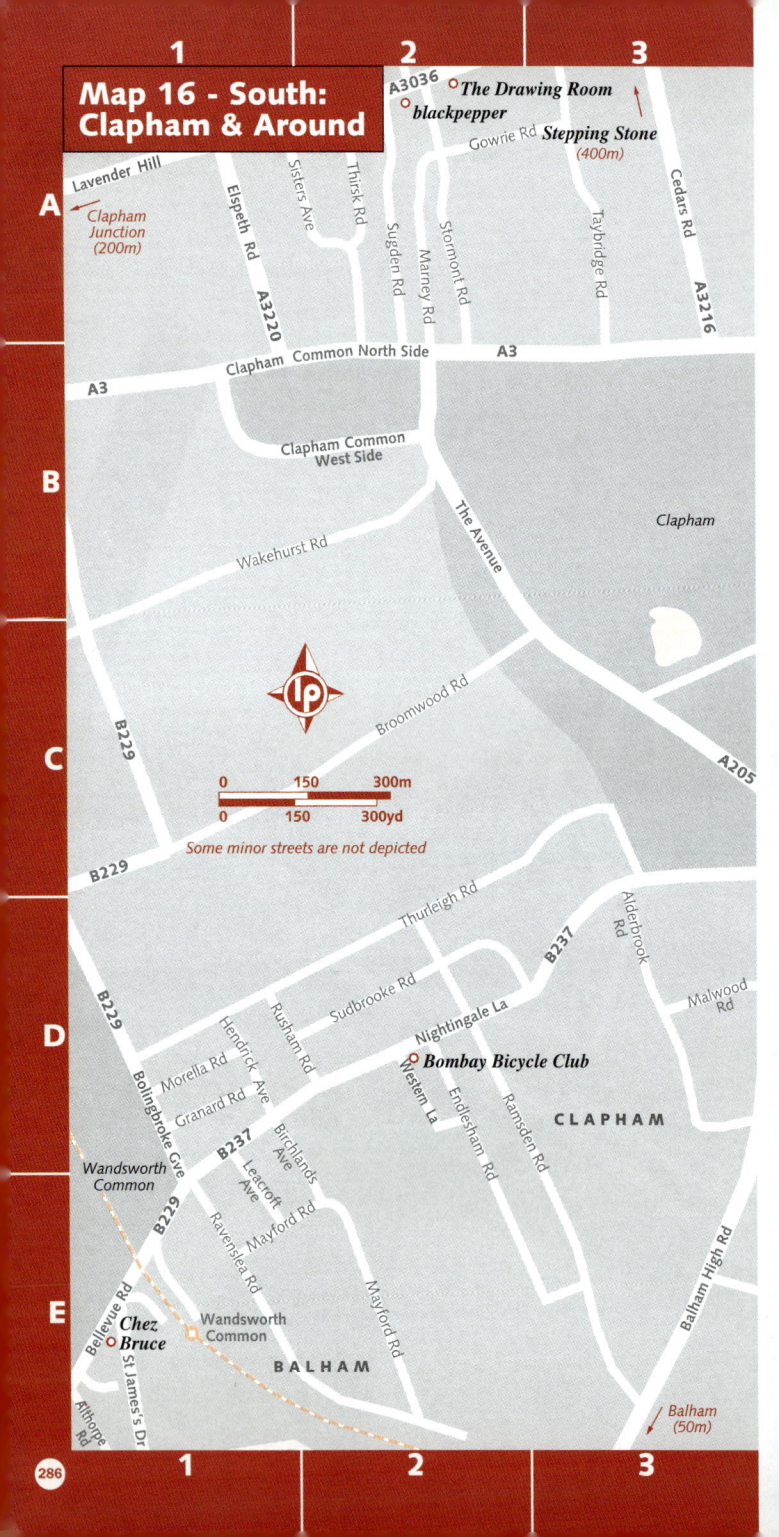

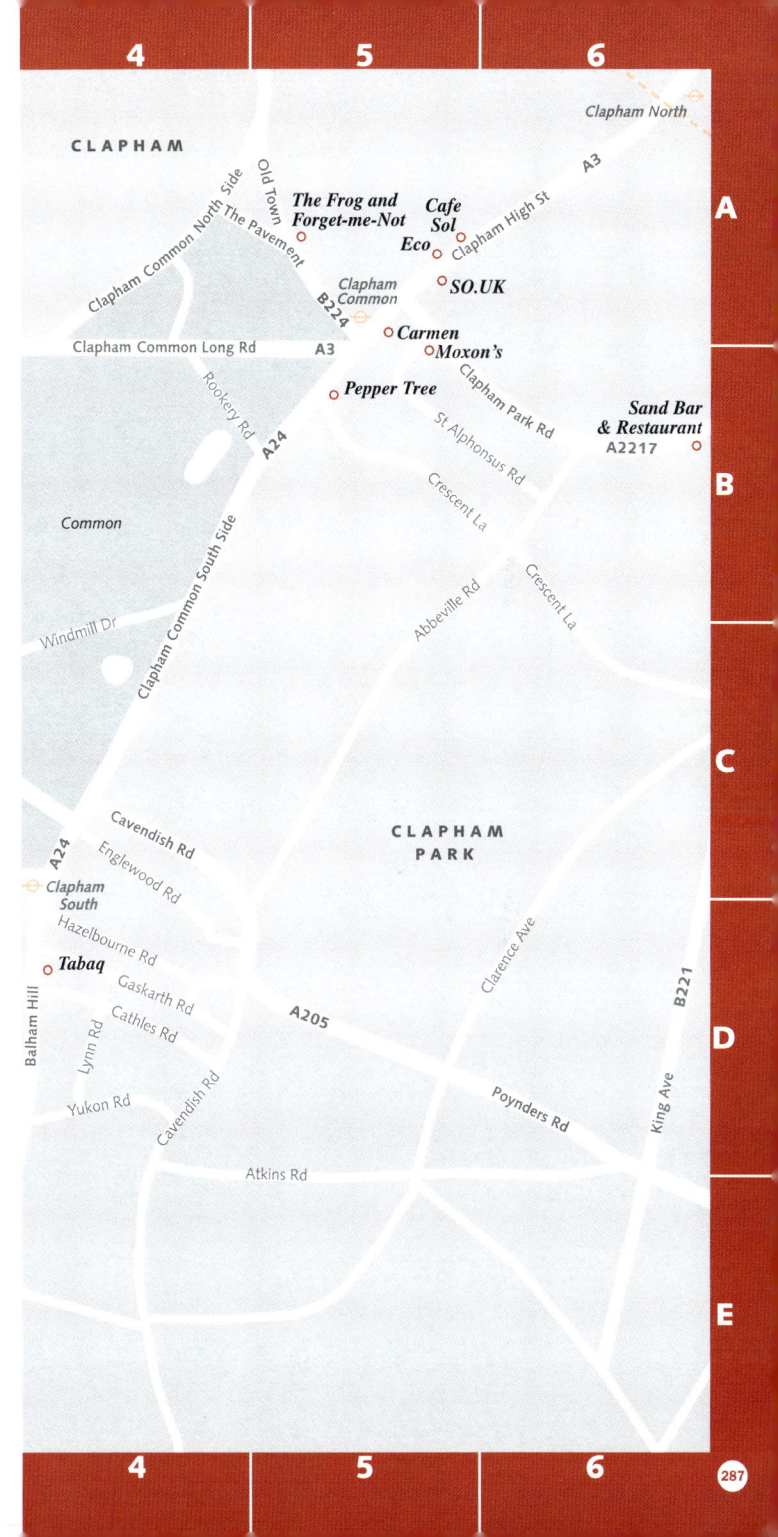

CLAPHAM

- Clapham North
- The Frog and Forget-me-Not
- Cafe Sol
- Eco
- SO.UK
- Carmen
- Moxon's
- Pepper Tree
- Sand Bar & Restaurant
- Tabaq

CLAPHAM PARK

Clapham South

Common

Map 17 - South: Brixton & Stockwell

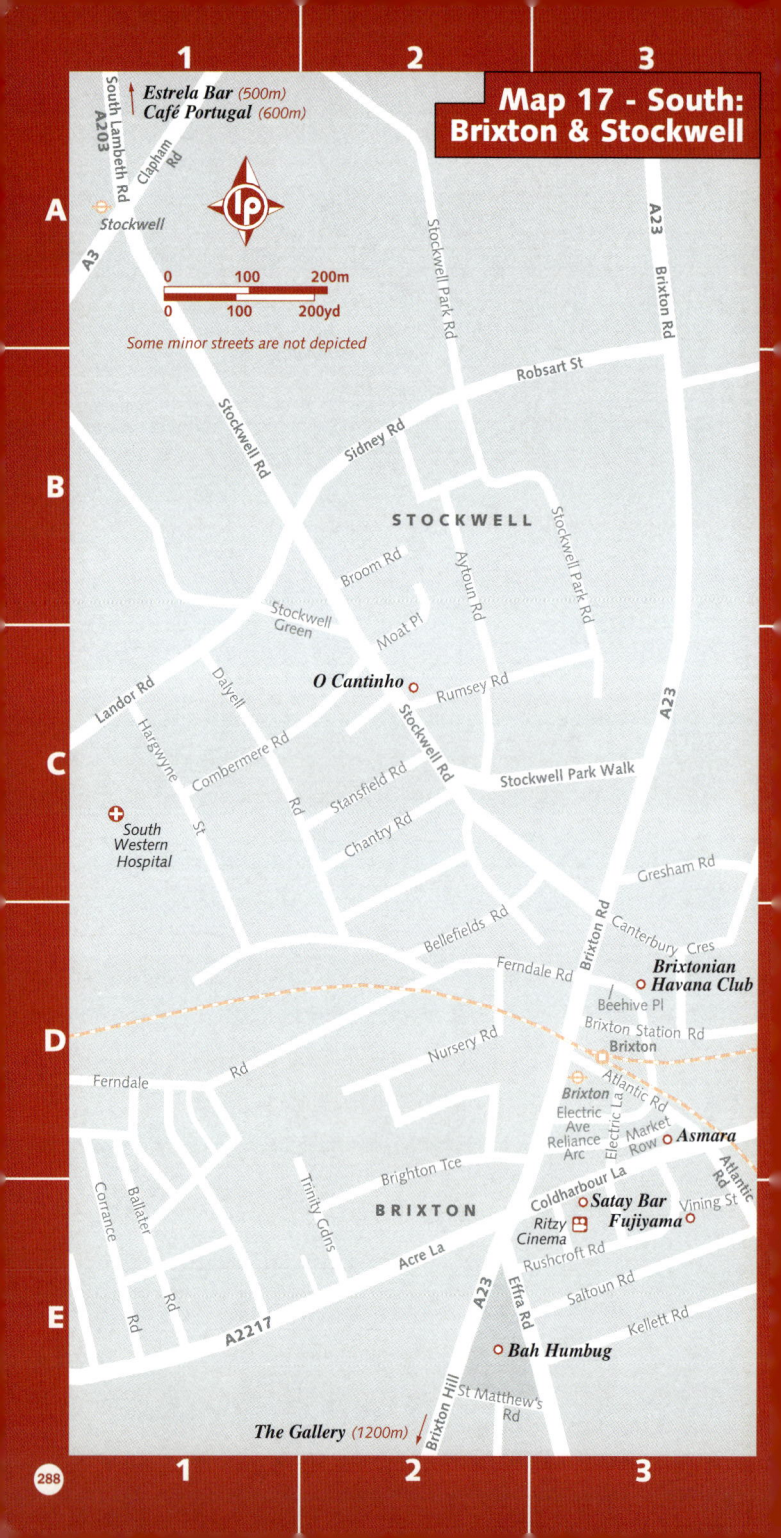

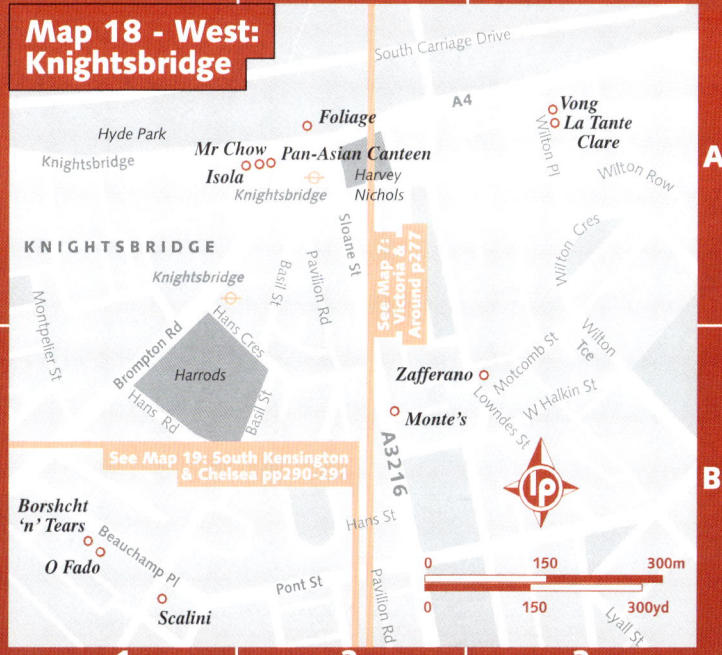

Map 18 - West: Knightsbridge

- Hyde Park
- Knightsbridge
- Foliage
- Mr Chow
- Isola
- Pan-Asian Canteen
- Harvey Nichols
- Knightsbridge
- Vong
- La Tante Clare
- Wilton Pl
- Wilton Row

KNIGHTSBRIDGE

- Montpelier St
- Knightsbridge
- Brompton Rd
- Hans Cres
- Basil St
- Harrods
- Hans Rd
- Pavilion Rd
- Sloane St
- Wilton Cres
- Wilton Tce
- Motcomb St
- Lowndes St
- W Halkin St
- Zafferano
- Monte's

See Map 7: Victoria & Around p277

See Map 19: South Kensington & Chelsea pp290-291

- Borshcht 'n' Tears
- Beauchamp Pl
- O Fado
- Pont St
- Scalini
- Hans St
- A3216
- Pavilion Rd
- Lyall St

0 — 150 — 300m
0 — 150 — 300yd

289

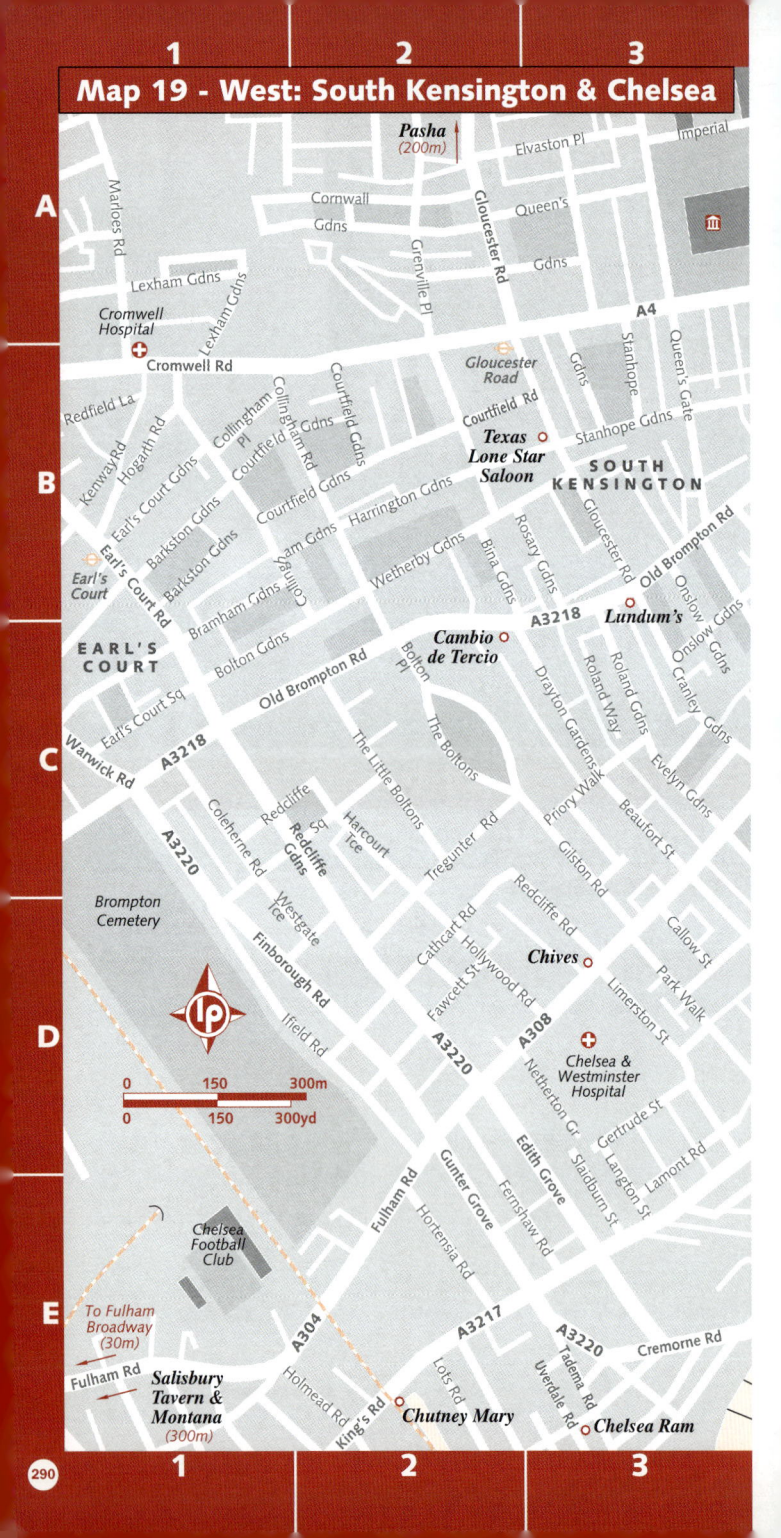

Map 19 - West: South Kensington & Chelsea

4
5
6
Prince's Gate Mews
Ognisko
College Rd
Science Museum
Exhibition Rd
Victoria & Albert Museum
Natural History Museum
Brompton Sq
A4
Map 18: Knightsbridge Map p289
Beaufort Gdns
Beauchamp Pl
Ovington Sq
Hans Pl
Pont St
A
Egerton Tce
Egerton Gdns
Brompton Rd
Walton St
Ovington St
Hasker St
First St
Lennox Gardens
Clabon Mews
Cadogan Sq
Cromwell Rd
Thurloe Pl
Thurloe Sq
Thurloe St
South Tce
Daquise
South Kensington
The Thai Bar & Restaurant
Milner St
Halsey St
Moore St
Pelham St
Draycott
Denyer St
Rawlings St
Bute St
Bibendum
Sloane Ave
Cadogan St
Sydney Pl
Onslow Sq
Sumner Pl
A308
Lucan Pl
Elystan St
B
Ave
To Sloane Square (150m)
El Rincón
Ixworth Pl
Whitehead's Grove
Pond Pl
Elystan Pl
King's Rd
Foulis Tce
Neville St
Fulham Rd
Royal Marsden Hospital
Cale St
Astell St
Lower Sloane St
Markham St
Markham Sq
A3217
Royal Avenue
St Luke's
St Luke's St
Sydney St
South Pde
Dovehouse St
Chelsea Sq
Britten St
Smith St
Chelsea Farmers Market
CHELSEA
C
Manresa Rd
Radnor Walk
Shawfield St
Smith Tce
Elm Pk
Phat Phuc Noodle Bar
Flood St
Old Chelsea Town Hall
Tedworth Sq
Old Church St
Carlyle Sq
Chelsea Manor St
Walk
Elm Park Rd
King's Rd
Redburn Street
Christchurch St
The Vale
Glebe Pl
Flood
B302
Bramerton St
Buona Sera at the Jam
A3217
Made in Italy
Oakley St
The Phene Arms
Gordon Ramsay
Rd
Swan Walk
Royal Hospital
Chelsea Physic Garden
Bluebird
Old Church St
Cheyne Gdns
D
Paultons Sq
Upper Cheyne Row
Cheyne Row
Walk
Chelsea Embankment
Beaufort St
Cheyne
Chelsea Old Church
Cadogan Pier
Albert Bridge
THAMES
Milman's St
Cheyne Walk
RIVER
Battersea Bridge
Carriage Drive North
E
Albert Bridge Rd
Anhalt Rd
Ransome's Dock
(See South: Battersea)
Battersea Park
A3031
Hester Rd
Echo St
Parkgate Rd
Buchan's
(See South: Battersea)
The Settle Inn (500m)
4
5
6

Map 20 - West: Notting Hill & Kensington

Brasserie du Marché aux Puces

Yum Yum (700m)
William IV (1100m)
& Astons (1200m)

Bali Sugar

The Cow

Mandola

192

Zucca

Portobello Rd Market

Beach Blanket Babylon

NOTTING HILL

Notting Hill Brasserie

Wiz

Julie's

Ladbroke Square Gardens

Notting Hill Gate

The Ladbroke Arms

HOLLAND PARK

Holland Park

Norland Square

Tootsies

KENSINGTON

Holland Park

4
5
6
A
B
C
D
E
Union Canal
Jason's Wharf
(See North: Maida Vale)
Blomfield Rd
Warwick Pl
MAIDA VALE
Senior St
Delamere Tce
Howley Pl
Warwick Ave
Harrow Rd
Bourne Terrace
Westbourne Tce Rd
Little Venice
London Waterbus Boats
A404
Westway
A40(M)
Lord Hills Br
Royal Oak
Ranelagh Br
Westbourne Terrace
Westbourne Park Villas
Paddington
Paddington Station
Gloucester Tce
Westbourne Park Rd
Porchester Rd
Orsett Terrace
A4206
Eastbourne Tce
Kildare Tce
Alexander St
Queensway
Bishop's Bridge Rd
Cleveland Tce
Westbourne Tce
Gloucester Tce
St
Hereford Rd
Newton Rd
Westbourne Grove
Chilworth
Tiroler Hut
Alwaha
Garway Rd
Inaho
L'Accento
Whiteley's Shopping Centre
Inverness Tce
Leinster Gdns
Cleveland Square
Devonshire Ter
Kensington Gdns Square
Leinster Square
Assagi
Porchester Gdns
BAYSWATER
Queen's Gdns
Prince's Sq
Chepstow Pl
Ilchester Gdns
Queensway
Queensborough Tce
Porchester Tce
Leinster Tce
Craven Hill
Bayswater
Hung To
Prince's Tce
Moscow Rd
St Petersburgh Pl
Lancaster Gate
A40
Ossington St
Clanricarde Gdns
B411
Mandarin Kitchen
Linden
Queensway
Bayswater Rd
North Walk
Notting Hill Gate
Kensington Palace Gdns
Palace Gardens Mews
Palace Gardens Tce
Speke's Monument
Lancaster Walk
Budge's Walk
0
150
300m
0
150
300yd
Kensington Gardens
Churchill Arms
Orangery
The Broad Walk
Round Pond
Brunswick Gdns
B405
Kensington Church St
Kensington Palace Green
Kensington Palace
Vicarage Gate
The Dial Walk
Palace Green
Palace Ave
Pitt St
A4204
Kensington Palace Barracks
Holland St
Maggie Jones's
Wodka (300m)
The Flower Walk
The Terrace
Kensington Rd
L'Anis

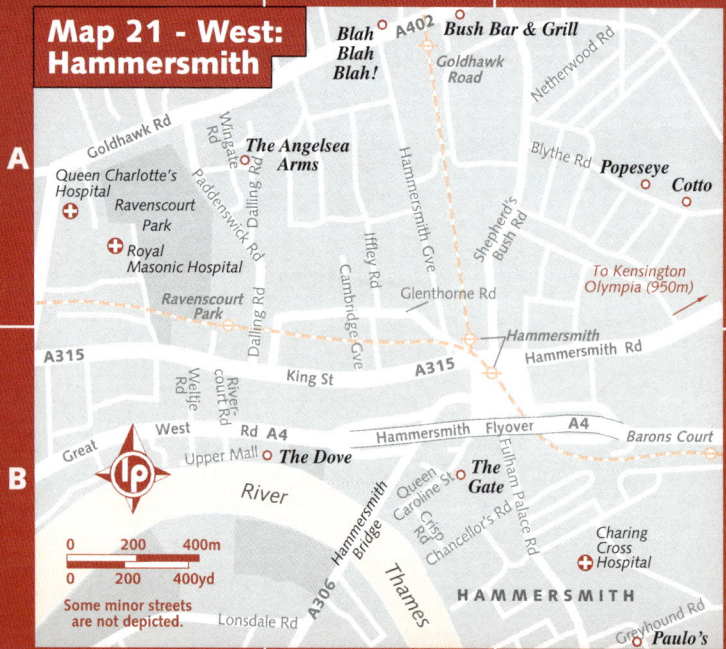

Map 21 - West: Hammersmith

A
- Goldhawk Rd
- Queen Charlotte's Hospital
- Ravenscourt Park
- Royal Masonic Hospital
- Wingate Rd
- Paddenswick Rd
- Darling Rd
- **The Angelsea Arms**
- Blah Blah Blah!
- A402
- Goldhawk Road
- **Bush Bar & Grill**
- Netherwood Rd
- Iffley Rd
- Cambridge Gve
- Hammersmith Gve
- Glenthorne Rd
- Shepherd's Bush Rd
- Blythe Rd
- **Popeseye**
- **Cotto**
- To Kensington Olympia (950m)

- Ravenscourt Park
- A315
- King St
- Rivercourt Rd
- Welfje Relfje
- A315
- Hammersmith
- Hammersmith Rd

B
- Great West Rd A4
- Hammersmith Flyover A4
- Barons Court
- Upper Mall
- **The Dove**
- River Thames
- A306 Hammersmith Bridge
- Queen Caroline St
- Crisp Rd
- **The Gate**
- Fulham Palace Rd
- Chancellor's Rd
- **Charing Cross Hospital**
- HAMMERSMITH
- Greyhound Rd
- **Paulo's**
- Lonsdale Rd

0 200 400m
0 200 400yd

Some minor streets are not depicted.

1 | **2** | **3**

294

Legend

○	Restaurant	Bank	Underground Station
✈	Airport	Hornsey	Railway with station
🚌	Bus Station/Stop	Greenwich DLR	Docklands Light Railway with station
	Church	Dundonald Rd	Tramlink with station
	Cinema		
✚	Hospital	Fulham Rd	Motorway, Major Road
ⓘ	Information	Belgrave Rd	Road
☪	Mosque	Georgiana St	Street
🏛	Museum	Gerrard Pl	Minor Street
P	Parking Area	SOHO	Area
•	Point of Interest		Parks, Gardens
	Pool		Buildings
✉	Post Office		Mall, Market
✡	Synagogue		
	Theatre	see map	Extents of Overlap
	Zoo		

295

London Underground

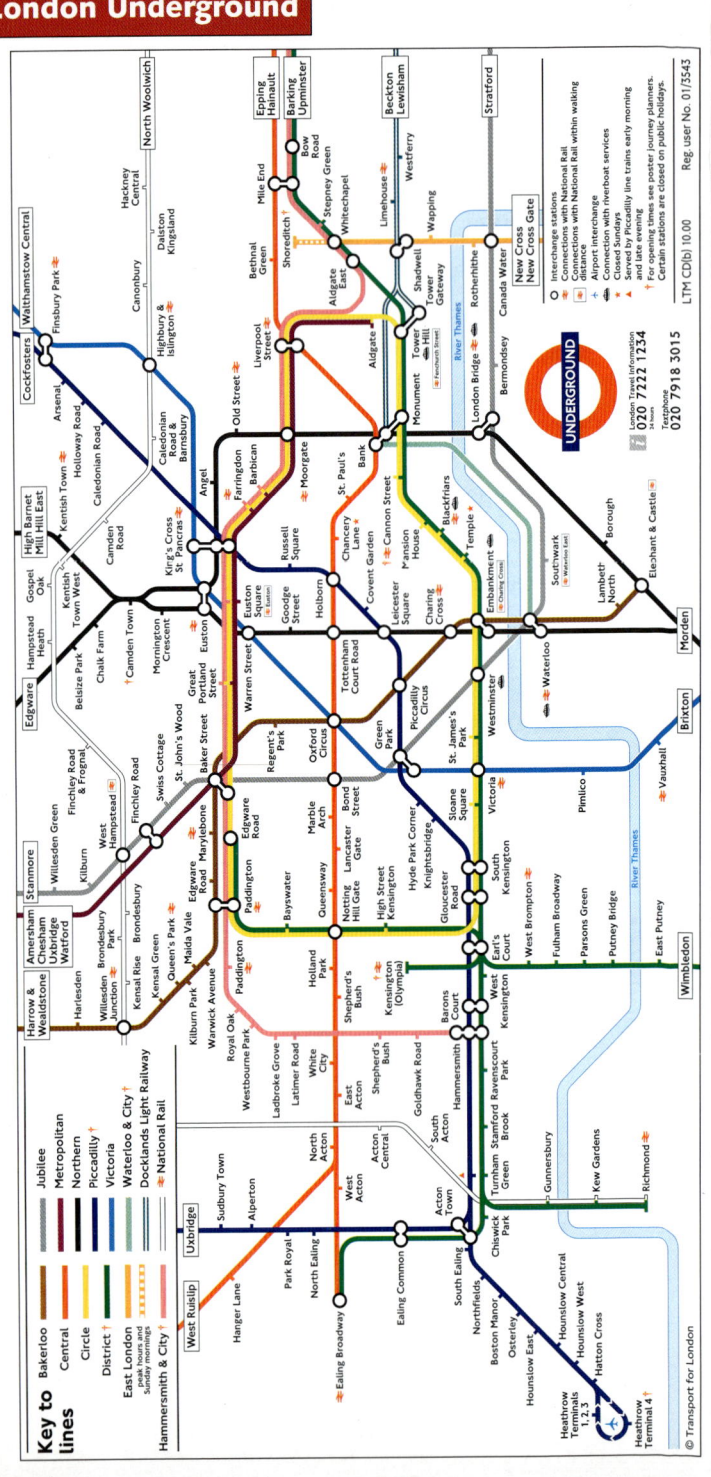